W9-BJF-480

Tricks of the
MS-DOS® Masters

HOWARD W. SAMS & COMPANY
HAYDEN BOOKS

Related Titles

The Waite Group's MS-DOS® Bible, Second Edition
Steven Simrin

The Waite Group's MS-DOS® Developer's Guide, Revised Edition
John Angermeyer and Kevin Jaeger

The Waite Group's Understanding MS-DOS®
Kate O'Day and John Angermeyer

The Waite Group's Discovering MS-DOS®
Kate O'Day

The Waite Group's MS-DOS® Papers
The Waite Group

The Waite Group's Advanced C Primer++
Stephen Prata

The Waite Group's C++ Programming (Version 2.0)
Edited by The Waite Group

The Waite Group's C Primer Plus, Revised Edition
Mitchell Waite, Stephen Prata, and Donald Martin

The Waite Group's Microsoft® C Bible
Naba Barkakati

The Waite Group's Microsoft® C Programming for the IBM®
Robert Lafore

The Waite Group's Turbo C® Bible
Naba Barkakati

The Waite Group's Turbo C® Programming for the IBM®
Robert Lafore

The Waite Group's Inside the Amiga® with C, Second Edition
John Berry

C Programmer's Guide to Serial Communications
John Campbell

QuickC™ Programming for the IBM®
Carl Townsend

Turbo C® Developer's Library
Edward R. Rought and Thomas D. Hoops

For the retailer nearest you, or to order directly from the publisher, call 800-428-SAMS. In Indiana, Alaska, and Hawaii call 317-298-5699.

Tricks of the MS-DOS® Masters

**John Angermeyer, Rich Fahringer,
Kevin Jaeger, and Dan Shafer; The Waite Group**

HOWARD W. SAMS & COMPANY

A Division of Macmillan, Inc.
4300 West 62nd Street
Indianapolis, Indiana 46268 USA

Copyright © 1987 by The Waite Group, Inc.

FIRST EDITION
FOURTH PRINTING — 1988

All rights reserved. No part of this book shall be reproduced, stored in a
retrieval system, or transmitted by any means, electronic, mechanical,
photocopying, recording, or otherwise, without written permission from the
publisher. No patent liability is assumed with respect to the use of the
information contained herein. While every precaution has been taken in the
preparation of this book, the publisher and The Waite Group assumes no
responsibility for errors or omissions. Neither is any liability assumed for
damages resulting from the use of the information contained herein.

International Standard Book Number: 0-672-22525-5
Library of Congress Catalog Card Number: 8-60389

The Waite Group Developmental Editor: *Mitchell Waite*
The Waite Group Managing Editor: *James Stockford*

Acquisitions Editor: *James S. Hill*
Editor: *Katherine Stuart Ewing*
Technical Reviewer: *Stan Kelly-Bootle*
Indexer: *Sandi Schroeder, Schroeder Editorial Services*
Designer: *T. R. Emrick*
Illustrator: *Wm. D. Basham*
Cover Artist: *Kevin Caddell*
Compositor: *Shepard Poorman Communications, Indianapolis*

Printed in the United States of America

To my mother, who was a source of inspiration in my endeavors. And to my father, to Daniel and Jeanette, to my grandmother, to Johanna and David and Richard and Maisie for their help and encouragement.

John Angermeyer

To Amparo

Rich Fahringer

For Branwyn

Kevin Jaeger

To my wife Carolyn

Dan Shafer

Contents

Legend   ■ Master Trick   □ Information

    ▤ Simple Trick   ◪ Caution

Contents

Chapter 4 Secrets of Tree-Structured Directories *91*

Contents

Contents

About the Authors

 **John Angermeyer** is an independent consultant specializing in microcomputer software development, technical writing, and desktop publishing. Previously a software engineer for a telecommunications company, Mr. Angermeyer has also worked as a consultant in the development of programmable control systems. He is co-author with Mitchell Waite of *CP/M Bible: The Authoritative Reference Guide to CP/M*, with Mitchell Waite and Mark Noble of *DOS Primer for the IBM PC & XT*, and with Kevin Jaeger of *MS-DOS Developer's Guide*.

 **Rich Fahringer** has been involved in the computing industry since 1969 when he began his career with IBM. His experience has included the design of distributed processing networks, point of sale systems, database management systems and on-line data collection systems. For the past eight years he has focused on software development for microprocessor based systems. He is presently the Manager of Operating Systems Development for Maxitron Corporation, a leader in the development of programmable controllers for factory automation.

 **Kevin Jaeger** is a computer systems design engineer specializing in software architecture. With a degree in computer science, Kevin Jaeger has worked in the telecommunications, graphics display, and process control industries. His specialities include personal computing and the design of realtime imbedded systems. His current project is the design of an operating system for a multiprocessor based realtime cell controller. He is co-author with John Angermeyer of *MS-DOS Developer's Guide*.

 **Dan Shafer** is an independent product consultant and freelance writer in California's Silicon Valley. He is also the coordinator of symposia for attorneys on the impact of Artificial Intelligence and expert systems on their profession. Dozens of his feature articles and product reviews have appeared in computer magazines. He is author of *Silicon Visions* and *AI on the Mac*. As publisher of a monthly newsletter, *Visions: The Shafer Report*, he analyzes future technological trends and impacts. Dan and his wife and four daughters live in Redwood City, California.

Preface

When we were approached by The Waite Group to write a book titled *Tricks of the MS-DOS Masters,* our immediate response was, "Who? Us?" We wouldn't want to be pretentious to the point of considering ourselves "masters." We're just people who have been lucky enough to find careers that allow us to indulge our interests in computers. Along the way, we have all shed a fair amount of sweat and tears discovering the secrets and finicky tastes of these beasts that supposedly serve us. It is that experience of discovery that The Waite Group has asked us to share with you.

Not all of the bits of information and tricks described in this book are based on discoveries made solely by the authors. Some are, but many are based on the discoveries and work of the large number of users of MS-DOS personal computers. To all these people a piece of the credit must be given. We can only hope that, with the release of this book, we can return the favor to all users by providing a comprehensive collection of tricks and tips in a single reference work.

In particular, this book depends heavily on all the people who have, for various reasons, released their software developments into the public domain and, through their altruism, have helped countless personal computer users of all types to increase their efficiency and enjoyment of their personal computers at low cost. The many individuals and companies who have distributed their software as "freeware" or "user-supported," and the many commercial firms that have produced useful software, have made all our lives easier.

Each of the four authors holds a different perspective on computing: John Angermeyer is a "user par excellence" and well-known writer. Rich Fahringer's twenty-one years in computing embody a wealth of experience distributed across mainframe computers, minicomputers, and today's microcomputers. Kevin Jaeger is a "nuts and bolts" person, always looking to see how things work. Dan Shafer's visions of artificial intelligence and the future of computing have gained him a prominent position in the industry. Each author has choosen topics that are of special interest to him, then has contributed to this book experiences and knowledge about those topics.

The result is *Tricks of the MS-DOS Masters,* a book that is not so much a broad, generalized description of MS-DOS as a collection of in-depth excursions into some areas of MS-DOS and IBM Personal Computers and compatibles that have escaped previous scrutiny. We believe *Tricks of the MS-DOS Masters* is the perfect book for MS-DOS users who have already read the basic books and don't want or need a library of specialty reference books.

This book does not supplant MS-DOS guides but is intended to be used in conjunction with them as the next step in seeking information once the basic texts have been exhausted. In addition, *Tricks of the MS-DOS Masters* contains information that has not been presented before in a work about MS-DOS: information on obtaining low-cost software, on expanding and configuring your computer system, and on the use and installation of "productivity tools," data encryption, and much more.

If you decide to pursue in greater detail the topics contained in this book, use the bibliography in Appendix A to continue your investigations with little delay.

Every one of the tricks, programs, and concepts contained in this book has been used in real situations on real computers. This is a book by real MS-DOS users for real MS-DOS users. Knowledge *is* power, and *Tricks of the MS-DOS Masters* contains the knowledge to change the average user into a "power user" and to make power users more powerful.

Acknowledgments

Three of the four authors have found employment at one time or another at Maxitron Corporation and would like to thank their friends and colleagues there for their support and contributions to the content of this work. Their many tips and intelligent comments about MS-DOS have been an invaluable resource and learning opportunity. We'd also like to express our thanks to Eric Chasanoff whose incredible energy and enthusiasm shed considerable light on the inner workings of MS-DOS. We're also grateful to Eric Jaeger of Digital Equipment Corporation for his insights on the history and practice of encryption.

The authors would like to express special thanks and appreciation to Jim Stockford of The Waite Group for helping to keep us on track through the long months of writing and preparation and to Katherine Stuart Ewing of Sams for her thorough and professional editing of this book while in its final stages. Their efforts in the creation of this book are no less important than those of the authors. Additional thanks are also given to Wm. D. Basham for his many fine illustrations, T. R. Emrick for the design of the book, Kevin Caddell for the fine work done on the cover art and Stan Kelly-Bootle and Ray Duncan for their technical reviews of the manuscript.

Finally, our thanks are also due to Mitchell Waite of The Waite Group and James S. Hill of Sams for giving us the opportunity to write this book and for helping make it a reality.

John Angermeyer
Rich Fahringer
Kevin Jaeger
Dan Shafer

Trademarks

All terms mentioned in this book that are known to be trademarks or service marks are listed below. In addition, terms suspected of being trademarks or service marks have been appropriately capitalized. Howard W. Sams & Co. or The Waite Group Inc., cannot attest to the accuracy of this information. Use of a term in this book should not be regarded as affecting the validity of any trademark or service mark.

AT and IBM are registered trademarks and PC DOS, PC*jr*, and XT are trademarks of International Business Machines, Inc.

BERNOULLI BOX is a trademark and Iomega is a registered trademark of Iomega Corporation.

COMPAQ is a registered trademark of COMPAQ Computer Corporation

CompuPro is a trademark of Vyasin Corporation.

Concurrent, Concurrent PC-DOS, Concurrent PC-DOS Expanded Memory, GEM, and GEM Desktop are trademarks and CP/M and CP/M-86 are registered trademarks of Digital Research Inc.

dBASE, dBASE III, and Framework are registered trademarks and dBASE III PLUS and Framework II are trademarks of Ashton-Tate.

Epson is a registered trademark of Epson America, Inc.

Intel is trademark of Intel Corporation.

1-2-3, Lotus, and Symphony are registered trademarks of Lotus Development Corp.

Microsoft Windows, Word, XENIX, Microsoft, and MS-DOS are registered trademarks of Microsoft Corp.

Multiscan is a trademark of Sony Corporation of America.

MultiSync is a trasdemark of NEC Corporation.

The Norton Utilities is a trademark of Peter Norton Computing, Inc.

OKIDATA and MICROLINE are registered trademarks of Oki America Inc.

ProKey is a trademark of RoseSoft, Inc.

Reflex, Sidekick, Superkey, Traveling Sidekick, Turbo BASIC, Turbo Lightning, Turbo Pascal, and Turbo Prolog are registered trademarks of Borland International.

Seattle Computers is a trademark of Seattle Computer Products, Inc.

SmartKey and SmartPath are trademarks of Software Research Technologies.

UNIX is a registered trademark of AT&T Bell Laboratories.

WordStar is a registered trademark of MicroPro International Corporation.

Conventions Used in This Book

To help you locate information for reference, certain important items are set within boxes and identified with icons as follows:

 INFORMATION: Indicates material to increase your knowledge about a particular subject.

 SIMPLE TRICK: Indicates a solution to a problem or describes a method of accomplishing a specific task.

 MASTER TRICK: Indicates a trick that is more advanced or generally more difficult to implement than a SIMPLE TRICK.

 CAUTION: Indicates a warning about possible problems, equipment damage, or personal injury that can occur.

In text, keys are shown with an initial capital letter:

the Enter key

The Ctrl-Break key combination

Items that you must replace with appropriate information are shown within brackets:

[filespec]

[input-file]

Output on screen and items that you are to enter are set apart from the rest of text and typeset in a special typeface. When a single illustration includes both your input and output on the screen, the material that you are to enter is highlighted:

```
A>debug
-n coldboot.com
-a 100
XXXX:0100 jmp f000:fff0
XXXX:0105
-rcx
:5
-w
-q

A>
```

Introduction

Chapter 1

MS-DOS and the IBM Personal Computer series represent a revolution in computing. The installed base of users running MS-DOS on IBM PC series or compatible computers comprises the single largest segment of computing today. Yet for all the popularity of the MS-DOS system and IBM PC series computers, this combination is without a doubt the least documented and understood. Why has this occurred?

MS-DOS and the IBM PC series computers are promoted as "turn-key" products for people who want *computing power*, without having to be *computing professionals*. You turn on the power and go! Unlike mainframe computers and minicomputers, no "priesthood" of support personnel is required, no voluminous manuals written in "computerese." Because users are not expected to have to do their own tinkering to use the system, the technically oriented hardware and software engineering notes that used to accompany previous "hobbyist" microcomputers are usually absent. MS-DOS and the IBM PC series are truly populist products for a populace that supposedly neither wants nor needs the extensive, complex documentation normally associated with computers.

In the last respect, the computer industry has been guilty of a terrible arrogance. In producing a computing system that can be used by those without extensive knowledge of computers, the manufacturers have assumed that their customers will never progress to the point where additional information is desired. The paternalistic attitude of the computer industry toward its customers often is responsible for the lack of information about MS-DOS and the IBM PC series and produces a veritable information desert where a cornucopia of knowledge should have been. *Tricks of the MS-DOS Masters* has been written to help provide the information needed to make the cornucopia a reality.

Who Is This Book For?

We have already alluded to the fact that the computer industry sees its customers as unprepared and unwilling participants in the information exchange. It is our belief that you, our reader, are neither.

This book is not an introduction to MS-DOS. We assume that you have previous experience with MS-DOS and with the IBM PC series or compatible computers. This is not to say that *Tricks of the MS-DOS Masters* cannot be of use to the beginning user. The information contained within is readily understandable, and certain sections of this book assume no prior knowledge of their topics. However, the novice user most likely will want to keep handy a general reference guide such as *MS-DOS Bible* (Sams #22408) to answer the more mundane questions that may arise.

This book is not a programmer's book, although it can be of great use to programmers, who are another type of user. Although some short examples are presented in assembly language for use with DEBUG, we assume no prior knowledge of any type of computer programming language, nor do we attempt to teach you any programming language. The assembly language examples used throughout this book need only be typed as shown, then run. If you are interested in learning how to program your IBM PC series or compatible computer under MS-DOS, we direct your attention to one of the numerous available books, such as *Assembly Language Primer for the IBM PC & XT* (New American Library), *Advanced MS-DOS* (Microsoft Press), or *MS-DOS Developer's Guide* (Sams #22409).

Then who is this book intended for? *Tricks of the MS-DOS Masters* is for the

- Serious business, professional, or personal user
- Software developer or software consultant
- Systems integrator or systems consultant
- "Power user," and those who would be "power users" of all types

Tricks of the MS-DOS Masters is a user's book. Much of what is contained in this book has been gleaned from countless articles, manuals, books about using MS-DOS, and from many hours spent in front of the "glowing green tube." The questions that we have attempted to answer are those that plague actual users. We feel that this book will make you more productive by

- Reducing the time you spend discovering how to perform certain operations
- More efficiently using the time you spend interacting with the computer

One other aspect of this book deserves notice. We have attempted to provide information that makes users more *independent*. Knowledge of system configuration, product compatibility, and the availability of features and products help make "average" users less dependent on the so-called experts, enabling them to act with decisiveness and authority on questions regarding computers and their use.

How To Use This Book

Tricks of the MS-DOS Masters is not a "cover-to-cover" book. It is not necessary to read the entire book to gain benefits from it. Each chapter has been written as a separate entity and stands on its own merits. Where one chapter draws on the work of another, we have included concise references to allow the reader to locate the referenced information and continue without delay. We do, however, recommend that the reader scan the entire book at least once to gain a knowledge of its contents. Some of the information contained in this book appears nowhere else at this time. Understanding the possibilities can be a great asset when difficulties arise.

The topics in this book fall into three basic groups: (1) in-depth information about "standard" MS-DOS commands and functions, (2) information about little known or underutilized enhancements for MS-DOS and MS-DOS programs, and (3) information about system configuration.

"Standard" MS-DOS Commands and Functions

Each of the chapters in this group contains in-depth descriptions of "generic" MS-DOS commands and programs. Each exposes uses, features, and liabilities that are not commonly known, showing you how to extract the last ounce of performance from your MS-DOS system.

This chapter, the *Introduction*, lists the different MS-DOS implementations and differences in commands and operation under the various versions of MS-DOS.

Chapter 2, *Secrets of the Batch File Command Language*, shows the power, and limitations, of MS-DOS's Batch Files. Hints for parameter manipulation, formatting the batch display, creating menus, and more are included.

Chapter 3, *Secrets of Redirection, Pipes, and Filters*, explains the concepts of data redirection, data pipes, and filter programs. Use of the reserved device names is also explained.

Chapter 4, *Secrets of Tree-Structured Directories*, covers not only directory basics, but the tools required for efficient management of large directory structures, including the search PATH and MS-DOS commands JOIN, ASSIGN, and SUBST.

Chapter 5, *Secrets of MS-DOS Commands*, presents the MS-DOS commands: what they are and what they do, how to invoke them, and how to abort them. Included is a comprehensive overview that correlates the commands with the various versions of MS-DOS.

Chapter 7, *Discovering Secrets: A Debugger Tutorial*, shows how to use MS-DOS' DEBUG program to examine and change your system and how to use assembly language programs provided in books, magazines, etc., even if you don't know assembly language.

Chapter 9, *Secrets of Files*, explains the different types of files and file formats under MS-DOS and goes further to show you how to recover damaged, lost, or erased files.

Appendix D, *Secrets of Diagnostics*, lists the various diagnostics error codes that your system can produce when a problem exists.

MS-DOS Enhancements

The chapters in this group all deal with topics beyond those encountered during "generic" operation of MS-DOS. Some of the features described are little known or used extensions to MS-DOS. Other topics cover the acquisition, installation, and use of "productivity" or "utility" tools under MS-DOS.

Chapter 6, *Secrets of Screen Manipulation*, features ANSI.SYS, the extended display control facility of MS-DOS, as well as tricks and tips for utilizing the keyboard effectively.

Chapter 8, *Obtaining and Using Free and Low-Cost Software*, discusses many public domain and user-supported programs: where to find them, how to use them, and some star performers.

Chapter 10, *Secrets of Add-On Software*, describes productivity tools such as "desktop accessories," DOS shells, directory managers, file searchers, RAM disks, and more. This chapter covers the benefits and liabilities of specific software and gives tips on installation and use.

Chapter 14, *Secrets of Data Encryption*, tells about data security for storage and transmission: the software and hardware products available, how to select the right one, and how to use them.

Appendix B, *Source Information*, lists sources for free and low-cost software, as well as distributors for commercial items discussed in the book.

Configuration

Three chapters cover aspects of setting up an MS-DOS system, from the initial hardware configuration and selection of storage and peripheral devices to customizing the system for your particular needs. This is the first time information has been presented on this subject outside of manufacturers' manuals.

Chapter 11, *Secrets of Add-On Boards*, describes selection, installation, and configuration of the hardware. This chapter also raises compatibility issues and shows how to resolve them.

Chapter 12, *Secrets of Add-On Mass Storage*, details the latest mass storage devices, including configuration and backing up.

Chapter 13, *Secrets of System Configuration*, covers the options and use of MS-DOS' CONFIG.SYS and AUTOEXEC.BAT configuration files and what they can mean to your system's use and performance. This chapter also goes beyond the standard configurations by describing modification of configuration commands.

Appendixes A and C contain an annotated bibliography and reference tables, respectively.

The Faces of MS-DOS

One of the most important points to understand about MS-DOS is that the name *MS-DOS* encompasses a large number of operating systems. The first version of MS-DOS Version 1.0 was based on a product from Seattle Computer Products known as *86-DOS*. Since 1981, when Microsoft and IBM released MS-DOS, the system has undergone three major and numerous minor revisions. Variants also have been provided for computers whose hardware bears little resemblance to the IBM series. The common thread that ties all these systems together has been that all systems are designed for the Intel 8086 family of processors (8088, 8086, 80188, 80186, 80286, and 80386) and use essentially the same higher level interface. To understand the role of the "higher level interface" and what it means for MS-DOS compatibility, we first must review the structure of MS-DOS.

The Pieces of MS-DOS

MS-DOS systems consist of three major parts. Taken in order from the lowest level (closest to the hardware) to the highest level (the user interface), these three components are as follows:

- The BIOS: The basic input/output system is that portion of the system responsible for the interface to the hardware and that handles such tasks as manipulating device registers and coordinating device interaction. Strictly speaking, the BIOS is not part of MS-DOS, but is supplied by the hardware manufacturer to provide a standard interface to what may be nonstandard hardware. The BIOS may vary significantly from computer to computer. However, its presence is critical.

- The MS-DOS Kernel: This portion of MS-DOS provides the system's program interface. It is responsible for interpreting the various commands issued by the application programs and passing them to the BIOS in a form recognizable to it. The kernel is the section documented in the *IBM Technical Reference Manual* or *Microsoft Programmer's Reference Manual* that may accompany your system. Because this piece is seen only by application programs, it is not the topic of this book.

- The MS-DOS Command Interpreter: This highest level section of MS-DOS, called the *command interpreter* or *shell*, is that which is actually seen by the user. Although this section is the most familiar to MS-DOS users, it has the least role in the identity of MS-DOS. That is to say, MS-DOS without the command interpreter would still be MS-DOS, but an MS-DOS system without the kernel or BIOS would simply fail to function.

Because only the MS-DOS kernel is constant among MS-DOS implementations (within a given revision), how is it possible to write a book on MS-DOS that professes to cover the spectrum of MS-DOS systems? Quite honestly, we don't. Instead, we note that the vast majority of MS-DOS systems has nearly identical components and that even the variants keep close to the "official" IBM line where possible. What are some of the variations that can be encountered?

On IBM Personal Computers (including the XT and AT) and compatibles, the BIOS is usually supplied in two pieces: a ROM BIOS, stored in Read Only Memory (ROM), and a loadable portion, read from the boot disk each time the system is initialized. However, the BIOS is not always in two pieces. Some MS-DOS implementations, such as PC-PRO for the CompuPro (Viasyn) series of computers, have no ROM BIOS and must read the entire BIOS from the disk. Regardless of the type of system, the differences between the methods used to supply the BIOS should only be apparent during the boot procedure and if and when incompatibilities arise.

The MS-DOS kernel *must* conform or the system is not MS-DOS. It is that simple.

The command interpreter or shell, often a program named COMMAND.COM, is fairly constant (within a given revision) from system to system. Because this is the piece of MS-DOS seen by the user, most manufacturers strive to use or emulate it so that they can most visibly demonstrate their compliance with MS-DOS. This book is addressed to users of COMMAND.COM and its close associates.

There are cases when an MS-DOS user would not interact with COMMAND.COM. Because COMMAND.COM is essentially an application program (albeit a sophisticated one) running under MS-DOS, it can be replaced by another program that performs a similar function but in a different format. A more likely case for a user not using COMMAND.COM would be when another *operating environment* is loaded on top of COMMAND.COM. Common examples of this are Windows from Microsoft, TopView from IBM, and GEM from Digital Research Inc.

In spite of the alternatives to COMMAND.COM, nearly all MS-DOS users have to get to know the generic operation of MS-DOS, if for no other reason than because so many useful application programs have been written with generic operation in mind. The user needs to understand the syntax, conventions, and assumptions of MS-DOS to make use of these programs.

The IBM Personal Computer Series and MS-DOS

Although MS-DOS, and its cousin for the IBM series of personal computers, PC DOS (actually called just plain *DOS* by IBM), have much in common, the popularity of the IBM standard has significantly affected what users *see* as MS-DOS. The impact is not evident so much in the actual operation of MS-DOS as it is in the assumptions PC DOS makes about the hardware environment. Storage devices may vary in implementation, but MS-DOS manages to make them all appear the same. The problems arise mostly in dealing with the keyboard, display device, and optionally, printer, that may be attached to the system.

To restate the problem in another form, MS-DOS commands and programs that deal with the file system, memory management, and program execution operate nearly identically from system to system. On the other hand, commands and programs that deal with display manipulation, advanced keyboard functions, and enhanced printer capabilities may suffer from serious incompatibilities when moved from a PC DOS system to an MS-DOS system.

MS-DOS attempts to overcome this problem by providing a basic compatibility mode of operation for the keyboard, display, and printer. When using this mode, which provides simple character I/O functions, MS-DOS systems can operate with such diverse hardware as an IBM keyboard and enhanced graphics adapter (EGA) or a simple terminal such as a Televideo 925. MS-DOS itself uses this compatibility mode as a default. Unfortunately, besides being rather boring, this mode offers little advanced functionality. (See Chapter 6 for more information on advanced operation of the IBM keyboard and display.) Whether to accept the defaults or go with the advanced capabilities thus becomes a trade-off between compatibility and more impressive features.

Other than the hardware support issues, very few differences can be found between generic MS-DOS and PC DOS. The majority simply reflect decisions by IBM to include or not include certain utilities or documentation material. A rule of thumb that applies to ninety-nine percent of the cases is that if a command or program works under generic MS-DOS, it will work under PC DOS. As we've just discussed, however, the reverse may not always be true. Table 1-1, which lists the MS-DOS commands, shows the differences between versions in more detail.

The Evolution of MS-DOS

In our discussion to this point, we have been referring to the MS-DOS kernel and command interpreter as "constant (within a given revision)." Now, we are ready to elaborate on that statement and explain the various versions of MS-DOS that have been produced so far. Beginning with MS-DOS version 1.0 in 1981, MS-DOS has been through three major revisions, and six minor revisions, ending at Version 4.0, which is currently publicly available only in Europe. (The rest of the world must make do with Version 3.2.) PC DOS has kept up with two of the major revisions (to PC DOS 3.2) and all but two of the minor revisions. In late 1986, both MS-DOS and PC DOS were holding at Version 3.2.

What changes have gone into MS-DOS during the past five years? Quite a few. Version 1.0 started as little more than a "well enhanced 16-bit version" of CP/M. Because neither Microsoft nor IBM supports versions of MS-DOS or PC DOS earlier than Version 2.0 and because Version 2.0 represented a radical change in MS-DOS, the earliest versions are not considered here.

The most significant changes incorporated in Version 2.0 were the hierarchical file structure and support for hard (fixed) disks and for user installable device drivers. The similarities to the UNIX operating system, plus the leverage of the IBM name, served to propel MS-DOS into the forefront of microcomputer operating systems.

Additional support for different media types was incorporated into the Version 3.0 and 3.2 releases, whereas support for networking applications was included in the 3.0 and 3.1 releases. Concurrent or multitasking operation, the capability of running more than one program at a time, is supposedly the next feature to be added. Unfortunately for owners of PC and XT type systems, current indications are that a multitasking version of MS-DOS will be supported only on the Intel 80286 processor, such as is used in the AT and COMPAQ 286 series, and on the Intel 80386 processor used in the COMPAQ Deskpro 386. On the other hand, should these events come to pass, some other operating system will undoubtedly fill the gap, such as Concurrent PC-DOS from Digital Research Inc.

Although the addition, enhancement, and repair of MS-DOS functions were all part of these releases, in this book, we are concerned primarily with changes to the user interface. (Readers desiring more information on the MS-DOS functions should turn to programmer's reference works such as *The MS-DOS Developer's Guide* by John Angermeyer and Kevin Jaeger, published by Howard W. Sams.)

Table 1-1 contains a list of MS-DOS and PC DOS commands and utilities available as of Version 3.2. This table should enable the reader to determine what commands and features are applicable to his or her particular system and may also help in deciding if an upgrade is called for. The table is necessarily incomplete. It concentrates solely on those versions where major changes have occurred since Version 2.0. More detailed descriptions of all the commands may be found in Table 5-3 (see Chapter 5).

Table 1-1.   MS-DOS Commands and Utilities[1]

Covered in Chapter 5						
MS-DOS Commands		2.0	2.1	3.0	3.1	3.2
ASSIGN	Assign drive to drive	X	X	X	X	X
ATTRIB	Set or clear file attributes			X	X	X
BACKUP	Backup hard disk	X	X	X	X	X
BREAK	Controls CONTROL-BREAK check	X	X	X	X	X
CHDIR	Change current directory (abbreviated CD)	X	X	X	X	X
CHKDSK	Validate disk & report	X	X	X	X	X
CLS	Clear screen	X	X	X	X	X
COMP	Compare files (IBM PC DOS only)	X	X	X	X	X
COPY	Copy files or devices	X	X	X	X	X
CTTY	Change console	X	X	X	X	X
DATE	Set or get current date	X	X	X	X	X
DEL	Delete file	X	X	X	X	X
DIR	Directory of files	X	X	X	X	X
DISKCOMP	Compare disk	X	X	X	X	X
DISKCOPY	Copy disk	X	X	X	X	X
ERASE	Delete file	X	X	X	X	X
EXE2BIN	Convert .EXE file to .COM file	X	X	X	X	X
EXIT	Terminate child shell	X	X	X	X	X
FC	Compare files (generic MS-DOS only)	X	X	X	X	X
FDISK	Configure fixed disk	X	X	X	X	X
FIND	Locate string within file(s)	X	X	X	X	X
FORMAT	Initialize disk	X	X	X	X	X
GRAFTABL	Access extended ASCII chars.				X	X
GRAPHICS	Print graphics screen	X	X	X	X	X
JOIN	Logically connect drive to directory				X	X
KEYBFR	Load keyboard layout for France			X	X	X
KEYBGR	Load keyboard layout for Germany			X	X	X
KEYBIT	Load keyboard layout for Italy			X	X	X
KEYBSP	Load keyboard layout for Spain			X	X	X
KEYBUK	Load keyboard layout for U.K.			X	X	X
LABEL	Set or change a disk's volume name			X	X	X
MKDIR	Create directory (abbreviated MD)	X	X	X	X	X

Table 1-1 (cont).

Covered in Chapter 5						
MS-DOS Commands		**2.0**	**2.1**	**3.0**	**3.1**	**3.2**
MODE	Configure device	X	X	X	X	X
MORE	Paginate screen text	X	X	X	X	X
PATH	Set command search path	X	X	X	X	X
PRINT	Print files in background	X	X	X	X	X
PROMPT	Set system prompt line	X	X	X	X	X
RECOVER	Recover damaged files or disk	X	X	X	X	X
REM	Remark	X	X	X	X	X
REN	Rename file	X	X	X	X	X
REPLACE	Selectively add or replace files					X
RESTORE	Restore hard disk from backup	X	X	X	X	X
RMDIR	Remove directory (abbreviated RD)	X	X	X	X	X
SELECT	Add international keyboard command to AUTOEXEC.BAT			X	X	X
SET	Set or get environment parameters	X	X	X	X	X
SHARE	Load file sharing support					X
SORT	Alphabetically sort input lines	X	X	X	X	X
SUBST	Establish virtual drive				X	X
SYS	Transfer operating system	X	X	X	X	X
TIME	Set or get current time	X	X	X	X	X
TREE	Display directory structure	X	X	X	X	X
TYPE	Display file on screen	X	X	X	X	X
VER	Display MS-DOS version	X	X	X	X	X
VERIFY	Controls verify on COPY mode	X	X	X	X	X
VOL	Display disk volume label	X	X	X	X	X
XCOPY	Copy directory tree and all files					X
Covered in Chapter 2						
Batch Commands		**2.0**	**2.1**	**3.0**	**3.1**	**3.2**
ECHO	Display string on screen	X	X	X	X	X
FOR	Iteratively execute commands	X	X	X	X	X
GOTO	Transfer control	X	X	X	X	X
IF	Evaluate conditional expression	X	X	X	X	X
PAUSE	Wait for user action	X	X	X	X	X
REM	Remark	X	X	X	X	X
SHIFT	Loop processing of commands	X	X	X	X	X
Covered in Chapter 13						
Configuration Commands		**2.0**	**2.1**	**3.0**	**3.1**	**3.2**
BREAK	Controls CONTROL-BREAK check	X	X	X	X	X
BUFFERS	Set number of MS-DOS disk buffers	X	X	X	X	X
COUNTRY	Set country specific values			X	X	X
DEVICE	Install device driver	X	X	X	X	X
FCBS	Set number of file control blocks			X	X	X
FILES	Set number of open files	X	X	X	X	X
LASTDRIVE	Set name of last drive			X	X	X
SHELL	Specify command interpreter	X	X	X	X	X
STACKS	Set size of MS-DOS stack					X

[1] X indicates generic, IBM, and most other implementations of MS-DOS.

MS-DOS Compatibility

There are many ways to view *compatibility* between operating systems. In considering MS-DOS, we have selected three ways that seem the most useful: How compatible is MS-DOS with PC DOS, how compatible are the different versions of MS-DOS, and how compatible is MS-DOS with foreign operating systems that claim compatibility?

MS-DOS versus PC DOS

The most common area of difference between generic MS-DOS and PC DOS is in those utilities that access the mass media devices directly, such as DISKCOPY, DISKCOMP, and FORMAT. The reason is that these utilities often bypass MS-DOS entirely, performing their own I/O with the hardware. Because the hardware varies between different makes of the system, providing the utilities to perform these functions is left to the manufacturer. As a result, one manufacturer's disk utilities, for example, often fail or work incorrectly when used on a different make of system.

Other differences can also exist between generic MS-DOS and PC DOS. Microsoft has proven to be somewhat more generous than IBM in providing utility programs to system purchasers. A generic MS-DOS Version 2.0 implementation for the CompuPro (called *MS-PRO*) included not only the standard development utilities DEBUG and LINK but also the Microsoft Macro Assembler (MASM), Librarian (LIB), and Cross Reference Utility (CREF). One other utility included with generic MS-DOS was a program called *FC*, for File Compare. This utility has definite advantages over the standard PC DOS compare facility, COMP, leaving one wondering why IBM left it out.

Compatibility between Versions

As mentioned previously, Microsoft no longer supports any of the Version 1.X revisions of MS-DOS, although many applications written for Version 1.X also run under newer versions. You should take this to mean that Microsoft no longer guarantees operation of Version 1.X software with any of its future releases.

Compatibility between the later versions, from 2.0 to 3.2, is a different matter. Unless applications are written specifically to take advantage of newer features, applications tend to be downwardly and upwardly compatible. This is an exceptionally good track record for an operating system.

Not surprisingly then, the most serious problems tend to occur not with running applications written for one version under another version, but with mixing the parts of the operating system itself. Most of the system utilities have built-in checks to prevent these types of errors. For example, attempting to run Version 3.2 FORMAT under Version 3.1 produces an error message. However, if you're clever enough, these checks can be defeated. Why would you? You may be strongly tempted to use XCOPY, a Version 3.2 utility, under Version 3.1. Resist these temptations! The version checks are usually there for a good reason, and a utility that appears to work properly under an earlier version may rear up some day and take a bite out of your hard disk, or some similar catastrophe.

Mixing system files from separate versions (Version 3.1 IBMBIO and Version 3.2 IBMDOS, for example) is a a special invitation to trouble. The files may appear to work together but, again, the possibility of an unknown bug is not worth the supposed benefits.

Sometimes all the elements are not under the control of the user. In one case, certain close compatibles of the IBM XT proved unable to boot PC DOS Version 3.2 when it was first released. The failure lay in the way the IBM PC DOS BIOS interacted with the compatible's ROM BIOS. A ROM BIOS that operated perfectly with earlier versions of PC DOS suddenly rolled over and played dead when it attempted to boot the new system. What is the solution in these cases? Report the problem to vendors that supply the compatibles. They need to maintain IBM compatibility in order to maintain sales and sooner or later, they will come up with a fix. In this particular case, a new ROM BIOS was made available at a reasonable fee. Once installed, the system booted PC DOS 3.2 without a hitch.

Compatibility with "Compatible" Operating Systems

A number of available operating systems are "compatible" with MS-DOS, such as Concurrent PC-DOS from Digital Research Inc. and DoubleDos from SoftLogic Solutions. In these two cases, the systems go considerably beyond MS-DOS, supporting the concurrent operation that has eluded Microsoft for so long. That constitutes a strong argument for using one of these systems. But the flip side of the coin is that these systems *replace* MS-DOS instead of depending on it. The consequences are that these systems tend to lag behind MS-DOS in implementing new features. Even worse, because they emulate MS-DOS, there is a chance that some unexpected compatibility issue may arise. If a newly written application or utility takes advantage of some MS-DOS idiosyncrasy, whether or not by the programmer's design, that program may not behave in a similar manner under a "compatible" operating system. The issue is not who implemented the feature correctly or incorrectly, but that a program depended on to behave in a certain way may fail to do so.

Whether to use a "compatible" operating system is a matter of trade-offs: between the enhanced functionality of the "compatible" operating system and the assured compatibility of using the "real thing."

Summary

Having read this far, you understand both the structure of this book and how it fits with the structure of MS-DOS. We've also covered, albeit briefly, what to expect from the different versions of MS-DOS. All this information should assist you in finding the answers you desire to your questions about MS-DOS and the MS-DOS environment.

Secrets of the Batch File Command Language

T he batch facility provided by MS-DOS is one of the major "productivity tools" available to MS-DOS users. With it, you can create *batch files* to reduce the number of keystrokes required to perform a task or series of tasks.

A single batch command file may contain several MS-DOS commands that are performed when the command file is executed. In addition to saving keystrokes, you are assured that the commands will be performed with no keystroke errors, quickly, and in correct sequence. Often, you can construct batch files that are capable of performing a sequence of lengthy tasks that may be run consecutively while you are away from your computer system. This "unattended" processing enables you to perform other work while your computer is performing a number of tasks or to start tasks that may be run overnight.

The beginning sections of this chapter show you how to create batch files and introduce you to the MS-DOS batch command language *subcommands,* which can add a great deal of power and flexibility to your batch files. Because one of the most difficult tricks in using MS-DOS is comprehending the vague and incomplete section of the MS-DOS manual describing batch files and commands, this chapter goes into greater detail about the basics than most chapters in this book.

After covering the fundamentals of creating and using batch files, some of the more advanced topics of batch files are described, such as executing a batch command file in another batch command file. The final sections of this chapter discuss using a few simple public domain software programs that provide some of the "missing links" not found in MS-DOS, links that extend the capability of batch files even more. Chapter 8 of this book gives additional information on how to obtain these public domain programs for your use.

What Is an MS-DOS Batch Command File?

An MS-DOS batch command file is a text file containing one or more commands, each command on a separate line of the text file. The filename extension of the text file must be .BAT. When the name of the file is entered on the MS-DOS command line (without the .BAT filename extension), MS-DOS executes the commands contained in the text file. For brevity, MS-DOS batch command files are often referred to as *batch* files, *command* files or *dot-bat* files.

The commands in an MS-DOS batch command file may be of any type: internal MS-DOS commands (for example, DIR and COPY), external commands (for example, BACKUP and SORT), batch command file subcommands (for example, IF and GOTO), or another batch command file. There are some restrictions on how one batch command file may be executed from within another batch command file. These restrictions are discussed later in this chapter. Chapter 5 of this book describes in more detail the types of commands used by the MS-DOS operating system.

Following is an example of a simple batch file containing four commands. The MODE command is an external command distributed with MS-DOS. The CHDIR command is an internal MS-DOS command. (It has a synonym named *CD*.) The remaining two commands are hypothetical external commands that you may have developed, purchased, or obtained from the public domain.

```
MODE LPT1:=COM1:
PRINTCTL /WIDE
CHDIR \LETTERS
WP
```

If you were to name the batch command file EDIT.BAT, each time you enter EDIT as a command, MS-DOS automatically executes the following commands for you:

1. Redirect the parallel printer output to an asynchronous communications adapter with the MODE command.

2. Execute a printer control utility named PRINTCTL that instructs your printer to print using a wide character font.

3. Change the current (default) directory of the current

(default) disk to the \LETTERS subdirectory with the CHDIR command.

    4. Execute your word processor named WP.

That's a pretty fair amount of work MS-DOS performs for you in exchange for just entering a few characters and pressing the Enter key. In the bargain, MS-DOS won't misspell the name of your directory before you use your word processor or ever forget to reassign your printer or execute your printer control program.

If you also use a spreadsheet program frequently, you may want to have another batch file named SPREAD.BAT that would look something like this:

```
MODE LPT1:=COM1:
CHDIR \FINANCE
PRINTCTL /NARROW
CALC \NOAUTOCALC
```

You now have the ability to use your word processor and spreadsheet without ever looking for memos in the wrong directory or printing spreadsheets with the wrong printer settings.

You can imagine the added convenience and time savings you might gain with other batch files you can create. Another advantage of batch files is that they quickly and automatically can execute commands immediately after exiting your word processor, spreadsheet, or other application program. This can be useful to reset your printer to "normal" mode, delete temporary work files from your disk, or clear your screen to remove the display of sensitive or confidential data. The following example uses the MS-DOS CLS command to clear the display screen after the CALC spreadsheet program is used to work with files in a subdirectory named PAYROLL.

```
MODE LPT1:=COM1:
CHDIR \PAYROLL
PRINTCTL \NARROW
CALC /NOAUTOCALC
CHDIR \
CLS
DIR
```

Now every time you exit the spreadsheet program, the screen is cleared and the files in your root directory are displayed on the screen. The important thing is that the batch file *never* forgets to perform specified actions and that it does it quickly.

How To Create a Batch File

Because batch files are simply text files with one or more commands on each line, they may be created easily with most word processors. A few word processors do not create files in the normal "text" file format, but most have an option to create such a file. The acid test is to display the file using the MS-DOS TYPE command. If the TYPE command displays on the screen the batch file created with your word processor without any strange characters, beeps, overlapping lines, or other anomalies, your word processor is probably capable of creating batch files. Word processing options that should *not* be used when creating batch files are: word wrap, line justification and auto-tab generation. The WordStar word processor nondocument mode's defaults have these options off and should be used when creating batch files.

If you do not have a word processor or yours is not capable of creating batch command files, you may use the EDLIN text editor that comes with MS-DOS. EDLIN is not very easy to use and you may want to replace it with another inexpensive editor. Several are available commercially and from the public domain. The Sidekick Notepad editor and similar memory resident program editors are useful for creating batch files. The MS-DOS COPY command may be used to create small batch files easily. Following is an example.

TRICK

USING THE COPY COMMAND TO CREATE AN MS-DOS BATCH COMMAND FILE

Creating a batch command file with the MS-DOS COPY command is quick and easy. Even if you have a word processor or text editor, you may want to use this method of creating a file quickly. The COPY command does have one important disadvantage: It cannot be used to modify an existing file. To create the modified file, the entire file must be reentered with changes. As big a problem as this is, it can be useful if you ever need to create a file on a system that has no editor or an editor that you do not know how to use. Whenever you use a system running under MS-DOS, you *always* have the MS-DOS internal COPY command at your disposal.

The following example shows the command line format to use when creating a batch file with the COPY command.

```
COPY CON: [filename].BAT
```

The first parameter to the COPY command, the reserved device name CON:, indicates that the input for the file to be created will come from the input "console" (another name for the keyboard). The keyboard input will be copied to the file named by the COPY command's second parameter.

When the COPY command is executed with the source filename of CON:, the cursor is displayed on the next line of the screen. Then, you may enter lines of text. Indicate the end of each line by pressing the Enter key. After the last line of the file to be created is entered, use the F6 key (or Ctrl-Z keystroke sequence), followed by the Enter key to indicate to the COPY command that this is the end of input from the keyboard. If you have redefined your F6 key using a keyboard enhancement program, the Ctrl-Z key must be used. The following example shows how to use the COPY command to create the batch file shown in the first example of this chapter.

```
A>COPY CON: EDIT.BAT
MODE LPT1:=COM1:
PRINTCTL /WIDE
CHDIR \LETTERS
WP
^Z
        1 File(s) copied


A>_
```

A ^Z is displayed by MS-DOS when you press the F6 key (or Ctrl-Z keystroke combination). It is *not* the two characters caret (^) and uppercase letter Z. After creating a file with the COPY command, check the contents of the file just created. The easiest way to do this is with the MS-DOS TYPE command.

```
A>TYPE EDIT.BAT
MODE LPT1:=COM1:
PRINTCTL /WIDE
CHDIR \LETTERS
WP


A>_
```

When you are entering lines of text using the COPY command, use the Backspace key to back up to an error on the same line. Then, correct the error and rekey the remainder of the line. If you discover an error in a previously completed line, you have no choice but to immediately exit the COPY command and start again to enter the entire file.

When creating batch files, you have a few limitations. Do not use control characters (because they can confuse MS-DOS when executing a batch file), add a filename extension of .BAT to the filename, and make the lines of text the commands you want MS-DOS to execute for you when the batch file is executed.

Several additional special MS-DOS commands are normally used only in batch files. They are often referred to in the MS-DOS manual as batch file subcommands. These subcommands can help you to create batch files with considerably more power and flexibility and are discussed later in this chapter.

Using Ctrl-Break To Terminate an Executing Batch File

If batch files are so great, what could go wrong? Like many things with extra power, a potential exists for extra problems. For example, suppose that during a brief lapse of concentration, you accidentally enter REPORTS on the command line with the intent of using your word processor. You subsequently realized that REPORTS.BAT is a batch file which starts up hours of printing you normally reserve for running at lunch time.

Fortunately, MS-DOS has a feature that you can use to terminate a batch file before it is completed. By pressing the Ctrl-Break (or Ctrl-C) key sequence, the currently running program is terminated before its normal completion and MS-DOS asks:

```
Terminate batch job (Y/N) ?_
```

You may reply with the letter N (for no) if you want to stop the current program but continue executing the remaining commands in the batch file or reply with a Y (for yes) to terminate the batch file and return to the MS-DOS prompt.

Some programs may not exit when you use the Ctrl-Break (or Ctrl-C) key sequence. In that case, use another way to terminate the program if there is one. Then, while MS-DOS is between commands, press the Ctrl-Break key. You'll probably have to be pretty fast at pressing Ctrl-Break after the current program ends but before the next command begins. Start pressing the key combination as soon as your program finishes. It won't hurt anything if you press Ctrl-Break several times.

Different programs use different keystroke combinations to exit before normal completion (abort). The most common combination is Ctrl-Break. However, not all programs follow this convention. Some programs have no preferred keystroke combination to abort. Still other programs have no way to abort. Refer to the program's reference manual to determine what the termination procedure is for the program. If you can't find the information in the manual, try using Ctrl-Break (or Ctrl-C) to terminate the program. Some programs respond to these keystrokes only after the BREAK ON command has been executed previously.

Putting Comments in Your Batch Files

When creating batch files, you should put in a few comments to remind you what you have done. What you are doing today may appear perfectly obvious while you are working on it, but when you return to make a few changes a month from now, the same "perfectly obvious" batch file probably will appear to be an impossible maze. Comments are especially important for large or complex batch files. The MS-DOS REM command, which is an abbreviation for REMark, is a convenient way to *document* what and why things are being done in a batch file.

As an example, let's take a look at our first batch file, EDIT.BAT, which we use to set up the desired directory and printer options before using a word processor. Adding a few REM commands to explain what you are using the PRINTCTL program to do and the other options that are available could save a considerable amount of time looking for and in your manual when you want to change printer options. The following example shows what your new documented EDIT.BAT file might look like now:

```
MODE LPT1:=COM1:
REM  Set the printer up to use the WIDE character font.
REM     Other options are \NARROW and \NORMAL.
REM     The options CANNOT be abbreviated.
PRINTCTL /WIDE
CHDIR \LETTERS
WP
```

Another advantage to documenting your batch files is that if you occasionally want to use your word processor with your printer set up in another mode, you can simply look at your EDIT.BAT file using the MS-DOS TYPE command. A quick glance at the file reminds you which directory to change to and what options are available for your printer using PRINTCTL.

After you make these changes to your EDIT.BAT file, you might notice something you don't like: every time you execute your EDIT batch file, these annoying REMarks, interleaved with the MS-DOS prompt and blank lines, flash by on the screen before the word processor finally begins. The next section of this chapter tells you about the ECHO batch file subcommand that is used to eliminate bothersome messages.

If you are familiar with the CP/M operating system SUBMIT facility, you may have tried putting comments in MS-DOS batch command files with a period (.) in the first column of the comment. Surprisingly, it works—although the MS-DOS documentation never mentions the feature. Although it may appear to be a handy feature, avoid using the period to identify comments. Undocumented features of MS-DOS (and especially PC DOS) have a tendency to disappear as new versions of the operating system are released.

Using the ECHO Subcommand To Let the User Know What Is Happening

The MS-DOS ECHO subcommand is another special command used only in batch files. It has four separate but related functions that it performs, depending on what follows the command name ECHO on the command line.

If nothing follows the ECHO command on the command line, the result is a message telling you whether *echo mode* is ON or OFF.

```
A>ECHO
Echo is ON


A>_
```

If the word ON (upper-, lower-, or mixed case) is the *first* word following the ECHO command on the command line, echo mode is set to ON, which causes MS-DOS to echo (display) *all* text in a batch file.

If echo mode was already ON, MS-DOS remains in echo mode and no harm is done. Echo mode ON is the "normal" mode that MS-DOS operates in and is usually the most convenient mode to use when not in a batch file. When your system is booted, echo mode ON is the default unless you have modified your COMMAND.COM file (see Chapter 13 for details on patching your version of COMMAND.COM).

If the word OFF (upper-, lower-, or mixed case) is the *first* word following the ECHO command on the command line, MS-DOS stops the display of the prompt line and commands on the screen as they are being executed. Setting echo mode OFF when it was already off does not do any harm. When in a batch file, echo mode OFF is usually the preferred way because it suppresses the display of all REMark and other commands the user is not interested in seeing.

If the *first* word following the ECHO command is *not* ON or OFF, everything following the command name ECHO is treated as a message to be displayed on the screen. If echo mode is ON when this form of the ECHO command is executed in a batch file, the entire ECHO command is displayed on the screen on one line followed by only the message on the next line. This redundant display of the message portion of the ECHO command makes the screen difficult to read. However, if echo mode is OFF when the ECHO command is executed, only the message portion of the command is displayed on the screen. When used with echo mode OFF, the ECHO command provides a convenient way to inform the user what is going on in a batch file. You can accomplish the same thing by using the REM command (with echo mode ON). However, the messages will be displayed on the screen interleaved with the MS-DOS prompt and blank lines. Using the ECHO command with echo mode OFF produces a much neater and more readable screen display.

The following illustrates the advantages of using the ECHO command with ECHO mode OFF. It also demonstrates a few other tricks that can be used with the ECHO command.

HINTS ON USING THE ECHO SUBCOMMAND

Several features and quirks of the MS-DOS ECHO subcommand are not explained in all versions of the MS-DOS documentation.

1. Replaceable parameters and environment strings are expanded when used with the ECHO subcommand. For example, ECHO %1 displays the value of the first parameter to the batch command rather than the characters %1. And ECHO %PATH% displays the current value of the PATH environment string rather than the characters %PATH%. These features make it convenient to display variable information with a single ECHO subcommand.

2. A single percent sign (%) may be displayed by using two percent signs. For example, the command ECHO %% displays a single percent sign.

3. Spaces following the ECHO command are treated as a single *delimiter* until the first nonspace character. The best way to indent messages displayed by the ECHO command is to follow the ECHO command with one space, the ASCII BackSpace character, the number of spaces desired, then the message to be indented. The ASCII BackSpace character is hexadecimal 08. You may be able to generate it with your word processor or text editor. WordStar users can generate the BackSpace character with the Ctrl-P command followed by Ctrl-H. Pressing Ctrl-H without preceding it with the Ctrl-P command causes WordStar to interpret the keystroke literally: The cursor is moved back one space instead of placing an ASCII BackSpace character into the file being edited. Be sure to read carefully the caution box *Avoiding TAB Characters in Batch Files*.

4. The ECHO subcommand can be used to append a line of text to a disk file by using the >> data redirection operator. An example is given in Chapter 3 of this book.

5. Do not use the symbols <, >, or ¦ with the ECHO subcommand unless you really intend to do data redirection or piping.

The following example illustrates some of these features of the ECHO command.

```
A>TYPE COPY2A.BAT
ECHO OFF
REM
REM COPY2A Batch file:  Copies one or more files to the
REM      disk in drive A:; wildcards may be used.
REM
DIR A: /W
ECHO ^H
ECHO WARNING:  This batch file erases 100%% of the files
ECHO ^H           on the disk in drive A:. If you do not
ECHO^H            want to lose these files, press the
ECHO ^H           Ctrl-Break keystroke combination now ! ! !
PAUSE
ERASE A:*.* < YES.INP
IF "%1" == "" GOTO COPYALL
:COPYNEXT
```

```
ECHO Copying %1 to A:
COPY %1 A: /V
SHIFT
IF "%1" == "" GOTO ENDBAT
GOTO COPYNEXT
:COPYALL
ECHO Copying *.* to A:
COPY *.* A: /V
:ENDBAT
DIR A: /W
```

DISPLAYING A BLANK LINE WITH THE ECHO SUBCOMMAND

When you use the ECHO subcommand to display messages on the screen during the execution of a batch file, separate related blocks of text with a blank line to improve the readability of the screen. Creating a blank line is one of the most basic and easy operations to perform with the ECHO subcommand. However, the command ECHO with nothing on the remainder of the command line instructs MS-DOS to display a message indicating the current status of echo mode, for example, Echo is ON or Echo is OFF.

One solution is to begin each message that is displayed with the ECHO subcommand with an unobtrusive character, such as the exclamation mark (!).

```
ECHO OFF
ECHO !
ECHO !    WARNING:   The next command will erase all files
ECHO !               on the disk in the A: drive.
ECHO !               Press Ctrl-Break now if you do
ECHO !               not want to continue.
PAUSE
FORMAT A:
```

Using the ! character works, but it is *not* the totally blank line that would improve readability even more.

MS-DOS Version 2.x users can cause the display of a blank line with the ECHO command followed by two or more blanks (ECHO). MS-DOS Version 3.x users can do the same with the ECHO command followed *immediately* by a period (ECHO.). Do not include a space or other character between the ECHO command and the period.

Unfortunately, what works for Version 2.x of MS-DOS does not work with Version 3.x, and vice versa. If you want to create batch files that are compatible with all versions of MS-DOS, two solutions are available.

The first solution is to patch the COMMAND.COM program for Version 3.x of MS-DOS to produce the same effect for an ECHO command followed by two blanks as Version 2.x of MS-DOS. Details on this patch are given in Chapter 13 of this book. If you are creating batch files that will be distributed to numerous MS-DOS users, this probably is not an effective solution because all Version 3.x users will have to have a patched COMMAND.COM file. When users restore crashed disks from backups or receive a new Version of MS-DOS, it will be necessary to reinstall the patch.

The second solution to creating batch files that display a blank line for all MS-DOS versions is to change the way the ECHO command is specified on the command line.

The ECHO command followed by a Space, then the ASCII BackSpace character (hexadecimal 8 or Ctrl-H) causes the display of a blank line on the screen for all versions of MS-DOS. The following example shows what the batch file used in the previous example would look like if the BackSpace character was used instead of the exclamation mark. The ^H indicates where the BackSpace character appears in the file. Many printers do not indicate the presence of a BackSpace in a file with ^H characters, but actually backspace the print head one space before printing the remainder of the line.

```
ECHO OFF
ECHO ^H
ECHO ^H      WARNING:   The next command will erase all files
ECHO ^H                 on the disk in the A: drive.
ECHO ^H                 Press Ctrl-Break now if you do
ECHO ^H                 not want to continue.
PAUSE
FORMAT A:
```

Using the BackSpace character has several advantages over the other methods used to cause the display of a blank line on the screen:

1. You don't have to patch the COMMAND.COM program file for your system.

2. BackSpace operates correctly when used with all current versions of MS-DOS (including 2.0, 2.1, 3.0, 3.1 and 3.2).

3. ECHO commands that have an indented message are indented when they are displayed on the screen. All MS-DOS command delimiter characters (space, tab, comma, semicolon, and equal sign) following the command name ECHO and preceding the first nondelimiter character on the command line are ignored when MS-DOS displays the message for an ECHO command.

4. If the first word in the message for an ECHO command is ON or OFF, the preceding BackSpace character causes the command *not* to be interpreted as an ECHO ON or ECHO OFF command. The fourth line of the batch file in the preceding example causes MS-DOS to set echo mode

ON and ignore the remainder of the command line (for example, the disk in the A: drive) if the BackSpace character is not present.

Many word processors and text editors provide a procedure to insert special control characters such as the BackSpace character in a file. If you are a WordStar user, use the Ctrl-P command followed by Ctrl-H to place a BackSpace in the file (it is displayed on the screen as ^H). If your word processor does not have this feature, create the batch file using asterisks where the BackSpace character is to be placed. Later, use the MS-DOS DEBUG command to change the asterisks to the BackSpace character (see Chapter 7 for more detail on using the DEBUG command).

DOCUMENTING BATCH COMMAND FILES WITH REM AND ECHO

Comments are very useful in a batch file. When creating a batch file containing comments, always begin the batch file by setting ECHO OFF. Then use the ECHO command to inform the user of what is going on while the batch file is executing. Use the REM (for REMark) command to provide additional information that the user does not need to be concerned with when using the batch file but that can be helpful in debugging or modifying the batch file later.

When using the ECHO command, be careful not to begin the comment with the words ON or OFF. If you do, MS-DOS interprets this as a command to change the state of the echo mode. For example, the command ECHO On Friday run the WEEKLY batch file does *not* display the message On Friday run the WEEKLY batch file, but rather sets the echo mode ON and the remainder of the command line is ignored.

You may use the REM command with no comments on the remainder of the line in order to provide improved readability of the batch file.

The following example shows a batch file named PRINTALL.BAT that does not set the echo mode OFF with the ECHO OFF command. It executes the PRINTCTL program shown in previous examples to indicate to the system printer what print size to use when printing the subsequent reports.

It also executes another hypothetical program named REPORT that formats a disk file and sends it to the printer. The remainder of the commands in the file are batch file REM subcommands that document what the file is doing as it executes. Following the listing of the batch file is an example of the screen output generated when the batch file is executed.

```
REM Print accounting reports batch file.
REM
CHDIR \REPORTS
REM
REM Print the General Ledger report using wide print.
REM
REM PRINTCTL parameters are /WIDE, /NORMAL or /NARROW
REM REPORT may be reconfigured using RINSTALL.
REM
PRINTCTL /WIDE
REPORT GL.RPT
REM
REM Print the Sales and Summary reports using normal print.
REM
PRINTCTL /NORMAL
REPORT SALES.RPT
REM
REM Copy the Summary report from another \ACCTG directory.
REM
COPY \ACCTG\SUMMARY.LST SUMMARY.RPT /V
REPORT SUMMARY.RPT
DEL SUMMARY.RPT
REM
REM Print the Inventory report using narrow print.
REM
REM Warning:  This is a 1.5 to 2 hour listing.
REM
REM It is printed last so that other reports
REM      are completed if printing must
REM      be stopped for other processing.
REM
PRINTCTL /NARROW
REPORT INVEN.RPT
REM Return printer to normal print font.
PRINTCTL /NORMAL
```

Here is what the output of the PRINTALL batch file looks like when the batch file is executed.

```
A>REPORT

A>REM Print accounting reports batch file.

A>REM

A>CHDIR \REPORTS

A>REM

A>REM Print the General Ledger report using wide print.

A>REM

A>REM PRINTCTL parameters are /WIDE, /NORMAL or /NARROW
```

```
A>REM REPORTS may be reconfigured using RINSTALL.

A>REM

A>PRINTCTL /WIDE

A>REPORT GL.RPT

A>REM

A>REM Print the Sales and Summary reports using normal print.

A>REM

A>PRINTCTL /NORMAL

A>REPORT SALES.RPT

A>REM

A>REM Copy the Summary report from another \ACCTG directory.

A>REM

A>COPY \ACCTG\SUMMARY.LST SUMMARY.RPT /V
        1 File(s) copied

A>REPORT SUMMARY.RPT

A>DEL SUMMARY.RPT

A>REM

A>REM Print the Inventory report using narrow print.

A>REM

A>REM Warning:  This is a 1.5 to 2 hour listing.

A>REM

A>REM It is printed last so that other reports

A>REM        are completed if printing must

A>REM        be stopped for other processing.

A>REM

A>PRINTCTL /NARROW

A>REPORT INVEN.RPT

A>REM Return printer to normal print font.
```

```
A>PRINTCTL /NORMAL

A>_
```

As the commands in the batch file are executed, the command line is echoed (displayed) on the screen. In addition, the comments in each REM command are echoed. This extra *screen clutter* can be eliminated by beginning the batch file with the ECHO OFF command to set the MS-DOS echo mode OFF.

With echo mode OFF, comments in the batch file using the REM subcommand are not displayed as the batch file executes. Information relevant to the batch file user can be given with the ECHO statement. These changes have been made to the PRINTALL.BAT file in the following example. Notice that the batch file contains more comments, which make the purpose of the commands easier to understand for anyone who may modify the batch file, yet the screen output displayed while the batch file is executing is much cleaner and easier to understand for the batch file user.

```
ECHO OFF
REM
REM      PRINTALL Batch File
REM
REM      Prints out all accounting reports.
REM
REM The General Ledger report is printed using wide print.
REM The Sales and Summary reports are printed using normal
REM print.  The Inventory report must be printed using the
REM narrow print.  At the end the printer is set to normal.
REM
REM The Summary report is named SUMMARY.LST in the \ACCTG
REM directory.  It must be copied into \REPORTS and renamed
REM SUMMARY.RPT for the REPORT program.  After being printed,
REM it is deleted in order to save disk space.  It may
REM be recopied in order to create another listing.
REM
REM The Inventory report is printed last in order to let
REM all of the shorter reports be completed in case
REM printing must be interrupted for other processing.
REM The batch file INVYONLY may be used to run the
REM Inventory report only.
REM
REM Notes:
REM    The REPORT program is configured to look for a
REM      setup file in the \DATABASE directory.  If this must
REM      be changed, run the RINSTALL program.
REM    The PRINTCTL program has the following parameters:
REM      /WIDE    wide print font.
REM      /NARROW  narrow print font.
REM      /NORMAL  normal print font.
REM
CHDIR \REPORTS
ECHO ^H
```

```
ECHO Printing General Ledger Report . . .
PRINTCTL /WIDE
REPORT GL.RPT
ECHO ^H
ECHO Printing Sales Report . . .
PRINTCTL /NORMAL
REPORT SALES.RPT
ECHO ^H
ECHO Printing Summary Report . . .
COPY \ACCTG\SUMMARY.LST SUMMARY.RPT /V > NUL:
REPORT SUMMARY.RPT
DEL SUMMARY.RPT
ECHO ^H
ECHO The Inventory report is about to be started.
ECHO ^H
ECHO Warning:  This is a 1.5 to 2 hour listing.
ECHO ^H
ECHO To bypass this report, press Ctrl-Break,
ECHO then reply with "y" followed by the Enter
ECHO key in response to the next question.
ECHO ^H
PAUSE
PRINTCTL /NARROW
REPORT INVEN.RPT
PRINTCTL /NORMAL
```

The following screen shows how much easier the screen display of the batch file is to read and understand.

```
A>REPORTS

A>ECHO OFF

Printing General Ledger Report . . .

Printing Sales Report . . .

Printing Summary Report . . .

The Inventory report is about to be started.

Warning:  This is a 1.5 to 2 hour listing.

To bypass this report, press Ctrl-Break,
then reply with "y" followed by the Enter
key in response to the next question.

Strike a key when ready . . .

A>_
```

Using the MS-DOS Batch Command File Subcommands

When Version 1.0 of MS-DOS was introduced, there were only two batch file subcommands: REM and PAUSE. Version 2.0 included the remaining subcommands: ECHO, FOR, GOTO, IF, and SHIFT. Versions 2.1, 3.0, 3.1, and 3.2 of MS-DOS have not added any additional batch file subcommands or modified the functionality of any of the subcommands with the exception of an annoying "glitch" introduced with Version 3.0 ECHO subcommand (see the *Displaying a Blank Line with the ECHO Subcommand* trick box earlier in this chapter). Because Version 1.x of MS-DOS is now considered obsolete, software developers tend to ignore the fact that several of the batch file subcommands are not available to Version 1.x users when creating batch files.

All batch file subcommands have a number of characteristics in common:

1. They are all *internal* MS-DOS commands. Consequently, no .COM or .EXE files are associated with these commands. You can also rename any of the commands by patching the COMMAND.COM file on your disk. Details on how to do this are given in Chapter 13 of this book. However, it is probably not a good idea to modify your COMMAND.COM file because your system is not able to run all batch files that you may receive with your purchased or public domain software.

2. Although they are intended for use in batch files, all may be executed directly from the MS-DOS command line. However, none of the subcommands is of much use except when used in a batch file.

3. Replaceable parameters and environment strings may be used with any of the batch file subcommands. Both of these subjects are covered in more detail later in this chapter.

The ECHO and REM subcommands were introduced in the sections of this chapter that describe the most suitable method of documenting and commenting batch files. The SHIFT command is covered in more detail after the related subject of replaceable batch file parameters is described. The following sections briefly introduce the remaining subcommands: FOR, GOTO, IF, and PAUSE. Where appropriate, tricks and cautions for each subcommand are given after each subcommand is discussed.

The FOR Subcommand

The FOR batch file subcommand is used to execute another command iteratively (a number of times). The following example of the FOR command executes the MS-DOS COPY command twice.

```
FOR %%F IN ( EXPENSE.WKS EXPENSE.RPT ) DO COPY %%F A: /V
```

This FOR subcommand produces the same results as the following two COPY commands.

```
COPY EXPENSE.WKS A: /V
COPY EXPENSE.RPT A: /V
```

The general format of the FOR subcommand is:

```
FOR %%[variable] IN ( [set] ) DO [command]
```

The value of [variable] is set sequentially to each member of [set], then the [command] is evaluated and executed. If any member of the [set] contains the filename wildcard characters * or ?, the [variable] is set to each matching filename in the current directory of the disk. Pathnames may not be specified for filenames using wildcard characters.

Parameters may be included in the [command] portion of the FOR command, occurrences of the %%[variable] in the [command] are replaced with the current value of the [variable] each time the command is executed. The [command] may not be another FOR command. An attempt to do so results in an error when the FOR command is executed. The message FOR cannot be nested is displayed on the screen and the execution of the batch file is terminated.

Note that the FOR command may be used at the MS-DOS prompt level or within a batch file. When used at the MS-DOS prompt, [variable] must be preceded by a single % character. When used within a batch file however, two % characters must precede [variable] so that "%[variable]" is literally produced when the command is executed.

Not all versions of the MS-DOS documentation point out some important facts pertaining to the FOR subcommand:

1. The [variable] must be a single letter. (Whereas you can use numbers and several special characters for a variable, it is not recommended because these may not remain compatible with future versions of MS-DOS).

2. The [variable] may be referenced by the command any number of times, including zero. Any references to the [variable] must be in the same case as the original variable. Therefore, the command FOR %%D IN (A B) DO DIR %%d: does *not* execute the commands DIR A: and DIR B: as expected. Instead, it executes the command DIR %d: twice.

3. The list of expressions in [set] must be separated by one or more command line delimiters (space, comma, semicolon, equal sign, or tab). The expressions in a set may not include any of these delimiters or any of the data redirection characters (<, >, and ¦). MS-DOS also provides no way to indicate the use of an asterisk or question mark other than when these characters are to be interpreted as a filename wildcard specification.

4. The [set] may have any number of members. If the [set] is null (empty), the [command] is never executed. All, some, or none of the members of the [set] may be a filename wildcard specification.

5. The %%[variable] has no special meaning outside the execution of a FOR subcommand.

6. If the [command] is a GOTO [label] subcommand, the GOTO causes execution of the batch file to resume at the command immediately following the [:label]. No additional iterations of the

---

HINTS FOR USING THE FOR SUBCOMMAND

The FOR command [set] specification may include replaceable batch file parameters. You can capitalize on this fact to quickly create batch files that accept a variable number of parameters. For example, the following one line batch file copies any number of files from a hard disk to a floppy disk in drive A:.

```
FOR %%X IN ( %1 %2 %3 %4 %5 %6 %7 %8 %9 ) DO COPY %%X A: /V
```

If the batch file is named COPY2A.BAT, the command COPY2A APPOINT.APP *.MEM results in the execution of the COPY command once with the [variable] set to the value of APPOINT.APP and once for *each* file in the current directory with a filename extension of .MEM.

FOR command are executed. If a FOR command is interrupted in this way and later reexecuted, the execution of the FOR command begins again with the first iteration.

7. If the length of the command line exceeds 127 after the [command] is evaluated, the results of the command's execution are unpredictable. They vary from execution of the command with missing parameters to a system halt requiring a power-off/power-on reset.

8. If the [command] is a batch file, execution of the current batch file is terminated. The named batch file executes normally. Consequently, only the first iteration of the FOR subcommand is executed. You can avoid this: see *Executing Batch Files within Batch Files* later in this chapter.

The GOTO Subcommand

The format of the batch file GOTO subcommand is quite simple:

```
GOTO [label]
```

When MS-DOS encounters a GOTO subcommand during the execution of a batch file, it searches the batch file for a line with a colon in column one followed immediately by the specified [label]. Execution of the batch file resumes with the command on the line immediately following the line containing the appropriate [label]. If the [label] is not defined in the batch file, the batch file terminates with the message Label not found.

The colon for the line defining the [label] *must* be in the first position of the line. Even a preceding space or tab character results in the [label] being incorrectly interpreted. If a batch file contains more than one definition of a [label], only the first occurrence of the [label] is recognized. A single [label] definition may be the target of any number of GOTO subcommands, including none. Thus, unreferenced [label]s may be defined and may provide a means of "commenting" a batch file. However, the REM command is used normally for that purpose.

There is no restriction as to which direction a GOTO command may jump. The direction of the jump may be forward (to a label following the GOTO command in the file), to skip commands in the file, or backward, to repeat commands. The following batch file repeats your favorite demonstration program "forever," or until the Ctrl-Break keystroke combination is pressed.

```
ECHO OFF
:DoAgain
CLS
MYDEMO
GOTO DoAgain
```

Normally, an infinite sequence of commands is not what is desired, so you need to have conditional logic that uses the IF subcommand to "break out" of the iterative sequence. When creating batch files that perform iteration in this manner, always be sure that the condition which signifies the end of processing for the loop is created in the loop.

You can encounter several problems when you develop batch files. These problems are due to the lack of a precise definition of what constitutes a valid [label] and are compounded by the fact that there is a slight difference between MS-DOS versions in the method of handling [label] values that are longer than allowed.

The following discusses these problems.

HINTS FOR USING THE GOTO SUBCOMMAND

The GOTO batch file subcommand was a welcome enhancement with Version 2.0 of MS-DOS. Version 3.0 of MS-DOS has significant improvements in the time required to perform a transfer of control to another command when a GOTO [label] command is executed. Unfortunately, some other undocumented changes also were made to the GOTO subcommand.

The MS-DOS documentation states that "a label in a batch file is defined as a character string where the first 8 characters are significant (make it different)." This implies that a GOTO Label1234 *goes to* any of the following labels: :Label123 or :Label1234 or :Label123A. Versions 3.0 and higher of MS-DOS operate in this way. However, lower numbered versions find :Label123 only. Therefore, the following batch file operates correctly only when used with Versions 3.0 and higher of MS-DOS. If the GOTO PrintReports subcommand is executed using Version 2.0 of MS-DOS, the message Label not found is displayed on the screen and execution of the batch file terminates.

```
ECHO OFF
REM
REM  This batch file is NOT valid for Versions 2.x of MS-DOS.
REM
IF NOT "%1" == "" GOTO PrintReports
ECHO ^G Parameter must be given to specify report filename.
GOTO EndBat
:PrintReports
REPORT %1
:EndBat
```

Another glitch to avoid is using special characters in [label] names. Because label begins with a colon (:), you can assume that this character cannot be used in a [label] name.

It is also obvious that the data redirection characters <, >, and ¦ must be avoided. Delimiter characters, such as the space character, tab character, and = also do not work. Less obvious, the [,], and + do not work. Several of the other characters may be used in [label] names, but only if they are not the first character of the name.

To improve the chances of creating batch files that are compatible with future releases of MS-DOS, the following guidelines are suggested:

1. Limit all [label] names to 8 or fewer characters.

2. Do not use *any* special characters in [label] names.

3. Always use an alphabetic character for the *first* character of a [label] name.

4. Use only alphabetic characters and numbers for the remaining characters of a [label] name.

Another characteristic of [label] names is that they are not case sensitive. Consequently, the command GOTO DoList goes to any of the following labels: :dolist, :DoList, or :DOLIST.

If MS-DOS executes a GOTO command and the [label] is not defined in the batch file, the message Label not found is displayed and the batch file terminates. If the label is defined several times in the batch file, the command following the *first* occurrence of the label is executed. If a label following a GOTO command is not defined but the GOTO command is never executed (it may be the command following an IF clause), the error is never detected by MS-DOS. This makes it possible to have a batch file that executes correctly with one set of parameters but terminates with the Label not found message when executed with another set of parameters.

A final caution about GOTO [label]s: replaceable parameters (%0 through %9) and environment string variables (%string-name%) are replaced by the proper values when they are encountered in a label name following a GOTO subcommand. For example, if the value of the first parameter is AR, the command GOTO %1REPORT is replaced with the command GOTO ARREPORT when it is executed. However, the label definition :%1REPORT is *not* replaced with :ARREPORT when the search for the label is made. Therefore, the label is never found and the batch file terminates with the Label not found message.

The IF Subcommand

The batch file IF subcommand enables batch files to be written using conditional logic. A common application of the IF command is to cause the execution of a batch file to conditionally "branch" to another location in the batch file. The following example shows the COPY2A.BAT batch file modified to copy the specified files to the disk in drive A:, but when no files are specified, *all* of the files are copied.

```
IF (%1) == () GOTO COPYALL
FOR %%X IN ( %1 %2 %3 %4 %5 %6 %7 %8 %9 ) DO COPY %%X A: /V
GOTO ENDBAT
:COPYALL
COPY *.* A: /V
:ENDBAT
```

The general form of the IF subcommand is

```
IF [condition] [command]
```

When the IF subcommand is executed, the [condition] is evaluated. If it is true, the [command] is evaluated and executed, otherwise the [command] is skipped, and the following command in the batch file is executed.

Three [conditions] may be specified with the IF subcommand. All three may be preceded by the logical operator NOT.

```
IF ERRORLEVEL number [command]
```

```
IF NOT ERRORLEVEL number [command]
```

```
IF [string1]==[string2] [command]
```

```
IF NOT [string1]==[string2] [command]


IF EXIST [file-specification] [command]


IF NOT EXIST [file-specification] [command]
```

The [condition] ERRORLEVEL [number] is true when the previous program has an exit code of [number] or higher. Programs may optionally set an exit code before they terminate. If they do not, MS-DOS assumes an exit code of zero. Beginning with Version 3.2 of MS-DOS, the FORMAT, REPLACE, BACKUP, and RESTORE commands set an exit code of non-zero if they terminate with an error. All other MS-DOS commands always terminate with an exit code of zero.

Conventionally, programs that use exit codes use zero to indicate normal execution and non-zero to indicate that an error condition was encountered. Until recently, very few programs made use of the error code feature of MS-DOS and thus have an exit code of zero. The feature is now becoming more commonly used. Consult the program documentation for your software to determine the values of any exit codes and their interpretation.

The condition [string1]==[string2] is true when [string1] and [string2] are identical. The case of the [strings] *is* important, therefore the [condition] AAA==aaa is *not* true. The [string] values may *not* include any command line delimiters (comma, equal sign, space, tab, or semicolon) or data redirection characters (<, >, or |). The [string] values *may* be partially or wholly composed of batch command file replaceable parameters, environment strings, and/or FOR subcommand [variables].

The condition EXIST [file-specification] is true if [file-specification] exists in the default directory of the specified drive. Pathnames are not allowed in the [file-specification]. The [file-specification] may be partially or wholly composed of batch command file replaceable parameters, environment strings, and/or FOR subcommand [variables].

The IF subcommand may be nested. The only constraint to the number of times it may be nested is the maximum length of a command line (127 characters).

The PAUSE Subcommand

The PAUSE subcommand suspends the execution of the batch file and displays the following message.

```
Strike a key when ready . . .
```

When a key is pressed, the execution of the batch file is resumed. A key is defined as "any data key," so pressing the Alt or Shift keys has no effect. Pressing the Ctrl-Break key combination allows termination of the execution of the batch file.

One common use of the PAUSE subcommand is to stop the execution of the batch file in order to allow the user to change disks in a floppy drive. Another common use is to warn the user that the batch file may destroy important data and gives the user the opportunity to terminate the batch file before data is lost.

A message may follow the command name PAUSE on the command line. This message is displayed when the PAUSE subcommand is executed only if echo mode is ON. If echo mode is OFF, any message to the user must be displayed on the screen with one or more ECHO subcommands. If a message is used with the PAUSE subcommand, the data redirection characters (<, >, and |) should not be used.

Creating a "Batch File for All Reasons" Using Replaceable Parameters

Now that we see how helpful batch files can be in making our work faster and more accurate, we examine some of the features of batch files that can make them even more powerful.

One of the features that provides more flexibility when using batch files is the use of replaceable parameters. A simple example shows how easy it is to use them. In the beginning of this chapter, we created a batch file named EDIT.BAT that made it easy to start a word processor. Many word processors allow an optional filename on the command line that indicates what file is to be created or modified. For example, our word processor might allow WP SAMPLE.MEM to indicate that the file SAMPLE.MEM is to be edited.

It would be convenient to modify our batch file to allow us to do the same thing, and fortunately, we can easily do just that.

```
CHDIR \LETTERS
PRINTCTL /WIDE
WP %1
```

Notice the %1 following the name of our word processor on the last line of the batch file. This corresponds to the first parameter on the command line following the name of our batch file EDIT when the batch file is executed. For example, entering EDIT FEB25.MEM instructs the batch file to execute WP FEB25.MEM (after changing to the directory named \LETTERS and executing our printer control program). Notice that when the batch file executes, the %1 is replaced with FEB25.MEM.

Up to nine replaceable parameters may be used within a batch file, which are referenced as %1 to %9. When the batch file is executed, each occurrence of a percent sign followed by a digit is replaced with the corresponding parameter on the command line.

Using Multiple Replaceable Parameters

A replaceable parameter may be referenced within a batch file an unlimited number of times. For example, if we create a batch file named EDITNEW.BAT to help us with the creation of a new document, it would look like this:

```
CHDIR \LETTERS
PRINTCTL /WIDE
COPY %1 %2
WP %2
```

After setting the current directory and executing our printer control program, the batch file copies the file named by the first parameter to the file named by the second parameter when the batch file is executed. The following example shows the batch file commands executed when the EDITNEW batch command is executed with two parameters.

```
A>EDITNEW SAMPLE.MEM JOESMITH.MEM

A>CHDIR \LETTERS

A>PRINTCTL /WIDE
```

```
A>COPY SAMPLE.MEM JOESMITH.MEM
    1 file(s) copied


A>WP JOESMITH.MEM


A>_
```

This batch command file is useful to copy a memo template to the file that we want to create, then execute our word processor with the name of the newly created file so that the memo template can be modified to produce the final form of the memo. Notice that the second parameter %2, which is replaced by JOESMITH.MEM, is referenced twice within the batch file.

Another rule for batch file parameters is that you don't have to reference a parameter at all. This is not generally useful except that when you are testing a partially completed batch file you won't get any annoying error messages. Be careful though. If you intend to use a parameter and forget, MS-DOS won't let you know about your error.

Now that we've seen how useful replaceable parameters can be, you may have a question—what if I want to have a percent sign in a batch file that does not represent a replaceable parameter? Fortunately, MS-DOS provides a simple way to do this:

USING THE PERCENT SIGN
IN BATCH FILES

In order to place a percent sign in a batch file that does not represent a replaceable parameter or environment string, simply use two percent signs together. MS-DOS replaces two consecutive percent signs with one. For example, if a batch file named PERCENT.BAT contained:

```
ECHO OFF
ECHO This is a sample batch file to show how
ECHO percent signs are interpreted by MS-DOS.
ECHO The following line is displayed on
ECHO the screen with only nine percent signs.
ECHO %% %%1234 %%abcd%% %%!@#$ %%%%%%%
ECHO ON
```

Executing the batch file by entering PERCENT on the MS-DOS command line results in the following display on the screen:

```
A>PERCENT

A>ECHO OFF
This is a sample batch file to show how
percent signs are interpreted by MS-DOS.
The following line is displayed on
the screen with only nine percent signs.
%  %1234  %abcd%  %!@#$  %%%%


A>_
```

Notice that each pair of percent signs in the next to last ECHO command is replaced with one percent sign when the batch file is executed.

Using the SHIFT Command for More Than Nine Parameters

For most uses of a batch file, nine replaceable parameters are sufficient. However, MS-DOS provides a way to access more than nine parameters when necessary. Do *not* use the notation %10 to indicate the tenth parameter, which is replaced with the first parameter value followed immediately by a 0.

The SHIFT command has no parameters. When executed, the value of each parameter takes on the value of the following parameter. For example %1 is assigned the value of the second parameter following the name of the batch file on the command line, %2 is assigned the value of the third parameter, etc. For example, suppose a batch file with the name SHIFTBAT.BAT has the contents:

```
ECHO OFF
ECHO First line   %1-%2-%3-%4-%5-%6-%7-%8-%9!
SHIFT
ECHO Second line  %1-%2-%3-%4-%5-%6-%7-%8-%9!
SHIFT
ECHO Third line   %1-%2-%3-%4-%5-%6-%7-%8-%9!
SHIFT
ECHO Fourth line  %1-%2-%3-%4-%5-%6-%7-%8-%9!
```

```
SHIFT
ECHO Fifth line   %1-%2-%3-%4-%5-%6-%7-%8-%9!
SHIFT
ECHO Sixth line   %1-%2-%3-%4-%5-%6-%7-%8-%9!
ECHO ON
```

When SHIFTBAT is entered on the command line with twelve
parameters as shown below, the screen display is as follows:

```
A>SHIFTBAT a b c d e f g h i j k l


A>ECHO OFF
First line   a-b-c-d-e-f-g-h-i!
Second line  b-c-d-e-f-g-h-i-j!
Third line   c-d-e-f-g-h-i-j-k!
Fourth line  d-e-f-g-h-i-j-k-l!
Fifth line   e-f-g-h-i-j-k-l-!
Sixth line   f-g-h-i-j-k-l--!


A>_
```

The hyphens and exclamation point demonstrate another feature
of SHIFTing replaceable parameters. When parameters have no value,
they have just that—*no value!* These are often referred to as *null*
parameters. In the sixth line of the example above, the %8 and %9 are
replaced with nothing, not even a space. Unexpected null parameters
can cause problems. For example, suppose that we execute our batch
file EDITNEW with only one parameter as follows:

```
CHDIR \LETTERS
PRINTCTL /WIDE
COPY %1 %2
WP %2
```

Recall that this batch file expects two parameters: a template
filename and the name of the file to be created. Here is what the screen
looks like after executing the batch file with a missing parameter:

```
A>EDITNEW SAMPLE.MEM


A>CHDIR \LETTERS
```

```
A>PRINTCTL /WIDE

A>COPY SAMPLE.MEM
File cannot be copied onto itself
        0 File(s) copied

A>WP

A>_
```

Notice that both places the %2 replaceable parameter appears in the batch file are replaced with nothing. As a result, the COPY command executes with only one parameter and does not copy any files, but gives an error message instead. On the next line, our word processor executes without the intended filename. The contents of your batch file determines whether a missing parameter causes problems. The next section shows how to check for a missing parameter.

CHECKING FOR MISSING PARAMETERS IN BATCH FILES

You may have several reasons for wanting to determine whether a replaceable parameter was specified on the command line when a batch file was executed. First, you may want to supply a default value if no parameter is given. Second, you may want to display an error message if no parameter was given, then exit the batch file. Finally, the batch command file may accept a variable number of parameters, so you need to determine how many parameters have been specified.

The following example shows how to test whether a parameter exists. The batch file, named WSPRINT.BAT, executes a program named WSSTRIP.COM with the file specified by the first parameter of the batch file as input and a temporary file named TEMP.TMP as output. The program reads in the input file, *strips* (removes) the high order bits from all characters in the file, and writes the characters to the output file. This allows the file to be listed on the printer. The batch file is useful to obtain a listing of a WordStar document "as is," including the WordStar "dot commands." The listed output is quite different than that printed using the WordStar print command, which reformats pages and adds header and footer lines and page numbers, etc. The temporary file TEMP.TMP is deleted before the batch file terminates in order to reclaim the disk space. The original file specified as a parameter to the batch file is not modified by the batch file at any time.

```
ECHO OFF
REM
REM  This batch file prints a WordStar files "as is"
REM
IF "%1" == "" GOTO NOPARM
WSSTRIP < %1 > TEMP.TMP
TYPE TEMP.TMP > PRN:
DEL TEMP.TMP
GOTO ENDBAT
:NOPARM
ECHO WARNING:  No filename was specified, exiting batch file.
:ENDBAT
```

Notice that the parameter being tested is within quotes and that it is compared to a pair of quotes.

You may question why the IF command is not written as:

```
A>IF %1 ==   GOTO NOPARM
```

```
Bad Command Name
```

This IF command is asking MS-DOS to compare the value of the first parameter to GOTO. If it is not equal, the command on the next line is executed. If the value of the first parameter is GOTO, MS-DOS attempts to execute the command NOPARM. Because you probably do not have a program on your disk named NOPARM, the message `Bad command name` is displayed and execution resumes at the command on the next line of the batch file.

Characters other than quotes may also be used. Some MS-DOS users prefer to use parentheses, for example: IF (%1) == ( ) GOTO NOPARM. You may use any character(s) you choose to make the IF statement readable, but avoid the characters <, >, and ¦, or MS-DOS attempts to perform data redirection or piping with the IF command.

The following trick box shows how to use checking for nonexistent parameters in order to process a variable number of parameters.

USING A VARIABLE NUMBER OF BATCH FILE PARAMETERS

One of the useful functions that a batch file can perform is executing a command a variable number of times depending on the number of parameters specified on the command line when the batch file is executed. The technique introduced in the preceding trick box, *Checking for Missing Parameters in Batch Files,* is used to determine whether additional parameters have been specified. When the parameter list is exhausted, the batch file terminates.

The following example is similar to the one in the previous trick box. It differs in that more than one WordStar file may be listed if desired each time the batch file is executed.

```
ECHO OFF
REM
REM  This batch file prints one or more WordStar files "as is"
REM
IF "%1" == "" GOTO NOPARM
:DOSTRIP
ECHO Processing file %1 . . .
WSSTRIP < %1 > TEMP.TMP
TYPE TEMP.TMP > PRN:
DEL TEMP.TMP
SHIFT
IF "%1" == "" GOTO ENDBAT
GOTO DOSTRIP
:NOPARM
ECHO WARNING:  No filename(s) specified, exiting batch file.
:ENDBAT
```

The SHIFT subcommand is used to make this type of *iterative* processing easy. The current file is always the parameter specified by %1. If the parameter was specified, it is processed and the next parameter is shifted to become %1, the new current file. When the current file has a null value (it is not specified), the batch file terminates with the GOTO ENDBAT clause of the IF subcommand.

CAUTION

AVOIDING TAB CHARACTERS
IN BATCH FILES

The ASCII TAB character (hexadecimal 09) is often used to represent several spaces. Many word processors and text editors use this convention in order to make files smaller when they are written to disk. Occurrences of consecutive ASCII Space characters (hexadecimal 20) are replaced with fewer TAB characters (or a combination of Space and TAB characters). A significant savings in the amount of disk space required for the file is often achieved. When the file is read by the same program and displayed on the screen, the TAB characters are *expanded* (replaced with multiple Space characters).

The significant disk space savings achieved with this technique may make it appear that you are getting something for nothing! Unfortunately, different programs interpret the TAB character in different ways. A discussion of the most common methods used to interpret the TAB character would require a lot of time and space. The important point is that problems can occur when one program writes a file with TAB characters and another program reads the file interpreting the TAB characters differently.

When your batch command is executed, MS-DOS reads each line of the batch file, finds the command name on the line, then attempts to execute the command. When the command is executed, the remainder of the line is "passed" to the command so that it may inspect the line for parameters.

This "passing" of the command line is done without any interpretation of TAB characters. Consequently, the manner in which TAB characters are interpreted depends on the individual command. One important point is that it is *impossible* for the command to interpret TAB characters in the same way as your word processor does because the command cannot know what modifications have been made to the command line it has received from MS-DOS (MS-DOS removes data redirection and file piping information before passing on the command line).

Fortunately, MS-DOS commands are consistent in their interpretation of the TAB character when it is used as a delimiter between parameters. Multiple occurrences of TAB characters, Space characters, or combinations of these characters are interpreted as a single delimiter. You do, however, get some surprises when the TAB character is used for something other than a delimiter. This could happen when you are using the MS-DOS FIND filter to find lines in a file containing multiple spaces. For example, suppose that you want to find all lines in a file containing the appearance of ten spaces followed by an asterisk.

```
FIND SAMPLE.TXT "          *"
```

Many word processors would convert the sequence of characters between the quotes to the four characters TAB TAB Space* as the batch file is written to disk. The MS-DOS FIND filter searches the file SAMPLE.TXT for sequences of these four characters, *not* ten spaces followed by an asterisk.

The MS-DOS REM and ECHO commands also interpret the TAB character differently than you intend. Comments carefully aligned for readability are displayed with apparently haphazard alignments.

The problems with MS-DOS commands can be annoying, and the problem with the FIND filter can be difficult to find if you are not aware of what is happening. These problems are minor, however, compared to those that can occur with programs purchased or obtained through the public domain.

Some programs attempt to expand the TAB character using the most common *standard* method used by word processors. Remember, however, that this *cannot* be done correctly because of the modifications MS-DOS may have made to the command line. Other programs convert each occurrence of the TAB character to a single Space character. A few programs simply exit when the first TAB character is encountered in the command line, usually displaying a message something like Invalid parameter. Another common method that programs use to handle the TAB character is to simply ignore it. This can lead to problems when the TAB appears as a delimiter because two adjacent parameters separated only by a TAB character are interpreted as a single parameter.

The obvious conclusion of this warning is: Don't create batch command files with word processors that replace multiple spaces with the TAB character. If your word processor has an option to override this feature, use it.

Otherwise, change to another word processor or text editor when creating batch files. The problems created when the TAB character appears in a batch file are not necessarily disastrous, but discovering the cause of the unexpected results can be very difficult.

EXECUTING BATCH FILES WITHIN BATCH FILES

A batch command file may be executed within another batch command file without causing any problems. However, unless you take care, the results may not be exactly what you intended. When a batch file that has been executed within another batch file terminates, MS-DOS returns to the command line. The batch file that invoked the second batch file does *not* resume processing at the command following the one that invoked the second batch file. A short example with two batch files named FIRST.BAT and SEC-OND.BAT illustrates this point.

```
A>TYPE FIRST.BAT
REM Hi!  I'm the FIRST batch file.
SECOND %0
REM Bye from the FIRST batch file.


A>TYPE SECOND.BAT
REM Hi!  I'm the SECOND batch file.
REM I was called by a batch file named %1.
REM Bye from the SECOND batch file.


A>FIRST


A>REM Hi!  I'm the FIRST batch file.


A>FIRST


A>REM Hi!  I'm the SECOND batch file.


A>REM I was called by a batch file named FIRST.


A>REM Bye from the SECOND batch file.


A>_
```

Notice that the REM command of the *first* batch file is not executed. Instead, MS-DOS returned to the command line when the *second* batch file completed execution. This implies that batch files can be executed from other batch files when the command invoking the second batch file is the *last* command in the calling batch file. This is often referred to as *chaining* batch files.

The only other time when it is appropriate to execute another batch file from within a batch file is when you do not require the remaining commands in the calling batch file to execute. The following example shows how this might be useful. After commands common to day-end, weekend, and month-end processing are executed, a batch file named MONTHLY, WEEKLY, or DAILY is executed, depending on the value of a parameter given to the ENDDAY command when it is executed.

```
A>TYPE ENDDAY.BAT
```

```
ECHO OFF
REM First, back up the transaction files.
ECHO Place transaction backup disk in drive A:
PAUSE
FOR %A IN ( *.TRX *.BCH ) COPY %%A A: /V
IF (%1) == () GOTO DoDaily
IF %1 == 'w' GOTO DoWeek
IF %1 == 'W' GOTO DoWeek
IF %1 == 'm' GOTO DoMonth
IF %1 == 'M' GOTO DoMonth
ECHO Warning:   Invalid parameter %1
GOTO EndBat
:DoMonth
ECHO Monthly reports will be generated.
MONTHLY
:DoWeek
ECHO Weekly reports will be generated.
WEEKLY
:DoDaily
ECHO Daily reports will be generated.
DAILY
:EndBat
```

Although these are useful features of batch command file processing, it would also be useful to be able to execute a batch file from within another batch file, then to resume processing of the original batch file at the command following the command that called the second batch file. Many MS-DOS users know that there is a way to do this, but avoid it because it must be complicated. In reality, it is quite easy to do: Simply execute the command named COMMAND with the parameter [/C] followed by the name of the batch file to be executed and any parameters required by the batch file. The following screen shows the general format.

```
COMMAND /C [command-with-optional-parameters]
```

The space following the [/C] is not required. The [command] that is to be executed may be any type of command (internal, external, or batch). However, the COMMAND command is generally useful only when executing a batch command. Do not attempt to execute a [command] that uses data redirection or piping. The redirection or piping applies to the COMMAND command, not the [command] that is to be executed. There is a slight disadvantage to executing commands in this manner. An additional amount of memory is required for the execution of the COMMAND program that executes the [command] following the [/C] parameter. As a result, some commands that normally execute successfully on your system may fail when executed in this way due to lack of sufficient memory.

The following example shows the two batch files FIRST.BAT and SECOND.BAT used in the first example of this trick box. Notice the small change made to the second line of the first batch file.

```
A>TYPE FIRST.BAT
REM Hi!  I'm the FIRST batch file.
COMMAND /C SECOND %0
REM Bye from the FIRST batch file.


A>TYPE SECOND.BAT
REM Hi!  I'm the SECOND batch file.
REM I was called by a batch file named %1.
REM Bye from the SECOND batch file.


A>FIRST


A>REM Hi!  I'm the FIRST batch file.


A>COMMAND /C SECOND FIRST


A>REM Hi!  I'm the SECOND batch file.


A>REM I was called by a batch file named FIRST.


A>REM Bye from the SECOND batch file.


A>


A>REM Bye from the FIRST batch file.


A>
```

Notice that because of the method in which the FIRST batch file called the SECOND batch file, the remainder of the FIRST batch file was executed following the execution of the SECOND batch file.

USING ENVIRONMENT VARIABLES WITH BATCH FILES

MS-DOS provides an *environment* that is made available to all MS-DOS commands and programs, including batch commands. The environment consists of a number of *environment variables* (or strings) that may be inserted in or deleted from the environment with the MS-DOS SET command accompanied by the appropriate parameters. The SET command with *no* parameters may also be used to display the variables currently in the environment.

Environment variables were an enhancement added to MS-DOS Version 2.0. Two environment variables are used by MS-DOS to determine the prompt that is displayed on the command line and the path searched when looking for external commands to be executed. These environment variables are named PROMPT and PATH and may be modified with the MS-DOS commands with the same name (PROMPT and PATH) or the SET command.

A few examples using the SET command will give you a better understanding of what the environment is and for what purpose environment variables might be used. The following example displays the current environment variables (there are none) using the SET command with no parameters, then creates two variables named ONE and TWO and displays the environment variables again.

```
A>SET


A>SET ONE=A:


A>SET two = b:


A>SET


ONE=A:
TWO = b:


A>_
```

Your environment already may have some variables defined by your AUTOEXEC.BAT file. A typical example follows.

```
C>SET
COMSPEC=C:\COMMAND.COM
PROMPT=Date: $d  Time: $t  $p $_$n$g
PATH=C:\;C:\COMMON;C:\MSOFT;C:\TURBO;C:\NORTON;C:\MASM
LIBPATH=\SYM
TERM=IBMMONO
LIB=\MODULA\EMLIB+\MODULA\DSLIB+\MODULA\MODULA
FF=\FILEFAC
ONE=A:
TWO = b:


A>_
```

There is a limited amount of memory that can be used to add variables to the environment. This limit can be changed to allow more extensive use of the environment. The method by which this limit may be increased varies depending on the version of MS-DOS your computer system is running. Chapter 13 of this book has more details on how to make this change to your system.

In order to access the value of an environment variable in a batch file, the name of the environment variable is specified by enclosing it in percent signs. For example, to access the variable named ONE in the example above, the string %ONE% is placed in the batch file. Before MS-DOS executes a command within a batch file, it first evaluates it, replacing all occurrences of replaceable parameters, environment variables, and FOR subcommand variables with their current value. Consequently, MS-DOS evaluates the command COPY *.* %ONE% /V as COPY *.* A: /V before it is executed.

The following batch file uses a program named LIST that requires two parameters. The first parameter to the LIST program is the name of a file to be listed on a printer, the second parameter is the number of lines per page. The batch file, named LISTN.BAT, lists up to ten files using the same lines per page parameter.

```
A>TYPE LISTN.BAT
ECHO OFF
REM
REM   LISTN Batch File:  First parameter is lines per page,
REM   followed by up to ten files to be listed.
REM
IF NOT (%1) == () GOTO SaveLPP
ECHO WARNING:  No lines per page parameter was given.
GOTO EndBat
:SaveLPP
REM Save first parameter (lines per page) in environment.
SET LPP=%1
REM Make parm 2 parm 0, parm 3 parm 1, parm 4 parm 2, etc.
SHIFT
SHIFT
REM List the file(s).
FOR %%P IN (%0 %1 %2 %3 %4 %5 %6 %7 %8 %9 ) DO LIST %%P %LPP%
REM Delete LPP environment variable.
SET LPP=
:EndBat
```

Environment variables can be used for a large number of purposes. You can save the current value of the PROMPT variable using SAVPROMPT=%PROMPT%, change the user's PROMPT for the duration of the batch file, then restore the original value of the PROMPT using PROMPT=%SAVPROMPT%.

Another common application of environment variables is to set up a number of predefined environment variables in the AUTOEXEC.BAT files for a number of different systems that specify which drive and pathname should be accessed to find certain files. Batch files that access these environment variables may be used on all of these systems without modification.

In addition to their usefulness for batch file processing, environment variables are becoming more commonly used by application programs to tell them which directories should be searched to find their data, overlays, configuration files, etc. As this trend continues, it will become easier to install applications software on your system. Programs will be able to access environment variables set up by your AUTOEXEC.BAT file to determine the "environment" in which they are operating.

TRICK   **DEBUGGING BATCH COMMAND FILES**

Obviously, some batch files can become very complex and should not be trusted to work properly unless they have been thoroughly tested. Because executing a batch file may require running lengthy reports or other time-consuming programs, it would be convenient to have a method of testing them efficiently.

Fortunately, you can test batch command files quite thoroughly without consuming an excessive amount of time. Simply precede time-consuming commands with the REM subcommand, remove any ECHO OFF commands, and run the batch file a number of times with various combinations of likely parameter values. Do not precede any of the batch subcommands (ECHO, FOR, GOTO, IF, SHIFT, PAUSE, or REM) with the REM command in order to allow iteration, branching, and conditional logic to take place while the batch file is tested.

As the test runs of the batch file are executed, the commands that would normally be executed are displayed on the screen with the replaceable parameters, environment variables, and FOR subcommand variables fully evaluated. Be sure to test the batch file with invalid parameter combinations to ensure that missing or incorrect parameters do not cause serious problems when the batch file is executed "for real." If you have a printer, you may press the Ctrl-P key combination before entering the batch command and parameters to be tested. This causes the display on your screen to be listed on your printer as your testing proceeds.

Summary

This chapter has shown how to use many of the batch subcommands provided in MS-DOS and has described some of the ways that files can be used to accomplish certain types of tasks. Many of the topics covered included features of batch processing that have been poorly documented in the MS-DOS technical documentation, and in some cases, not documented at all. Batch files can be a lot of fun if you are willing to take the time to experiment with their known and newly discovered capabilities. Throughout the rest of this book, batch file examples are provided, many of which incorporate the features discussed in this chapter. As a logical extension of MS-DOS commands and batch files, the next chapter deals with the features of redirection and pipes that were introduced in MS-DOS Version 2.0.

Secrets of Redirection, Pipes, and Filters   Chapter 3

All the features discussed in this chapter were introduced in version 2.0 of MS-DOS. The MS-DOS redirection, pipe, and filter features are similar to an equivalent set of features in the UNIX operating system. The concept of data redirection is quite simple: Data normally originating from the keyboard or destined for the screen can be "redirected" to come from or go to another device or a disk file. Piping is the redirection of data directly from one program into another. Filters are special programs that read data from the keyboard, process the data, and write it to the screen. Filters are often used with data redirection, but the use of data redirection is optional.

Although the redirection features of MS-DOS are very useful, they have not been as fully utilized as you might expect. The documentation for using redirection is not overwhelmingly clear in the MS-DOS manuals. In addition, CP/M users were not accustomed to having data redirection available. Many applications avoided reliance on the feature when it was introduced in order to maintain compatibility with version 1.0 of MS-DOS. Now that MS-DOS version 1.0 is nearly extinct, use of the redirection features is becoming more common. The examples and tricks presented in this chapter will help you make use of these powerful MS-DOS features.

Redirection of Output Data

One of the most practical applications of output redirection also provides a simple example. The MS-DOS DIR command is used to display the contents of a disk directory on the screen. At times, you might rather have the directory contents listed on a printer. This is accomplished easily by using output redirection:

```
A>DIR > PRN:
```

The directory display that normally would be printed on the screen is listed on the printer. The > following the DIR command indicates redirection of output data. The > sign must be followed immediately with the name of an output device or disk file. In this example, the printer output device is used, indicated by the reserved device name PRN:. Parameters for the DIR command are allowed before or after the redirection designation (> PRN:) on the command line. For example, to display the directory information for all batch files in the wide format, use any of the following commands:

```
DIR > PRN: *.BAT /W
DIR *.BAT > PRN: /W
DIR *.BAT /W > PRN:
```

The *.BAT parameter specifies that directory information is to be displayed only for files with a filename extension of BAT. The /W parameter instructs the DIR command to display the directory in the wide format. The > PRN: specifies to MS-DOS that output for this command is to be redirected to the printer—it is *not* a parameter to the DIR command. Placing any redirection specifications on the end of the command line (as in the third line of the above example) is usually the preferred format, although only to improve the readability of command lines as we see them on the screen. MS-DOS is capable of interpreting equally well all the formats of the command line shown.

All the preceding examples redirect screen output to the printer output device. Redirecting screen output to a disk file is just as easy: Specify the name of a disk file after the output redirection symbol (>). For example, the command

```
A>DIR \REPORTS > DIRINFO.LST
```

```
A>_
```

sends the directory information for the directory named \REPORTS to a file named DIRINFO.LST in the current directory. If you want to view the directory information on the screen, enter TYPE DIRINFO.LST on the command line. Using redirection with the following command, the contents of the DIRINFO.LST file can also be listed on the printer.

```
A>TYPE DIRINFO.LST > PRN:
```

Saving directory information in a file in this manner is often useful for the comparison of directory contents before and after a program or batch file executes.

Now that you are familiar with the basics of output redirection, you have an easy-to-use but powerful trick that has many useful applications. Be sure to read the information boxes in this chapter for additional ideas on using redirection. Use care to avoid overwriting files that contain data you do not want to lose. MS-DOS replaces existing files with a new file *without warning* when output redirection is specified to a file that already exists. The following trick shows how you can avoid this accidental loss of data within MS-DOS batch command files.

HOW TO AVOID OVERWRITING DISK FILES IN A BATCH FILE

Redirecting screen output to a disk file is allowed within MS-DOS batch command files. Any command in the batch file can use the > followed by a device or disk filename to indicate output redirection. Because MS-DOS simply opens a disk file and writes any screen output to the file, the possibility exists that the original data in the file will be lost if a file with the same name already exists. In some cases, this may be what you intend for the batch file to do—if a file with the same name already exists, replace it with the new file.

When you do *not* want to lose the existing file, the batch file subcommand IF with the EXIST parameter may be used to check for the existence of a disk file before overwriting. The following batch file, named SAVEDIR.BAT, creates a file with output from a DIR command in a file named DISKINFO.LST *only if the file does not already exist:*

```
ECHO OFF
REM
REM   SAVEDIR.BAT batch file.  Saves the directory
REM   information for the file(s) given by the
REM   batch file parameter in a disk file named
REM   DISKINFO.LST.  If the file already exists,
REM   it is not overwritten and an error message
```

```
REM  is displayed.
REM
IF NOT EXIST DISKINFO.LST GOTO DOLIST
ECHO Warning:  The file DISKINFO.LST already exists!
ECHO           Exiting batch file WITHOUT creating
ECHO           a new file.
GOTO ENDBAT
:DOLIST
ECHO Creating directory information file DISKINFO.LST . . .
DIR %1 > DISKINFO.LST
:ENDBAT
ECHO ON
```

The batch file user could be given the choice of exiting the batch file or overwriting the DISKINFO.LST file by changing a few of the commands that follow the IF subcommand.

When you are redirecting screen output to a device (such as PRN: or AUX:), the device must actually exist or the results are unpredictable. In some cases, the data is merely lost. However, the system also may "crash," requiring a system power-off/power-on restart. Redirecting screen output to the screen (reserved device name CON:, for console) is acceptable, but redundant. See the *Reserved MS-DOS Devices* information box at the end of this chapter for more detail on redirecting data to devices.

ELIMINATING "SCREEN CLUTTER" USING REDIRECTION IN BATCH FILES

Several MS-DOS commands display progress information on the screen as the command is performing its function. Whether this information is useful depends on the context in which the command is used. Using output redirection is a convenient way to make this output optional.

When the output is not wanted, redirect the command output to the null device with > NUL:. The null device is just what its name implies—nothing! Any output redirected to it is gone forever, so be sure that the output is unwanted before you redirect it to the null device.

When batch command files are executed with ECHO OFF, the output from commands may be confusing to the person using the batch command file. For example, the MS-DOS command sequence COPY FORE-

CAST.WKS A: /V generates the message 1 file(s) copied when it is executed. With ECHO OFF, the COPY command line is not displayed during the execution of the batch file, and the 1 file(s) copied message seems to appear out of context. Redirecting the output of the COPY command to the NUL: device can eliminate this confusion. The ENDDAY.BAT batch command file in the following example uses this technique combined with progress messages displayed with the ECHO command to inform the user of the progress of the batch command file as it executes.

Output that clutters the screen but is to be saved should be redirected to a disk file. This technique can be used to suppress verbose screen displays while a batch file is executing but preserves the data normally displayed if it is required for review at a later time.

The suppressing of command output is generally useful only within batch files. The following example is the ENDDAY.BAT batch file used to back up important files at the end of each workday:

```
ECHO OFF
REM
REM  ENDDAY.BAT batch file.  Backs up all report,
REM  transaction, and memo files on disk.
REM
ECHO Put REPORT backup disk in drive A:
PAUSE
ECHO Backing up REPORT files to disk . . .
COPY \REPORTS\*.RPT A: /V > NUL:
REM
ECHO Put TRANSACTION backup disk in drive A:
PAUSE
ECHO Backing up TRANSACTION files to disk . . .
COPY \TRANSACT\*.TRX A: /V > NUL:
REM
ECHO Put MEMO backup disk in drive A:
PAUSE
ECHO Backing up MEMO files to disk . . .
COPY \MEMOS\*.MEM A: /V > NUL:
REM
ECHO ON
```

Notice that the output of each COPY command is redirected to the null device using > NUL:. After the batch file execution is completed, its entire output remains visible on the screen. If the COPY command output is not suppressed, the name of each file copied is displayed on the screen with each filename on a separate line. When several files are backed up using this version of the batch file (without redirecting COPY output to the null device), the verbose output of the COPY command causes the screen to scroll and useful information is lost from sight before the batch file has completed execution.

Suppressing screen output must be done with care. Many MS-DOS commands are inconsistent in the way they display error messages. Some are directed to the "standard error device," which means they are always displayed on the screen despite any output redirection specified for the command. Other error messages are directed to the "standard output device" and are not displayed on the screen when output redirection is used. It would be preferable if MS-DOS commands would be consistent about sending error messages to the standard error device and progress messages to the standard output device.

Because of the arbitrary behavior of MS-DOS commands, it is usually more reliable to redirect output that clutters the screen to a log file that may be examined later if problems are encountered.

Appending Output Data to an Existing File

We have seen how easy it is to redirect the screen output of a program to a newly created disk file. With MS-DOS, it is just as easy to add redirected output data from a program to the *end* of an existing disk file. The symbol for appending redirected output to a file is $>>$, *two* greater-than signs rather than one. For example, to create a file named DIRINFO.LST that contains the directory information for two disk directories, enter the commands

```
A>DIR \REPORTS >  DIRINFO.LST
```

```
A>DIR \MEMOS    >> DIRINFO.LST
```

```
A>_
```

The first command creates the file DIRINFO.LST, which contains the information for the REPORTS disk directory. The second command appends the information for the MEMOS disk directory to the end of the data already in the DIRINFO.LST file created by the first DIR command.

A few features of appending redirected screen output should be observed:

1. Appending redirected output to a device (such as PRN:) has no special effect. Thus, using > PRN: and > > PRN: are always

equivalent. Whether any data was previously redirected to the device is irrelevant.

2. Appending redirected output to a disk file that does not exist creates a new file with no data, then appends the redirected data to the newly created empty file. This feature makes appending to a file that does not already exist equivalent to redirecting data using the > symbol. This is a nice feature of MS-DOS, but be aware that no warning message is displayed.

3. When output is redirected to a disk file that contains an end-of-file marker (hexadecimal 1A), the screen data is correctly appended after the end file marker. However, many MS-DOS commands and other programs treat text files in a special way and ignore the contents of the file following the end-of-file marker.

The consequences of the manner in which MS-DOS appends to files with an end-of-file marker can result in what appears to be very mystifying behavior. Suppose that you have a file named TEST which ends with an end-of-file marker. The command DIR > > TEST would append the directory information for the current directory to the end of the file. When you examine the file size of the file before and after the append operation, you observe that the file has increased in size by the appropriate number of characters. However, if you TYPE the contents of the file to the screen, the file *appears* to remain unchanged. This is due to the fact that the MS-DOS TYPE command (and many other programs, such as WordStar) ignores all data in a text file after the first end-of-file marker encountered. The data does exist, but most programs hide it from view.

If the data hidden after the end-of-file marker is important, it may be recovered using the DEBUG command. See Chapter 7 for an example. The best cure, however, is an ounce of prevention. The following offers a batch file that can be used to remove any end-of-file markers from text files before redirected data is appended to them.

REMOVING END-OF-FILE MARKERS FROM TEXT FILES

When you use the MS-DOS redirection feature to append output to the end of a disk file, problems can occur if the file to be appended to ends with one or more end-of-file markers (hexadecimal 1A). Several commonly used programs (such as WordStar) create text files with trailing end-of-file markers for compatibility with operating systems other than MS-DOS. A number of programs exist that modify a file to eliminate this problem, but all that is needed is to use some of the lesser known parameters of the COPY command that comes with MS-DOS. The following batch file, named STRIPEOF.BAT, shows the COPY command parameters used to strip the end-of-file marker:

```
ECHO OFF
REM
REM   STRIPEOF.BAT batch file.  Requires one parameter,
REM   the name of a text file that is to have the end-
REM   of-file marker removed.  Uses a temporary file
REM   that is not overwritten if it already exists.
REM   If disk space is exhausted during the COPY
REM   operation, the original file is untouched.
REM
IF NOT EXIST TEMP1.$$$ GOTO DOCOPY
ECHO Warning:  The file TEMP1.$$$ would be replaced,
ECHO           batch file will terminate without
ECHO           modifying the file %1.  RENAME or
ECHO           ERASE the TEMP1.$$$ file and rerun.
GOTO ENDBAT
:DOCOPY
ECHO Modifying text file %1 . . .
COPY %1 /A TEMP1.$$$ /B
IF NOT EXIST TEMP1.$$$ GOTO NOSPACE
ERASE %1
RENAME TEMP1.$$$ %1
GOTO ENDBAT
:NOSPACE
ECHO Warning:  The file %1 cannot be modified,
ECHO           probably due to insufficient disk
ECHO           space.  Correct the problem and
ECHO           rerun STRIPEOF to modify the
ECHO           text file %1.
:ENDBAT
ECHO ON
```

The COPY command with the correct parameters is all you need to create a file without any end-of-file markers. The remainder of the batch file, however, serves the useful function of ensuring that no data is lost accidentally.

The parameter /A following the source filename instructs the COPY command to "treat all characters up to, but not including, the first end-of-file marker as input data." The parameter /B following the target filename instructs the COPY command to "write the data to the file but do *not* follow the data with an end-of-file marker."

HOW MS-DOS KNOWS WHERE YOUR FILE ENDS

Many features of the MS-DOS operating system are patterned after the CP/M operating system, which is the most commonly used operating system for 8-bit microcomputers. Text files under the CP/M operating system were always terminated with an end-of-file character (hexadecimal 1A or Ctrl-Z) to indicate the precise end of the text file. This was necessary because CP/M disk files were allocated in sizes that were a multiple of the disk sector size, normally 128 bytes. If a text file, such as a memo, was 120 bytes, a 121st byte end-of-file marker was added to the file to indicate that the remaining seven bytes of the file should be ignored when processing the file.

MS-DOS also allocates disk files in "blocks," the size of the block varies from disk to disk. Under MS-DOS these allocation "blocks" are called *clusters* and often range in size from 1K to 4K bytes. The MS-DOS directory entry is maintained for each file on the disk. MS-DOS also has more information in the directory entry than does the CP/M operating system. The additional information includes the date and time the file was created and the size of the file in bytes (called the *byte count*).

With the additional byte count information available for each file, it is not necessary to use the end-of-file marker to indicate where the end of useful information in a file is located. However, to maintain some compatibility with CP/M disk files and applications, several MS-DOS commands that process text files use the end-of-file marker as an end of file indication. Many applications that were ported to the MS-DOS environment also continued to use the end-of-file marker to indicate the end of valid data in a text file. WordStar is an example of an application that makes use of the end-of-file character under MS-DOS.

The end-of-file character is therefore redundant within MS-DOS text files and creates a problem: The *byte count* for a text file may not coincide with the occurrence of the end-of-file marker. An example of this is when output from a command is concatenated or appended (using the > > redirection operator) to a WordStar file that ends with an end-of-file character. Programs that operate on the resulting file treat the file differently depending on the method the program uses to determine the end of valid data in the file.

Currently the trend is for programs to ignore any occurrence of end-of-file markers in a text file and rely on the byte count in the directory entry for a file as the true end-of-file indication. This approach has two advantages: The end-of-file character may be used within the file for other purposes (such as control information), and all files (text files and data files) have one and only one method of determining the exact amount of data in a file. However, with the large number of programs currently in existence that create or depend on the existence of the end-of-file marker, the day of one consistent method for determining the end of a file is quite some time in the future.

APPENDING REDIRECTED OUTPUT
TO LOG FILES

It often is helpful to maintain a log of the batch files that have been executed. You may be attempting to do this now with a word processor. Maybe your batch file is set up so that when it is executed, the word processor is invoked to update manually the log file with the time, date, batch filename, and name of the person executing the batch file. You may have even attempted to "automate" the process by giving a few instructions within the batch file using the ECHO command, then invoking the word processor.

Using the MS-DOS output redirection feature, you can fully automate this process. As an example, suppose that you have a batch file named REPORTS.BAT for which you want to maintain an execution log file. Here's how to start the batch file:

```
ECHO OFF
TYPE CRLF.INP >> REPORTS.LOG
ECHO Starting batch file REPORTS.BAT >> REPORTS.LOG
DATE < CRLF.INP >> REPORTS.LOG
TIME < CRLF.INP >> REPORTS.LOG
ECHO ^H
ECHO ^H
ECHO Enter your name followed by the F6 key, then the Enter key
ECHO ^H
COPY CON: REPORTS.TMP > NUL:
TYPE REPORTS.TMP >> REPORTS.LOG
TYPE CRLF.INP >> REPORTS.LOG
ERASE REPORTS.TMP
. . .
(remainder of batch file commands)
```

This example assumes the existence of a file named CRLF.INP that contains two ASCII characters, the carriage return (hexadecimal 0D) and line feed (hexadecimal 0A) characters. These two characters are generated when you press the Enter key on your keyboard. The CRLF.INP file may be created quickly using the MS-DOS COPY command.

```
A>COPY CON: CRLF.INP
```

```
^Z
```

```
      1 File(s) copied


A>_
```

Notice the blank line following the COPY CON: CRLF.INP command. The Enter key is pressed twice, once to execute the COPY command and again to generate the carriage return and line feed that are copied into the CRLF.INP file. After the second time the Enter key is pressed, press the Ctrl-Z or F6 key to indicate end-of-file, followed by the Enter key again. Be careful, if you have redefined the F6 key for your keyboard, you must use the Ctrl-Z keystroke combination to indicate the end-of-file. Pressing the Ctrl-Z or F6 key causes the display of the ^Z characters on your screen.

When the REPORTS.BAT batch command file is executed, the following is displayed on the screen:

```
A>REPORTS
A>ECHO OFF


Enter new date:
Enter new time:


Enter your name followed by the F6 key, then Enter key


Pat
^Z


. . .
(remainder of batch file display)


A>_
```

Notice that MS-DOS fails to redirect the prompts for entering the date and time to the log file. Some MS-DOS commands are somewhat arbitrary about what messages are sent to the screen using the standard output device, which creates this minor annoyance. There are also variations on what messages use the standard output device between the different versions of MS-DOS, so your system may place these messages in the output redirection file. Also notice that several ECHO ^H commands are executed in order to provide the user of the batch file a more readable screen. See Chapter 2 for more information on the ECHO batch file subcommand.

The command TYPE CRLF.INP >> REPORTS.LOG is used to output blank lines to the log file to improve its readability. Here is what the log file looks like after the batch file has executed:

```
(previous contents of file)
. . .


Starting batch file REPORTS.BAT
Current date is Thu  7-03-1986

Current time is 18:23:41.19

Pat
```

A common pitfall when using the ECHO command in batch files is to enclose the function keys with the < and > characters, such as "the <F6> key." On a command line, however, this instructs MS-DOS to redirect the program input from a file named *F6* and redirect the output to a file named *key*! An alternate format, such as the reference to "the F6 key" in the previous example, avoids this problem: The data redirection symbols < and > were omitted.

The automatic logging feature is very useful also as a security feature. If you include a similar set of batch file commands in your AUTO-EXEC.BAT file (without the prompt for user name) you can detect whether anyone has turned on your computer while you are away by examining the contents of the REPORT.LOG file. See Chapter 13 for more information on the AUTOEXEC.BAT batch file, which is automatically executed whenever the computer is reset.

Redirecting Keyboard Input

The < is used to redirect standard input *into* a program. Input that normally would be input from the keyboard is instead input from the file or device that follows the < sign. For example, to delete *all* files from the current directory, the MS-DOS ERASE (or DEL) command with a wildcard file specification of *.* is used. When all files in a directory are to be deleted, the ERASE command requires a confirmation from the keyboard before the deletion is performed. Therefore, entering ERASE *.* on the MS-DOS command line results in the display of the following prompt:

```
A>ERASE *.*
Are you sure (Y/N)? _
```

You have to reply with a Y (to delete all files) or an N (to bypass the delete operation). Versions of MS-DOS 2.0 or higher also require the Y or N to be followed by the Enter key. The Ctrl-Break or Ctrl-C keys also may be used. They terminate the command without performing the delete operation. The reply may be in upper- or lowercase.

If you are certain that you will always want to reply with a Y to the Are you sure (Y/N)?_ prompt, the ERASE command is a good candidate for redirection of input. If a file named YES.INP resides in the current directory and contains a Y followed by the Carriage Return character (hexadecimal 0D and 0A), the preceding erase operation can be performed with the following command:

```
A>ERASE *.* < YES.INP
Are you sure (Y/N)? Y

A>_
```

This results in the ERASE command being a "hands off" command that requires no keyboard input. Notice that the prompt for input Are you sure (Y/N)?_ and the reply from the file named YES.INP (in this case, a Y) are still echoed to the screen. Notice also that this is now potentially very dangerous if the current disk and current directory are not correctly set. Hands off commands can be very useful and efficient, especially when used in batch files. However, they must be used with great care. Because the input for several MS-DOS commands (including the ERASE command) has changed slightly with new versions of MS-DOS, you may wonder whether you need to create several versions of the YES.INP file if you intend to use the ERASE command with redirection in several versions of MS-DOS. Fortunately, this usually can be avoided. The following explains how files for input redirection may be created to be compatible with all versions of MS-DOS.

Of course, entering ERASE *.* < YES.INP requires more keystrokes than entering ERASE *.*, waiting for the prompt, then pressing the Y and Enter keys. However, in a batch file that will be used several times, input redirection not only reduces the required number of keystrokes but also makes the batch file a hands off process.

CREATING INPUT FILES FOR
REDIRECTION TO MS-DOS COMMANDS

As MS-DOS has evolved, several commands have been modified to require a confirmation from the keyboard before an action is taken. These minor "enhancements" provide some insurance that potentially dangerous actions that could destroy data are not performed accidentally.

Although these changes provide increased protection against accidental data loss and other errors, there is a corresponding minor decrease in MS-DOS version compatibility.

Fortunately, these MS-DOS version incompatibilities usually can be overcome when redirecting input from a data file to an MS-DOS command. For example, the MS-DOS LABEL command (which is used to add, change, or delete a volume label) was modified with MS-DOS version 3.1 to prompt for a confirmation before deleting a volume label. When the command was introduced in MS-DOS version 3.0, no keyboard input was required for confirmation. If you are creating a batch file that uses the LABEL command to delete a volume label, always redirect an input file with the correct response into the command. When the batch file is executed on a system with a version of the LABEL command that requires no input, the input redirection does not do any harm as long as the input file can be found on disk. When executed on a system with a version that requires input, the correct response is redirected into the command.

Another minor incompatibility between MS-DOS versions are a few commands that previously required a response with *any* data key now require a response with the Enter key. Because the Enter key is considered a data key by versions that accept any data key, always use the Enter key in response files created for redirection into these commands. A few commands that previously responded to questions with a response of Y or N require the response to be followed with the Enter key. A response file that contains the proper response followed by the Enter key (hexadecimal 0D and 0A) works properly for redirection into these commands with all versions of MS-DOS.

Two important things to remember when creating files that will be used to redirect keyboard data into a program are

1. Redirecting data into a program that does not require input from the keyboard does not do any harm. The existence of the input file is verified and if found, the command executes normally and the contents of the file are ignored.

2. Redirecting more data into a program than the program requires does not do any harm. As long as the beginning data characters in the file are the correct responses to execute the program as desired and terminate it, any excess characters that follow are simply ignored.

Keeping these facts in mind when creating files for input redirection can be helpful in producing more portable files for other programs as well as MS-DOS commands.

Note that input may be redirected into MS-DOS commands that require *no* keyboard input. For example, the DIR command can be entered as DIR < YES.INP and still perform the directory display normally. No problems arise from this use of unnecessary input redirection. Because it serves no purpose, it is not recommended. In addition to adding an element of confusion, the execution of the DIR command is slowed slightly because the input file is searched for in the specified directory before the DIR command is executed. The fact that the file is not required is not known before the command executes and therefore the time spent searching for the file is wasted. In addition, if the file is not found, the message File not found is displayed and the execution of the DIR command is bypassed.

Redirection of keyboard input must be done with much care. For example, the only time most MS-DOS commands request keyboard input is to confirm that an action which destroys data (such as deleting files or formatting a disk) is to be performed. Redirecting input to these commands when the wrong disk is inserted in a floppy drive or from the wrong directory on a hard disk serves only to automate the destruction of data.

Input may be redirected from devices as well as disk files. The device must be an input device (AUX:, COM1:, etc.). Output only devices, such as PRN: (the printer), may not be used. Redirecting data from the console device (CON:) is an exercise in redundancy: Input that would normally come from the keyboard is redirected to come from the keyboard!

For practical reasons, it is usually tricky to redirect input from a device (such as a modem). If the device used is not working properly or fails before the command using input redirection is completed, no facility within MS-DOS exists to interrupt the program execution. To continue, a system reset using Ctrl-Alt-Del is usually required.

The most frustrating problem encountered when using input direction is the *short* input file. If a program using redirected input from a disk file executes and exhausts the contents of the file before the program has completed execution, the program "hangs," waiting for more input from the keyboard. A "hung" program can be even more difficult to detect if the screen output is redirected to the NUL: device or a RAM disk because evidence of the program's progress is not evident on the screen or blinking disk lights. Because MS-DOS does not provide any facility to interrupt the program, the only means to return to the MS-DOS command line is to reset the system using Ctrl-Alt-Del. The condition created with a short input file does not really "crash" the system. In fact, any memory resident program, such as Sidekick, continues to be available.

Another problem with using redirected input occurs with some programs that use "conditional logic" to determine whether keyboard input is required. For example, many programs check for a floppy disk in a drive before accessing the disk. If a floppy disk is found, program execution continues, using the disk. If the floppy disk is *not* found, a prompt asking you to insert the disk, then press the Space Bar is displayed. There is no facility within MS-DOS to *conditionally* press the Space Bar when using redirected input. If you cannot ensure conditions that will induce a program to request keystrokes in a predictable manner, the use of input redirection is of questionable value.

Using MS-DOS Filters

A program that receives its input from the standard input device, processes the data, and sends its output to the standard output device is referred to as a filter. Consequently if a filter is executed and no data redirection is specified, the input is from the keyboard and the output is to the screen. Although many filters perform only relatively minor processing of the data presented, they provide a very useful function.

MS-DOS versions 2.0 and higher are distributed with three standard filters: FIND, MORE, and SORT. The FIND filter finds lines of text that contain an ASCII string specified by a parameter. The MORE filter displays screen data one screenful at a time. And the SORT filter creates an output file of sorted records from the input file. For more information on these filters, see the information box titled *MS-DOS Filters*.

Because filters always use the standard input and output devices, they are often used effectively with data redirection for input, output, or both. Although it is often convenient to use redirection with filters, it is not necessary. For example, the following is an application of the SORT filter using input directly from the keyboard. Only the output of the SORT filter is redirected.

```
A>SORT > SORTCOL1.OUT
```

```
first
second
third
fourth
^Z


A>TYPE SORTCOL1.OUT
first
fourth
second
third


A>_
```

The output file SORTCOL1.OUT is produced with the inputted records sorted into alphabetical order. The SORTCOL1.OUT output file just created can be used as an input to the SORT filter:

```
A>SORT /+2 < SORTCOL1.OUT > SORTCOL2.OUT


A>TYPE SORTCOL2.OUT
second
third
first
fourth


A>_
```

The /+2 parameter for the SORT filter indicates the column of text in which to begin the comparison for the sort. Notice also that the name of the input file is *not* the same as the name of the output file. The following caution box explains what problems identical input and output names can cause.

CAUTION

REDIRECTING INPUT AND OUTPUT
ON THE SAME COMMAND

When using data redirection, MS-DOS allows the input and the output of a program to be redirected at the same time. There are, however, a few precautions that must be taken. *First, NEVER redirect input and output to the same file.* MS-DOS does not detect this condition and the results are unpredictable. However, one common result requires that the system be reset using Ctrl-Alt-Del or even a power-off/power-on restart.

Similar problems occur if files created, modified, or deleted by the command are also used for the redirection of input or output. The results are unpredictable. However, you can be sure they usually are not the results intended. An example of this would be to redirect the output of the MS-DOS TYPE command to the file being "typed." The result is that the original file is "lost," and a new file with the same name is created with a length of zero.

```
A>DIR *.TXT

     Volume in drive A has no label
  Directory of  A:

BIGMEMO.TXT      40960  10-06-86    8:41a
     1 File(s)      38272 bytes free

A>ECHO IMPORTANT:  The following is NOT recommended!
IMPORTANT:  The following is NOT recommended!

A>TYPE BIGMEMO.TXT > BIGMEMO.TXT

A>DIR *.TXT

     Volume in drive A has no label
  Directory of  A:

BIGMEMO.TXT          0  10-06-86    8:42a
     1 File(s)      79232 bytes free

A>_
```

Whenever commands are inadvertently executed with these conditions, run the MS-DOS CHKDSK command immediately to ensure that no disk problems have been generated. (Use the /F option for MS-DOS Versions 2.0 and higher.) The CHKDSK command also frees any disk space that has been allocated but is not in use.

Using the MS-DOS Piping Facility

MS-DOS "pipes" are a shorthand for redirecting output from one program into another program. For example, the following MS-DOS commands produce a screen display of directory information sorted by filename:

```
A>DIR > TEMP.XXX


A>SORT < TEMP.XXX


. . . sorted directory display . . .


A>ERASE TEMP.XXX


A>_
```

First, the output of the DIR command is redirected to a file named TEMP.XXX. Then, the TEMP.XXX file is redirected into the SORT command, which sorts the records from the file and displays them on the screen. The same results can be accomplished on one command line using the MS-DOS piping facility.

```
A>DIR | SORT


. . . sorted directory display . . .


A>_
```

The preceding command line may be read as "send the output of the DIR command to the SORT command." MS-DOS performs data piping (designated by the ¦ character) in a manner similar to the first example in this section: Output from the first command (DIR) is redirected to a temporary file on the disk. When the second command (SORT) executes, its input is redirected from the temporary file created by the first command. When all commands have completed, the temporary files are deleted. The temporary files created are named %TEMP1.$$$ and %TEMP2.$$$ in the root directory of the current disk. The actual filenames and number of temporary files created during the piping process differ between versions of MS-DOS, but the point is that the piping process is effectively the same as redirecting output from one command to a disk file, redirecting the disk file as input to the next command, then erasing the created temporary file(s) from disk.

The ¦ symbol, which designates piping on the command line,

must be followed immediately by the name of the program into which the piped data is to be sent. One or more spaces may be used for readability. However, all parameters for the previous command must be specified before the ¦ symbol on the command line.

Data may be piped several times within one command line. For example, DIR ¦ SORT ¦ MORE is a valid command line. There is no limit to the number of times piping may be specified on one command line, although the maximum length of the command line does impose some limitations. In practice, piping data between numerous programs, or programs that have a lengthy execution time, is not recommended because the temporary files will not be available for restarting should problems arise. The temporary files (%TEMP1.$$$ and %TEMP2.$$$) are erased from the disk when the commands using the piping facility are completed.

REMEMBERING WHAT SYMBOLS REPRESENT WHICH DIRECTION

First-time users of data redirection may have difficulty recalling which redirection symbol is associated with each redirection feature. Although you may not assign intuitively the symbols <, >, > >, and ¦ to their respective functions, an easy trick can help you picture what each symbol represents. If you imagine the < sign as the head of an arrow, the direction of the arrow accurately indicates that the flow of data is *from* a disk file (or device) *to* a program.

```
Program-Name   <-- Input-Disk-File-Name
```

You can remember the symbol for redirection of output with the same trick: the greater-than sign forms the head of an arrow representing the flow of data *from* a program *to* a disk file or device.

```
Program-Name   --> Output-Disk-File-Name
```

The symbol for a pipe is the vertical bar, so maybe you have to stretch your imagination a little to make your mind jump to plumbing whenever you encounter the ¦ symbol, but it is close enough. The symbol used to specify redirection of output when *appending* to an existing file (rather than creating a file) is *two* greater-than signs, a modification of the normal output redirection symbol.

CREATING INPUT REDIRECTION FILES USING SUPERKEY OR PROKEY

One of life's little frustrations is creating input files for redirecting data into a program. When the input file does not contain exactly the required characters to run the program correctly, the results are obviously not exactly what was intended. Unfortunately, one of the most common results is that the program hangs, waiting for more input from the keyboard after all the characters from the input file have been exhausted. Because MS-DOS does not accept keyboard input to complete the program execution, a system reset using Ctrl-Alt-Del is required.

Generating large files for input redirection requires considerable patience in order to refine the contents of the file. Running the program for which the input file is being created and writing down each required keystroke is a time-consuming and error-prone process. Keyboard enhancement programs such as Superkey and ProKey can be helpful in performing this task more quickly.

The procedure is similar for all keyboard enhancement programs: Execute the target program, begin a macro definition for the keyboard enhancement program, enter the keystrokes required to perform the desired function, end the macro definition, and save the macro definition on disk.

The .MAC file created by the macro definition process can now be printed and referenced to create an accurate data file for input redirection. For most applications, the file can be created using any word processor.

If the file must contain *control* characters (such as Ctrl-A, Esc, etc.), only word processors that allow the insertion of these characters into a data file may be used. If your word processor does not allow the entry of the required characters, the MS-DOS DEBUG command can be used to create the data file. Word processors are preferred over DEBUG because you can insert and delete characters more easily. WordStar, for example, allows easy entry of all the control characters from hexadecimal 1 through 1D except 1A (the Ctrl-Z or end-of-file marker character) using the Ctrl-P prefix.

Whereas keyboard enhancement programs can be helpful in creating data files for input redirection, they also can cause problems. Keyboard macros created for use with a program *cannot* be used when input is redirected from a disk file. Keyboard enhancement programs monitor the input directly from the keyboard. When a keystroke designating a macro is detected, the macro definition's keystrokes are placed into the keyboard buffer. When MS-DOS is redirecting input from a disk file, there is no keyboard activity for the keyboard enhancement program to monitor. A keystroke that normally would be expanded by a macro definition (if entered from the keyboard) is read from the disk file and placed directly into the keyboard buffer—*no macro expansion takes place.*

The lack of any macro expansion of keystrokes while input is being redirected from disk requires special attention when creating files for input redirection. Macro definitions for the keyboard enhancement program must be *cleared,* then all keystrokes to perform the desired functions must be entered in full.

HOW MS-DOS OPERATES USING DATA REDIRECTION

To use the data redirection features of MS-DOS, you do not need to have a detailed understanding of how they work. However, learning a few more facts about how MS-DOS redirection operates can be helpful in determining whether these features will work with certain programs.

When MS-DOS encounters one of the data redirection symbols (>, > >, <, or ¦) on the command line, it performs several functions before executing the associated command. The redirection symbol and its associated device or filename are removed from the command line so that when the command executes it does not attempt to interpret the redirection specification information as parameters. If input redirection is specified from a filename, MS-DOS attempts to locate the file on disk. If output redirection to a filename is specified, MS-DOS attempts to create the file on disk. If these operations are not successful, an error message is displayed and MS-DOS returns to the command line *without* executing the command. If these operations are successful the command is executed. While it is executing, the command has no indication that input or output is being redirected.

If output redirection is specified, any data that the command writes to the *standard output device* is redirected by MS-DOS to the specified device or disk file. In a similar manner, any data read from the *standard input device* is redirected from the specified device or disk file if input redirection is specified. All data redirection is performed directly by MS-DOS, so the command has no indication that redirection is being performed.

The term *standard output device* refers to one of the techniques that a program may use to write data to the screen. Programs may use several other techniques for screen display, including writing to the *standard error device* and moving data directly to the screen display area in memory. Only programs that use the standard output device to display data on the screen may be used with output redirection. Programs may use a combination of several different techniques to display screen data, which accounts for the fact that some screen output is redirected and other data is displayed on the screen.

Programs also may use several alternate techniques to accept input from the keyboard. Only input that programs read from the standard input device is redirected by MS-DOS. If input redirection is used with a program that uses a combination of keyboard input techniques, only some of the data is redirected from the specified device or disk file, whereas other data is input directly from the keyboard. An example of a program that uses a mixture of keyboard input techniques is the MS-DOS MORE command. The input text file is read using the standard input device and may originate from a disk file if input redirection is specified. The data characters that cause the screen to scroll when the --MORE-- prompt is displayed are read directly from the keyboard input port and must originate directly from the keyboard.

How can you tell if a program uses the standard input device? First, look at the program documentation. If that does not indicate whether input may be redirected, try executing the program and press Ctrl-Break when prompted for input. If the program terminates, it is a likely candidate for input redirection. Determining whether a program uses the standard output device is done in a similar manner. If pressing Ctrl-Break while a program is displaying data on the screen terminates the program, the program is a likely candidate for output redirection. Another test that can be made is pressing Ctrl-Num Lock to see whether the screen display stops scrolling until a data key is pressed.

Programs that do not stop scrolling certainly will not work with input redirection. In most cases, these tests will give you an accurate indication of whether data redirection is possible, although there are exceptions.

Unfortunately, the only way to be certain whether a program works with data redirection is to try it and see what happens. Although this may not be the miracle news you were hoping for, there is some good news. Trying redirection with programs that do not make use of redirection does not do any harm. Of course, if normal execution without redirection of the program would destroy large amounts of data, the results probably will be the same when using redirection.

Testing output redirection on a program is usually not difficult. The easiest technique is to redirect the output to the printer device using the > PRN: specification on the command line. Redirected output normally visible on your screen is output to your printer while the command is executing. Depending on how your printer buffers the data it receives, the printer output may be a few lines behind what would be displayed on the screen.

Testing input redirection can be a much more trying experience. While a program is reading keyboard input from a disk file, the keyboard is "locked out." Even the Ctrl-Break key is ineffective. You can expect to go through the three-finger restart procedure (system reset using Ctrl-Alt-Del) several times before getting the input file working properly.

One helpful hint when testing input redirection files: Always execute the BREAK ON command before starting your testing. If you see things begin to go wrong, the BREAK ON command helps to *increase* the chances that the Ctrl-Break key will terminate your program. This is not a sure thing, but sometimes you are lucky and the Ctrl-Break key takes effect during an interval when an output operation of the program is executing. After suffering through the exasperating experience of waiting for the reset cycle to complete numerous times, any measure that increases your odds is welcome.

Most MS-DOS commands that request keyboard input may be used with input data redirection. There are a few exceptions, such as the MORE command, which has two inputs as described previously.

Most screen output of MS-DOS commands also may be redirected. The exceptions to redirected screen output include the several commands that display error messages on the screen using the standard error device, which does not allow them to be redirected. New versions of MS-DOS often have minor undocumented changes that modify how screen information is displayed, so use caution when transferring applications that use redirection from one version of MS-DOS to another. In most cases, the differences between MS-DOS versions do not have any significant impact.

Using data redirection for commands within batch files is allowed by MS-DOS and is often very useful. Using redirection for an *entire* batch file, however, is an exercise in futility. Any input redirection for the batch file is ignored (after a check to make sure that the file destined to be "unused" exists). Any output redirection file created is an empty file. Ordinarily, no harm is done by specifying redirection for the batch file, although redirecting input from a nonexistent device may cause a system "hang," and redirecting output to an important disk file replaces the file with an empty file.

STANDARD MS-DOS FILTERS

Three filters are distributed with MS-DOS versions of 2.00 and higher. These are the FIND, MORE, and SORT filters. This information box gives a brief description of each of these filters along with a few hints about their use and undocumented glitches. Information about their syntax and parameters is available in your MS-DOS manual. Since the introduction of the data redirection facility in MS-DOS Version 2.00, improved versions of the standard MS-DOS filters and numerous additional filters have become available commercially and through public domain sources.

The MS-DOS FIND filter command "finds" occurrences of a string in text files. The standard input is a text file (which may be redirected from a device or disk). The output is a text file with each line of text that contains the specified string. The FIND filter is very useful when searching a large number of files for a particular string. Unfortunately, there are a number of restrictions. The program is case sensitive and not word-oriented, so a search for the string red outputs all lines containing the strings credit, Fred, and redirection but does *not* output lines containing the strings Red or RED.

Another limitation is that "white space" cannot be ignored. White space is normally defined as text characters that cannot be seen when printed, such as spaces, tabs, null characters, line feeds, and carriage returns. Several commercial and public domain programs are available that overcome these shortcomings and offer additional features. These programs are often named something like *grep,* which is the name of the UNIX counterpart to the MS-DOS FIND command.

The MS-DOS MORE filter command reads a file from the standard input device (which may be redirected from a device or disk) and displays it on the screen one screenful at a time pausing with the message --MORE--. Pressing any data key causes the display of another screenful of data until the input file is exhausted. The MORE filter is convenient for displaying large text files on the screen. An alternate method would be to TYPE the file and use the Ctrl-Num Lock key to manually halt the screen display when data is about to be scrolled out of sight. The MORE command is a simple yet elegant method of doing the same thing. Although the output of the MORE command may also be redirected to a device or disk file, this use of the command is unlikely to be useful.

The MS-DOS SORT filter command reads data from the standard input device, sorts the data, then outputs the data to the standard output device. The filter is very useful for sorting the output of another MS-DOS command before it is displayed on the screen. For example, DIR ¦ SORT is an easy way to sort by filename the information for a disk directory and display the information on the screen. The SORT filter is also useful for sorting small files created with a word processor, such as a name and address file. Every line of text in the file must have the data field to be sorted on in the same position within the line, so a name and address file with more than one line per entry is jumbled after being sorted unless the name is repeated in the same place on each line. Tab characters are not expanded by the SORT filter. If your word processor automatically inserts tabs, you probably need to place the data field to be sorted on so that it begins in the first column of each text line.

The documentation for the SORT filter states that files larger than 63K cannot be sorted. Unfortunately, attempting to sort a large file does not result in a "user friendly" message stating that the file is too large. The typical result is a system "hang" that requires a Ctrl-Alt-Del system reset. Even on files under 63K in size, the SORT filter is not fast and requires considerably more time to complete as the input file increases in size. If you are likely to be performing file sorts frequently, you should probably purchase a dedicated sorting program or find a suitable one among the public domain software.

The SORT filter is capable of sorting in ascending or descending ASCII sequence. The ASCII character set begins with numbers (0 through 9), capital letters (A through Z), followed by lowercase letters (a through z). Special characters (#, $, %, etc.) are interspersed before, after, and between these groups of characters. Consequently, sorting your list of favorite restaurants may give you the unexpected sequence of

13 Main

Zack's

l'Orangerie

See Appendix C for a complete table of the ASCII character set.

When the input and output of the SORT filter are disk files, you can easily make a simple mistake that can cause lost data, system resets, and general aggravation. When redirecting data, *never* specify input redirection and output redirection using the same filename. Rename the input file, SORT the file using the renamed file as input to the output file, examine the output file for correctness, then delete the original renamed file. A simple batch file can be created to perform this function.

RESERVED MS-DOS DEVICES

The source or destination of redirected data is always a disk file or a device. When redirection is from or to a device, the syntax is similar to the syntax used for disk file redirection: The redirection symbol (<, >, or >>) is followed by one of the MS-DOS reserved device names. This information box provides some advice on how to use these reserved device names and includes a table of the reserved names available in MS-DOS.

All reserved device names may be specified with or without a trailing colon (for example, CON or CON:). MS-DOS interprets these references in the same manner. Using the colon is normally preferred, however, because a reference without the colon is ambiguous to anyone who has not memorized the information contained in Table 3-1.

Table 3-1. Reserved MS-DOS Device Names

Reserved Name	Input/ Output	Description and Comments
CON:	Both	When used as output, CON: represents the display screen. When used as input, it represents the keyboard. As an input device, the F6 key or Ctrl-Z keystroke combination is used to generate an end-of-file indication, which ends CON: as the input device.
AUX:	Both	Normally assigned to COM1:, first asynchronous communications adapter port.
COM1:	Both	First asynchronous communications adapter port.
COM2:	Both	Second asynchronous communications adapter port.
PRN:	Output	Normally assigned to LPT1:, first parallel printer.
LPT1:	Output	First parallel printer.
LPT2:	Output	Second parallel printer.
NUL:	Both	The null device, a nonexistent or dummy device useful for testing applications or suppressing unwanted output data. When NUL: is used as an input device, an immediate end-of-file is generated. When used as an output device, NUL: is the "bit-bucket."

MS-DOS ignores the extensions of filenames that are identical to a reserved device name. Consequently, you cannot name the auxiliary dictionary for your spelling checker AUX.DIC because this filename is interpreted as the AUX: device.

When a device name is used for redirection, it must exist. Otherwise, the results are unpredictable. Unfortunately, no method is available to determine whether a device exists, so using device redirection within a batch file is an act of faith. Reserved device names are not used exclusively with data redirection. They also can be used without redirection in place of filenames for several MS-DOS commands. For example, the MS-DOS COPY command may have the source and/or destination of its data specified with device names. The command COPY CON: PRN: redirects input from the keyboard to the printer.

When a reserved device name is used, any preceding drive specifier or following filename extension is ignored. For example, DIR > B:PRN.LST is equivalent to DIR > PRN: but far more confusing. Reserved device names are not case-dependent, therefore prn:, PRN:, Prn: and prN: are all interpreted by MS-DOS as the reserved device name for the first parallel printer (or other device if the PRN: device has been reassigned).

Summary

This chapter has shown some of the advanced features introduced in MS-DOS Version 2.00 and have been retained and enhanced in subsequent versions of MS-DOS. The redirection, pipe, and filter features of MS-DOS, "borrowed" from the UNIX operating system, provide the MS-DOS user with considerably more power to perform various tasks at the MS-DOS command prompt level than previously available. The ability to perform these tasks, such as redirecting the output of a *sorted* directory listing to a file, can greatly simplify daily use of MS-DOS without our having to create complex batch procedures or custom programs. Despite the restrictions of the redirection, piping, and filter features pointed out in this chapter, they can be very useful when used with care.

Combining what you've learned in this chapter with the information on batch files in Chapter 2 can further enhance the usefulness of the redirection, piping, and filter features, often resulting in very powerful command procedures that perform tasks beyond some of your wildest dreams. Many of the features described in this chapter are used extensively throughout the rest of this book. The next chapter describes the concept of tree-structured directories and related features and commands.

Secrets of Tree-Structured Directories   Chapter 4

Most computer systems, including the IBM PC and its compatible systems, limit the user to a certain number of directory entries on a disk. With the IBM PC, the total number of available file directory entries depends on the type of disk in use. The limits are shown in Table 4-1.

Table 4-1. Directory Entry Limits by Disk Type

Disk Type	Directory Entries
Single-sided 40-track disk	64
Double-sided 40-track disk	112
High-capacity 80-track disk	224[1]
Hard disk	512+[2]

[1] A "high-capacity disk" is always a double-sided 80-track floppy disk.
[2] Depends on the size of the hard disk.

A consequence of this limit—which is imposed because MS-DOS has to know how much space to reserve for the directory entries—is that you might find yourself running out of directory space for new files long before you have run out of disk space on which to store the *contents* of those files.

MS-DOS 2.0 and higher versions implemented a means of "getting around" this limitation. This technique is called the *tree-structured directory*. It permits you to create subdirectories, each occupying only one directory entry on the disk. Each subdirectory, in turn, can hold a theoretically unlimited number of subdirectory and file entries. This is because a subdirectory is in fact a file. Because file sizes are not limited except by total disk capacity, their contents—directory entries—can grow theoretically to an infinite size. As a result, you can have an almost unlimited number of files stored on an MS-DOS computer's floppy or hard disk.

Why Use Tree-Structured Directories?

If this increased ability to store large numbers of file entries were the only reason for tree-structured directories, they still would be one of the handier features of MS-DOS. However, there are several other major advantages to this feature.

Manageability of Data

By using tree-structured directories intelligently (more on that subject throughout this chapter), you can make our data files more manageable. You can store all of our accounting files in one subdirectory, all of your payroll files in another, all of your disk utility programs in yet another, and so on.

This makes it easier to know where your data is and to keep track of its updating and backup storage.

Increased Speed of Access

By their nature, individual subdirectories contain fewer files and less information than would an entire disk. If you don't use subdirectories, every time you need MS-DOS to find a program, the program would have to search through the entire disk directory until it found the file. Particularly on hard disks where the number of files may be in the 1,000-plus range, the use of subdirectories makes locating files far easier—and therefore faster—for MS-DOS.

Programs like WordStar (prior to Version 4.0), Lotus 1-2-3, and others that make extensive use of program "overlay" files run more quickly and efficiently if they are stored in subdirectories than if they must search through entire disk directories to locate each overlay as it is needed.

Logical Arrangement of Information

When you are using an MS-DOS computer for a large variety of tasks related to one or more management functions, you find yourself frequently relying on your memory to know what steps to take next, which files are needed for which reports, and similar instructions. If you group programs and their related data files together in subdirectories, your ability to remember such information is vastly improved, eliminating the time-consuming need to refer to directory listings. Subdirectories essentially make you a much more efficient user of the system.

As far as efficiency goes, subdirectories are much like well-thought-out file folders in a filing system. If you keep all your correspondence in a single folder, finding a letter to Allyn Derage from September, 1983, is going to be a great deal more challenging and time-consuming than if you keep your correspondence alphabetically, chronologically, or both.

Screen Display Simplification

Some programs, notably DIR, maintain or provide a screen display of all the files in a directory. When all the files don't fit on one screen, the display becomes less and less useful. By using subdirectories, you can help ensure that the only files shown on the screen at any moment are those relevant to and usable by the program you're running.

An Overview of Tree-Structured Directories

Now that we've looked briefly at some of the reasons you might want to implement a tree-structured directory on your MS-DOS system, suppose that we turn our attention to an examination of how these tree-structured directories are organized and how they work. First, we look at what is called the "root" directory. Then we examine subdirectories and their organization. Creating new subdirectories is covered before we discuss how to copy material between subdirectories.

After we discuss how to move from a subdirectory level "deep" in the tree structure back to the *top* or *root* level directory, we point out some considerations to take into account when using hard disk backup and restore routines with subdirectories. Finally, we discuss how to remove a subdirectory and what to take into account when doing so.

The Root Directory

Every disk formatted by MS-DOS—floppy or hard—contains a root directory. This is the only directory present until and unless you create subdirectories.

The term *root directory* should convey the impression that you can use this directory as the basis for building a multileveled set of subdirectories that, when drawn in diagram form, resembles a tree. Unless you've created an AUTOEXEC.BAT file that changes the usual procedure (see Chapter 2), when you first boot MS-DOS, you find yourself in the root directory.

TRICK   **FINDING OUT WHERE YOU ARE**

As you follow the discussions in this chapter, redefine your system prompt to tell you where you are. At the system prompt, which is probably now a C> (the drive name may differ), type:

```
prompt $p$g
```

(The PROMPT command, by the way, is discussed in greater detail in Chapter 6.) The immediate effect of this change is that the system prompt changes to C:\>. The backslash indicates that you are currently in the root directory. You'll see the usefulness of this as you study the examples in this chapter.

What Are Subdirectories?

A *subdirectory* is an entry in the root directory (or, in the case of *nested* subdirectories, an entry in another subdirectory). In a DIR display of the root directory, subdirectory entries look the same as those for other files with two exceptions: They normally have no extensions, and their size is not given. The following sample DIR listing demonstrates a portion of a directory showing two subdirectories and three other files.

```
Volume in drive C has no label


Directory of C:\


LETTER1   TXT   12   03-17-86   7:14p
MEMO424          8   04-24-86   9:11a
BSNSPLAN      <DIR>   01-01-86   12:14p
AGENDA1   TXT   24   06-11-86   01:01a
BUDGETS       <DIR>   06-30-86   4:59p
```

Notice that where a directory entry for a file indicates its size, the two subdirectories called BSNSPLAN and BUDGETS have the abbreviation <DIR>. Each of these subdirectories, in turn, can contain files and other subdirectories, and their directory entries would be identical in format.

Naming Conventions and Rules

A subdirectory's name must follow the same rules as those for other kinds of filenames. In other words, each name can be up to eight characters long, consist of any combination of letters, numbers, and certain special symbols, and have an optional extension three or fewer characters long. Because of an inherent limit on the length of a whole *path* list, you're sometimes wise to use subdirectory names that are shorter than eight characters and have no extensions. That issue is discussed more fully shortly.

The same conventions applied to file naming should generally be taken into account in naming subdirectories. The names must be meaningful to you, and you can't give two subdirectories in one directory the same name.

The . and .. Directories

Each subdirectory you create has two pseudo-directory entries automatically placed in it. One of these subdirectories is called " . " and the
other is called " . .". As shown in the following example, they appear in
a DIR listing exactly as any other subdirectory entry.

```
C:\>dir \bsnsplan


Volume in drive C has no label


Directory of C:\BSNSPLAN


.              <DIR>        01-01-86   12:14p
..             <DIR>        01-01-86   12:14p
EXECSUMM  TXT         24    01-08-86   11:04a
```

These pseudo-directory entries are sometimes called directory
markers. The . marker is a pseudo-directory entry that always refers to
the current directory. The .. marker, on the other hand, always refers
to the parent directory, the directory from which the current directory
branches. The . marker serves no useful purpose for most commands,
whereas the .. marker is particularly useful when it comes to moving
among subdirectories, a subject covered a little later in this chapter.

Nesting Subdirectories

As described, a subdirectory can contain files or other subdirectory
entries. Each subdirectory entry in a subdirectory has the same
properties and naming rules as a subdirectory in the root directory.

You might use subdirectories nested inside other subdirectories
for even better logical access to files. For example, you might wish to
have a correspondence file that has subdirectories for several different
alphabetic subdivisions for easier storage and retrieval of letters. Such
a subdirectory setup could look like the following.

```
C:\>DIR \CORR                        ← the first subdirectory is called
                                       CORR for correspondence

A-F       <DIR>     02-02-86  11:11a  ← nested subdirectory for A-F

G-L       <DIR>     02-02-86  11:12a  ← nested subdirectory for G-L
```

```
M-R        <DIR>      02-02-86   11:13a   ← nested subdirectory for M-R

S-Z        <DIR>      02-02-86   11:15a   ← nested subdirectory for S-Z

FORMLTR1  TXT   4     01-30-86   4:13p
```

Name Length Limit: It's Important

The number of levels of subdirectory nesting that you can do in MS-DOS has no *theoretical* limit, but there is a very important *practical* limit.

The total length of a path (discussed later in this chapter), which tells MS-DOS how to get from one subdirectory to another through the tree and back to the root directory, cannot exceed 63 characters. This means, for example, that if you use the full eight characters for each subdirectory name, you can have seven levels of nesting below the root directory. Each subdirectory name has eight characters, and subdirectory names are separated from one another by backslashes.

If you engage in a great deal of subdirectory nesting, be sure to plan ahead. You don't want to find yourself in a situation where you can't include a directory for your program in a path that is already 63 characters in length.

Creating Subdirectories with MKDIR

Let's actually create a couple of subdirectories so that you can begin to see how these useful devices can work for you. To set up a subdirectory in MS-DOS, use the MKDIR (make directory) command, or its abbreviated form, MD. For the rest of this chapter, we assume that you are working with a computer with a hard disk as drive C. If you are using a floppy-based system, you need to change the drive name from C to A or B.

Be sure that the prompt indicates that you are at the root directory (which it is unless you've created a subdirectory and changed over to it deliberately). It should look like the following (assuming that you have previously set the prompt command as described earlier):

```
C:\>_
```

Figure 4-1 is a diagram of the tree-structured directory that you are about to create. To help you follow the procedures for creating subdirectories, refer to Figure 4-1 as you progress through the examples.

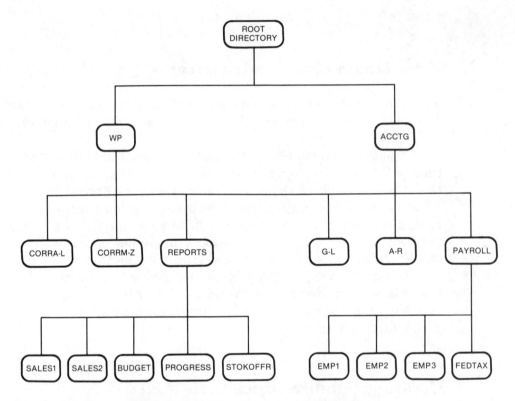

Figure 4-1.   Tree-Structured Directory

Because most of us like to deal with things in a top-down approach, especially when looking at a computer screen, Figure 4-1 shows the directory tree as an "upside down" or "inverted" tree. In keeping with this concept, we work from the top of Figure 4-1 down, so that the root directory is at the top of the structure. Now create the first two subdirectories: WP for word processing files and ACCTG for accounting department files.

```
C:\>MD WP

C:\>MD ACCTG

C:\>DIR \WP                           ← the first backslash
                                        means root directory


Volume in drive C has no label
```

```
Directory of C:\WP

.              <DIR>      08-11-86  4:13p
..             <DIR>      08-11-86  4:13p
        2 File(s)      1234567 bytes free

C:\>DIR \ACCTG

.              <DIR>      08-11-86  4:14p
..             <DIR>      08-11-86  4:14p
        2 File(s)      1234567 bytes free
```

You have now created two subdirectories from the root directory and examined a DIR listing of the contents of each. At this point, because you have not placed anything into them, their only directory entries are the markers . and .. about which we have already talked briefly.

Using MKDIR Inside Subdirectories

Both of the subdirectories that you have just created are connected with the root directory. But as you can see from Figure 4-1, you're going to create some subdirectories within subdirectories. To do so, you still use the MKDIR or MD command. This time, though, you must either change the current directory so that you are in the appropriate subdirectory or you must specify enough of the pathname so that MS-DOS knows where to put the subdirectory. Because we discuss moving between subdirectories later in this chapter, we focus on providing the pathname with the MD command.

To create the subdirectory called CORRA-L (meaning *Correspondence, A-L*) within the WP subdirectory, type:

```
MD WP\CORRA-L
```

By specifying the WP subdirectory, you override MS-DOS's usual method of assigning subdirectories to the root directory. Now if you ask for a directory of the WP subdirectory, you find a new entry:

```
C:\>DIR \WP


Volume in drive C has no label
Directory of C:\WP
```

```
  .              <DIR>      08-11-86   4:13p
  ..             <DIR>      08-11-86   4:13p
CORRA-L          <DIR>      08-11-86   5:09p
         3 File(s)      1234567 bytes free
```

Similarly, to create the other subdirectories to the WP and ACCTG subdirectories shown in Figure 4-1, type the following sequence of commands:

```
C:\>MD WP\CORRM-Z
```

```
C:\>MD WP\REPORTS
```

```
C:\>MD ACCTG\GL
```

```
C:\>MD ACCTG\AR
```

```
C:\>MD ACCTG\PAYROLL
```

TRICK

DIRECTORY NAME SHORTCUTS

Use the .. shortcut directory name mentioned earlier to reduce the amount of typing in directory creation. The . directory name can also be used with a command, but its use has the opposite effect of a shortcut. For example, it is perfectly permissible in MS-DOS to type

```
C:\WP>DIR .
```

to display the files in the current directory. But the effect is exactly the same as entering the command without the . directory name, as shown in the following example.

```
C:\WP>DIR
```

Therefore, even though the . directory entry is available for use with commands, it serves no useful purpose when you consider that almost all commands treat the current directory as the default if no subdirectory parameters are specified. However, you may find . useful for some commands that require both source and destination drives, directory paths, and filenames. For example, the BACKUP command requires that you specify both the source and destination drives and paths, so if you want to make sure that you back up all the files in the current directory to drive A, you type:

```
C:\WP\REPORTS>BACKUP . A:
```

Compared to the . directory entry, the .. directory entry has considerably more potential use. You can use it to refer to the directory directly above the current directory, also called the *parent* directory instead of specifying the entire directory path originating from the root directory. For example, you can type:

```
C:\WP>CD ..\ACCTG
```

or slightly more elaborately,

```
C:\WP\CORRM-Z>CD ..\REPORTS
```

Using the .. directory entry as a command parameter can save a great deal of typing, particularly if repetitive subdirectory changes are involved.

Both the . and .. directory entries can be used as parameters with all standard MS-DOS commands that accept directory path- and file-related parameters.

The creation of the next-level subdirectories shown in Figure 4-1 follows a similar pattern. We show you the first one and leave the others for you to do yourself.

```
C:\>MD WP\REPORTS\SALES01
```

Copying between Subdirectories

If you want to follow along with this discussion, you should start by using your favorite text editor or word processor to create two small files. Each need be only one or two lines long, and the text should give you some clue as to which file you are looking at. Save these files in your root directory. Call one of them FILE1 and the other FILE2 so that you can follow this discussion.

For the purposes of copying, directories are much like separate disks. They can be "addressed" as if they are entirely different floppy or hard disks. Copying from one subdirectory to another, then, is quite simple. The format for the COPY command is as follows:

```
COPY [source-path]\[filename] [[destination-path][\[filename]]]
```

As with copying files between disks, the use of the destination's filename is unnecessary unless you want to have it stored under a different name. Specifying the destination filename isn't always necessary because as long as the path is different, MS-DOS treats the files as different even though they have the same filename.

To copy FILE1 from the root directory to the WP subdirectory, type:

```
COPY FILE1 WP
```

You can confirm that this file is indeed in the WP subdirectory by using the DIR command as shown previously. Now, copy the same file to the ACCTG subdirectory.

```
COPY FILE1 ACCTG
```

The FILE1 disk now has *three* files: one in the root directory and one each in the WP and ACCTG subdirectories.

COPYING BETWEEN SUBDIRECTORIES THE SHORT WAY

As with the COPY command, you can use the .. directory shorthand in copying files. In other words, you can type

```
C:\WP>COPY ..\DIR1\FILE1 FILE2
```

and eliminate the necessity of typing the entire directory path from the root to the parent directory and the DIR1 subdirectory below the parent directory. The command sequence shown in the previous example could be rephrased to "Locate FILE1 by moving up one directory level, then down to the subdirectory DIR1, then copying FILE1 to FILE2." In the example, WP, which is the current subdirectory, and DIR1, both have the same parent directory, the root directory.

Copying files between sub-subdirectories and between different subdirectory levels is just as easy. The key thing to remember is that the filename is not the whole story. The pathname is an essential part of identifying a file on a disk or hard disk. As long as the pathnames are different, the files can coexist on the disk without confusing MS-DOS.

Changing Directories

So far, you've accessed subdirectories by typing their names explicitly in MS-DOS commands. This is often unnecessary and cumbersome. If you're going to do any appreciable amount of work involving one subdirectory, you should make that subdirectory your currently active directory. Do this with the CHDIR (change directory) command (abbreviated CD). Specify the complete pathname of the directory to which you want to change. From that point on, all references to the first backslash in a pathname are taken to mean the currently active directory.

If you have set the prompt to show the currently active subdirectory, you can keep track of where you are quite easily. In the following examples, we assume that you have set up the prompt so that it displays the current directory.

```
C:\>CD WP

C:\WP>CD CORRA-L

C:\WP\CORR-AL>CD REPORTS
```

Invalid Directory   ← REPORTS is not a subdirectory of WS\CORR-AL

```
C:\WP\CORRA-L>CD ..\REPORTS
```
← the ..\REPORTS is a shorthand pathname

```
C:\WP\REPORTS>CD ..
```
← shorthand for moving up one directory

```
C:\WP>CD \ACCTG

C:\ACCTG>CD \WP\REPORTS\STOKOFFR
```

```
C:\WP\REPORTS\STOKOFFR>CD \          ← shorthand for "go to root directory"

C:\>
```

From the preceding examples, you should be able to deduce the following rules and hints about moving between subdirectories.

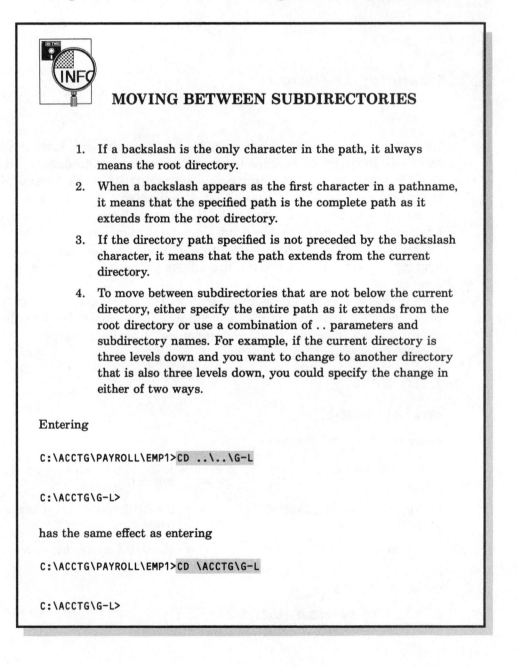

MOVING BETWEEN SUBDIRECTORIES

1. If a backslash is the only character in the path, it always means the root directory.

2. When a backslash appears as the first character in a pathname, it means that the specified path is the complete path as it extends from the root directory.

3. If the directory path specified is not preceded by the backslash character, it means that the path extends from the current directory.

4. To move between subdirectories that are not below the current directory, either specify the entire path as it extends from the root directory or use a combination of .. parameters and subdirectory names. For example, if the current directory is three levels down and you want to change to another directory that is also three levels down, you could specify the change in either of two ways.

Entering

```
C:\ACCTG\PAYROLL\EMP1>CD ..\..\G-L

C:\ACCTG\G-L>
```

has the same effect as entering

```
C:\ACCTG\PAYROLL\EMP1>CD \ACCTG\G-L

C:\ACCTG\G-L>
```

Subdirectories and Backup Routines

One of the small aggravations about setting up and using subdirectories is that when you want to back up data stored in subdirectories, you must be more explicit about your instructions than you do when all your data is stored in one large root directory. This is obviously a small price to pay for the convenience of subdirectories, without which you might well find your MS-DOS computer systems overly limiting. But bear in mind that subdirectories are treated differently sometimes by routines that you use to make archival and backup copies of your data.

Subdirectories and DISKCOPY

The MS-DOS DISKCOPY command does not differentiate between subdirectory entries and any other file entry. As a result, if you have set up subdirectories on a floppy disk and use DISKCOPY to make a backup copy of the information, any subdirectory and its contents are copied to the destination disk.

Subdirectories and COPY

Using the MS-DOS COPY command to copy specifically identified files, you must, of course, supply the full MS-DOS pathname as it relates to the current directory. The subdirectory identifier is part of that name, so no other special precautions need be taken.

Subdirectories and BACKUP/RESTORE

DISKCOPY can only be used with floppy disks. An attempt to use DISKCOPY to back up a hard disk results in an error condition. COPY can, of course, be used to copy files from a hard disk to a floppy disk and vice versa, but COPY's disadvantage is that it requires a great deal of typing because you specifically have to back up files on every individual MS-DOS path. Wildcard characters (* and ?) can be used for filenames, but they are not usable in pathnames where a subdirectory is expected.

Many users of systems equipped with hard disks use the MS-DOS commands BACKUP and RESTORE to archive data to a floppy disk and retrieve it later. When you use these commands, you usually want to use the /S parameter that instructs MS-DOS to back up and restore files in all subdirectories *at all levels beyond the specified directory.* Table 4-2 shows several sample BACKUP commands and indicates which files would be backed up by their use.

Table 4-2.   BACKUP Commands with /S Parameter

Command	Files Backed Up
BACKUP C:*.TXT A:	All files in root directory with .TXT extension but no subdirectory files regardless of extension.
BACKUP C:*.TXT A:/S	All files in root directory and all files in all subdirectories with .TXT extension.
BACKUP C:\WP*.TXT A:	All files in WP subdirectory with .TXT extension.
BACKUP C:\WP*.TXT A:/S	All files in WP subdirectory with .TXT extension and all files with that extension in any subdirectory associated with WP subdirectory. No other .TXT files in other subdirectories are backed up.
BACKUP C:\WP\REPORTS*.* /S	All files in REPORTS subdirectory of WP subdirectory. Regardless of name or extension, all files appearing in any subdirectory associated with REPORTS subdirectory.
C:\WP>BACKUP . A:	All files in current directory of of current drive. The . subdirectory marker is used because BACKUP requires that both source and destination be specified.

Table 4-2 does not include some of the other options of the BACKUP command, notably the /M parameter, which limits the BACKUP process to those files that have been modified since the last time they were backed up, and the /D parameter, which permits you to specify the earliest date of last modification the system should use for the BACKUP procedure. The focus of Table 4-2 is on subdirectories and their impact on the BACKUP and RESTORE operations.

When you use BACKUP to store data from your hard disk on floppy disks, some planning permits you to take advantage of the subdirectory capability of MS-DOS to group your archives so that related files are together on one set of floppy disks. When it's time to restore one of these files, you find the convenience of limiting the number of disks and files to search through to find the file you want to restore more than pays for the extra time spent during the BACKUP process.

When you have backed up some files using the BACKUP command with the /S parameter, then want to restore them, you need to use the same parameter in the RESTORE command. As with the BACKUP command, the /S parameter in the RESTORE command begins with the specified subdirectory and restores all files at levels beyond that of this subdirectory. An example helps to clarify.

Assume that you have backed up a floppy disk with the following command:

```
C>BACKUP C:\WP\REPORTS\*.* A: /S
```

As you know from what you just learned, this command backs up all the files in the WP\REPORTS subdirectory and all the files of its descendant subdirectories on the set of floppies used for this BACKUP procedure. After you've backed up, if you lose all your files with the .DAT extension from one of these subdirectories (say, for example, the SALES1 subdirectory) and wanted to restore just those files, typing the command

```
C>RESTORE A: C:\WP\REPORTS\*.DAT /S
```

does *not* have the desired effect. This restores files with the .DAT extension from all the subdirectories associated with the WP\REPORTS path. These probably include some data files that you have changed since this backup and could result in a very serious data loss.

USE THE /P PARAMETER WITH RESTORE

To prevent this problem, get into the habit of always using the /P parameter when you use RESTORE to retrieve files stored with the BACKUP command. The /P parameter causes MS-DOS to prompt you before it restores any file that was changed since the backup was made. It can save you hours of time and a lot of frustration.

The command that has the desired effect of restoring only files in the WP\REPORTS\SALES1 path with a .DAT extension is

```
C>RESTORE A: C:\WP\REPORTS\SALES1\*.DAT
```

Alternatively, you could switch to the subdirectory to which you want the files restored and type the command more simply (we have assumed here that the PROMPT pg command was previously entered).

```
C:\WP\REPORTS\SALES1>RESTORE A: C:*.DAT
```

RESTORE RE-CREATES DELETED DIRECTORIES

TRICK

If you use the /S parameter to back up and restore files, you should be aware of one peculiarity: If you use BACKUP to archive some files, then later delete a subdirectory (we show you how to do so shortly), you find that RESTORE with the /S parameter re-creates that obsolete subdirectory. Sometimes this is a desirable result (as when you delete the subdirectory because it had no current use but later needed to retrieve it and all its contents to revise something). It never causes a serious problem because you can easily delete the subdirectory if its restoration was unintentional (unless free space on the disk is limited).

Removing Subdirectories

Once you have finished using a subdirectory and want to free the space it occupies on your disk, you can remove it using the RMDIR (remove directory) command (abbreviated RD). A safeguard is built into the RD command: It does not remove a directory that has in it any files other than the subdirectory markers. This means that any subdirectory that has data files, program files, *or another subdirectory* in it cannot be deleted before all of those items are removed. Note that this is true even if the only item in the subdirectory is the name of another subdirectory that is empty.

The MS-DOS Search Path

We have made several references to the *path* in an MS-DOS file's address. Now it's time to focus attention for a few moments on what a path is and how it is used by MS-DOS.

You *Can* Get There from Here!

Viewed simply, an MS-DOS search path is just a list of the subdirectories through which MS-DOS must travel to get to the file whose name appears at the end of the path. Each subdirectory is separated from the others in the path and from the filename by backslashes (\). Assuming that you are in the root directory, the pathnames for the WP, REPORTS, and SALES1 files that you have been working with so far in this chapter appear as follows:

```
WP                    ← No need for backslash because subdirectory is in
                        current directory

WP\REPORTS

WP\REPORTS\SALES1
```

These pathnames are, of course, the same ones used to make the directories in the first place.

Pathnames tell MS-DOS how to get from *where you are* to the file that you are trying to find or use. If the path is continually *downward* on the tree (see Figure 4-1), you need specify only that portion of the path that is below the currently active directory.

Finding the Current Directory

If you use the PROMPT pg command described earlier in this chapter, the prompt always lets you know exactly where the current MS-DOS path is. Because this command is an internal command, there is no reason not to use it, and you'll find that knowing where you are at all times is convenient and useful.

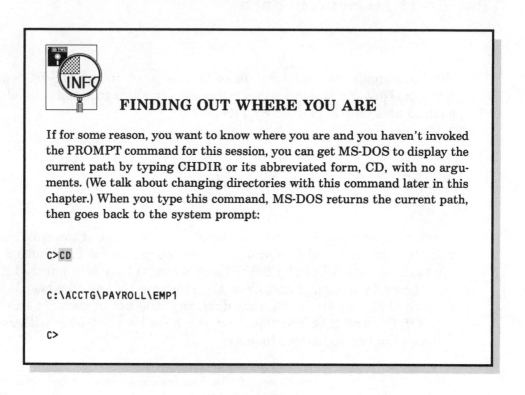

FINDING OUT WHERE YOU ARE

If for some reason, you want to know where you are and you haven't invoked the PROMPT command for this session, you can get MS-DOS to display the current path by typing CHDIR or its abbreviated form, CD, with no arguments. (We talk about changing directories with this command later in this chapter.) When you type this command, MS-DOS returns the current path, then goes back to the system prompt:

```
C> CD

C:\ACCTG\PAYROLL\EMP1

C>
```

How MS-DOS Uses the Path

Whenever you enter a command in MS-DOS (other than a built-in command that doesn't require a .EXE or .COM file to run), MS-DOS searches for the appropriate file to execute to carry out your instructions. It first looks at the current directory and, if it doesn't find it there, it looks for a setting for the [path] variable stored in the environment. This is *not* the same as the *current* path.

DETERMINING THE CURRENT PATH

You can determine what is assigned to the [path] variable by entering PATH at a system prompt without any arguments. The current value of the [path] variable, along with all other system environment variables, can be seen by typing SET with no arguments.

The sequence in which the subdirectories are assigned to the [path] variable determines the order in which the subdirectories are searched. The search begins with the leftmost subdirectory and continues until the file is found or the path list is exhausted. If MS-DOS cannot find the appropriate command file, it informs you by displaying the error message `Bad Command or File Name`.

Changing the Path

You alter the sequence of subdirectories in which MS-DOS looks for command files by using the PATH command. The PATH command is not particularly tricky. You provide MS-DOS with a list of subdirectories, each subdirectory separated from the others by semicolons, to indicate the path sequence you wish DOS to use in searching for command and batch files.

When you first start MS-DOS, the default condition is that no path is specified. You can return to this condition by defining a path consisting only of a semicolon:

`PATH;`

With this situation in effect, MS-DOS does not search anywhere but the current directory for any command file.

To extend the search path, however, you need to enter one or more subdirectories as arguments to the PATH command. For example, suppose that you have a command file called D.COM in a subdirectory called NEATSTUF. (The program D.COM actually exists. It provides a sorted directory listing that shows all kinds of files, even those invisible to MS-DOS's DIR command. More about the D.COM command file is found in Chapter 8.) You want to be able to use this command from within any of several directories that are used primarily for word processing.

If you set a path with the following command, your system finds the D.COM file from whatever path is currently active.

```
PATH C:\NEATSTUF
```

One potential problem with this path, however, is that you also may have a number of commands in your root directory for which MS-DOS needs to search from time to time. You can overcome this problem by defining the path as follows:

```
PATH C:\;C:\NEATSTUF
```

Now, whenever MS-DOS is asked to run a command, it searches first in the root directory, then in the subdirectory called NEATSTUF. If MS-DOS finds the command in either place, it runs the command without further searching. Failure to locate it in either directory results in the error message reproduced earlier.

Things To Consider

By now, you're getting the idea that subdirectories can provide very powerful ways of organizing information, particularly on a hard disk that is used for a number of different functions. When you are defining the path, however, you want to be conscious of a few possible problems that could arise if you use it incorrectly.

For example, if you have two programs on your system with the same name (a situation you should normally avoid but one which is theoretically possible and harmless under most circumstances), you could accidentally invoke the wrong program or version by designing a path that has in it more than one subdirectory that contains a program of that name.

It can be quite frustrating to set up a PATH command to guide MS-DOS cleanly and efficiently to the place where the command that you want performed is stored, only to find that it doesn't work because of the software you are using.

NOT ALL PROGRAMS KNOW ABOUT THE MS-DOS PATH

Another thing to be aware of is that some programs—among them most notably WordStar (prior to Version 4.0)—do not use MS-DOS pathing at all and thus do not lend themselves to this kind of design. WordStar was one of the first MS-DOS programs to use file overlays. In other words, the main program file calls on program segments stored in other files as it needs them. The WS.COM file, the main command file, can be placed on a sub-directory in a current path setting and be located properly by MS-DOS. But its overlay files are not found if they are not on the currently active subdirectory. This problem no longer exists in WordStar Version 4.0 and above.

Finally, remember that although you can make your directory tree as deep as you want, the path specified with a command cannot exceed 63 characters in length. This will probably never be a problem, but it's worth noting.

TRICK

PACKING MORE CAPABILITY INTO THE MS-DOS SEARCH PATH

If you are using MS-DOS 3.x or higher, you can use the SUBST command (explained later in this chapter) to pack more searching capacity into a single pathname.

Managing the Whole Subdirectory Structure

MS-DOS includes the command TREE.COM that permits you to take a look at the entire structure of your disk, including all subdirectories and, optionally using the /F switch, all files in each subdirectory. You occasionally may want to run TREE (or one of its fancier public-domain equivalents discussed in following text and in Chapter 8) with your printer on (and output *redirected* to the printer as described in Chapter 3 or using the Ctrl-PrtSc combination) so that you can look at a "map" of your tree structures. This becomes particularly important as you add subdirectories at deeper and deeper levels of directory identification.

Using the DOS TREE Command

Frankly, the TREE command is rather limiting. But it *does* provide a means of finding where your files are and how your subdirectories relate to one another. Its syntax is simple. To get a complete listing of all subdirectories, enter TREE. The following is what TREE prints after we have set up the structure shown in Figure 4-1.

```
C:\>TREE

DIRECTORY PATH LISTING FOR VOLUME MISC

Path: \WP

Sub-directories: CORRA-L
                 CORRM-Z
                 REPORTS


Path: \WP\CORRA-L

Sub-directories:  None


Path: \WP.\CORRM-Z

Sub-directories:  None


Path: \WP\REPORTS

Sub-directories: SALES1
                 SALES2
                 BUDGET
                 PROGRESS
                 STOKOFFR


Path: \WP\REPORTS\SALES1
```

Sub-directories: None

Path: \WP\REPORTS\SALES2

Sub-directories: None

Path: \WP\REPORTS\BUDGET

Sub-directories: None

Path: \WP\REPORTS\PROGRESS

Sub-directories: None

Path: \WP\REPORTS\STOKOFFR

Sub-directories: None

Path: \ACCTG

Sub-directories: G-L
                 A-R
                 PAYROLL

Path: \ACCTG\G-L

Sub-directories: None

Path: \ACCTG\A-R

Sub-directories: None

Path: \ACCTG\PAYROLL

Sub-directories: FEDTAX
                 EMP1
                 EMP2
                 EMP3

Path: \ACCTG\PAYROLL\FEDTAX

Sub-directories: None

Path: \ACCTG\PAYROLL\EMP1

```
Sub-directories:  None


Path: \ACCTG\PAYROLL\EMP2

Sub-directories:  None


Path: \ACCTG\PAYROLL\EMP3

Sub-directories:  None
```

You can optionally specify a drive with the TREE command. For example, if drive C (normally the hard disk) is the default and you want to see the subdirectory structure of the disk in drive B, type

```
TREE B:
```

and the display shows the entire structure of the subdirectories on that disk.

With or without the drive designator, you can opt to have MS-DOS include in the TREE display a listing of the files in each subdirectory. The command to do this is

```
TREE /F
```

or with the drive designator:

```
TREE B: /F
```

The following shows a portion of a display with the /F switch included in a TREE command.

```
DIRECTORY PATH LISTING FOR VOLUME MISC

Files:            LETTER1 .TXT
                  MEMO424
                  AGENDA1 .TXT
                  FILE1


Path: \WP

Sub-directories:  CORRA-L
                  CORRM-Z
                  REPORTS

Files:            FILE1
                  WS      .COM
```

```
WSMSGS  .OVR
WSOVLY1 .OVR
```

Path: \WP\CORRA-L

Sub-directories: None

Files: None

Path: \WP\CORRM-Z

Sub-directories: None

Files: None

Path: \WP\REPORTS

Sub-directories: SALES1
                   SALES2
                   BUDGET
                   PROGRESS
                   STOKOFFR

Files: None

Path: \WP\REPORTS\SALES1

Sub-directories: None

Files: None

Path: \WP\REPORTS\SALES2

Sub-directories: None

Files: None

Path: \WP\REPORTS\BUDGET

Sub-directories: None

Files: None

Path: \WP\REPORTS\PROGRESS

Sub-directories: None

Files: None

Path: \WP\REPORTS\STOKOFFR

Sub-directories: None

Files: None

Path: \ACCTG

Sub-directories: G-L
                   A-R
                   PAYROLL

Files: FILE1

Path: \ACCTG\G-L

Sub-directories: None

Files: None

Path: \ACCTG\A-R

Sub-directories: None

Files: None

Path: \ACCTG\PAYROLL

Sub-directories: FEDTAX
                   EMP1
                   EMP2
                   EMP3

Files: None

Path: \ACCTG\PAYROLL\FEDTAX

Sub-directories: None

Files: None

Path: \ACCTG\PAYROLL\EMP1

Sub-directories: None

Files: None

```
Path: \ACCTG\PAYROLL\EMP2

Sub-directories:   None

Files:             None


Path: \ACCTG\PAYROLL\EMP3

Sub-directories:   None

Files:             None
```

Public-Domain Improvements on TREE

Chapter 8 discusses a number of useful public-domain programs that are available and have similar functions to TREE. One particularly useful programs is the popular D.COM. This program goes by a number of different names, many of which begin with SDIR (for sorted directory or super directory). Generally, SDIR24.COM is the same program as D and SDIR.

SDIR is a very powerful replacement for MS-DOS's admittedly limited DIR command. Not only does SDIR provide a *sorted* list of all the files that you ask for in the subdirectory, it can also provide a completely sorted listing of all subdirectories and all files within each subdirectory or of all files in all subdirectories sorted into one large list showing the subdirectory in which each resides. You'll find, by the way, that naming this file D.COM saves you lots of typing and is easier to remember than its more "legal" name, SDIR (which usually also has some numbers following it to indicate the version number). If you run the following command after renaming SDIR.COM as D.COM, you can obtain a complete directory listing of drive C's files, sorted by subdirectory and filename within the subdirectory:

```
D C: /TF
```

If you want to have all the names of all the files in all subdirectories sorted as a group and their subdirectory locations displayed, type:

```
D C: /TA
```

Chapter 8 contains information that no IBM PC hard disk owner should be without about the other useful options in this public-domain program.

Commercial Improvements on TREE

A number of commercial programs extend and enhance the MS-DOS TREE command. One of the best known and most popular is XTREE. This program provides a graphic display of the tree structure of your disk and simultaneously shows the files associated with each subdirectory as you move through the display with the cursor keys. It also permits the mass copying, deleting, and renaming of files, a feature you'll find quite handy.

WHEREIS That File?

As useful as XTREE and SDIR are, they both require you to look at a complete display or printout of the subdirectories on your hard disk to see where things are located. Sometimes, you only want to know in which subdirectory you stuck that obscure file that your boss is suddenly breathing down your neck to get. In those circumstances, try the WHEREIS public-domain utility.

This utility takes a filename as an argument and displays any and all subdirectory paths in which that filename is located. See Chapter 8 for details.

Moving Quickly between Subdirectories

When you work with tree-structured directories, you frequently find the need to move from one subdirectory to another at a lower or higher level. Two tricks save typing time as you do so.

The . and .. Subdirectories

You can move up one subdirectory level without having to type the name of the next subdirectory by using its "nickname," which is two periods. If, for example, you are in a subdirectory called WP\REPORTS\SALES1 and want to get back to the REPORTS subdirectory, type:

```
C:\WP\REPORTS\SALES1>CD ..
```

```
C:\WP\REPORTS>CD ..
```

```
C:\WP>CD ..
```

```
C:\>
```

Notice that at each subdirectory level, the .. nickname applies to the next higher level of the subdirectory path. This directory or subdirectory is referred to as the *parent* of the current subdirectory.

When Not To Type the Backslash

Because the backslash key is not situated in a particularly convenient location on many keyboards, many people experience difficulty in reliably pressing it while touch-typing. As a result, they find themselves forced to take their eyes from their work to use this key. You can minimize this interruption if you remember a simple rule:

The backslash key stands for the root directory and can be omitted in any command meant to apply to or extend the current subdirectory. If you are moving to the root directory, however, it must be typed.

For example, if you are already at the WP subdirectory and want to change to the REPORTS subdirectory, the backslash is not needed because REPORTS is a subdirectory of the current directory:

```
C:\WP>CD REPORTS
```

```
C:\WP\REPORTS>
```

One other use of the backslash: Alone (that is, used without a subdirectory name following it), it always refers to the root directory:

```
C:\WP\REPORTS\SALES1>CD \

C:\>
```

(Even the space after the CD command is optional and is inserted in the text only for readability. In practice, we don't need to use a space deliberately.)

Controlling Storage with Programs Used Many Places

Storing data files in a hierarchical tree-structured directory is a good idea and one that can save a great deal of time and energy. However, one major problem occurs with this approach to disk management: Program files may also have to be "distributed" (that is, duplicated) throughout the system. That can be extremely inefficient in disk usage.

This section addresses the problem and some alternative approaches to solving it.

Example: Writers and Their Word Processors

Writers who work on several projects at once and want to have all the data files associated with each project stored in a single subdirectory are good examples of the kind of problem dealt with here. As writers switch from one subdirectory to another, they find that the word processing program being used all the time must be present in each subdirectory before it works.

Although this problem does not arise with all word processors (or with all of any other type of program), it occurs often enough to warrant taking time to understand how to solve it if you encounter it.

MS-DOS Version 2.x Solutions

If you are running under MS-DOS Version 2.0 or later, but *not* Version 3.0, your ability to deal with such situations is limited to three main approaches: using the ASSIGN command if the program simply defaults to an inconvenient drive, using the PATH command if the only problem is that the program needs to be somewhere in the path, and taking advantage of a public-domain type of program such as DPATH or a commercial enhancement like SmartPath. We describe each of these approaches briefly in the next few sections.

ASSIGN the Right Drive

As already mentioned, WordStar (prior to Version 4,0), among other popular programs for the IBM PC, does not take advantage of MS-DOS pathing capabilities for its overlay files. If, for example, you wish to put one copy of the WordStar program and overlay files on your hard disk but use subdirectories to store individual files related to projects, you find recurring device errors. The program is attempting to access drive A, where it expects to find certain files not in the current directory area. The result is any of several different kinds of error conditions.

You can "fool" WordStar into thinking that drive C, the hard disk, is really also drive A, the floppy drive (or one of the two floppy drives). You do this with the ASSIGN command, as follows:

```
ASSIGN A=C
```

The above example shows how you can tell MS-DOS to "assign drive A to drive C." Note that the : is never used with the drive specifiers when the ASSIGN command is used.

After you have ASSIGNed drive A to drive C, any time WordStar tells MS-DOS to look on drive A for something, MS-DOS instead looks at drive C. That overcomes one problem with WordStar. The program still does not run quite correctly in a tree-structured directory, but this problem—defaulting to an incorrect drive—may be found in other programs as well. If this is the only reason your favorite program won't run on a hard disk without multiple copies of the program lying around, you've just learned a way of saving lots of disk space.

```
┌─────────────────────────────────────────────────────────────┐
│  ┌─────────┐                                                  │
│  │ CAUTION │                                                  │
│  │  [hand] │                                                  │
│  │  image  │    MS-DOS LOSES THE DRIVE!                       │
│  └─────────┘                                                  │
│                                                               │
│  If you use the ASSIGN command, then later in the same        │
│  session and without rebooting or resetting the system, you   │
│  execute a DIR or other built-in command with the replaced    │
│  disk as the target, MS-DOS still uses the substituted drive  │
│  assignment. Type the ASSIGN command with no arguments to     │
│  clear this problem or reset the system with Ctrl-Alt-Del.    │
└─────────────────────────────────────────────────────────────┘
```

Informing MS-DOS What Path That It Should Use

If the reason a particular program won't run in a tree-structured directory under MS-DOS 2.x is related to the fact that the program isn't "smart" enough to look elsewhere for the needed program files, you can set up an MS-DOS path (as described in detail previously) that includes the subdirectory in which the program files are located.

Using DPATH and Related Products

DPATH (see Chapter 8 for details) is a public-domain program that allows you to establish a path that even programs which don't take advantage of MS-DOS pathing use correctly. Its syntax is identical to that of the MS-DOS PATH command, so learning how to use it is very easy. Using DPATH and SmartPath is the only way we've found to allow WordStar program files to exist in one place and run from subdirectories of text files on an IBM PC hard disk.

Place the program files in a subdirectory or the root directory. Here, we assume the program and overlay files are in the subdirectory \WS from the root directory. Set both the PATH command and SmartPath (the program filename is called SPATH.COM) to look to that subdirectory for files if they are needed:

```
PATH C:\WS;\
```

```
SPATH C:\WS;\
```

These commands can be entered from the keyboard or embedded

in a .BAT file (see Chapter 2 for details) so that they are easy to execute whenever you wish. They can also, obviously, be stored in your AUTOEXEC.BAT file if they are configurations that you use most of the time.

MS-DOS 3.x Solutions

If you have MS-DOS 3.1 or later, you have, in addition to the options outlined previously for earlier versions of MS-DOS, two commands that prove helpful in dealing with the problem of program files that don't "find themselves" correctly in tree-structured directories: SUBST and JOIN.

The SUBST Command

The MS-DOS 3.0 SUBST command permits a great deal of power and flexibility in the use of subdirectories with programs that do not support MS-DOS pathing. Essentially, SUBST (which stands, logically enough, for SUBSTitute) permits you to treat a subdirectory path as if it were a disk drive of its own. You assign it a letter and from that time on you can obtain its directory, *log* to it (that is, cause it to be the currently active "drive"), and in all other ways treat it as if it actually were a separate disk drive.

SUBST PROBLEMS

Although SUBST generally has the desired result, you should be aware that some users have reported problems and potential bugs in working with MS-DOS 3.1's SUBST command. These problems have been reported to disappear when Version 3.2 is used.

Continuing with the WordStar example, you can store all of your WS program and overlay files (*.OVR) in a subdirectory called \WS, then store the document files related to specific projects in individual subdirectories. If we had three projects called PROJ1, PROJ2, and PROJ3, for example, we could assign each of these project subdirectories a disk drive letter with the following set of commands:

```
C:\>SUBST D: C:\WS\PROJ1
```

```
C:\>SUBST E: C:\WS\PROJ2
```

```
C:\>SUBST F: C:\WS\PROJ3    ← see note below about maximum drive letter
                              usage
```

Now you can run WordStar from its own subdirectory and use its built-in log command to log to drive D to work with PROJ1 files, drive E to work with PROJ2 files, or drive F to work with PROJ3 files. With versions of WordStar prior to 4.0 and the many other programs that do not support MS-DOS pathing completely or at all, this approach is nearly as efficient as using DPATH or SmartPath, although a combination of the two approaches may well be the best for your needs.

**FILE LETTER DESIGNATIONS
IN MS-DOS VERSION 3.x**

In MS-DOS Version 3.1 and later, you can use virtual disks (see Chapter 12) and "fake" disks like those with SUBST and treat them as if they were real physical disk drives. You must, however, be sure to tell MS-DOS how high your lettering scheme goes. This requires use of the LASTDRIVE command, described in detail in Chapter 13. If you attempt to use SUBST and call for a drive whose letter exceeds the maximum one you've told MS-DOS about, you won't be successful in the substitution attempt.

Summary

In this chapter, you have learned to make full use of subdirectories in MS-DOS. You have seen how directories and subdirectories relate to disk storage, filename limitations, and other aspects of MS-DOS usage. You have looked also at some public-domain and commercial programs that can greatly facilitate finding your way through the often tangled mess of directories and subdirectories that can arise from indiscriminate overuse of these features.

Along the way, you've learned a few tricks about when and how to use certain command configurations for most efficient use of the MS-DOS system with which you are working.

Secrets of MS-DOS Commands

Chapter 5

T his chapter provides general information about the MS-DOS commands, including discussions of the *path* MS-DOS uses to find commands; command parameters such as filename specifications, wildcards, and switches; command line editing; the concept of the current (or default) drive and directory path; using the reserved device names; and the break, print, and halt keystrokes for controlling command execution. These subjects are relevant to most MS-DOS commands as well as to a large proportion of the commands (or programs) available commercially and through the public domain. There are numerous exceptions to the "general rules" that apply to all commands. These exceptions are mentioned in various chapters in connection with a discussion of the commands pertinent to those chapters' subject matter. Exceptions are also included in the *MS-DOS Reference Manual.*

In some cases, common commands are described to explain tricks and techniques as well as pitfalls to avoid. For example, the COPY command, one of the most commonly used commands, is described in great detail to explain previously poorly documented features such as concatenating (combining) two or more files together, the differences between COPY's handling of binary and text files, and so on.

Data redirection and piping, another subject that applies to all commands in general, is covered fully in Chapter 3 of this book. MS-DOS's configuration commands (which are entered in the CONFIG.SYS file, not on the MS-DOS command line) are covered in detail in Chapter 13.

No attempt has been made to fully describe the functions and parameters relevant to each individual MS-DOS command. Listed in the bibliography are several books that are tutorial in nature and introduce the specifics of each command. Of course, the manual that comes with your copy of the operating system is another reference source. Most of the chapters in this book provide a full explanation of the commands that are relevant to their subject.

At the end of the chapter, Table 5-5 summarizes each MS-DOS command and provides information about changes made for the different versions of MS-DOS. (Table 13-1 [see Chapter 13] gives similar information for each of the configuration commands that are associated with the MS-DOS CONFIG.SYS file.)

What Is an MS-DOS Command?

A *command* is something you use to tell MS-DOS what to do. All commands are entered on the MS-DOS *command line* following the prompt (normally A> or C>) at the left of your display screen. A more detailed description is given in the information box titled *What Is the MS-DOS Command Line?* When you give MS-DOS a command, it executes the command, then returns to the MS-DOS command line to wait for another command. The MS-DOS command line consists of the MS-DOS prompt followed by the cursor, which is what MS-DOS uses to "prompt" you to enter another command. The phrases *enter the command at the MS-DOS prompt* and *enter the command on the MS-DOS command line* are equivalent.

WHAT IS THE MS-DOS COMMAND LINE?

The MS-DOS command line is the MS-DOS prompt followed by the cursor and space for you to enter a command. The MS-DOS prompt is what MS-DOS displays to let you know that it is ready to accept another command. The cursor points to the area where the command is displayed as you enter it from the keyboard.

The default MS-DOS prompt is *normally* the two characters A> for most computers with only floppy disk drives, and *normally* C> for most computers with a hard disk. These facts cannot be stated with certainty because different computer configurations with RAM disks, assigned disk drives, add-on hard disks, etc., can alter the prompts associated with various devices.

The default *cursor* is a thin blinking line about twice the size of the underscore character. When you press a key on the keyboard, the character for the key pressed is displayed at the cursor's position, and the cursor moves forward to the next space.

These are *default* descriptions of the prompt and cursor. The default descriptions apply when your computer is turned on for the first time after it arrives "straight from the factory." Like many things in MS-DOS, the prompt and cursor are *configurable,* so they may be changed to make your system easier to use. These features of MS-DOS make it much more flexible and powerful, but the fact that certain basic elements of the system are variable also makes it difficult to learn and describe. Even experienced MS-DOS users can have problems when they begin using another system that is configured differently than the system to which they are accustomed.

The maximum allowable length of a command is 128 characters, which means that the MS-DOS command line can take more than one line on the display screen. If you attempt to enter a command larger than allowed, MS-DOS responds with a beep, and the cursor does not advance.

HOW TO MODIFY THE MS-DOS PROMPT

Beginning with Version 2.0, one of the nice additions to MS-DOS is the PROMPT command, which allows you to modify the default prompt for your system. The default A> or C> characters may be replaced with any text you choose, such as Enter next command: or Speak to me!. In addition to text, you may include any of the following information: current time, current date, current directory, current drive, or MS-DOS version number. These variables are referred to as *meta-strings* in the MS-DOS documentation. They are embedded in the prompt by specifying a dollar sign ($) followed by a lowercase letter associated with each meta-string. The following example shows how to create a prompt line with the time, date, and directory on one line followed by the current drive on the following line.

```
C>PROMPT Date: $d  Time: $t  $p $_$n$g

Date: Wed 10-08-1986  Time: 16:05:02.83  C:\LOTUS
C> _
```

Notice that the prompt is now on two lines of the screen. Additional meta-strings are available to enter characters that are not normally allowed in the text for a prompt. For example, the > character could not appear as text for a prompt on the command line for the PROMPT command because this character would redirect the output of the PROMPT command to a file. All characters that may follow the $ character in the prompt text for the PROMPT command are shown in Table 5-1.

Table 5-1.   Prompt Text Characters

Character	Meaning
$	Must precede any of the following characters
t	The current time
d	The current date
p	The current directory of the current drive
v	The version number
n	The current drive
g	The > greater-than character
l	The < less-than character
b	The ¦ vertical bar character
q	The = equal-sign character
h	The backspace and erasure of the previous character
e	The ESC escape character
_	The CR-LF character sequence (the prompt continues on the beginning of the next screen line)

The PROMPT command setup in the previous example is very useful, especially for hard disk users, because the minimal information displayed is the current directory. By including the PROMPT command as part of your AUTOEXEC.BAT batch command file (which is executed during system start-up), you eliminate the need to type a relatively complex command each time your computer system is reset.

To restore the prompt to the default prompt, execute the PROMPT command with no *prompt text* following the command.

```
Date: Wed 10-08-1986  Time: 16:05:02.66  C:\LOTUS
C>PROMPT


C>_
```

The smallest prompt possible consists of a single space, which cannot be done with the PROMPT command simply by following it with spaces because spaces are interpreted as *no* prompt text by the PROMPT command. The Space character can be created with the nonprintable hexadecimal 255 character, which may be entered on the numeric keypad while holding down the Alt key.

When the PROMPT command is executed, the prompt text becomes one of your "environment" strings. The current PROMPT value can therefore be examined using the MS-DOS SET command with no parameters. The *name* of the environment string is also PROMPT. This fact can be exploited within batch command files. The current PROMPT can be saved in another environment variable, then restored later. The following example uses an environment string named XPROMPT to save the original value, then removes the XPROMPT string from the MS-DOS environment after the original prompt is restored. The new prompt used within the batch file is the ASCII BELL character (hexadecimal 07 or Ctrl-G), which causes a beep to sound when each command in the batch file completes and the command line is displayed. This may be useful or annoying, depending on the nature of the commands that you are executing within the batch command file.

```
SET XPROMPT=%PROMPT%
PROMPT ^G
REM
REM Normal batch commands go here with new prompt text.
REM
SET PROMPT=%XPROMPT%
SET XPROMPT=
```

Types of MS-DOS Commands

There are three primary categories of MS-DOS commands: *internal* commands, *external* commands, and *batch* commands. An understanding of the differences between these categories can be very helpful in using the commands, particularly when things go awry. The following three sections provide a description of the different command types and explain some of the terminology associated with each. Unfortunately, there is no authoritative source of definitions for much of the MS-DOS terminology. As a consequence, many terms and phrases with shades of differences in meaning are used interchangeably. The following sections will be of help when going though your manuals, documentation, magazines, and other publications, including this book.

WHAT IS THE MS-DOS COMMAND.COM PROGRAM?

COMMAND.COM is an MS-DOS command that provides the interface between you and your computer system. All commands that you enter on the MS-DOS command line are interpreted by COMMAND.COM, which finds the command to be executed. (Where COMMAND.COM finds commands is described under the heading *How MS-DOS Finds Commands To Execute* in this chapter.) If no command can be found, COMMAND.COM displays the Bad command or file name message and redisplays the MS-DOS prompt so that you can try again. If the command is found, COMMAND.COM loads the command into the computer system's memory and passes control to the command to execute it. When the command is completed, control is returned to COMMAND.COM, which redisplays the MS-DOS prompt and waits for the next command to be interpreted, loaded, and executed.

The COMMAND.COM program is also called the *command processor, command interpreter,* or *system shell.* You can substitute another "shell" as an interface between you and the system with the SHELL configuration command in the CONFIG.SYS file. The way to do this is described in Chapter 13 of this book.

The COMMAND.COM program makes use of other system resources that provide functions available to all commands executed in your computer system. These "resources" are contained in the hidden system files and the ROM BIOS.

The hidden system files have names that vary from version to version of MS-DOS. In the IBM personal computer series systems they are called IBMBIO.COM and IBMDOS.COM and must be the first two files in the root directory of any disk used to *bootstrap* the MS-DOS operating system.

For a disk to be "bootable," the disk must also contain a *boot record* (which is stored on the disk with the MS-DOS FORMAT command) and the ordinary (nonhidden) COMMAND.COM file. The MS-DOS SYS command transfers all of the elements required to make a previously formatted disk bootable except a copy of the COMMAND.COM file, which may be copied with the MS-DOS COPY command. If the /S parameter is used with the FORMAT command, the boot files (including COMMAND.COM) are copied to the disk after it is formatted.

The ROM BIOS (read-only memory basic input/output system) is a collection of routines that are part of the hardware of your computer system. The BIOS contains computer instructions that perform some diagnostics on your system when it is powered on or reset, then loads the *boot record* from a disk. The boot record loads the hidden system files, which in turn, load the system shell, normally COMMAND.COM.

Internal Commands

Internal commands are commands that are interpreted and performed directly by the COMMAND.COM shell program. These commands appear in a table within the COMMAND.COM program. All internal commands are part of the MS-DOS operating system and are described in your MS-DOS Manual. They are available for use whenever your system is at the MS-DOS prompt. Examples of MS-DOS internal commands are BREAK, COPY and DATE. Several of the internal commands have synonyms, such as DEL and ERASE, a command that *deletes* (or *erases*) files from a disk.

You can change the names of internal commands or even replace internal commands with external commands you have written or purchased. These are advanced tricks that must be done carefully and are not for the fainthearted.

CHANGING MS-DOS COMMAND NAMES

If you ever wanted the compare program to be named COMPARE rather than the less descriptive COMP, this trick is for you. Use the MS-DOS RENAME (or REN for short) command to change the filename COMP.COM to COMPARE.COM. Any external command can be renamed in this manner. Most external MS-DOS commands have a related disk file with the same name as the command followed by the filename extension .COM. The few exceptions to this rule have a filename extension of .EXE.

A program can determine what name is used to execute it, and a few commercially available programs do rely on this feature to perform slightly different functions depending on their name. No MS-DOS external commands (as of version 3.2) use this feature to function differently, so renaming any external command is a "safe" thing to do. However, a few disadvantages to renaming MS-DOS external commands should be taken into consideration before renaming everything on your disk.

First, all batch command files you are currently using that reference any renamed command will not be able to find the command to be executed. The relatively quick task of renaming a few command files might also require the relatively tedious, time-consuming, and error-prone task of modifying numerous batch command files. In addition, any purchased software you acquire in the future may have batch command files that are intended to assist in the installation or configuration of the product. Any references to renamed commands made within these batch command files again will cause the nuisance of the Bad command or file name problem to arise.

The second disadvantage can be the embarrassment and frustration of appearing to know nothing about MS-DOS when you are using a friend's or colleague's computer system after bragging "Oh, yeah, I can fix that in a minute."

Before changing all your MS-DOS .COM files to one-character names in order to save keystrokes, consider the possible consequences.

In addition to the possibility of giving MS-DOS external commands non-DOS command names, you may also want to give a non-DOS command an MS-DOS command name. You could, for example, rename COMP.COM to MS-COMP.COM and create your own version of compare, which performs the same or similar functions as the MS-DOS COMP command. You could also add enhancements to the command that are invoked only when additional parameters are present on the command line. As long as your program is reliable, you can have the advantages of the MS-DOS command and the added capabilities of your own creation at the same time. A few programs are available in the public domain that qualify for this purpose of renaming MS-DOS commands. (For more information, see Chapter 8, *Obtaining and Using Free and Low-Cost Software;* Appendix A, *Annotated Bibliography*; and Appendix B, *Source Information.*)

External Commands

External commands are programs loaded by the COMMAND.COM shell program and executed. For each external command, an associated disk file with a filename extension of .COM or .EXE is available. Other disk files may be required to execute the program, but there *always* must be either a .COM or .EXE file present on a disk and available to the system in order to execute an external command.

Because external commands (or programs) constitute a very common type of command, the terms *command* and *program* are often used synonymously, although their meanings are not always identical. The phrases *at the MS-DOS prompt, type the command name and press the Enter key* and *at the MS-DOS prompt, type the program name and press the Enter key* have the same meaning only when the command being discussed is an external command.

A number of external commands are distributed with MS-DOS:

the .COM and .EXE files on the floppy disk that comes with your operating system. Programs you have purchased, obtained through the public domain, or those you or your friends have written are also usually external commands.

Some programs, such as BASIC programs written using several different BASIC *interpreters,* are *not* external commands. These programs are often saved on disk with a filename extension of .BAS. The BASIC interpreter loads the file from disk and executes or *interprets* the program. The BASIC interpreter itself is an external command, such as the BASIC.COM and BASICA.COM programs that come with PC DOS. The programs written using BASIC are not external commands because the .BAS files created by them cannot be executed directly from the MS-DOS command line. Some BASIC interpreters have an option to create a .COM or .EXE version of a BASIC program that can be executed directly from the MS-DOS prompt, so some programs written in BASIC are external commands and some are not.

The same is true for programs written in other languages that are often interpreted rather than executed. If a program is executed from within the language interpreter, the program is *not* an external command. If the program can be executed from the MS-DOS command line, the interpreter probably has a "compile" option that allows the creation of external commands.

The name of any external command is the same as the name of the .COM or .EXE file on disk. For example, the command named DISKCOPY corresponds to the DISKCOPY.COM file supplied with MS-DOS. External commands distributed with MS-DOS are often referred to as *MS-DOS commands, MS-DOS programs,* or *MS-DOS utilities.*

External commands purchased or obtained through the public domain are seldom referred to as *commands* (although they are external commands). They are more likely to be called simply *programs, utilities,* or *applications.* Application programs are programs that perform a function fundamental to the primary objective of your use of a personal computer, such as word processing, spreadsheets, and database managing. Utilities are programs that serve a useful function secondary to the objective, such as disk backup, file compression, and file encryption.

Some examples of MS-DOS external commands are DISKCOPY, FORMAT, MORE, and SORT. These commands have associated disk filenames of DISKCOPY.COM, FORMAT.COM, MORE.COM, and SORT.EXE. The MORE and SORT commands belong to a special class of programs called filters. (See Chapter 3 for more information on filter programs.) Some examples of external commands that are *not* MS-DOS commands are WS, 123, and SK. The associated disk filenames for these programs are WS.COM, 123.EXE and SK.COM, which are the disk filenames for the well known MicroPro WordStar, Lotus 1-2-3, and Borland Sidekick programs.

Batch Commands

Batch commands, like external commands, always have an associated disk file. For batch commands, the files always have a filename extension of .BAT and are referred to as *batch command files* or *dot bat* files. The name of a batch command is the same as the first part of its associated filename, so a batch command named INSTALL has an associated disk file named INSTALL.BAT.

A batch command file is a text file that contains one or more commands to be executed. The commands may be internal commands, external commands, other batch commands (with some restrictions), or batch subcommands. Batch subcommands are a special class of MS-DOS internal commands typically used only within batch files. Although they may be executed directly from the MS-DOS command line, the functions performed by subcommands are normally useful only within batch files. Some of the functions that batch subcommands can perform are commenting batch files, conditionally executing commands, and executing a group of commands more than once. Chapter 2 of this book covers the subject of creating and using batch command files.

Although batch commands are available in Version 1.0 of MS-DOS, the batch subcommands ECHO, IF, FOR, SHIFT, and GOTO were introduced with Version 2.0. Most batch commands currently distributed with software operate only in MS-DOS Version 2.0 or later.

Batch files are fairly easy to create and are indispensable for serious users of personal computers. The few minutes required to make and test a batch file are usually worthwhile even if it will be used only a few times. Batch command files do more than save time by eliminating keystrokes. A good batch file ensures that all the commands required to perform a function are consistently performed in the correct order and with no keystroke errors.

Batch commands are seldom sold separately, although they are often included with purchased software packages to perform functions such as installing and configuring the companion software. Probably the best known batch command is the AUTOEXEC command automatically executed by MS-DOS when your computer is reset (booted). The associated disk file is the AUTOEXEC.BAT file, which easily can be created or modified to add any commands that you want automatically executed when your computer is turned on or reset. See Chapter 13 for more details on the AUTOEXEC batch command file. Another example of a batch command is the PCJRINST command sometimes supplied with a software product to modify the software so that it operates on the IBM PC*jr*. A PCJRINST.BAT file is supplied with Superkey and several other software products.

Because you may have several batch files with the same name but different contents, you need to know which batch file is processed when you enter a command. The next section of this chapter describes how MS-DOS finds commands to execute.

How MS-DOS Finds Commands To Execute

When you enter a command on the MS-DOS command line, a very predictable algorithm is used to locate the command to be executed. If you understand what search path MS-DOS follows to locate a command, you can have some control over what command is executed by changing the default disk, default directory, and contents of the PATH environment string variable. The following paragraphs describe this search path.

When a command is entered on the command line, the first place MS-DOS looks for the command is in a table of internal command names within the COMMAND.COM program. If the name of the command is found in the table, the command is an internal command and is executed directly by the COMMAND.COM program.

If the command is not an internal command, MS-DOS looks for a disk file in the current directory on the current disk with a filename of [command-name].COM. (The [ ] signs here and throughout this book indicate a variable within a command.) For example, if the name of the command entered on the command line is BEEP, MS-DOS looks for a program file named BEEP.COM. If the file is found,

COMMAND.COM loads the file into your computer's memory, then executes the program. When the program has completed execution, COMMAND.COM redisplays the prompt and waits for another command.

If no .COM file is found, COMMAND.COM searches the current directory on the current disk for a program file named BEEP.EXE. If found, the file is loaded, executed, and the MS-DOS prompt is displayed.

If no .EXE file is found, COMMAND.COM searches the current directory on the current disk for a batch command file named BEEP.BAT. If found, the batch command file is processed. When processing is completed the MS-DOS prompt is displayed.

If no .COM, .EXE, or .BAT file is located in the current directory on the current disk, the paths named in the PATH environment string are searched. The search continues looking for a .COM file, then an .EXE file, then a .BAT file, in the first named path in the PATH environment string. It then looks for a .COM file, then an .EXE file, and so on, in the second path in the PATH environment string until a command to execute is located.

If no command is located after all paths named in the PATH environment string are searched, MS-DOS displays an error message `Bad command or file name` and redisplays the prompt. The amount of time required to determine that no command exists increases proportionally with the number of paths in your PATH environment string. The trade-off is that adding more paths to your PATH environment string allows you to keep command files in several different disk directories, thus permitting you to keep your disk files well organized. The best solution is to order your path so that the most commonly executed commands are in directories near the beginning of the list of paths specified in your PATH environment string.

The search path previously described is also followed when a command is encountered within a batch command file. When the command is found and executed, MS-DOS returns to the next command in the batch file, not the command line. The only exception is when a *batch* command is encountered within a batch command file. In this case, the *new* batch command file is executed, then MS-DOS returns to the command line, *not* the next line in the calling batch file. The remainder of the original batch file that invoked the second batch command is ignored. If the second batch command was the last command in the original file, no unexpected results or problems occur. A technique that can be used to get around this limitation of executing batch commands within batch command files is described in Chapter 2.

With versions of MS-DOS prior to 2.0, you cannot have sub-directories on a disk. Consequently, the search for a command to be executed is far more simple. The name of the command is searched for in the shell (normally COMMAND.COM), followed by a search for a .COM, an .EXE, or a .BAT file on the current disk. Environment strings are not available in MS-DOS Version 1, so no PATH environment variable is available to direct MS-DOS to search other disks.

When you enter a command on the command line, you may specify a filename extension for the command. For example, to perform a disk copy, the command DISKCOPY.COM A: B: works just as well as DISKCOPY A: B:. Be careful, though, because the filename extension is *ignored* by MS-DOS. In fact, the command DISKCOPY.BAT A: B: performs the same function as the previous two examples—even though no DISKCOPY.BAT file exists anywhere on your disk.

Another idiosyncrasy of MS-DOS is that if you specify a command name that is longer than eight characters, the extra characters in the name are ignored. For example, the DISKCOMP command executes normally when you give the command DISKCOMPARE A: B:.

Versions of MS-DOS numbered 3.0 and higher have a small but extremely useful enhancement: The pathname of an external command may be specified on the command line preceding the command to be executed. Suppose that you have two files on your hard disk named FF.COM: The version you use to send a form feed to the printer is located in a directory named \COMMANDS, and the other version is the Norton file-find utility located in a directory named \NORTON. Assume that the MS-DOS PATH command most recently executed was

```
PATH C:\DOS;C\;C\COMMANDS;C:\LOTUS;C:\WORDSTAR;C:\NORTON
```

When the command FF is entered at the MS-DOS prompt, the search path for finding the command is the

command table in COMMAND.COM

current directory

\DOS directory

root directory

\COMMANDS directory

The FF.COM file in the \COMMANDS directory is executed and sends a form feed to the system printer. To execute the Norton file-find utility program, you have to enter the command \NORTON\FF at the MS-DOS prompt. As mentioned, this feature works only in Versions of MS-DOS numbered 3.0 and higher. For other versions of MS-DOS, you may get around this limitation using one of the following methods: Modify the search path with the MS-DOS PATH command, copy the FF.COM file from the \NORTON directory to the current directory, or change the current directory to the \NORTON directory with the MS-DOS CD (or CHDIR) command. Another more permanent solution is to rename one of the command files. For example, rename the form feed program to FORMFEED.COM and the file-find command to FILEFIND.COM.

When the command pathname is explicitly given for a command to be executed, such as \NORTON\FF, the search path is limited to the specified path *only*. Commands in the current directory or in paths named in the PATH environment string are ignored. If the command is not found in the explicitly stated directory, the Bad command or file name message is displayed and MS-DOS returns to the command line.

Parameters for MS-DOS Commands

Parameters are items that can be included on the MS-DOS command line following the command name. They are used to specify additional information to the command when it executes. Some commands, such as the MS-DOS VER command, have *no* parameters. Other commands, such as the MODE command, *require* parameters in order to perform anything useful. Most commands have *optional* parameters. That is, if you do not include one or more parameters, the command provides a default value. The default values provided by commands vary considerably from command to command, so you must check documentation for each command to know what default values are provided

The most common parameter given for a command is a disk filename or *file specification*. The number of filenames allowed (if any), types of files that may be specified and defaults provided are different for each command, but the standard format normally followed is

```
[drive:] [path] [filename.extension]
```

The items enclosed in brackets ([and]) indicate variables within the command.

Another type of parameter common to MS-DOS commands is the command line *switch*. Switches are often represented on the command line with a slash (/) followed by a letter or number. (Many programs, especially those derived from the UNIX operating system, use the hyphen (–) character to precede a switch on the command line.) For MS-DOS commands, the case of a letter following the slash is not important. Therefore, the switches /w and /W are interpreted the same way by MS-DOS. In practice, most documentation shows command names, filenames, and command switches in uppercase letters, but most users enter these items in lowercase letters. Such is life! For software obtained commercially or through the public domain, consult the documentation to determine if the case of any alphabetic switch parameters is important.

Command-line switches usually may be placed anywhere on the MS-DOS command line following the name of the command to be executed. Their order is usually not important, and spaces between switches are allowed but optional. Therefore, the following commands are all equivalent.

```
A>DIR/W/P
```

```
A>DIR /W /P
```

```
A>DIR     /w      /p
```

```
A>DIR     /p      /w
```

There are exceptions to these rules for a few commands. Consult your MS-DOS manual for the proper command line format for each command. An example of an exception to these rules is the /A and /B parameters for the COPY command. The /A switch must immediately follow the filename of each file that is to be treated as an ASCII file. The /B must follow files to be treated as binary files. Additional confusion is caused by the fact that certain default values for file types are assumed if these file type switches are not given for the filename parameters of the COPY command.

Again, these rules only apply to MS-DOS commands. Purchased and public domain software tends to have numerous exceptions regarding the ordering and spacing of command line switches.

A final "common" element of command-line parameters is the *delimiter characters*. Command line delimiters separate parameters that appear on the command line and include space, comma (,), semicolon (;), equal sign (=), and tab character. In practice, only the space character is used, with the occasional use of the equal sign. With the exception of switches, all parameters must be separated from other parameters and the command name by a delimiter. A general rule of thumb: If a delimiter may or must be at a particular place in a command line, one or more delimiters may appear at that place. For example, all of the following commands are interpreted identically by MS-DOS:

```
A>DIR *.*
```

```
A>DIR =*.*
```

```
A>DIR          *.*
```

```
A>DIR ;;,,== *.*
```

As you might guess, these general rules have exceptions. For example, for the SET command, you *must* put an equal sign after the name of the environment string to be added (or modified) and the new value of the string. In addition, spaces following the equal sign *are* significant.

```
A>SET EXAMPLE1 This is invalid because no equal sign appears
```

```
A>SET EXAMPLE2=This string's value will have no leading space
```

```
A>SET EXAMPLE2= This string's value will have a leading space
```

The MS-DOS MODE command is another exception to the general rule that multiple occurrences of delimiters are equivalent to a single delimiter. Successive commas indicate missing parameters that are given default values by MS-DOS. For example, the command MODE COM1:12,,,P is interpreted as MODE COM1:12,1,7,1,P. Replacing the three commas with a single comma would produce unexpected results.

Most purchased and public domain software is more rigid in interpreting command-line delimiters. Consult the documentation accompanying the software to determine the proper command-line format for each program.

One of the most difficult errors to detect is when a word processor that is used to place commands in a batch file has added spaces as delimiters. Many word processors replace multiple spaces with the tab character to save file space when possible. Numerous programs have difficulty interpreting the tab character correctly. When a command is executed in a batch file, the program can't "know" how many spaces are represented by a tab character in the command line.

WHAT IS THE MS-DOS DEFAULT DRIVE AND PATH?

The *default drive* is the one whose assigned letter is displayed by the MS-DOS prompt. For example, when the prompt is A >, floppy disk drive *A* is the default drive. The default drive is also called the *current* drive.

If a filename specification *without* the optional drive specification is used as a parameter, most commands use the current drive for the file. For example, executing the MS-DOS CHKDSK command with no parameters performs a disk check on the current drive. This can lead to problems when using programs that destroy data, such as the MS-DOS FORMAT command. See *Making Formatting Disks Safer* for a technique to avoid losing everything on your hard disk.

The *default path* is the path displayed by the MS-DOS CD (or CHDIR) command when no parameter is given, or by the MS-DOS prompt if you use the $p meta-string with the MS-DOS PATH command. The default path is also called the *current* path.

The default drive and path are significant when MS-DOS executes a command (see the *How MS-DOS Finds Commands To Execute* section of this chapter for more details). In addition, most commands search the current drive and path for data files on which to operate when no explicit drive or pathname is specified with a filename.

When your system is reset, the current drive and path are the root directory of the disk drive from which the system was booted (unless changed by your AUTOEXEC.BAT file). The current drive may be changed by entering the drive letter followed by a colon at the MS-DOS prompt. For example, A: changes the current drive to drive A, B: to drive B, etc.

The current path for the current drive may be changed with the CD (or CHDIR) command followed by the desired pathname. The current path for any other disk may be changed by executing the CD command followed by the drive letter and pathname. For example, if the current drive and path is

C:\, executing the command CD A:\LETTERS\JULY changes the current path for the A drive to \LETTERS\JULY if it exists, or displays the message Invalid directory, if it does not exist. The current drive and path (C:\) remain unchanged.

MAKING FORMATTING DISKS SAFER

The MS-DOS FORMAT command formats (or initializes) a disk so that it may be used with your computer system. FORMAT command options include placing a working copy of the MS-DOS operating system files on the disk and giving the disk a volume label (name). As vital as the FORMAT command is, it is also very dangerous—disks containing MS-DOS files that are reformatted no longer contain the original files!

As previously stated, when no drive letter is specified, some MS-DOS commands assume that the drive on which to operate is the current drive. Unfortunately, the FORMAT command is no exception, and the results can be disastrous. If you want to format a few new floppy disks for use with your system and are operating on a system with a hard disk, the default drive is likely to be the hard disk. Executing the FORMAT command without the drive specifier attempts to format the default disk—your hard disk! You are asked to verify that you want to format a fixed disk, a response of Y Enter destroys all 10Mb (more if you have a larger hard disk) of data on your disk.

This points out the value of backing up your disk frequently and of user friendly software. The Y Enter response to the FORMAT prompt is identical to your typical response to the FORMAT command's Do you want to format another (Y/N) ? prompt when you want to format several floppies.

The potentially disastrous use of the FORMAT command has finally been resolved in Version 3.2 of MS-DOS. The FORMAT command requires a drive specifier in order to format a disk because no default disk drive is assumed. In addition, if the disk to be formatted is a fixed disk, the volume label of the disk must be entered before the format operation is performed. If you are using Version 3.2 of MS-DOS, be sure to give your hard disk(s) a volume label when formatting or use the LABEL command to give your hard disks a label *now*.

If you are using a version of MS-DOS below 3.2, another solution is strongly recommended, easy to do, and could save you from the trouble of losing all the data on your hard disk. First, rename the FORMAT.COM file on your hard disk to FORMAT1.COM. Next, create the following batch file named FORMAT.BAT.

```
C>COPY CON: FORMAT.BAT
IF (%1) == () GOTO :ENDBAT
FORMAT %1
:ENDBAT
^Z
          1 File(s) copied


C>_
```

The batch file helps avoid formatting your hard disk accidentally if you execute the FORMAT command and forget to specify a drive letter with the command.

If you accidentally format your disk, don't touch anything until you buy a program to restore everything. Formatting a disk with existing data files on the disk does not really "destroy" the data on the disk, but it does make the data on the disk inaccessible to MS-DOS.

The fact that the information on a disk may be "unerased" by a special utility program also points out that reformatting your disk does not "wipe out" the contents of the disk. Therefore, be sure that you use a wipe out program to really erase everything if your data is confidential. An example of a "wipe out" program is WIPEDISK, which is included with the Norton Utilities software package. Never use the WIPEDISK program rather than FORMAT unless you have to.

The ASSIGN Command

The MS-DOS ASSIGN command has one, and only one, virtue—it allows you to run certain application programs using your hard disk or a RAM disk. For example, Version 1.10 of EasyWriter only recognizes drives A and B as drives that it can use to read or write files. This limitation can be circumvented by using the ASSIGN command.

The ASSIGN command tells MS-DOS to route all requests for one disk drive to another. For example, the command ASSIGN A=C causes all references to drive A to be directed to drive C. Note that the ASSIGN command does not accept drive specifications with a colon (that is, ASSIGN A:=C: is incorrect). After the command is executed, the two commands DIR A: and DIR C: are identical. The command displays the directory that is on physical drive C. When the ASSIGN command is executed, any previous drive assignments are *undone* and only the assignments specified for the last ASSIGN command are effective. More than one assignment may be made when the ASSIGN command is executed. For example, to route all disk requests that normally are intended for floppies to your hard disk, execute ASSIGN A=C B=C. The ASSIGN command with no parameters undoes all drive assignments.

Now that you know everything good about the ASSIGN command, here's the bad news: MS-DOS gets very confused when drives are reassigned with the ASSIGN command. Several commands such as DISKCOPY and DISKCOMP totally ignore the assignments, as do several popular programs, such as Lotus 1-2-3. The PRINT command should *never* be used while drives are reassigned. In general, memory-resident programs active when the ASSIGN command is used have a potential to become very confused and may destroy data.

The MS-DOS BACKUP command has a number of problems that might not become evident until you attempt to restore data saved while drives were assigned. Several commands that check for inconsistent parameters can have problems, such as the COPY command, which normally does not allow a file to be copied onto itself.

If you think MS-DOS gets confused, try using the ASSIGN command to reassign your hard disk as a floppy and vice-versa, your RAM disk as another floppy and vice-versa, then copy some files around and delete the files after they are copied. If this sounds dangerous, take it as a sign that ASSIGN should be used only when it is necessary to run an application that otherwise cannot be run. After the application has been run, and before using MS-DOS from the command line or running other applications, immediately execute ASSIGN with no parameters to undo any previous assignments.

The following is a sample batch command file that can be used to run EasyWriter Version 1.10 from a hard disk. It is a useful model to use for all applications where the ASSIGN command is required. All uses of the ASSIGN command should be done within a batch file in this way—use ASSIGN to reassign drives as required for the program to be executed, execute the desired application, then use ASSIGN with *no* parameters to unassign the assigned drives.

```
ECHO OFF
ECHO WARNING:  Drives A and B are now assigned to drive C
ECHO           If you use Ctrl-Break to exit from this
ECHO           batch file, be sure to execute the ASSIGN
ECHO           command with no parameters to undo these disk
ECHO           assignments before continuing.
PAUSE
ASSIGN A=C B=C
```

```
EW
ASSIGN
ECHO NOTE:  Drives A and B are now assigned normally.
ECHO ON
```

You may also add other commands to the batch file to perform functions normally required before using your word processor, such as setting up and restoring printer controls, changing to a directory where documents to be edited are stored, etc. Most programs requiring the use of the ASSIGN command were developed for earlier versions of MS-DOS and have been updated to eliminate the need for using it. If you use a program frequently, the best solution probably is to upgrade to a more recent release of the product.

The MS-DOS JOIN and SUBST commands were introduced with Version 3.1 and offer more effective methods of performing the function of the ASSIGN command. If you are using a version of MS-DOS that offers these commands, you should consider the ASSIGN command obsolete and replace its use with one of these more advanced commands.

Entering MS-DOS Commands

Several keys have special functions to help you correct mistakes when you are entering commands on the MS-DOS command line. Use either the Backspace key or the Left Arrow key to erase the character preceding the cursor and move the cursor one position to the left. The Esc key can be used to cancel the current command, which causes MS-DOS to display a backslash (\) character at the end of the current command and position the cursor at the beginning of the next line. The current command is *not* executed and a new command can be entered on the next line. This is convenient when you have made several mistakes on the current line, and it is easier to reenter the entire command than use the Backspace key to correct the command.

There are two additional command line editing keys that may be used while entering a command. The use of these keys is not recommended because not all programs correctly interpret the characters that are inserted into the command line when these commands are used. These keys are the Tab key, which may be used to move forward to the next tab stop, and the CTRL-Enter key combination, which may be used to move the cursor to the beginning of the next line to continue a command.

The command line editing features of MS-DOS are described in the next section of this chapter. These features are not one of MS-DOS's strong points. The *Retrieving MS-DOS Commands* section describes a program that can make "life on the line" a much easier proposition.

Modifying the Previous MS-DOS Command

In addition to the relatively meager options that you can use to edit the command you are entering on the command line, MS-DOS provides a facility for editing the previous command entered so that it may be reexecuted. This is a handy feature when you want to make a correction to an incorrect command that failed or execute several similar commands in succession. The previous MS-DOS command executed is saved in a command buffer. Several editing keys may be used to copy the saved command, delete parts of the command, or insert new characters into the command. Table 5-2 lists the available editing keys and describes their function.

Table 5-2. Functions of Editing Keys

Key	Function
Esc	Cancels the current command and does not update the command buffer
Tab	Moves the cursor to the next tab stop
Ins	Allows the insertion of characters into a command
Del	Skips over one character in the command buffer
F1	Copies the next character from the command buffer
F2	Copies all characters from the command buffer up to a specified character
F3	Copies all remaining characters from the command buffer
F4	Skips over all characters in the command buffer up to a specified character
F5	Copies the current command line into the command buffer without executing the command

The MS-DOS command line editing keys are nearly useless. They are difficult to use because they do not display the previous command for reference while you edit. The most useful is the F3 key, which copies the entire previous command to the current command line if no other keys have been used. Then, the Backspace key may be used to erase part of the previous command and reenter any desired changes before executing the modified command. The Esc key is also useful to "cancel" the current command and start over.

Several keyboard enhancement programs, such as Superkey and ProKey, have the capability of building a "stack" of previous commands entered on the MS-DOS command line. These programs allow you to retrieve commands from the stack of commands that has been saved. These commands then may be (optionally) modified and reexecuted. The editing capabilities of these programs are not very powerful, but they do offer more power and ease of use than the built-in capabilities of MS-DOS.

RETRIEVING MS-DOS COMMANDS

An inexpensive program named RETRIEVE gives you all the command line editing features that you wish were built into MS-DOS. RETRIEVE allows you to easily display previously executed MS-DOS commands, edit them if desired, then reexecute them. The keystrokes used to recall and edit commands are logical and easy to use.

The RETRIEVE program also allows abbreviations to be used for frequently used commands. This feature can be very useful to save keystrokes and reduce errors while entering MS-DOS commands. Because these command abbreviations are not keyboard macros, which redefine keystrokes for your keyboard, their use does not interfere with the use of the keyboard when running an application program.

The RETRIEVE program is a memory-resident program compatible with most other popular memory-resident programs, such as Borland's Turbo Lightning, Superkey and Sidekick utilities.

The RETRIEVE program is part of the "Utilities I" package available from *The Directory—Personally Developed Software for IBM Personal Computers*. The phone and address are provided in Appendix B.

If you don't mind using unsupported software (or can't tell the difference), you may want to check out the command line editor named CED, available through the public domain. CED has many features similar to the RETRIEVE program, and, of course, is priced right. See Chapter 8 for more information on the CED command editor.

Controlling MS-DOS

A number of keystroke sequences have special meaning to MS-DOS when you are entering commands on the command line and when commands are being executed. Table 5-3 lists these keystroke sequences and gives a description of their function.

Table 5-3.   **Keystroke Sequences and Their Functions**

Key	Function
Ctrl-C or Ctrl-Break	Interrupts a command and returns to the MS-DOS command line. From the MS-DOS command line, cancels the entry of the current command
Ctrl-P or Ctrl-PrtSc	Echoes the screen display to the printer. Pressing Ctrl-P or Ctrl-PrtSc again toggles this function off
Ctrl-S or Ctrl-Num Lock	Stops the screen display. Pressing any other key restarts the display
Shift-PrtSc	Prints the contents of the screen on the printer
Ctrl-Alt-Del	Restarts MS-DOS (system reset)

These keystroke sequences are always in effect from the MS-DOS command line and when you are executing programs supplied with MS-DOS. A program may inhibit the normal MS-DOS action for these keystroke sequences, except the Ctrl-Alt-Del keystroke sequence. Most purchased and public domain software that displays screen information on the bottom line of the screen and scrolls the screen display up does not inhibit the use of these keystroke combinations. Most software that uses the entire screen and allows "cursor control" keys to move the cursor and enter information at various places on the screen normally inhibits the use of all of the above keystroke sequences except Shift-PrtSc function, which prints the contents of the entire screen on the printer.

The effect of the Ctrl-C and Ctrl-Break keys is determined by the use of the MS-DOS BREAK command. If the last execution of the BREAK command had a parameter of OFF (or the BREAK command has never been executed), you can interrupt the execution of commands only when they are displaying information on the screen or asking for input from the keyboard. If the last execution of the BREAK command had a parameter of ON, you can interrupt the execution of a program more easily. See Chapter 13 for more information on the use of the BREAK command.

HOW TO "MONITOR" YOUR SYSTEM WITHOUT ONE

With the exception of the more mechanical components of your system—printers, plotters, and the like, your monitor (screen, video terminal, or CRT) is the most likely candidate for failure. Because all computer components tend to know when you most critically need them, you should have some idea of how to survive until your monitor can be fixed or replaced should it "go south." The easiest way is to simply redirect the screen output to your system's printer.

If the image on your monitor disappears, you won't be able to run most "screen-oriented" programs (such as spreadsheets or word-processors) effectively because their output cannot usually be redirected to your printer. If you must try, you can use the MS-DOS print-screen (Shift-PrtSc) function repeatedly. For most purposes, this is far too time-consuming. In addition, the printed image of the screen does not give an indication of the current cursor position.

Most MS-DOS commands are "line-oriented" programs—they display one line at a time on the bottom of your screen as they scroll the previous screen display up one line. Consequently, they are not difficult to use if their "screen display" is listed on your printer instead. To accomplish this, simply press the Ctrl-PrtSc (or Ctrl-P) keystroke combination after your system starts.

One shortcoming of this method is that MS-DOS does not normally output a print line to the printer until the entire line is completed. Consequently, any command that you are entering is not printed until you have entered the command. If you feel you have made a mistake, press the Esc key and reenter the entire command. This is not as convenient as using the Backspace key, but it reduces the possibility of making an error. In addition, some commands prompt you for keyboard input before continuing or exiting. For example, the MS-DOS COMP command inquires `Compare more files?` when it completes its current comparisons. Any response other than a Y or N causes the message to print on the printer and be redisplayed on your screen. With more dangerous commands, such as FORMAT or ERASE, you can use the more time-consuming (but less error-prone) approach of printing the screen when these commands prompt for input.

Obviously, this trick is not going to let you make any heavy-duty use of your system, but it does allow you to monitor what is going on enough to make some copies of files to a disk so that they may be transferred to another system until your monitor gets back "Real Soon Now."

Changing the MS-DOS Default
SWITCHCHAR Value

The normal "switch" character used to specify an MS-DOS parameter is the forward slash (/) character. You can change the value of this character to the hyphen (-) character to make MS-DOS commands more compatible with the UNIX operating system. When the switch character value is changed, the slash character can be used as the pathname separator (normally the backslash (\) character). Changing the value of the switch character is commonly done by real UNIX aficionados, who then are able to use both operating systems alternately with fewer adjustments and confusion. Chapter 13 of this book describes how to modify the value of the MS-DOS switch character for different versions of MS-DOS.

You should be aware of several problems before you reconfigure your system to take advantage of this feature. First, the feature is not documented in IBM PC DOS manuals. This means that it is not likely to be supported on future versions of the product. It is already becoming more difficult to change the default switch character value with newer versions of the operating system.

A second disadvantage is that some programs that create files using one value of the switch character become confused when the files are used later with another value for the switch character. Examples are the BACKUP and RESTORE programs, which should *never* be executed when the switch character is set to anything other than the default slash character.

Another disadvantage of using a nonstandard switch character is the confusion you can cause yourself when you switch to another system that uses the normal default switch character. A good example of this is the following command.

```
C>COPY A:*.* /V
```

When the switch character is the normal slash, the preceding command copies all files from the floppy disk in drive A to the current directory on the hard disk drive C. The copy is verified because of the presence of the /V parameter.

When the switch character is *not* the default slash character, MS-DOS interprets the command much differently. The A:*.* is interpreted as the *source* filename specification. The /V is interpreted as the *destination* filename specification. Therefore, all files on drive A are copied to the default directory on drive C and renamed /V. If the disk in drive A has more than one file, each file copied after the first file replaces the previously copied file because all files copied are named /V in the target directory (the current directory on drive C). As a result, only the last file copied remains in the current directory, and its name is /V.

The probability that you really want to copy numerous files, only save the last one, and name it /V is very small. The probability that you will do this if you are unaccustomed to a nonstandard switch character is high. The conclusion: If you want to avoid looking silly working on another system, don't mess around with the switch character on your own system.

Using Wildcards for Filename Specifications

Many programs accept a command-line parameter that specifies the name of a file on which the program is to perform its processing. Two *types* of file specifications may be given: *unambiguous* file specifications and *wildcard* file specifications.

An unambiguous file specification is what its name implies: One and only one file is specified. If no disk drive is given in the file specification, the current (or default) disk drive is assumed. Similarly, if no pathname is given, the current path is also assumed. Because duplicate filenames are not allowed to exist in the same directory on the same drive, only one disk file can possibly be referred to with an unambiguous file specification.

A wildcard file specification allows you to refer to more than one file. All wildcard file specifications have one or both of the * and ? wildcard characters. The ? wildcard character means "match any character in the filename in this position." Therefore, the wildcard file specification MEMO?.TXT matches files named MEMO1.TXT, MEMOA.TXT, MEMOZ.TXT, and many others. The following example shows the contents of all the files in a directory using the MS-DOS DIR command and the directory display resulting from three wildcard file specifications.

`A>DIR`

```
Volume in drive A has no label
Directory of  A:


RECEIVE   BAT      256    7-01-86   11:01a
REPORTS   BAT      384    8-16-86    4:26p
REPORTS   BAK      364    8-16-86    4:23p
REPORTS   DOC      624    7-01-86    3:33p
GLEDGER   RPT     1784   10-04-86    2:18p
INVEN     RPT     2628   10-04-86    2:41p
PAYABLES  RPT     1544   10-04-86    1:27p
RECEIVE   RPT      826   10-04-86    9:21a
SEP30     RPT     3357   10-03-86    2:22p
AUG31     RPT     3718    9-03-86    3:05p
OCT01     RPT      820   10-02-86    1:18p
OCT02     RPT      694   10-03-86    2:32p
OCT03     RPT      922   10-04-86    4:51p
OCTMTD    RPT      540   10-05-86    2:20p
       15 File(s)      69344 bytes free
```

```
A>DIR REPORTS.BA?
```

```
Volume in drive A has no label
Directory of  A:


REPORTS   BAT      384    8-16-86    4:26p
REPORTS   BAK      364    8-16-86    4:23p
        2 File(s)      69344 bytes free
```

```
A>DIR OCT??.RPT
```

```
Volume in drive A has no label
Directory of  A:


OCT01     RPT      820   10-02-86    1:18p
OCT02     RPT      694   10-03-86    2:32p
OCT03     RPT      922  ·10-04-86    4:51p
        3 File(s)      69344 bytes free
```

```
A>DIR OCT???.RPT
```

```
Volume in drive A has no label
Directory of  A:


OCT01     RPT      820   10-02-86    1:18p
```

```
OCT02     RPT      694  10-03-86   2:32p
OCT03     RPT      922  10-04-86   4:51p
OCTMTD    RPT      540  10-05-86   2:20p
        4 File(s)      69344 bytes free
```

Notice the slight difference between the wildcard file specification OCT??.RPT and OCT???.RPT. The second specification includes the file named OCTMTD.RPT, whereas the first does not.

The asterisk is the second wildcard file specification character. The asterisk wildcard character means "fill the remainder of the filename with question marks." Therefore, the wildcard specifications OCT?????.RPT and OCT*.RPT match the same files.

A file "name" consists of two parts: a filename of up to 8 characters and an optional filename extension of up to 3 characters. When the asterisk wildcard character is used in the filename extension, it is equivalent to one, two, or three question marks depending on the position of the asterisk in the filename extension. When the asterisk is used in the filename, the question arises: "Does an asterisk in the filename portion of a file specification match files with *any* file name extension?" The answer is not a simple yes or no. It depends on the program for which the filename specification is used. The MS-DOS DIR command interprets a trailing asterisk in a filename to include a wildcard for the extension also. In other words, the filename specification REPORT* is the same as REPORT*.*. However, the MS-DOS ERASE (or DEL) command is more restrictive. The filename specification REPORT* is interpreted as REPORT??? so that files with *any* extension are not deleted.

Consequently, using the DIR command to display a list of the files to be deleted with the ERASE command does not always give an accurate display. Fortunately, the ERASE command is more restrictive in its interpretation of the asterisk wildcard character and never deletes *more* files than the DIR command displays. However, it sometimes deletes *fewer* files depending on the names of the files within the directory being operated on.

Not all programs and MS-DOS commands accept file specifications containing wildcards. For example the MS-DOS TYPE command does not type the contents of all files when given a wildcard file specification. Instead, the TYPE command indicates that the file specified could not be found.

```
A>TYPE *.RPT
File not found
```

Whether a program or command accepts wildcard file specifications is usually indicated in the documentation for the command. Some commands (such as the COMP command) that did not accept wildcard file specifications in earlier releases of MS-DOS have been enhanced to accept wildcards. It is a good idea to review documentation when upgrading to a new version of MS-DOS. A small improvement like this can be a real timesaver.

Another difference between commands is in the way *no* filename specification is interpreted. Some commands, such as the MS-DOS DIR command, interpret no filename specification to mean *all* files. Therefore, the commands DIR and DIR *.* cause the display of all files in the current directory. Other commands, such as the MS-DOS ERASE command, interpret no filename specification to mean *no* files. The message `Invalid number of parameters` is displayed and no files are removed from the directory. The difference in the way a no file specification parameter is interpreted by various commands is generally what is convenient for the user rather than a real inconsistency.

However, the MS-DOS ERASE (or DEL) command has an inconsistency that can be dangerous. When the ERASE command is used to specify the name of a directory, the command is interpreted to mean "delete *all* files in the named directory." Fortunately, the message `Are you sure?` is displayed and requires a positive confirmation before all files in the named directory are deleted.

GETTING EVERYTHING YOU WANTED— AND MORE

The ability to use wildcards for filename specifications in MS-DOS is a very powerful and time-saving feature. Instead of executing the COPY command fifty times to copy all of the files from one directory to another, only one COPY command need be executed. The only attitudes to have toward wildcards are positive, right? *Wrong!*

Wildcards also have some potential hazards if they are not well understood. Suppose that you have five long letters named LETTER1.TXT through LETTER5.TXT in a directory and that you want to make changes to all the files, but first you decide to make a backup copy of each letter to be on the safe side. You do this with the COPY command: COPY LETTER?.TXT LETTER?X.TXT. After hours of work, you now have modified each letter, printed it, and verified that it is correct. You no longer need the backup copies of the letters, so you issue the command ERASE *X.TXT to remove them from your disk.

So much for being on the safe side. You have erased all of your backup copies *and* all your hard work on your newly modified .TXT files. The wild-card specification *X.TXT is equivalent to *.TXT. If you are careful enough to make backup copies of files about to be modified, you are also probably careful enough to verify the results of the ERASE command and can now pull out your Norton Utilities disk and QUICK UNERASE your lost files before they are gone forever.

Any characters following an asterisk wildcard character in the *filename* portion of a filename specification are ignored until the period (.) preceding the filename extension. Any characters following an asterisk in the *extension* portion of a filename specification are also ignored. Consequently, *all* of the following wildcard specifications delete *all* of the files in the current directory:

```
A>ERASE *.*
```

```
A>ERASE *X.*
```

```
A>ERASE *.*X
```

```
A>ERASE *X.*X
```

If you are not sure which files will be affected by a wildcard filename specification, the best verification is to execute the DIR command first with the wildcard being considered. The DIR command may display more files than the ERASE command will erase, but it never fails to display files that the ERASE command will erase.

Using the COPY Command as an Editor

For a simple "no frills" editor, nothing can beat the MS-DOS COPY command. The big disadvantage to using the COPY command as an editor is that files can only be created, not modified. However, there are advantages, like creating a short file is fast. The biggest advantage is that the COPY command is an internal MS-DOS command, so it is *always* available on every system running the MS-DOS operating system.

The technique for creating a text file with the COPY command is quite simple: The input "file" is specified as the console device, using the reserved device name CON:. The specified output file is the name of the file that is to be created. The following example creates a simple batch file named APPEND.BAT:

```
A>COPY CON: APPEND.BAT
ECHO OFF
IF NOT EXIST %1.TXT GOTO :NEWFILE
COPY %1.TXT %1.BAK > NUL:
ECHO Appending to file %1.TXT . . .
ECHO Add lines to be appended. End with Ctrl-Z
TYPE %1.TXT
COPY %1.BAK/A + CON: %1.TXT > NUL:
GOTO :ENDBAT
:NEWFILE
ECHO Creating new file %1.TXT . . .
ECHO Enter lines for new file. End with Ctrl-Z
COPY CON: %1.TXT > NUL:
:ENDBAT
^Z
        1 File(s) copied


A>_
```

When using the COPY command as an "editor" in this way, you cannot correct mistakes made in previous lines of the file being created. Terminating the COPY command and starting over is the only way to correct a mistake. Any mistakes in the current line may be corrected by using the Backspace key, then rekeying the remainder of the line.

The file APPEND.BAT created in the previous example is another useful way to use the COPY command. It allows lines of text to be appended to the end of an existing text file. You can create another useful batch file called INSERT.BAT, which inserts lines of text before the lines of an existing text file. It is very similar to the APPEND.BAT batch file except the seventh line is modified to read

```
COPY CON: /A + %1.BAK/A %1.TXT > NUL:
```

which causes the input from the console device (keyboard) to be copied to the modified file *before* the original contents of the file are copied.

Using the COPY Command To Combine Files

The MS-DOS COPY command can do more than copy files. It also can combine or *concatenate* them. Concatenate means to join end to end in a series (as opposed to *merge,* which means to mix or interleave). When the COPY command is used to concatenate files, the names of the files to be concatenated are specified in the order that they are to be combined. The filenames are separated with the plus (+) sign. After one (or more) spaces, the name of the destination or *target* file is given. If the target file already exists, it is overwritten and the original information in the file is lost.

The capability of concatenating files was introduced with the version of the COPY command distributed with MS-DOS Version 1.1. If you have a lower numbered version of MS-DOS, the operations discussed in this section do not function correctly with your version of the COPY command. Other features of the COPY command added with Version 1.1 are the /B (binary file) and /V (verify after copy) parameters.

If any of the original source files to be concatenated are text files that may end with the ASCII end-of-file indicator (Ctrl-Z character), the /A (for ASCII) command line parameter should follow the name of the file. If the source files are binary files and the end-of-file character should *not* be interpreted as the end of the file, the /B (for binary) command line parameter should follow the name of the file. The following example shows how to combine three text files into one large file named MEMOS.TXT.

```
A>COPY MEMO1.TXT/A + MEMO2.TXT/A + MEMO3.TXT/A   MEMOS.TXT /V
```

When concatenating files, you can use wildcards for the source filenames. You can also combine text and binary files with the COPY command. If one of the source files named in the list of source files does not exist, the COPY command combines all the files that do exist into one file.

If you are naming the target file with the same name as one of the source files, the source file with the same name must be the first file to be concatenated. If you want the target file to have the same name as any of the source files other than the first source file, you must rename the source file before the COPY command is executed. An alternate method would be to give the target file a temporary name and rename the target file after the COPY command is executed.

Using the Reserved Device Names as Filenames

One feature common to many programs is the capability of accepting as a parameter a "device name" where a filename would normally be specified on the command line. Replacing a filename with a device name can be very useful when you want to treat a device the same way that you treat a file. The most common example is to create a file using the COPY command with input from the keyboard (console input device). The previous section, *Using the COPY Command as an Editor*, gives several examples of this.

The CON: device may also be used as an output device with the COPY command. In this case, the output of the COPY command is directed to your screen (console output device). As the following example illustrates, the results are similar to displaying the file with the MS-DOS TYPE command.

```
C>COPY AUTOEXEC.BAT CON:
ASTCLOCK
PROMPT Date: $d  Time: $t  $p $_$n$g
PATH    C:\;C:\COMMON;C:\MSOFT;C:\TURBO;C:\NORTON;C:\MASM
SET     LIBPATH=\SYM
SET     TERM=IBMMONO
SET     LIB=\MODULA\EMLIB+\MODULA\DSLIB+\MODULA\MODULA
SET     FF=\FILEFAC
FILEFAC /I /P
RETRIEVE ALIASES
        1 File(s) copied


C>TYPE \AUTOEXEC.BAT
ASTCLOCK
PROMPT Date: $d  Time: $t  $p $_$n$g
PATH    C:\;C:\COMMON;C:\MSOFT;C:\TURBO;C:\NORTON;C:\MASM
SET     LIBPATH=\SYM
SET     TERM=IBMMONO
SET     LIB=\MODULA\EMLIB+\MODULA\DSLIB+\MODULA\MODULA
SET     FF=\FILEFAC
FILEFAC /I /P
RETRIEVE ALIASES


C>_
```

A more exotic example of using the devices as files is to receive input from your modem and output it to your printer with the COPY command.

```
A>COPY AUX: PRN:
```

Although substituting devices as files is often performed with the COPY command, many other programs also accept input or output from a device. The fact that devices may be used in place of files is not always mentioned in the documentation for a program. In fact, sometimes the author of the program is not even aware that this feature is useful or even possible.

Reserved device names for MS-DOS are given in a table at the end of Chapter 3. One device that should not be underrated is the NUL: device. It is often useful to direct unwanted listings or large files to this device in order to save time when executing a program.

The Versions of MS-DOS

Seven "major" versions of the PC DOS operating system have been released. The version numbers and their related "primary" enhancements are shown in Table 5-4. Releases of MS-DOS versions are roughly analogous to PC DOS versions. If your version of MS-DOS has more than one number following the decimal point, the second number can be ignored. For example, Version 2.12 of MS-DOS is about the same as Version 2.1 of PC DOS. The only significant version of PC DOS not mentioned in the table is Version 1.05, which has numerous bug fixes to the BASIC interpreter and is available free of charge to purchasers of Version 1.0 of PC DOS. In general, versions of MS-DOS (or PC DOS) *earlier than* 2.0 are considered obsolete, and software developers accept the fact that their software does not operate on these versions.

Table 5-5 lists all MS-DOS commands and gives a brief description of their function. Short hints or warnings concerning the use of a command are also given, along with an indication of the type of the command: internal, external, filter, and so on. (See Chapter 13, Table 13-1, for a list of system configuration commands that may be included in the CONFIG.SYS file.)

Comprehensive information regarding the MS-DOS version number in which a command or significant modifications were introduced also is given in the table. Some modifications, such as support of a new disk type for the FORMAT, DISKCOMP, and DISKCOPY commands,

Table 5-4.   DOS Versions and Their Enhancements

Version Number	Date of Release	Primary Reason for New Release
1.0	August, 1981	First release
1.1	May, 1982	Double-sided disk drives supported Enhanced serial communications supported
2.0	March, 1983	Fixed-disk drive supported (PC/XT) Data redirection, subdirectories environment variables, enhanced batch file subcommands, device drivers, and system configuration commands added
2.1	October, 1983	Half-height drives supported (PC*jr* and portable)
3.0	August, 1984	1.2Mb floppy disks supported (PC/AT)
3.1	March, 1985	IBM network supported
3.2	December, 1985	3 1/2" disks supported (PC Convertible)

for each new version are not specifically mentioned. Minor changes, such as improvements to the display output, are not mentioned unless these subtle differences could cause unexpected results when using a command.

One important command that is not included in the alphabetized list of commands is the [letter]: command, which changes the default drive to the disk drive specified by the [letter]. By default, the system "knows" about 16 drives (A through P). Beginning with Version 3.0, the LASTDRIVE configuration command can be used to expand the number of disk drives up to 26 (A through Z).

Table 5-5.   Summary of MS-DOS Commands

Command	Description
ANSI.SYS	A device driver that allows the use of special character sequences to be generated by programs that control the cursor position, graphics attributes, display mode, and keyboard key reassignment. The ANSI.SYS device driver was introduced with Version 2.0 of MS-DOS.
ASSIGN	An external command that reassigns drive letters so that requests for a given drive are routed to another drive. The primary purpose of this command is to allow programs that expect to work only with two disk drives under Version 1.x of MS-DOS to work on a system with a hard disk. The ASSIGN command was introduced with Version 2.0 of MS-DOS.
ATTRIB	An external command that allows you to set or display the read-only attribute of a file, which protects files from being changed or erased. The ATTRIB command was introduced with Version 3.0 of MS-DOS. Beginning with Version 3.2 of

Table 5-5 (cont).

Command	Description
	MS-DOS, the ATTRIB command can also set and clear the archive attribute of a file.
BACKUP	An external command that makes a copy of one or more hard disk files onto floppy disks for backup purposes. BACKUP also can be used to transfer a file that is larger than the capacity of one floppy onto multiple floppies. Files copied with the BACKUP command *must* be restored using the RESTORE command. The BACKUP command was introduced with Version 2.0 of MS-DOS. Beginning with Version 3.0, enhancements were added to BACKUP and RESTORE to support fixed and floppy disks as the target and/or source devices for backing up files.
BASIC	This is the BASIC interpreter. Version 1.05 of PC DOS removed a large number of bugs that were in Version 1.0 of the PC DOS BASIC interpreter.
BASICA	This is the advanced BASIC interpreter. Version 1.05 of PC DOS removed a large number of bugs that were in Version 1.0 of the PC DOS BASICA interpreter.
BREAK	An internal command that controls how often MS-DOS checks for a break request (Ctrl-Break or Ctrl-C) from the keyboard. The break request interrupts a program's operation and returns to MS-DOS. Normally, MS-DOS checks for a break request only during screen, keyboard, printer, or auxiliary device operations. If BREAK ON is executed, MS-DOS checks for a break request during any MS-DOS function (such as disk operations). Executing BREAK OFF restores MS-DOS to its normal break checking. Executing BREAK with no parameters causes a display of the current break mode. The BREAK command was introduced with Version 2.0 of MS-DOS.
CD	Same as CHDIR.
CHDIR	Also CD. An internal command that changes the current directory from one path in a disk's directory tree to another. The current directory can be set independently for each disk drive on a system. With no parameters, the CHDIR command displays the current directory of the current disk. The CHDIR command was introduced with Version 2.0 of MS-DOS.
CHKDSK	An external command that analyzes directories on a disk and checks file allocations against the FAT (file allocation table). Provides information about the disk (number of files, disk space available for use, available disk space not in use) and memory (bytes available, bytes in use). If disk errors are discovered while analyzing the disk, CHKDSK frees disk space that is allocated but not in use, and also creates files with allocated space not in use. Beginning with Version 2.0 of MS-DOS, the corrective actions of CHKDSK became optional.
CLS	An internal command that clears the screen. The CLS command was introduced with Version 2.0 of MS-DOS.

Table 5-5 (cont).

Command	Description
COMMAND	This is the MS-DOS shell program. The COMMAND command may be executed more than once to have multiple copies of the shell in memory at one time. The most useful purpose of doing so is to execute a batch command file within another batch command file. See Chapter 2 for more details on how to execute a batch file within another batch file.
COMP	An external command that compares the contents of two files and reports any differences. Beginning with Version 2.0 of MS-DOS, the two file specification parameters to the COMP command may be wildcards.
COPY	An internal command that copies one or more files from one disk to another or one directory to another. The newly created file(s) may also be renamed. The source and/or target file may be one of the reserved MS-DOS device names. Beginning with Version 1.1 of MS-DOS, files may also be concatenated, treated as binary files (/B parameter), and verified (/V parameter).
CTTY	An internal command that allows a remote terminal to be used in place of the primary console device (standard screen and keyboard). The assignment of the console also may be reversed to restore the screen and keyboard as the standard input and output devices. The CTTY command was introduced with Version 2.0 of MS-DOS.
DATE	An internal command that displays and/or changes MS-DOS's record of the current date. Add-on boards that have a clock feature usually include software that makes use of this command unnecessary on system start-up. If your computer doesn't have a clock feature, include this command in your AUTOEXEC.BAT command file. Prior to Version 1.1 of MS-DOS, this was an external command.
DEBUG	A program debug utility that can be used to examine and/or modify the contents of memory, disk files, and disk sectors. DEBUG can also be used to execute programs under close control to "trace" the computer's operations and "patch" the contents of variables and registers as necessary. A complete tutorial of the nonprogrammer-oriented DEBUG commands is presented in Chapter 7. The DEBUG COMPARE command was introduced in Version 1.1 of MS-DOS along with the ability to load files larger than 64K. The DEBUG ASSEMBLE command was introduced in Version 2.0 of MS-DOS.
DEL	See ERASE.
DIR	An internal command that displays information about files in the directory of a disk. DIR displays the entire directory or a portion specified by a filename or wildcard specification. The information displayed by DIR includes the filename and extension, the file size in bytes, and the date and time the file was created. Beginning with Version 2.0 of MS-DOS, DIR also displays the volume identification of the disk, names of

Table 5-5 (cont).

Command	Description
	subdirectories in the directory, and the amount of available space left on a disk. MS-DOS versions lower than 2.0 did not record the time a file was created in directory information for a file. Therefore, the DIR command does not display the time information for files created on these versions of MS-DOS.
DISKCOMP	An external command that compares disks sector for sector to see whether they match exactly. Disks that have the same files copied in a different order would normally be functionally equivalent. However, DISKCOMP reports that the disks are not identical. In addition, if unused portions of the disk are not identical, DISKCOMP also reports that the disks are not identical. The most useful purpose of the DISKCOMP command is to verify that disks created with the DISKCOPY command are correct.
DISKCOPY	Makes an exact copy of another disk of the same size. All areas of the disk are copied sector for sector, including unused data portions of the disk. Although DISKCOPY does not require the target disk to be formatted, use the FORMAT command first to determine whether the target disk has bad sectors. DISKCOPY does not adequately check for or report on bad copies of the disk being created. The DISKCOMP command should also be used after the copy to verify the results of the DISKCOPY command. With the problems inherent in DISKCOPY, it is usually simpler to use the COPY command with a file specification of *.* to make a functionally equivalent copy of a disk. With Version 3.2 of MS-DOS, the XCOPY command may also be used to copy files. XCOPY tends to perform multiple file transfers much faster than the COPY command.
DRIVER.SYS	A device driver that allows access to a disk device by referencing a logical drive letter. The DRIVER.SYS device driver was introduced with Version 3.2 of MS-DOS.
ECHO	An internal command that controls whether batch file commands are displayed on the screen. ECHO ON displays the commands, which allows you to see exactly what is happening. ECHO OFF suppresses the display of commands, useful when they may be irrelevant or confusing. ECHO with a message displays the message on the screen. ECHO with no parameters displays the current state of MS-DOS (ON or OFF). The ECHO command was introduced with Version 2.0 of MS-DOS.
EDLIN	A crude line-oriented editor for working with ASCII text files. Several new EDLIN commands and other improvements were added with Version 2.0 of MS-DOS.
ERASE	Also DEL. An internal command that erases (deletes) one or more files from a disk. When a disk file has been erased, it has not really been destroyed, but it cannot be recovered by ordinary MS-DOS methods. If, and only if, no additional disk files have been created or modified, you may be able to recover

Table 5-5 (cont).

Command	Description
	the file using DEBUG. Recovering a file in this manner is very difficult and error prone, especially if the file resides on a directory other than the root directory. The use of a disk utility software package (such as the Norton Utilities) is recommended. Beginning with Version 2.0 of MS-DOS, you must press the Enter key after responding to the ERASE command's Are you sure? prompt displayed when all files in one directory are being erased.
EXE2BIN	An external command that converts programs from the .EXE format to the .COM format. Not all programs can successfully be converted to the .COM format, and this program is intended for use by the developers of a program only. This command was introduced with Version 1.1 of MS-DOS.
EXIT	A shell command that removes the most recently executed version of COMMAND.COM (the MS-DOS shell) from memory. This is not recommended if memory resident programs have been installed since the last copy of the shell was placed in memory. Attempting to remove the last remaining copy of the shell does no harm, and the last copy of the shell remains in memory.
FDISK	An external command that initializes and partitions a hard disk so that it may be used with more than one operating system (MS-DOS, XENIX, etc.). The FDISK command was introduced with Version 2.0 of MS-DOS.
FIND	A filter command used to locate those lines in a file of ASCII text data that contain some particular character or string. The FIND command was introduced with Version 2.0 of MS-DOS.
FOR	A batch command file subcommand used to repeat a command for each item in a list. The FOR subcommand was introduced with Version 2.0 of MS-DOS.
FORMAT	An external command used to prepare disks for use. Normally, purchased disks cannot be written to until they have been initialized with the FORMAT command. The /S parameter causes the FORMAT command to include a copy of MS-DOS on the disk being formatted. The /V (introduced in Version 2.0 of MS-DOS) parameter instructs the FORMAT command to prompt for a volume identification that is placed on the disk. Beginning with Version 3.2, the FORMAT command does not format the current disk when no disk specifier is given. In addition, if the disk to be formatted is a hard disk, the volume label of the disk must be entered. These enhancements make the accidental formatting of a disk and loss of a substantial amount of data much less likely.
GOTO	A batch command file subcommand used to jump to another part of the batch file. The direction of the jump may be forward (to skip over unwanted commands) or backward (to repeat commands). The GOTO subcommand was introduced with Version 2.0 of MS-DOS.

Table 5-5 (cont).

Command	Description
GRAFTABL	An external command that loads a memory resident table which allows the extended ASCII character set to be used when in graphics mode. Normally the extended ASCII character set is available only in text mode. The GRAFTABL command was introduced with Version 3.0 of MS-DOS.
GRAPHICS	An external command that loads a resident program which allows the Shift-PrtSc keystroke combination to print the image of a graphics display screen. The GRAPHICS command was introduced with Version 2.0 of MS-DOS. Support for several additional printers was added with Version 3.0 of MS-DOS.
IF	A batch file command used to test for some logical condition (such as the equality of two strings, the existence of a file, or an error in a previous program). The result determines whether the following command is executed. The command conditionally executed by the IF subcommand is often a GOTO subcommand. The IF subcommand was introduced with Version 2.0 of MS-DOS.
JOIN	An external command that connects a disk drive to a directory on another drive to create a new directory structure. Files on several drives may then be accessed using only one drive specifier. The JOIN command was introduced with Version 3.1 of MS-DOS.
KEYB??	External commands named KEYBFR, KEYBGR, KEYBIT, KEYBSP and KEYBUK are memory resident programs that provide alternate keyboard translation and date-time formats for use of MS-DOS in countries other than the United States. These commands were introduced with Version 3.0 of MS-DOS.
LABEL	An external command that adds, changes, or deletes disk volume labels. A disk volume is one or more disk surfaces treated logically as one disk, thus the terms *disk, volume,* and *disk volume* are usually synonymous. The disk volume label is also called the *volume identification* or *volume id.* The label for the disk is displayed when you use the DIR, CHKDSK, and TREE commands. The LABEL command was introduced with Version 3.0 of MS-DOS. Beginning with Version 3.1 of MS-DOS, a response from the keyboard is required for verification before a volume label may be deleted.
LINK	Combines parts of a program, called *object modules* and *libraries*, to form an executable file (.EXE file). LINK is used in the development of commands for MS-DOS and most other programs (with the exception of those that are interpreted, such as BASIC programs).
MD	See MKDIR.
MKDIR	Also MD. An internal command that creates new subdirectories as part of a disk's directory tree. The MKDIR command was introduced with Version 2.0 of MS-DOS. Several

Table 5-5 (cont).

Command	Description
	bugs in MS-DOS commands involving directory names with extensions were removed in Version 3.0 of MS-DOS.
MODE	An external command that controls the mode of the printer, display, or communications line. Several important revisions were made to improve serial communications with Version 1.1 of MS-DOS.
MORE	A filter command used to keep display output from scrolling off the screen before it can be viewed. A data key is pressed to display the next screenful of data. The MORE command was introduced with Version 2.0 of MS-DOS.
PATH	An internal command that instructs MS-DOS where to look for commands to be executed. The PATH command creates or modifies an environment string variable named PATH. Using the SET command to create or modify the PATH environment string (SET PATH=[pathlist]) performs a similar function but confuses some versions of MS-DOS. The [pathlist] may include a number of directories on different disk drives. Each path must be separated by a semicolon. The PATH command was introduced with Version 2.0 of MS-DOS.
PAUSE	A batch file subcommand that displays a message and waits for a keyboard response.
PRINT	An external command that loads a memory resident program which prints disk files on the system printer in the *background,* allowing the computer to be used in the *foreground* for other purposes while the files are printing. A number of better *print spoolers* are available commercially or bundled with add-on memory boards. The PRINT command was introduced with Version 2.0 of MS-DOS. Beginning with Version 3.0, the PRINT command uses a *time-slice* method of operation that allows the command to print a file more quickly than in previous versions when a computation-intense program is running in the foreground.
PROMPT	An internal command that changes the prompt on the MS-DOS command line. For fixed disk users, a prompt with (at least) the current pathname is recommended (see the *How To Modify the MS-DOS Prompt* section earlier in this chapter). The PROMPT command was introduced with Version 2.0 of MS-DOS.
RECOVER	An external command that recovers files which cannot be used because of defective portions on a disk. Also used to recover directories and regain access to files in the directory. RECOVER is *not* capable of recovering accidentally erased files or directories. The RECOVER command was introduced with Version 2.0 of MS-DOS.
RD	See RMDIR.
REM	A batch file subcommand that does nothing. Normally, the REM subcommand is used with ECHO mode OFF so that the

Table 5-5 (cont).

Command	Description
	command does not display on the screen when a batch file is executing. In this way, the REM command may be used to place comments (REMarks) in a batch file.
REN	See RENAME.
RENAME	Also REN. An internal command that renames disk files.
REPLACE	An external command that selectively replaces files on the target disk drive or directory with files of the same name from the source disk drive or directory. A variation copies only files that do *not* exist to the target drive or directory. Disk subdirectories may also be searched. The command is also useful to find and replace all occurrences of a disk file with an updated version. The REPLACE command was introduced with Version 3.2 of MS-DOS.
RESTORE	An external command that restores files (which were copied to a disk with the BACKUP command) to a hard disk. When files have been copied with the BACKUP command, they *must* be restored with the RESTORE command. The RESTORE command was introduced with Version 2.0 of MS-DOS. Beginning with Version 3.0, enhancements were added to BACKUP and RESTORE to support fixed and floppy disks as the target and/or source devices for backing up files.
RMDIR	Also RD. An internal command that removes directories from a disk's directory tree. Any files in a directory must first be deleted using the ERASE (or DEL) command. RMDIR removes directories created by the MKDIR command. The RMDIR command was introduced with Version 2.0 of MS-DOS.
SELECT	An external command that allows selection of an alternate keyboard and date-time format to be used by MS-DOS. Related to the KEYB?? commands and COUNTRY CONFIG.SYS command. The SELECT command was introduced with Version 3.0 of MS-DOS.
SET	An internal command that creates, modifies, displays, or deletes string variables in the MS-DOS *environment*. Environment strings may be accessed by batch command files (using %[string-name]%) and programs. The use of environment strings to determine video characteristics, search paths for program overlays, and/or data files, etc., has become increasingly popular as an easy way to provide configuration data to programs. The SET command was introduced with Version 2.0 of MS-DOS.
SHARE	An external command that loads a memory resident program which provides file sharing support for MS-DOS. File sharing is used when computers are connected on a network. The SHARE command was introduced with Version 3.0 of MS-DOS. Improved network support was provided with Version 3.1.

Table 5-5 (cont).

Command	Description
SHIFT	A batch command file subcommand that shifts batch file parameters over one place. SHIFT may be used to access more than ten batch file parameters. It is also useful to process batch files that may accept a variable number of parameters. The SHIFT command was introduced with Version 2.0 of MS-DOS.
SORT	A filter command used to rearrange the lines of an ASCII text file in alphabetical (or reverse alphabetical) order. The SORT command was introduced with Version 2.0 of MS-DOS.
SUBST	An external command that substitutes a drive letter for another drive or a disk directory. The files on the specified drive or directory then may be referred to by using the substituted drive letter. Useful for application programs that do not recognize paths or tree-structured directories such as WordStar. The SUBST command was introduced with Version 3.1 of MS-DOS. It is preferred over the ASSIGN command introduced with Version 2.0 of MS-DOS.
SYS	An external command that transfers the hidden files and other information to a disk in order to create a workable copy of MS-DOS. The SYS command is often used to transfer MS-DOS to a disk that is copy-protected or update the version of MS-DOS on a disk. Using the FORMAT command with the /S parameter to format a disk is the same as using the FORMAT command without the /S parameter, then executing the SYS command.
TIME	An internal command that displays and/or changes MS-DOS's record of the current time. Add-on boards that have a clock feature usually include software that makes the use of this command unnecessary on system start-up. If your system doesn't have a clock feature, include it in your AUTOEXEC.BAT command file. Prior to Version 1.1 of MS-DOS, this was an external command.
TREE	An external command that displays the entire directory structure (tree) of a disk. The TREE command was introduced with Version 2.0 of MS-DOS. Bugs involving directories with filename extensions and not displaying files in the root directory were removed with the TREE command in Version 3.1 of MS-DOS.
TYPE	An internal command that displays the contents of an ASCII text file on the screen.
VDISK.SYS	A device driver that installs a "virtual" or RAM disk in memory. The driver may be installed several times to create more than one RAM disk. A RAM disk appears to be another disk drive to MS-DOS. However, it resides in the memory and thus has much a faster access time than a hard or floppy disk. When a computer system is reset or turned off, all data on a RAM disk is lost. The VDISK.SYS device driver was introduced with Version 3.0 of MS-DOS. However, a listing of

Table 5-5 (cont).

Command	Description
	the source for a similar driver was included in the manual of Version 2.0 of MS-DOS and higher.
VER	An internal command that displays on the screen the number of the MS-DOS version that is being used. The VER command was introduced with Version 2.0 of MS-DOS.
VERIFY	An internal command that instructs MS-DOS whether to verify if data written to disk was written correctly. When VERIFY is executed with the ON parameter, MS-DOS begins verifying disk writes. When VERIFY is executed with the OFF parameter, MS-DOS stops verifying disk writes. When VERIFY is executed with no parameters, it reports MS-DOS's current state of disk write verification (ON or OFF). OFF is the default state of disk write verification when a computer system is reset. The VERIFY command was introduced with Version 2.0 of MS-DOS.
VOL	An internal command that displays the volume label (or volume identification) of a disk. Volume labels may be placed on a disk when they are formatted with the MS-DOS FORMAT command /V parameter (Version 2.0 or higher) or with the MS-DOS LABEL command (introduced with Version 3.0 of MS-DOS). The VOL command was introduced with Version 2.0 of MS-DOS.
XCOPY	An external command that copies groups of files which can include lower level subdirectories. The XCOPY command can select files based on several criteria, including the file specification, file archive attribute, or file date. In addition, options allow the display of a prompt preceding the copying of each file, the prompt requires a Y/N response. Another option causes the XCOPY command to copy files from all subdirectories below the specified directory to the target, optionally creating the subdirectories on the target if required. Copying from or to the reserved device names is *not* supported. The buffering techniques used by XCOPY tend to make it faster than the COPY command for copying large or multiple files. The XCOPY command was introduced with Version 3.2 of MS-DOS.

Summary

This chapter has shown some of the subtleties in the use of MS-DOS internal and external commands. Most of the information dealt with ways in which MS-DOS commands can be used that are poorly described in the technical manuals or with techniques that were not previously described at all. The information presented can help you in your daily use of MS-DOS commands. The techniques and tricks covered in this chapter are implemented in examples throughout the book to further enhance the way you use your system. The next chapter deals with more advanced use of programmable function keys and screen manipulation.

Secrets of the Screen and Keyboard   Chapter 6

After working with your computer system for a period of time, you will probably begin to notice that in spite of the work being performed, your programs and batch commands have a "raw" appearance. Although this is nice for impressing friends and colleagues with how much productivity you are achieving, most likely you would appreciate getting a more "polished" look. Frankly, the key to a polished look is using better input methods and providing an orderly, pleasing display. When people look at your work, most often they judge, for better or worse, its appearance. That is what this chapter is about: appearance!

The techniques presented in this chapter deal with getting the most from your keyboard and display. Topics covered are making use of extended keyboard keys, erasing and placing text, changing colors, and speeding up the entry of common commands. Some of these techniques are available from the command line and batch files. Others require some programming. Whatever the means of access, all of them can do something towards creating that "professional" look that distinguishes a quick fix from a true product.

Character and Keyboard Basics

Many of the features introduced in this chapter require the use of special characters or sequences of characters. Although you undoubtedly are familiar with the standard keys on your keyboard, how to go about using these special keys and characters is not always obvious. For this reason, this chapter begins by explaining the mysteries of the ASCII character set and the IBM PC, XT, and AT keyboards.

A Nomenclature for Keys and Characters

Because certain keys on your keyboard do not display recognizable characters, we must find an alternate method of letting you, the reader, know just what keys and characters we are talking about. When a key or character has a printable equivalent, we just use the character itself, as in A, z, or $. When a key or character cannot be printed directly, we indicate it by capitalizing the initial character of its name, as Esc or Enter. Each time you see a character or word with an initial capital letter, we are referring to a single key or character of that name. The distinction between keys and characters is established by the case: All uppercase denotes the character (as in ESC). Where typesetting restrictions allow, keys are shown with the same legend that they bear on the IBM PC standard keyboard.

Some characters require that more than one key be pressed at the same time. We indicate these keys by linking them with hyphens (Ctrl-A or Alt-A), or sometimes abbreviated as Alt-Ctrl-A. In these cases, the indicated character is formed by holding down the key(s) shown on the left side, typing the key that appears on the right, then releasing the key(s) on the left. For example, Alt-Ctrl-B means a character is generated when holding down the keys marked Alt and Ctrl on your keyboard, typing a B, then releasing the Alt and Ctrl keys. Note that although we indicate a control character to be entered with Ctrl-X, the convention for most systems, including PC DOS and MS-DOS, is to use a leading *circumflex* when specifying control characters. For example, Ctrl-A can be shown as ^A. We also follow this convention for the sake of brevity when displaying control characters.

We also use square brackets to indicate replaceable parameters, as in [param]. What we are telling you is that when you enter the command that contains [param], you must replace the parameter with a value of your own choosing, usually from a list of allowed values. When we indicate a replaceable parameter we use lowercase. The brackets prevent confusion with the unprintable characters.

Relationships among the Characters and Keys

A very interesting pattern exists among the standard ASCII characters. The ASCII character set defines 128 characters (codes 0 through 127), but not all of these appear on the keyboard. Instead, patterns of shifts and controls are used to generate the additional characters. Table 6-1 shows the 128 ASCII characters, laid out as a matrix of 8 rows of 16 columns.

Table 6-1. The ASCII Standard Character Set

Least Significant Hex Digit (columns); **Most Significant** (rows)

	0	1	2	3	4	5	6	7	8	9	A	B	C	D	E	F
0	NUL	SOH	STX	ETX	EOT	ENQ	ACK	BEL	BS	HT	LF	VT	FF	CR	SO	SI
1	DLE	DC1	DC2	DC3	DC4	NAK	SYN	ETB	CAN	EN	EOF	ESC	FS	GS	HOM	NEW
2	SPA	!	"	#	$	%	&	'	(	)	*	+	,	-	.	/
3	0	1	2	3	4	5	6	7	8	9	:	;	<	=	>	?
4	@	A	B	C	D	E	F	G	H	I	J	K	L	M	N	O
5	P	Q	R	S	T	U	V	W	X	Y	Z	[	\	]	^	_
6	`	a	b	c	d	e	f	g	h	i	j	k	l	m	n	o
7	p	q	r	s	t	u	v	w	x	y	z	{	¦	}	~	DEL

The two and three letter codes for characters 0 through 1F that appear in Table 6-1 are the standard abbreviations of the ASCII codes, except for EOF (end-of-file), which is SUB (substitute) in standard ASCII. You should also note that the characters for HOM (home) and NEW (newline) are also used for RS (record separator) and US (unit separator), respectively. The meanings of these abbreviations appear in Table 6-2.

The hexadecimal values of the characters in Table 6-1 are found by combining the row number with the column number. For example, ESC, shown as ESC, is in row 1, column B, and therefore its hexadecimal value is 1B. We have shown the rows together in four groups for a reason. These four groups are known as:

Rows 0 and 1 (characters 00 through 1F): control characters
Rows 2 and 3 (characters 20 through 3F): punctuation characters
Rows 4 and 5 (characters 40 through 5F): standard characters

Rows 6 and 7 (characters 60 through 7F):   shifted characters

Table 6-2.   ASCII Standard Nomenclature
for Control Characters

Abbreviation	Meaning
NUL	Null
SOH	Start of heading
STX	Start text
ETX	End text
EOT	End of transmission
ENQ	Enquiry
ACK	Acknowledge
BEL	Bell
BS	Backspace
HT	Horizontal tab
LF	Linefeed
VT	Vertical tab
FF	Form feed
CR	Carriage return
SO	Shift out
SI	Shift in
DLE	Data link escape
DC1	Device control 1
DC2	Device control 2
DC3	Device control 3
DC4	Device control 4
NAK	Negative acknowledge
SYN	Synchronous idle
ETB	End transmission block
CAN	Cancel
EM	End medium
EOF	End of file
ESC	Escape
FS	File separator
GS	Group separator
HOM	Home
NEW	Newline
SPA	Space

When you look at the table and at your keyboard, notice that there is not an exact correspondence between characters and shifted characters, especially within the Punctuation group. That is, although Shift [leads to {, Shift ^ is meaningless because ^ is already shifted. However, one area of exact correspondence exists.

Each control character may be created by holding down the Ctrl key and typing the character with a number 40 hex greater than its own. BEL is created with Ctrl-G, EOF with Ctrl-Z, and even HOM with Ctrl-^. This can be a very useful tool, as is shown in the next section on accessing keys and characters.

Note that three control characters *appear* to be generated from characters that are already shifted. In actuality, the Ctrl and Shift keys perform exclusive functions. Use of the Ctrl key disables the Shift function so that the keys Ctrl-A and Ctrl-a both generate the same code. As a result, for the three control characters created from shifted keys, the Shift key is superfluous: You don't need to hold down the Shift key when creating these characters. These characters, NUL (from Ctrl-@), HOM (from Ctrl-^), and NEW (from Ctrl-_), may also be created with the unshifted key strokes Ctrl-2 (for NUL), Ctrl-6 (for HOM), and Ctrl-→ for NEW).

To complicate matters further, Ctrl-2 (and thus Ctrl-@) is treated as a special case by MS-DOS. To begin, the *keyboard* reports this key as *two* NUL characters to avoid confusion with the leading NUL of an extended code. (Extended codes are explained in the following text.) On the other hand *MS-DOS* traps this sequence and replaces it with Ctrl-C (code 03). However, the uninterpreted key is still available to those editors or programs that read the keyboard directly.

In yet another special case, Del on the IBM keyboard does not generate the ASCII DELete character (hex 7F). That character is created by Ctrl-Backspace. The Del key itself generates an extended character sequence, as we shall see now.

The Alternate and Extended Keyboard

You may have noticed that the ASCII character set, which contains 128 characters, can be generated entirely by using the standard ASCII keys (or a combination of keys) on your keyboard. However, most IBM PC and compatible keyboards have more keys than that, including the function keys (usually to the left or above the main keyboard), and the *numeric keypad* (usually to the right of the main keyboard). The question then is if the standard keys use up 128 codes, what are the remaining keys encoded as?

The answer is *not* the codes from 128 through 257. Instead, IBM chose to use *extended* key codes. What they have done is define each of those keys as a *two character sequence*. Each sequence's first character is always the NUL character (code 0). For example, pressing the key marked F1 on your keyboard produces the two key code sequence NUL and ;. Actually, these keys are intended never to be echoed to the keyboard, so the second character returned need not be a printable character, and often isn't. Rather, these keys are meant to be interpreted by programs, which then perform special functions.

Table 6-3, Sections A through D, lists the extended key codes that can be produced from the standard IBM or compatible keyboard. Remember that the codes listed in Table 6-3 are the *second* codes and that each sequence begins with a NUL character. To make the table easier to use, we have shown each code in both its hexadecimal and decimal formats, with the hexadecimal number listed first. Alt refers to the key labeled *Alt* on your keyboard, which works in a manner similar to the Shift and Ctrl keys.

Table 6-3.   The Set of Extended Character Keys

Section A
Function Key Second Codes

Key	Normal HEX	Normal DEC	Shift HEX	Shift DEC	Control HEX	Control DEC	Alt HEX	Alt DEC
F1	3B	59	54	84	5E	94	68	104
F2	3C	60	55	85	5F	95	69	105
F3	3D	61	56	86	60	96	6A	106
F4	3E	62	57	87	61	97	6B	107
F5	3F	63	58	88	62	98	6C	108
F6	40	64	59	89	63	99	6D	109
F7	41	65	5A	90	64	100	6E	110
F8	42	66	5B	91	65	101	6F	111
F9	43	67	5C	92	66	102	70	112
F10	44	68	5D	93	67	103	71	113

Section B
Numeric Keypad Second Codes

Key		Normal HEX	Normal DEC	Shift ASCII[1]	Control HEX	Control DEC	Alt
Home	7	47	71	7	77	119	(no code generated)
Up	8	48	72	8	none		(no code generated)
PgUp	9	49	73	9	84	132	(no code generated)
Right	4	4B	75	4	74	116	(no code generated)
Blank	5	4C	76	5	none		(no code generated)
Left	6	4D	77	6	73	115	(no code generated)
End	1	4F	79	1	75	117	(no code generated)
Down	2	50	80	2	none		(no code generated)
PgDn	3	51	81	3	76	118	(no code generated)
Ins	0	52	82	0	none		(no code generated)
Del	.	53	83	.	FF	128	(no code generated)

[1] Single-character code without leading NUL.

Table 6-3 (cont).

Section C																
Alternate ASCII Key Second Codes																
(Created by holding Alt and typing key shown)																
Alt Key	Code		Alt Key	Code		Alt Key	Code		Alt Key	Code	
	HEX	DEC		HEX	DEC		HEX	DEC		HEX	DEC
Q	10	16	A	1E	30	X	2D	45	5	7C	124
W	11	17	S	1F	31	C	2E	46	6	7D	125
E	12	18	D	20	32	V	2F	47	7	7E	126
R	13	19	F	21	33	B	30	48	8	7F	127
T	14	20	G	22	34	N	31	49	9	80	128
Y	15	21	H	23	35	M	32	50	0	81	129
U	16	22	J	24	36	1	78	120	–	82	130
I	17	23	K	25	37	2	79	121	=	83	131
O	18	24	L	26	38	3	7A	122			
P	19	25	Z	2C	44	4	7B	123			

Section D										
Special Second Codes										
Key	Code			KEY	Code		KEY	Code	
	HEX	DEC			HEX	DEC		HEX	DEC
Ctrl-2	03	03		Shift-Tab	0F	15	Ctrl-PrtSc	72	114

Special Keyboard Functions

Not all keys return key codes to the system. Some key sequences are trapped by the system's BIOS (basic input/output system) or DOS and are used to invoke certain system actions. These special key combinations are as follows:

Ctrl-Alt-Del: Reset and reboot the system.

Ctrl-Break: Issue an interrupt 1B, which aborts the current program as soon as it calls DOS.

Ctrl-Num Lock: Pause the entire system until any key except Num Lock is pressed.

Shift-PrtSc:	Causes the entire contents of the display to be printed on the printer device.
Ctrl-PrtSc:	Second code 72 hex, 115 decimal (DOS trap) toggles echoing characters to the printer (may be disabled by an applications program).
Ctrl-2:	Double NUL sequence translated to code 03 by MS-DOS; acts as Ctrl-C to abort current program (may be trapped by an applications program).

Except for the last two, these key sequences are interpreted by the system's keyboard handler. The last two are interpreted by MS-DOS. In addition to these, other key sequences and functions are interpreted by the system command interpreter, COMMAND.COM. Refer to Chapter 5 for more information on MS-DOS commands.

Accessing Control Keys and the Extended Character Set

One of the first problems that you encounter when exploring the various key codes is that although your keyboard generates them, the DOS command interpreter or application program probably does not understand them. We now turn to that topic: the ability to access the various keys and characters.

Entering Control Characters into Text Files

There are many times when you want to use control codes within a file. One of the most important uses is in batch files, where control or ANSI sequences (which are discussed in the next section) can be used to reformat or clear the screen. Unfortunately, as you have probably noticed, most control characters cannot be just typed into the file.

However, there is a way to produce them. We are going to show you how to get a control character into a file, in this case ESC.

Although ESC is normally an unprintable character, and more often than not Esc is used as a control key by editors, nearly all editors provide an input mode for entering control characters into a text file. This is usually done in one of two ways.

TRICK

ENTERING THE ESCAPE CHARACTER IN TEXT FILES

The first method is the "control" mode, which is a means to tell the editor that the next character entered is to be translated into a control character. One example of a control mode is supplied in the EDLIN editor. The control mode is typically intended to translate A through Z into Ctrl-A through Ctrl-Z. However, we can take advantage of the fact that ESC, which occurs after Ctrl-Z, can also be expressed as Ctrl-[, since the [character occurs after Z in the ASCII table.

To get an ESC character into your file with EDLIN, first enter the "control mode" key for EDLIN, Ctrl-V. Now, type the character that you want translated into a control character, in this case [. As you type, you first see ^V echoed, then [. However, when you list the line you see ^[: the representation of Ctrl-[in EDLIN, which is also known as ESC.

Note that EDLIN differs from most programs and editors by displaying the ^ *after* the control character. The convention followed by nearly all other programs, and MS-DOS itself, is to place the ^ *before* the character, for example, ^C as a representation for Ctrl-C.

The second way to enter control characters in a text file is the "quote" mode, which tells the editor that the next character is to be entered into the file exactly as specified. If your editor supports this option, type the control sequence for quote mode followed by the Esc key. In WordStar, for example, the "quote" character is Ctrl-P, so to enter an ESC into your file, type Ctrl-P followed by the Esc key. WordStar displays ESC as the character sequence ^[.

Note that the extent of the quote mode varies among editors. Some editors, WordStar among them, only accept control characters, and not all of them at that. WordStar, for example, won't let you enter a NUL by using Ctrl-@. Perhaps this is because NUL serves no discernible purpose in a text file. Other editors, such as Epsilon from Lugaru Software, allow entry of the complete range of control and alternate keys.

The Extended Character Set

As you may know, the IBM PC family (PC, XT, and AT) and compatibles support not 128, but 256 standard characters. This character set contains symbols for use in math, games, rudimentary graphics, foreign languages, and some characters that are aesthetically pleasing. Table 6-4 lists these extended characters by number (both hexadecimal and decimal). By glancing at Table 6-4, you can see that we have also included the characters associated with the standard ASCII control characters, codes 01 through 1F (hex).

Table 6-4. Standard Graphics Character Set

DEC X_{10}	HEX X_{16}	ASCII	DEC X_{10}	HEX X_{16}	ASCII
0	00		34	22	"
1	01	☺	35	23	#
2	02	☻	36	24	$
3	03	♥	37	25	%
4	04	♦	38	26	&
5	05	♣	39	27	'
6	06	♠	40	28	(
7	07	•	41	29	)
8	08	◘	42	2A	*
9	09	○	43	2B	+
10	0A	■	44	2C	,
11	0B	♂	45	2D	-
12	0C	♀	46	2E	.
13	0D	♪	47	2F	/
14	0E	♫	48	30	0
15	0F	☼	49	31	1
16	10	►	50	32	2
17	11	◄	51	33	3
18	12	↕	52	34	4
19	13	‼	53	35	5
20	14	¶	54	36	6
21	15	§	55	37	7
22	16	▬	56	38	8
23	17	↨	57	39	9
24	18	↑	58	3A	:
25	19	↓	59	3B	;
26	1A	→	60	3C	<
27	1B	←	61	3D	=
28	1C	∟	62	3E	>
29	1D	↔	63	3F	?
30	1E	▲	64	40	@
31	1F	▼	65	41	A
32	20		66	42	B
33	21	!	67	43	C

Table 6-4 (cont).

DEC X_{10}	HEX X_{16}	ASCII	DEC X_{10}	HEX X_{16}	ASCII
68	44	D	118	76	v
69	45	E	119	77	w
70	46	F	120	78	x
71	47	G	121	79	y
72	48	H	122	7A	z
73	49	I	123	7B	{
74	4A	J	124	7C	¦
75	4B	K	125	7D	}
76	4C	L	126	7E	~
77	4D	M	127	7F	⌂
78	4E	N	128	80	Ç
79	4F	O	129	81	ü
80	50	P	130	82	é
81	51	Q	131	83	â
82	52	R	132	84	ä
83	53	S	133	85	à
84	54	T	134	86	å
85	55	U	135	87	ç
86	56	V	136	88	ê
87	57	W	137	89	ë
88	58	X	138	8A	è
89	59	Y	139	8B	ï
90	5A	Z	140	8C	î
91	5B	[	141	8D	ì
92	5C	\	142	8E	Ä
93	5D	]	143	8F	Å
94	5E	^	144	90	É
95	5F	_	145	91	æ
96	60	`	146	92	Æ
97	61	a	147	93	ô
98	62	b	148	94	ö
99	63	c	149	95	ò
100	64	d	150	96	û
101	65	e	151	97	ù
102	66	f	152	98	ÿ
103	67	g	153	99	Ö
104	68	h	154	9A	Ü
105	69	i	155	9B	¢
106	6A	j	156	9C	£
107	6B	k	157	9D	¥
108	6C	l	158	9E	P_t
109	6D	m	159	9F	ƒ
110	6E	n	160	A0	á
111	6F	o	161	A1	í
112	70	p	162	A2	ó
113	71	q	163	A3	ú
114	72	r	164	A4	ñ
115	73	s	165	A5	Ñ
116	74	t	166	A6	ª
117	75	u	167	A7	º

Table 6-4 (cont).

DEC X_{10}	HEX X_{16}	ASCII	DEC X_{10}	HEX X_{16}	ASCII
168	A8	¿	212	D4	╘
169	A9	⌐	213	D5	╒
170	AA	¬	214	D6	╓
171	AB	½	215	D7	╫
172	AC	¼	216	D8	╪
173	AD	¡	217	D9	┘
174	AE	«	218	DA	┌
175	AF	»	219	DB	█
176	B0	░	220	DC	▄
177	B1	▒	221	DD	▌
178	B2	▓	222	DE	▐
179	B3	│	223	DF	▀
180	B4	┤	224	E0	α
181	B5	╡	225	E1	β
182	B6	╢	226	E2	Γ
183	B7	╖	227	E3	π
184	B8	╕	228	E4	Σ
185	B9	╣	229	E5	σ
186	BA	║	230	E6	µ
187	BB	╗	231	E7	τ
188	BC	╝	232	E8	Φ
189	BD	╜	233	E9	Θ
190	BE	╛	234	EA	Ω
191	BF	┐	235	EB	δ
192	C0	└	236	EC	∞
193	C1	┴	237	ED	φ
194	C2	┬	238	EE	ε
195	C3	├	239	EF	∩
196	C4	─	240	F0	≡
197	C5	┼	241	F1	±
198	C6	╞	242	F2	≥
199	C7	╟	243	F3	≤
200	C8	╚	244	F4	⌠
201	C9	╔	245	F5	⌡
202	CA	╩	246	F6	÷
203	CB	╦	247	F7	≈
204	CC	╠	248	F8	°
205	CD	═	249	F9	·
206	CE	╬	250	FA	·
207	CF	╧	251	FB	√
208	D0	╨	252	FC	η
209	D1	╤	253	FD	²
210	D2	╥	254	FE	■
211	D3	╙	255	FF	

These characters are also associated with the keyboard, just as the standard ASCII characters are, but not in an obvious way. A variety of methods is available for accessing these characters, depending on the type of editor or program that you are running.

Specifying Characters by Number

Built into the keyboard handler of the IBM family and compatibles is a means to generate any single key code. As you may have noticed in Table 6-3, Section B, the numeric keypad does not generate codes while the Alt key is pressed. The reason for this is that while the Alt key is being held down, the numeric keypad can be used to specify any character from 0 through 255, with the character being generated when the Alt key is released.

Let's run through that again. Suppose that you want to generate the Greek lowercase *mu* often used to indicate "micro." You can find mu as character 230 in Table 6-4. To generate character 230, depress and *hold* the Alt key. While Alt is held down, type the numbers 2, 3, and 0 on the *numeric* keypad. Now, release the Alt key and you see the symbol for mu.

It may surprise you to learn that many editors, including EDLIN and WordStar, accept extended characters when entered in this manner. However, beware if you generate control characters (codes 0 through 1F hex) in this manner because they are interpreted just as if you had pressed the control sequence for that particular key. For control characters, you still need to resort to the methods outlined previously. Note that even though your editor may interpret control characters as special codes during printing, chances are that typing the file to the screen (via MS-DOS' TYPE command) will produce the desired results. For example, even though WordStar uses Ctrl-B as the command for boldfacing during printing, it is displayed as the "happy face" when the file is typed to the display.

Some Interesting Restrictions

Unfortunately, some symbols of the extended character set just cannot be displayed through MS-DOS. These are the symbols represented by characters 07 (BEL), 08 (BS), 0A (10 decimal, LF), and 0D (13 decimal, CR). These characters have a dual use: Each is not only associated with a symbol in the extended character set (See Table 6-4), but is also and *primarily* used to direct a special function of the display driver, for example, producing the *bell* tone or indicating movement of the cursor.

Does this mean that the symbols associated with them are forever lost, unable to be displayed? By no means. It just means that you have to bypass the display driver to display the desired symbols. *You must write the character codes directly into display memory!* However, in order to do that, some programming is required, which is beyond the scope of this book.

The problem of not being able to access certain symbols is not an uncommon one in MS-DOS. For example, use of the angle brackets < and > is severely restricted by MS-DOS ' proclivity for interpreting these characters as *redirection* commands, which explains why the MS-DOS PROMPT command must supply a special code to generate the right angle bracket, >.

Other Means of Accessing the Extended Character Set

At some time, you may attempt to use the Alt method of generating extended characters, only to have your editor ignore your efforts. This usually happens when you're using editors that do their own key processing, such as Epsilon from Lugaru Software. However, in these cases, another method that may work is to use the quote function of the editor and enter the character as Alt-[ASCII key sequence].

To use the example of the mu character again: First, find the equivalent character on the normal ASCII chart (it's easier to use hex). Mu is character E6 (hex), so subtract 80 hex to translate it into the standard ASCII range. The resulting character, 66 hex, is a lowercase *f.* Type the quote key, followed by Alt-f. You may see the mu character, or you may see a sequence of characters (such as M-f), or you may see just plain f. To see what actually happened, you have to close the file and TYPE it to the display. If your editor accepted the Alt character, you see the character as a mu. If this works, the same technique should apply to alternate control characters, such as Alt-Ctrl-D, which generates the German umlaut (an *a* with two dots over it).

Printing the Extended Characters

Once you have enhanced your displays by using characters from the extended character set, you may desire to print some of the fruits of your efforts. Two methods may be used to print the extended characters. The easiest method is to use an IBM Printer or IBM Graphics Printer. These printers contain the complete IBM character set in a ROM, and faithfully reproduce any text that can be displayed on your screen, including the extended characters.

When an IBM Printer is not available, another method may work in some cases. If your printer has the ability to define characters, sometimes referred to as *down-loading* characters, you may be able to teach your printer how to print the extended characters. However, this is not an easy task and almost always involves some programming. In addition, nearly all printers limit the number of custom characters that may be defined, meaning that you must choose which extended characters to support. Lastly, the definable characters almost surely will not have the same character codes as the extended character codes. Taken all together, unless you are seriously into programming and have some time on your hands, probably the least expensive means of printing the extended character set is to purchase an IBM printer with this capability built in.

Summary of Keys and Characters

Now that we have been through the characters and keyboard codes, what can you do with this information? Quite honestly, the greatest benefits are apparent if you decide to do some programming, which is when you can take full advantage of the extended keys and character set to customize your programs. However, there are also applications for the nonprogramming user.

Knowledge of the various key and character codes is required if you are to be able to use the features of the ANSI driver (discussed in the following section). This knowledge is also useful for entering printer control codes into your text files. Many printer control codes, which differ between the various makes of printers, contain the ESC character and other nonstandard characters. You should now know how to define the proper characters to use a printer's letter quality mode, superscript, subscript, and so forth.

Yet another application of this information is in using the extended character set (shown in Table 6-4) to draw boxes and charts in your batch files. Simply design the boxes with your editor and preface the strings with the ECHO command. With ECHO off, you can display the boxes from the batch file. Specifics for producing charts and boxes depend on the editor you are using and the type of display you wish to generate. In any event, understanding the basics of key and character codes is one of the necessary building blocks of understanding MS-DOS.

Using the ANSI Screen Handler

A relatively easy method of gaining additional control over your system's display is to use ANSI (American National Standards Institute) control sequences. These special character sequences can be used to perform various actions with your display, including moving the cursor, erasing all or part of the display, and changing display modes and attributes. In addition, ANSI sequences can be used to create simple keyboard macros.

ANSI control sequences are not normally part of your system's repertoire. You must explicitly install ANSI capabilities in your system.

Installing ANSI.SYS

Support for the ANSI control sequences is provided by a device driver. This device driver is contained in a file named ANSI.SYS that is supplied with MS-DOS releases (Version 2.0 or later) for the IBM PC series and some compatible computers. It is also included with some MS-DOS releases for compatible computers. If you are not one of the lucky ones, don't despair. Public domain versions of ANSI.SYS may be available for your noncompatible computer if it is running MS-DOS. Lastly, public domain versions of ANSI.SYS for the IBM PC XT and AT family and compatibles extend the basic services contained in the version provided with PC DOS.

The ANSI.SYS device driver is installed by inserting the line

```
DEVICE=[d:][path]ANSI.SYS
```

in your CONFIG.SYS file. If you do not have a CONFIG.SYS file, you need to create one in the root level directory on the boot device. Briefly, the command line tells MS-DOS to find the file ANSI.SYS located on drive [d] in directory [path] and load the file as an MS-DOS device driver. Assuming that ANSI.SYS is where you indicated, the ANSI device driver is loaded the next time you boot your system. Further details on device drivers and setting up your CONFIG.SYS file may be found in Chapter 13.

The standard ANSI.SYS device driver provided with PC DOS

replaces the MS-DOS console device driver (CON) normally loaded during bootup. The new driver contains the additional code necessary to interpret and execute the ANSI standard control sequences listed in Table 6-5.

Note that the features of the ANSI device driver are available to any program that writes to or reads from the standard console device. This includes command entries, files TYPEd to the screen, batch files, and programs that access any of the standard devices: *standard input, standard output*, and *standard error*.

The ANSI Codes

Every ANSI standard sequence has the same basic format:

`ESC [ [parameters] [identifier]`

The first two characters of each command are the ASCII ESC character (Hexadecimal 1B, Decimal 27, Ctrl-[), followed by an opening square bracket ([). It is interesting to note that ESC itself can be represented by the *control* character of the opening square bracket. If there is anything beyond coincidence in that fact, it is news to us.

The next section of an ANSI control sequence is the [parameter]. The exact value or character that appears here depends upon the individual subfunction that is being performed. What determines the function itself? The last section, the [identifier]. This item, which is usually a single ASCII character, determines the actual action that is performed.

The standard ANSI codes supplied in ANSI.SYS are shown in Table 6-5, Sections A through E.

The ANSI standard goes much further than what is supplied by IBM with PC DOS. Additional sequences, functions, and subfunctions are defined that provide even greater control. Many public domain versions of ANSI.SYS support these additional sequences. If you would like to obtain a more featured version of ANSI.SYS, a good place to start looking is with the PC Special Interest Group (PC-SIG) listed in Appendix B.

The first hurdle to overcome when using ANSI commands is generating the proper ANSI header, ESC [. You can't just type Esc at the system prompt because that's the command interpreter's method of "erasing" the input line. If you try typing Esc, you find that

Table 6-5. ANSI Standard Control Sequences Supported by the Default ANSI.SYS

Section A *Cursor Control Command Sequences*			
Name/ Command	Parameter	Default Value	Function Operation
SET POSITION ESC [r ; c H --or-- ESC [r ; c f	r row # c column #	1 1	Move the cursor to the specified position. Values of r and c are specified in ASCII decimal (that is, row 10 is indicated by the character 10). Both rows and columns are numbered starting at 1.
MOVE UP ESC [lA	l # of lines	1	Move cursor up specified number of lines or until top of screen is reached. Column position is not changed.
MOVE DOWN ESC [lB	l # of lines	1	Move cursor down specified number of lines or until bottom of screen is reached. Column position is not changed.
MOVE RIGHT ESC [cC	c # of columns	1	Move cursor right specified number of columns or until right edge of screen is reached. Row position is not changed.
MOVE LEFT ESC [cD	c # of columns	1	Move cursor left specified number of columns or until left edge of screen is reached. Row position is not changed.
SAVE CURSOR POSITION ESC [s	none		The current cursor position is saved (remembered by ANSI.SYS). Only the last saved position is remembered.
RESTORE CURSOR POSITION ESC [u	none		Move cursor to the location saved by the last SAVE CURSOR POSITION COMMAND.
REPORT CURSOR POSITION ESC [6n	none		Causes the current cursor position to be reported in the form: ESC [r;cR where r is the current cursor row and c is the current cursor column. The response is

Table 6-5 (cont).

returned from the standard
input device.[1]

[1] This feature is normally used under program control, where a program issues the "Report Cursor Position" sequence, and reads the response from s t d i n, usually without echo. Operation at the DOS prompt is possible with batch files, but meaningless.

Section B
Screen Erase Command Sequences

Name/ Command	Parameter	Default Value	Function Operation
ERASE SCREEN ESC [2J	2^2	2	Erase entire display and move cursor home position.
ERASE LINE ESC [0K	0^2	0	Erase line from cursor position to the right margin, inclusive Cursor position is not changed.

[2] Both of these commands are subsets of the full ANSI standard. Although they operate equally well when the parameter is omitted or of a different value than specified, we recommend use of the parameter shown in order to maintain upward compatibility.

Section C
Screen Attribute Command Sequences

Name/ Command	Parameter	Default Value	Function Operation
SET SCREEN ATTRIBUTE ESC [$p_1;p_2;...;p_n$m	See table following	none	Also known as SET GRAPHICS RENDITION, this command sets the default character display mode. The parameter list consists of at least one numeric code, with additional codes separated by semicolons.

p_n	Parameter Meaning
0	Normal (white on black)
1	High intensity
4	Underscore (monochrome display only)
5	Blink
7	Reverse video (black on white)
8	Invisible
$3x$	Set foreground color where x is one of:
$4x$	Set background color where x is one of:

Table 6-5 (cont).

Color Selection for Foreground and Background

$x = 0$	Black
1	Red
2	Green
3	Yellow
4	Blue
5	Magenta
6	Cyan
7	White

Section D
Display Mode Command Sequences

Name/ Command	Parameter	Default Value	Function Operation
SET MODE ESC [=mh --or-- ESC [?7h[3]	m See table following	0	Change screen width, type, or wrap characteristics as determined in the associated table. Parameter 7, setting line wrap, causes characters typed beyond the end of a line to be displayed on the next line(s).
RESET MODE ESC [=ml --or-- ESC [?7l[3]	m See table following	0	Change screen width, type, or wrap characteristics as determined in the associated table. Actions of parameters 0 through 6 is identical to SET MODE. Parameter 7, reset line wrap, causes characters typed beyond the end of a line to be discarded.

m	Parameter Meaning
0	Set 40 column by 25 line black and white mode
1	Set 40 column by 25 line color mode
2	Set 80 column by 25 line black and white mode
3	Set 80 column by 25 line color mode
4	Set 320 by 200 color graphics mode
5	Set 320 by 200 black and white graphics mode
6	Set 640 by 200 black and white graphics mode
7	Set/reset wrap at end of line

[3] The alternate forms, ESC [?7h and ESC [?7l, are for use only when changing the line wrap characteristics and may not be used with other parameter values.

Table 6-5 (cont).

Section E
The "Key Macro" Command Sequence

Name/ Command	Parameters	Function Operation
DEFINE KEY ESC [k;p_1;...;p_np	k key code	Also known as REASSIGN MACRO KEYBOARD KEY, this command is used to associate a sequence of characters with a keyboard key. The key code is specified by its numeric ASCII value. Extended keys are specified with a two-number sequence, beginning with 0. The parameters p_1 through p_n consist of ASCII codes or strings enclosed in quotation marks. Each parameter must be separated by a semicolon. For example, to define the F1 key as the sequence ESCdir, the following command is used: `ESC [0;59;27;"dir";13p` This command is interpreted as follows. Note that the leading ESC (code 27) in the new defined sequence causes the command interpreter to discard the previously entered line, and is not interpreted as an ANSI sequence by the command interpreter.
ESC [0;59 27;"dir";13 p	← Standard ANSI header ← Code for F1 key ← ESCdirEnter ← Key redefinition function code	

MS-DOS blanks the previous line and gives you a new line on which to enter your command. The new text is interpreted as if the text you typed before never existed. For this reason, it is often most convenient to store ANSI command sequences in text or batch files.

Using ANSI Control Sequences in Text and Batch Files

You have already seen how you can insert control characters into a text file. In addition to typing such files to the screen, ANSI sequences may also be part of the ECHO command's parameters in a batch file. This can allow you to "edit" the messages from a batch file, dispensing with the *echo off* line, for example. The following sequence shows how this is accomplished.

```
echo off
echo ESC [1AESC [KESC [1A
```

This sample moves the cursor up one line (to the line that says *echo off*), deletes it, and moves up another line so that the (necessary) line feed at the end places the cursor where the echo off first appeared. Note that the ESC[1A sequence moves the cursor up *without changing the column*. The only reason that all of the echo off line is erased by the ESC[K is that the ECHO command starts displaying text in column 1. If the ANSI movement and erase sequences appear after the start of the echo command, not all of the preceding text is erased. Consider the following sequence of echo commands in a batch file.

```
echo off                      ← turns echo off
echo xxxxxxxxESC [1AESC [K    ← 1st echo command line
echo yyyy                     ← 2nd echo command line
```

The first echo command displays eight x's, moves up one line, erases the two f's from the echo off line, and moves the cursor to the beginning of the next line. The second echo command then overwrites the first four x's with y's. The final result, assuming a default system prompt, would appear as

```
C>echo o
yyyyxxxx
```

Playing with Colors

Among the other features of ANSI.SYS is the ability to control the color and attributes of the characters. Referring to Section C of Table 6-5, we can set up a command sequence to cause all subsequent characters to be displayed in reverse video. For example, in a batch file, the command

```
echo ESC [7m    **** WARNING ****    ESC [0m
```

displays the message

```
"    **** WARNING ****    "
```

in reverse video, then changes back to normal video. That's something guaranteed to get anyone's attention!

If you are using a color monitor with a Color or Enhanced Graphics Adapter, you can change the color of both the characters and the background they are displayed against. Many people consider green to be a restful color. To see your work displayed in black against a green background, the command:

```
echo ESC [30;42m
```

in a batch file sets this up for you. As with reverse video, judicious use of color can make a point quite effectively. And best of all, we're not limited to using these commands only from batch files or programs.

Using an ANSI Control Sequence in the System Prompt

Although we said that ANSI sequences cannot be entered directly at the system prompt, there is a way to do so, with a little help from the PROMPT command. You see, the PROMPT command can be used to generate the ESC character, and the ANSI device driver doesn't care where the characters come from as long as they appear. By telling PROMPT to generate the ESC character, we can generate a standard ANSI command sequence. The way to do this is with the $e PROMPT option, as in:

```
prompt $e[
```

This command, entered at the MS-DOS command line, causes PROMPT to generate ESC [as the system prompt. When you type the command, you see a blank line appear. Now you can play with the ANSI command sequences by typing the remaining characters of a command sequence. For example, if you type J (uppercase J), you see the entire display go blank.

Remember that COMMAND.COM is still receiving the typed characters, so we want to "dump" the J. We can do that by typing the Esc key, causing COMMAND.COM to ignore the J. At this point you can type prompt to turn off the ANSI header being generated or press the Enter key again, to get another ANSI header, and continue experimenting.

By itself the ANSI header is not especially useful as a prompt. By combining additional elements, however, you can do wonders. For example, many people like the "path" prompt that provides the name of the current default directory but dislike the fact that long pathnames can severely limit the amount of room on the prompt line. (This doesn't cut down the number of characters that can be entered. It only makes it look cluttered.) Through the PROMPT escape sequence and ANSI command sequences, you can have the best of both worlds. Consider the PROMPT command:

```
prompt $e[s$e[1;1H$e[0m$e[K$e[7m $d / $t : $p $e[0m$e[u$n$g
```

This rather cryptic looking command accomplishes the following:

$e[s	Save current cursor position
$e[1;1H	Move to upper left corner of the display
$e[0m	Set normal mode display
$e[K	Erase topmost line of display
$e[7m	Set reverse video mode
$d	Display current date
$t	Display current time
$p	Display current drive and path
$e[0m	Set normal mode display
$e[u	Return to the original cursor position
$n	Display the current drive
$g	Display the prompt character >

All spaces and other characters (such as / and :) are displayed as shown. The end effect is to display at the top of the screen in reverse video the date, time, and path in the form

```
Fri  8-15-1986 / 10:14:25.72 : C:\BOOKS\CHAPTER6\DRAFT
```

and at the original cursor position a short, standard prompt of the form C>. From this short example you can see that with ANSI control sequences the possibilities are almost endless.

Using the ANSI "Keyboard Macro" Facility

Another feature of the ANSI.SYS driver is somewhat unexpected because it deals with keys rather than the display. Section E of Table 6-5 presents the format for assigning a *macro* to a key on the keyboard and also included a short example on defining the F1 key to display the current directory.

Unfortunately, this facility cannot be used to directly associate ANSI command sequences with keys. The reason is that COMMAND.COM interprets the key definition exactly as if it had been typed on the keyboard, and as we have already seen it is not possible to enter an ESC character directly.

Of course, indirect methods are still available, such as defining a key as `type ansi.cmd` and so forth (where ansi.cmd is a file containing an ANSI command sequence). The following presents an example of this technique that may prove useful. Our example actually consists of two macros, one macro to "remember" the current directory, and the other macro to change the directory back to the remembered directory.

Saving and Restoring the Current Directory—An Example

We implement our feature using three files: two batch files and one data file. Note that wherever ESC appears, you must insert the ESCape character in the file, as discussed earlier. The first batch file, which we have named INSTALL.BAT, defines the key that remembers the current directory. Here are the contents of INSTALL.BAT:

```
echo off
echo ESC [0;67;"\markdir";13p
```

What we have done is define function key F9 (code 67 decimal) to issue the command \markdir. This invokes our second batch file, MARKDIR.BAT, which we have located in the root directory. Now, what does MARKDIR do? It contains the following commands:

```
echo off        ← shut off echo to see just what we want
type \DEF10     ← type the ANSI Define Key header sequence
cd              ← get the text of the current directory
echo ";13p      ← finish the ANSI Define Key sequence
```

MARKDIR actually implements an ANSI key definition macro of its own. It first types our third file, DEF10 (for DEfine Function 10), which contains the *beginning* of the ANSI command sequence to define function key F10 (see following). DEF10 leaves the definition uncompleted. After DEF10 has been typed to the display, MARKDIR issues a cd command, which causes the current directory to be displayed. However, because a key definition is still pending, the current directory string is not displayed on the video display. Instead it is included as part of the key definition. The last step that MARKDIR performs is to "close" the key definition for function key F10, by echoing the string ";13p.

DEF10, the last file, is also located in the root directory and contains only the single following string:

ESC [0;68;"cd   ← a space follows cd and there is *no* carriage return at the
                   end of this line!

Note that the cd in DEF10 is part of the string definition for key F10, which changes the directory when the F10 macro is executed. Contrast this with the cd that appears in MARKDIR, which is used to display the current directory path for inclusion in the F10 macro.

Therefore, when F9 is pressed, it is expanded as the key sequence \markdir, which in turn is processed by DOS as a batch file. MARKDIR defines a key sequence for function key F10 containing the string cd [current path]. After that, pressing F10 gets us back to wherever we were when F9 was last pressed.

Why couldn't we have dispensed with typing DEF10 to the screen and simply echoed the header sequence to the display as we did in INSTALL.BAT? If we had echoed the string, or if there had been a carriage return after the cd[space] in DEF10, F10 would be defined with a carriage return in the middle and be expanded as the *two* lines:

```
cd
[current path]
```

Executing this sequence would inform us of the current directory, then give us an error as MS-DOS attempted to execute the pathname as a command. It is thus very important that the definition for F10 appear as a single line.

Saving and Restoring the Current Directory—A Second Example

The same effect might also be accomplished using a prompt command in the MARKDIR.BAT batch file, thus dispensing with the file DEF10. Such a file might appear as shown below:

```
echo off                         ← quiet lets us do our work
prompt $e[0;68;"cd ";"$p";13p    ← prompt will define key F10
echo on                          ← echo on to display prompt
echo off                         ← echo off
prompt $p$g                      ← reset prompt to normal
```

In this case, we are using the prompt command itself to issue the proper character sequence to define the F10 key. The cd that used to appear as a command in MARKDIR is no longer required because the $p prompt command serves to obtain the name of the current directory. Note also that it is necessary to turn echo on momentarily to cause the system prompt to be displayed because the prompt string itself defines the key macro for function key F10!

The reason for using batch files throughout the above examples is that we needed a method to issue the proper commands *without* having the commands themselves appear in the definitions. Using an echo off line at the command level only suppresses the system prompt, not the commands entered.

Summary

This chapter has shown some of the features available on IBM PC and compatible computers, features that allow you to increase the functionality and aesthetic aspects of MS-DOS commands. Although not all of the features described may be available on your computer, you can always put the information learned to good use in the process of discovering what the capabilities of your machine are. The next chapter provides a description on how to use MS-DOS' DEBUG program to further explore the capabilities of your system.

Discovering Secrets: A Debugger Tutorial   Chapter 7

T
he DEBUG program is a powerful utility that is distributed with the MS-DOS operating system. The primary purpose of the program is to *debug* or remove bugs from other programs or from DEBUG itself. Although the subject of debugging programs is not within the scope of this book, many of the features of the DEBUG program are useful for other purposes. The DEBUG program provides features that allow you to modify disk files at a very "low level." For example, you can insert special nonprintable characters in text files, which some word processors do not allow.

Because the DEBUG program is often ignored by nonprogrammers who use MS-DOS, the format of this chapter is more tutorial in nature than most of the chapters of this book. A number of trick boxes demonstrate how to apply some of the power of the DEBUG program to create files for use with other features of MS-DOS, such as input redirection and batch files. At the end of the chapter is an information box with a summary of all the DEBUG commands and their parameters.

One caution about the DEBUG program: It is not very user friendly. When you have an alternate method of examining, modifying, or creating a file, the alternate method probably is easier to use and less error prone. The "low-level" way in which DEBUG works with files means that no special interpretation of data is performed when the data is read, displayed, modified, or written. Because of this, there are times when DEBUG is the *only* way to examine or modify a file. The file you want to examine may cause your word processor to crash because of some combination of binary data, or you may need to insert some special characters into a file that your word processor does not support. These are the times when you'll be happy to have the DEBUG program to use, despite its lack of friendliness.

HOW THE COMPUTER BUG GOT ITS NAME

Most people who work with computers daily hear the term "bug" as a reference to a problem with a computer's hardware or software. Outsiders, however, are often curious about the use of a phrase indicating that an insect has somehow crawled into such an intangible thing as a computer program. There is, however, an interesting legend behind the term.

In the summer of 1945, Grace Murray Hopper, a Navy captain and one of its first computer programmers, was working with some associates at Harvard University on the Mark II, a predecessor to today's computers. A problem developed with one of the relays in the long, glass-enclosed computer. Finally, someone uncovered the cause of the problem and removed it with a pair of tweezers. The culprit, it turned out, was a moth. The term "bug" was born.

Hopper, now a distinguished person in the computing industry referred to as "amazing Grace," retired from the Navy as Rear Admiral in August of 1986 at the age of 79, but still has the historical moth taped in her 1945 logbook. Talk about good documentation! A picture of the bug appeared in the July, 1981, issue of the *Annals of the History of Computing*.

The use of the term "bug" may have been applied to mechanical difficulties long before the computer was invented. In the March 11, 1889, edition of the *Pall Mall Gazette,* a reference was made to Thomas Edison spending several nights discovering the cause of "a bug" in his phonograph.

Use the DEBUG Program with Caution

The DEBUG program offers several powerful features: You can write files to a disk; write sectors to a disk; execute portions of a program, modify the content of the registers or memory, then continue with the program execution; or input and output data to your computer system's hardware ports. These features make the DEBUG program very useful. However, they also make it potentially dangerous to use. Always use the DEBUG program with great care. When you're not sure exactly what you have done, always exit the DEBUG program with the Q (Quit) command at the – prompt. If you are not able to return to the DEBUG – prompt, restart your system with the Ctrl-Alt-Del keystroke sequence.

When you are learning DEBUG, create a new disk containing the DEBUG program and a copy of any files you will be modifying. Insert the floppy into a disk drive and change the default drive to the drive with the newly created floppy. Read and write files using the default drive only. This precaution greatly reduces the possibility of losing important data on your hard or floppy disk.

After you are familiar with the DEBUG program, you will feel more comfortable about making changes to files and similar operations directly to the files on a good disk. Even after you are familiar with using DEBUG, you need to follow good computing practices: Never operate on a file without first making a backup copy of the file, periodically create a backup copy of everything on your good "production" disks, and always double check your work. The most dangerous commands (such as writing to sectors on a disk) should be performed on a temporary disk whenever possible, then any altered files can be copied to a good disk. When this is not possible, the operation should be practiced on a temporary disk first before it is applied to a disk with valuable data.

What Is a Byte?

The DEBUG program displays memory in units of one *byte*. A byte is eight *bits* or binary digits. Consequently, a byte may have two to the eighth power unique values (256 decimal values in the range 0 through 255). The terms *byte* and *character* are often used interchangeably, as in the expressions "the file is 256 characters long" or "the file is 256 bytes long."

The term *character* often has a more restrictive meaning, in that a byte may be interpreted strictly numerically (having a value of 0 through 255) or as a character (having a value of a letter, numeric digit, special character, or control character).

When looking at a text file using the DEBUG program, the bytes in the file are always interpreted as characters. Fortunately, most computers and related peripherals (such as printers, screens, plotters, etc.) use the same byte values to represent the same characters. This standard set of codes is referred to as the *American Standard Code for Information Interchange* or *ASCII* character set.

The ASCII character set includes nonprintable or "control" characters (such as the tab, carriage return, and line feed characters) and *printable* characters (such as the lower- and uppercase letters of the alphabet, the digits 0 though 9, and special characters like the asterisk and percent sign). ASCII characters with values greater than 127 decimal are normally referred to as the *graphics* characters or *extended ASCII character set* for the IBM PC series and compatible systems. These characters have *no* standard ASCII definition. Table 7-1 summarizes the ASCII character codes.

Table 7-1.   American Standard Code for Information Interchange (ASCII)

Hexadecimal	Decimal	Description
00 through 1F	0 through 31	Control characters
20 through 7E	32 through 126	Printable characters
7F	127	Rubout control character
80 through FF	128 through 255	Graphics characters

When looking at nontext or *binary* files using the DEBUG program, you cannot know how to interpret the byte values in the file unless you are familiar with the format of the file. For example, in an executable binary file (a file with .EXE or .COM filename extensions), some of the data may be ASCII characters for messages that the program displays on the screen, some of the data may be numerical data that the program uses as variables during execution, and some of the data may be uninitialized buffer space that has no meaning to the program until a sector of data is read from disk to the buffer in memory.

The DEBUG program DUMP command displays data on the screen in two formats. First, the byte is displayed in binary format using two hexadecimal digits to represent the value of the byte. Next, the ASCII representation of the byte is displayed, with a period used to indicate occurrences of a nonprintable character. The hexadecimal notation is convenient to use because one hexadecimal digit can have 16 values (0 through F), and four binary bits may have two to the fourth (16) different values. Consequently, one hexadecimal digit can be used to represent exactly four bits or one-half of one byte. The term for four bits or a half byte is a *nibble*.

The hexadecimal digits A through F used to represent the digits above hexadecimal 9 have standard names that are used within the computer industry. These names are Able, Baker, Charlie, Dog, Easy, and Fox. The first letter of each name obviously indicates the hexadecimal digit to which each name refers.

In the examples for this chapter, all numbers are in hexadecimal notation because all input and output of the DEBUG program is in hexadecimal. However, unless otherwise noted, all numbers in the text of this chapter are in the decimal numbering system. For example, hexadecimal numbers are shown in the format X'dddd' where 'dddd' is the number.

General Description of DEBUG

The DEBUG program is a command-driven program. It has eighteen commands, each abbreviated by a single letter of the alphabet. Most of the commands are followed by parameters that give additional information to the command. For example, the DUMP command may be followed by an address that tells the command at which memory location to begin the display of information. Many of the commands have several different forms with different combinations of parameters. In some cases, a parameter for a command is optional: The DEBUG program supplies a default value for any omitted parameter. The *Summary of DEBUG Program Commands* information box gives a listing of all DEBUG commands with a description of their various parameter formats.

When you execute the DEBUG program, it responds with a hyphen (-) as a prompt character (versions of the MS-DOS DEBUG program before Version 2.0 use the > prompt character). After the prompt character, you enter a one-character command followed by any required parameters. The command is not case-sensitive, which means that the DUMP command may be specified by a lowercase d or an uppercase D. All numeric parameters used with DEBUG commands must be entered in hexadecimal notation. No convention is provided for entering decimal numbers. All numeric data displayed by the DEBUG program is also in hexadecimal notation. If you are not familiar with the hexadecimal numbering system, refer to the information box titled *A Short Course in the Hexadecimal Numbering System*.

When you are modifying a file using DEBUG, you first "load" a copy of the file into memory (loading a file is DEBUG's terminology for reading a file from disk into memory). While the file is in memory, you may modify the copy of the file in memory and display its contents using several of DEBUG's commands. After modifying the file, you may write the file back to the disk. *Modifying the copy of the file in memory does not change the file on disk.* If you modify a file and decide you do not want to change the file as it appears on disk, you may simply quit the DEBUG program using the QUIT command. No matter how many changes you make to the copy of the file in memory, the disk image of the file does *not* change until you write the file from memory to the disk with the WRITE command.

A SHORT COURSE IN THE HEXADECIMAL NUMBERING SYSTEM

The hexadecimal numbering system is another name for the base 16 numbering system. Just as the decimal numbering system (base 10) has ten digits 0 through 9, the hexadecimal numbering system has sixteen digits 0 through F. The ordering of these digits in ascending sequence is 0, 1, 2, 3, 4, 5, 6, 7, 8, 9, A, B, C, D, E, F. The letters used as digits are conventionally named Able, Baker, Charlie, Dog, Easy, and Fox.

The two-digit number 10 in hexadecimal is equivalent to the decimal value of sixteen, the numbering system's base, just as the number 10 in decimal is ten. The term *hexadecimal* is often abbreviated *hex*. Hexadecimal numbers are often written in the form X'123', '123'X, 0x123, 0123h, H123, $123, or with some similar notation to distinguish them from decimal numbers. In this chapter, the notation X'123' is used in text. In examples, no special notation is used because *all* numbers that are input to or output from the DEBUG program are in hexadecimal notation.

Counting in hexadecimal is similar to counting in decimal. However, X'19' is followed by X'1A' and no carry is made to the next most significant digit position of a number until a digit position reaches the digit F. Thus, the number X'1F' is followed by the number X'20', X'2F' by X'30' and so on.

The most common operation using hexadecimal notation required for use with DEBUG is converting hexadecimal numbers to decimal and vice versa. For this purpose, a calculator that can perform these conversions *is strongly recommended*. Several calculators are available that have this feature. Several programs also are available that have a calculator option. The programs are most useful if they are *memory resident*, which means that they can be resident in your computer's memory while another program, such as DEBUG, is executing. Sidekick is an example of a popular memory resident program that includes a calculator capable of converting numbers from hexadecimal to decimal.

Although a conversion calculator is recommended, it is useful to go through an example of converting a number from hexadecimal to decimal in order to become more familiar with the hexadecimal notation.

The general approach to converting a hexadecimal number to decimal is to convert each hexadecimal digit in the original hexadecimal number and multiply it times a "number," then sum all of these products to yield the decimal result.

The "number" to use when multiplying a digit is 16 raised to the zero power for the rightmost digit, 16 to the first power for the next digit to the left, 16 to the second power for the next digit to the left, and so on. Table 7-2 provides the multipliers needed to convert hexadecimal numbers up to five digits in length.

Table 7-2.   Hexadecimal to Decimal Conversion

Digit Position of Hex (Counting from Right)	Multiplier To Convert to Decimal	Power of 16
1	1	0
2	16	1
3	256	2
4	4096	3
5	65536	4

For example, to convert the hexadecimal number X'123' to decimal:

1. Multiply the rightmost hexadecimal digit, a 3, by 1. The result is 3.

2. Multiply the next digit to the left, a 2, times 16. The result is 32.

3. Multiply the next digit to the left, a 1, by 256. The result is 256.

4. Sum the products of the three multiplications above:

$$3 + 32 + 256 = 291$$

Converting the hexadecimal number X'10CA' to decimal is slightly more difficult because two of the hexadecimal digits must be converted to decimal before the multiply operation. Here are the steps required:

1. Convert the rightmost hexadecimal digit, an A, to decimal 10 and multiply by 1. The result is 10.

2. Convert the next digit to the left, a C, to decimal 12 and multiply by 16. The result is 192.

3. Convert the next digit to the left, a 0, to decimal 0 and multiply by 256. The result is 0.

4. Convert the next digit to the left, a 1, to decimal 1 and multiply by 4096. The result is 4096.

5. Sum the products of the four preceding multiplications:

$$10 + 192 + 0 + 4096 = 4298$$

General Information about DEBUG Commands

All DEBUG commands begin with a single letter that is an abbreviation for the command name. Most commands are followed by additional parameters, some of which are optional.

You can also use the MS-DOS command line editing keys F1 through F5, Del, Ins, and Esc when entering DEBUG commands if you have not redefined the use of these keys with a keyboard enhancement program (such as Superkey). See Chapter 5 for a description of the function of these keys when editing a command.

Several of DEBUG's commands require parameters that specify a *block* of data to be operated on. For example, the DUMP command dumps (or displays) the contents of a block of data on the screen. You may give the parameters that specify what block of data to operate on for all these commands in one of two similar formats. The first format allowed is [start-address] [end-address] and the second format is [start-address] L [block-length]. The DEBUG program distinguishes between these two formats by the presence of the L character that precedes the length of the block when the second format is used.

The DEBUG program has a fairly flexible command format. Delimiters are required only to separate consecutive hexadecimal values. A space, the tab character, or a comma may be used as the delimiter. In practice, the space is most commonly used because it improves the readability of commands. The examples in this chapter follow these conventions. They will help to familiarize you with the most common DEBUG command format found in most technical journals.

You should note that all characters in commands shown in upper-case can actually be typed in upper- *or* lowercase. These include: the command itself (such as *D* for the DEBUG DUMP command), the *L* that precedes a command length parameter, and the register names used with the REGISTER command. This convention is followed only for improved readability. The text in this chapter mentions when the use of uppercase characters is *not* optional.

DEBUG Memory Address Notation

The DEBUG program displays and accepts addresses in the format [segment:offset], where [segment] and [offset] are both hexadecimal numbers in the range X'0' to X'FFFF'. When inputting address parameters to the DEBUG program, the [segment] portion of the address is optional. If the [segment] is not specified, the DEBUG program supplies a default segment.

The DEBUG program keeps track of four different segment values: code, data, stack, and extra. Different segment values are supplied as defaults to different DEBUG commands. Except for files with a filename extension of .EXE or .HEX, the four segment values for the DEBUG program are identical.

When using DEBUG to debug a program, the values of the different segments are relevant. *However, when using the DEBUG program only to examine, modify, and create files, the segment portion of any addresses may be ignored as long as the file is less than 64K bytes in length.* DEBUG always supplies the same default segment for all commands when loading files, modifying data, or writing files. For more information on working with files greater than 64K bytes in length, see the *Breaking the 64K Barrier* trick box.

Using the DEBUG Program To Display Memory

One of the easiest functions to perform using the DEBUG program is to display a block of memory with the DUMP command. Although displaying the contents of various areas of memory in the computer is useful normally only to programmers, it is a worthwhile first step to learning to use the DEBUG program. Later, when we have learned to read a file from disk into memory, the ability to display the memory where the disk file is located will be a more practical use of the DUMP command.

The letter D is DEBUG's command for dumping (or displaying) memory. Optional parameters indicate to DEBUG the beginning location and size of the block of memory that is to be displayed. If the size of the block to be displayed is not indicated, the DEBUG program supplies a default of 80 (hexadecimal) bytes with an 80 (decimal) column system display format for the screen or 40 (hexadecimal) bytes for a 40 (decimal) column system display format. If the starting memory location to be displayed is omitted, the DEBUG program uses the location following the last location displayed as the default. If no previous DUMP command was entered, the default starting location is X'100' of the current default segment of memory.

The current default segment of memory is the first part of memory that is available to the DEBUG program to read in a file without overwriting information in memory that is required to operate the system (that is, the MS-DOS operating system and any memory resident programs). DEBUG uses the default when reading a file from disk, displaying data, modifying data, or writing a file to disk. These convenient DEBUG defaults mean that nonprogrammers do not normally need to be concerned with the current segment unless they are working with a file larger than 64K bytes (65,536 decimal bytes).

We now have enough background information to start using the DEBUG program to display memory. After you execute the DEBUG program by entering DEBUG on the command line, the - prompt appears. To display a block of memory, type the letter D and press the Enter key. The screen now looks something like this:

```
A>DEBUG
-D
432B:0100  C9 44 3C 02 73 01 C3 A0-48 02 3C 17 73 01 C3 E8   ID<.s.C H.<.s.Ch
432B:0110  76 00 FE C0 A2 70 46 A2-6F 46 A2 6E 46 04 02 A2   v.~@"pF"oF"nF.."
432B:0120  6C 46 C3 E8 87 00 87 DA-E8 86 F0 E8 DE FA 0E 00   lFCh...Zh.ph^z..
432B:0130  9F 86 C4 50 86 C4 B0 01-EB 0B E8 C6 F5 9F 86 C4   ..DP.D0.k.hFu..D
432B:0140  50 86 C4 32 C0 E8 28 00-58 86 C4 9E C3 5E 87 DE   P.D2@h(.X.D.C^.^
432B:0150  56 E8 3C F0 5E 87 DE 56-EB E3 E8 6A 00 5E 87 DE   Vh<p^.^Vkchj.^.^
432B:0160  56 E8 2C F0 5E 87 DE 56-E8 A1 FA 0E 0E 00 B0 02   Vh,p^.^Vh!z...0.
432B:0170  02 06 D4 44 2A 06 37 46-9F 86 C4 50 86 C4 E8 12   ..TD*.7F..DP.Dh.
-
```

The exact appearance of your screen may be different depending on the contents of the memory block that is displayed. However, the general format of the screen display should be the same. In response to the D command, the DEBUG program displays eight lines of data. All eight lines have the same format. The group of numbers on the left side of the screen is the beginning address of the sixteen bytes of data displayed on the remainder of the line. These addresses are in the [segment:offset] format: The segment, in this case, is the default segment because we did not enter any segment address as a parameter to the DUMP command.

The default segment for your system is probably different from the one in the above example and varies depending on the version of MS-DOS you are using, the memory resident programs you have loaded (such as Sidekick), and the configuration parameters supplied to your system on startup. The offset part of the address is 0100 (hexadecimal) in this case because this is the first time we have used the DUMP command since starting the DEBUG program. Entering D, again with no parameters causes the DEBUG program to display memory for the same segment, beginning with an offset of 180 (hexadecimal). Subsequent use of the DUMP command would use the offsets 200, 280, 300, 380, etc., unless a beginning address parameter is given with the command.

Following the memory address is the value of the sixteen bytes beginning at the specified address. The values for each byte are given in hexadecimal notation: Two hexadecimal digits represent the value of each byte. A hyphen appears between the eighth and ninth pair of hexadecimal digits to help delineate between the first eight bytes and the last eight bytes displayed on each line.

After the sixteen bytes are displayed in hexadecimal format, the same sixteen bytes are displayed in ASCII format. The high-order (leftmost) bit of the byte is ignored when the byte is converted to ASCII. For example, the bytes with a hexadecimal value of '41' or 'C1' are displayed on the right as an ASCII uppercase A. This feature can be useful because some word processors use this bit with printable characters to "flag" the byte with a special meaning. For example, WordStar uses this bit to indicate that an end-of-line break may begin after this byte. The DEBUG program displays the ASCII value regardless of the value of this bit.

Another ASCII display feature of which you should be aware is that all the nonprintable ASCII control characters (hexadecimal 00 through 1F and hexadecimal 7F) are indicated by the . (period) ASCII character. To know what the value of a byte represented with a period is, you must look at the value in the hexadecimal display of bytes on the left.

Later, when we read in a disk file to look at with the DEBUG program, we will use the DUMP command to display the contents of the file. Compared to most other programs, DEBUG displays the data in a very low-level manner: What you see is what you get. This is quite a contrast to what would be displayed for the same file with your word processor.

The nonprintable control characters often are used in text files by word processor programs as a prefix to the printable characters. These characters display the text as highlighted, reverse video, or underlined characters or displayed with other video options. Even the relatively simple MS-DOS TYPE command displays a text file with certain control characters interpreted in a special way. For example, the carriage return-line feed control characters cause the next printable character to be displayed on the beginning of the following line of the screen, and the tab control character is expanded to display several spaces before the next printable character. These *enhanced* display modes are useful in viewing the data in a file. Sometimes, however, to know a file's precise contents, you need to look at its data in raw form.

Now that you have "peeked" at the memory of your computer, you are ready to exit DEBUG and return to the MS-DOS command line. Enter Q for the DEBUG QUIT command. The remainder of this section explains the various formats for the DEBUG DUMP command. You may wish to execute the DEBUG program a few more times and play with displaying different parts of your computer system's memory to become familiar with the different formats of the DUMP command.

If you are somewhat familiar with your computer's hardware, you can display different portions of memory, such as the interrupt vectors, parts of the ROM BIOS, or even your screen's display memory. As long as you don't *modify* any of the memory or write anything to a disk file, you cannot harm your system using DEBUG. Remember that to exit the DEBUG program, at the - prompt, press the Q key, then the Enter key.

The four formats for the DEBUG program DUMP command are

```
D
```

```
D [start-address]
```

```
D [start-address] L [length]
```

```
D [start-address] [end-address]
```

All four formats perform the same function: The block of the computer's memory is displayed on the screen in hexadecimal and ASCII character format. The beginning address of the display block is determined by the [start-address] parameter that you give with the DUMP command. If you do not supply a [start-address], DEBUG provides a default value of one past the last address displayed, or X'100' for the current segment if you have not entered a DUMP command during current execution of the DEBUG program.

The size of the block displayed is determined by the value that follows the L parameter of the DUMP command. If no length is given, the DEBUG program supplies a value depending on the current display mode for your screen. Normally, the default length value is 80 (hexadecimal) for a display mode of 80 (decimal) characters. For the fourth format of the DUMP command shown in the preceding list, the length is determined by the value of the [end-address] relative to the [start-address]. The actual length of the block of memory displayed is determined by the calculation [end-address] minus [start-address] plus one.

Command Line Errors for the DEBUG Program

In DEBUG, only one error message is displayed for invalid command syntax: Error. The message is displayed with the ^ symbol, which indicates *approximately* where the error was found in the command. The MS-DOS manual doesn't give much of an indication as to what conditions cause the error to display, but following is a summary of some of the more common problems.

```
D L100
 ^ Error
```

The DUMP command does not allow a length parameter without a preceding [start-address]

```
D 300 200
    ^ Error
```

The [start-address] for the DUMP command must be less than or equal to the [end-address]

```
D CS:100 CS:200
         ^ Error
```

The segment used for an [end-address] is always identical to the segment for the related [start-address], whether the [start-address] segment was explicitly given or a default. No segment can ever be given with an [end-address].

```
D 8C00 L9000
         ^ Error
```

The address of the last byte displayed cannot be greater than X'FFFF'. In this example, the last byte displayed would be X'11BFF', which exceeds the maximum. This is one of the most difficult errors to find when using DEBUG. When a DUMP command begins at location X'100', the largest valid value for the length parameter is X'FF00'. (X'FEFF' for some versions of the DEBUG program. See the caution box titled *A Little Bug in DEBUG*.)

```
B 100 L80
^ Error
```

DEBUG has no B command.

```
D 100 180 L80
          ^ Error
```

Only an [end-address] or [length] parameter is allowed.

A LITTLE BUG IN DEBUG

It seems only fitting that the program designed to "remove bugs" from programs has at least one bug to call its own. This irony more or less helps the DEBUG program justify its existence. Fortunately, the bug described here is a relatively innocuous one. The DEBUG program works with *segments* of memory. A segment is a block of memory that is 64K (65,536 decimal) bytes long. Most of the DEBUG commands, however, do not allow access to the last byte of a segment. For example, the DUMP command D FFFF L1 should display the last byte of the current segment. However, an error message is displayed instead.

The bug does not normally create much of a problem because it merely restricts the number of bytes to 64K minus one (that is, 65,535 bytes in decimal) that can be viewed in a file. There is also a way to circumvent the bug by changing or overriding the value of the default segment. If you need to look at this elusive byte hiding at the end of a segment, see the *Breaking the 64K Barrier* trick box.

Like the jester who has no smile and thus demonstrates to humanity the need for his existence, the DEBUG program bug lives on. It is the one bug that we hoped would never get debugged. Unfortunately, it has been zapped since MS-DOS Version 3.0.

Examining a File with DEBUG

Now we are ready to do something really useful with the DEBUG program. We already know everything necessary to look at a file except reading (or loading) it into memory. The easiest way to do this with the DEBUG program is to give the name of the file on the MS-DOS command line when the DEBUG program is executed:

```
A>DEBUG AUTOEXEC.BAT
-D
432B:0100  41 53 54 43 4C 4F 43 4B-0D 0A 50 52 4F 4D 50 54   ASTCLOCK..PROMPT
432B:0110  20 44 61 74 65 3A 20 24-64 20 20 54 69 6D 65 3A    Date: $d  Time:
432B:0120  20 24 74 20 20 24 70 20-24 5F 24 6E 24 67 0D 0A    $t  $p $_$n$g..
432B:0130  50 41 54 48 09 43 3A 5C-3B 43 3A 5C 43 4F 4D 4D   PATH.C:\;C:\COMM
432B:0140  4F 4E 3B 43 3A 5C 4D 53-4F 46 54 3B 43 3A 5C 54   ON;C:\MSOFT;C:\T
432B:0150  55 52 42 4F 3B 43 3A 5C-4E 4F 52 54 4F 4E 3B 43   URBO;C:\NORTON;C
432B:0160  3A 5C 4D 41 53 4D 0D 0A-53 45 54 09 4C 49 42 50   :\MASM..SET.LIBP
432B:0170  41 54 48 3D 5C 53 59 4D-0D 0A 53 45 54 09 54 45   ATH=\SYM..SET.TE
-Q
```

The file that is named on the MS-DOS command line following the DEBUG command is loaded into memory at the default segment starting at offset X'100'. Entering a D (for the DEBUG DUMP command) starts at offset X'100' to display the first X'80' bytes in the default segment, so the first X'80' bytes of the file are displayed.

After reading a file into memory, it is often useful to know the size of the file. The R (REGISTER command) with no parameters displays the contents of your computer system's registers. Immediately after a file is loaded into memory by the DEBUG program, the BX and CX registers contain the size in hexadecimal bytes of the file. If the size of the file is less than 65,536 bytes, the BX register contains zero and the file size is in the CX register.

To convert a file size from hexadecimal to decimal, convert the hexadecimal value in register CX to decimal. If the value displayed for register BX is zero, you are done. Otherwise, you must convert the value in register BX to decimal, multiply that by 65,536 (decimal), then add the value for register CX after you convert it to decimal.

For example, to determine the size of the AUTOEXEC.BAT file examined in the previous example, execute the DEBUG program again giving the filename on the MS-DOS command line following the DEBUG command:

```
A>DEBUG AUTOEXEC.BAT
-R
AX=0000  BX=0000  CX=01EE  DX=0000  SP=FFEE  BP=0000  SI=0000  DI=0000
DS=432B  ES=432B  SS=432B  CS=432B  IP=0100     NV UP DI PL NZ NA PO NC
432B:0100 41              INC       CX
-Q
```

When the DEBUG program prompt appears, use the R (REGISTER command) to display the current values for the computer's registers. Don't be concerned if the display appears confusing. The only values that need to be understood when working with files are the two sets of numbers following the BX= and CX= labels. Because the value for the BX register is zero, determining the file size is a matter of converting the value for the CX register from hexadecimal to decimal. Using a calculator that performs this conversion quickly yields an answer of 494 bytes. The MS-DOS DIR command verifies this calculation:

```
A>DIR AUTOEXEC.BAT

Volume in drive A has no label
Directory of  A:\

AUTOEXEC BAT      494    8-26-86  10:48a
         1 File(s)     20896 bytes free
```

TRICK   LOCATING THE NTH BYTE OF A FILE

Locating a file's byte to display or modify it might seem like something that should be straightforward with the DEBUG program. Unfortunately, the procedure required to locate a byte is more cumbersome that one might hope. The problem is that if you know the position of a byte in the file in decimal, you must convert this position to an address that the DEBUG program understands.

Suppose that you want to look at the 150th character (or byte) in the file. At first, the calculation required may appear to be a little complicated but with some practice it becomes easier. Because all input to the DEBUG program is in hexadecimal, the 150 must be converted first to hexadecimal notation. If you have Sidekick or another program with a calculator that converts from decimal to hexadecimal, you can make these conversions much faster. The hexadecimal value of 150 decimal is X'96'. Because the file was loaded into memory at offset X'100', you must now make an adjustment for this load address. The first byte of the file is at location X'100', the fifth byte at location X'104', etc. The adjustment to add to the X'96' to account for the initial load address is X'FF'. However, when doing the arithmetic in your head, it is easier to add X'100', then subtract one. The sum of X'96' and X'100 is X'196', minus one is X'195', therefore the DEBUG command 'D 195 L1' displays the 150th byte of the file.

We already know that the first byte of the file is at offset X'100', but going through the same conversion process again to find the first byte in a file may help to make the reasoning more clear. Because we are looking for byte 1 (decimal) of the file, the 1 is converted to hexadecimal, which is also 1 (hexadecimal). Add X'100' to get X'101', then subtract 1, which is X'100'. This verifies what we already knew: The first byte of the file is at offset X'100'.

One of the tricky details that must be remembered when trying to locate a particular byte in a file is that there is a difference between the *position* and the *offset* of a byte in a file. The byte at the *first position* of a file is at offset 0 of the file, the byte at the *second position* in a file is at offset 1, etc. The offset of a byte is always its position in the file minus one. There is no way to logically deduce this fact. It is a matter of the difference between the definition of the related terms *position* and *offset*.

An Alternate Way of Loading a File into DEBUG

The previous section shows one method of loading a file into memory using the DEBUG program. An alternate method exists that requires the use of two DEBUG commands but also has a few advantages. First, the DEBUG N (NAME command) is used to tell the DEBUG program the name of the file to be loaded. If the file does not exist,

DEBUG does not inform you. (This is not an oversight because the NAME command is also used to specify the name of a new file when it is created.) Then, the DEBUG L (LOAD command) is used to tell DEBUG to load the named file. If no [start-address] is given as a parameter with the LOAD command, the file is loaded into the default segment starting at offset X'100'.

```
A>DEBUG
-N AUTOEXEC.BAT
-L
-R
AX=0000  BX=0000  CX=01EE  DX=0000  SP=FFEE  BP=0000  SI=0000  DI=0000
DS=432B  ES=432B  SS=432B  CS=432B  IP=0100    NV UP DI PL NZ NA PO NC
432B:0100 41            INC    CX
-D
432B:0100  41 53 54 43 4C 4F 43 4B-0D 0A 50 52 4F 4D 50 54   ASTCLOCK..PROMPT
432B:0110  20 44 61 74 65 3A 20 24-64 20 20 54 69 6D 65 3A    Date: $d Time:
432B:0120  20 24 74 20 20 24 70 20-24 5F 24 6E 24 67 0D 0A    $t  $p $_$n$g..
432B:0130  50 41 54 48 20 20 20 20-43 3A 5C 3B 43 3A 5C 43   PATH    C:\;C:\C
432B:0140  4F 4D 4D 4F 4E 3B 43 3A-5C 4D 53 4F 46 54 3B 43   OMMON;C:\MSOFT;C
432B:0150  3A 5C 54 55 52 42 4F 3B-43 3A 5C 4E 4F 52 54 4F   :\TURBO;C:\NORTO
432B:0160  4E 3B 43 3A 5C 4D 41 53-4D 0D 0A 53 45 54 20 20   N;C:\MASM..SET
432B:0170  20 20 20 4C 49 42 50 41-54 48 3D 5C 53 59 4D 0D      LIBPATH=\SYM.
-Q
```

One advantage of loading a file using this method is that you do not have to exit the DEBUG program in order to load a new file into memory. The first file to be examined can be loaded by specifying the filename following the name of the DEBUG program on the MS-DOS command line. Subsequent files can be loaded and examined by using the NAME and LOAD DEBUG commands.

Another advantage of using the DEBUG NAME and LOAD commands is that a [start-address] may be specified as a parameter to the LOAD command. This allows you to load multiple files into memory at one time without overlaying the previously loaded files. The files can now be compared, combined, and written to a single file or have other operations performed on them that could not be done with a single file in memory at one time.

Notice that each time a new file is loaded, the values of the BX and CX registers are updated with the file size of the most recently loaded file. The previous contents of these registers is lost, so in order to know the size of a previously loaded file, you need to inspect the value of these registers *before* the next file is loaded.

If the file being loaded cannot be found, the error message File not found is displayed when the L (LOAD command) is executed. The N (NAME command) does not care if the file exists. This feature comes in handy when you want to create a new file that does not already exist on disk. The N (NAME command) is used to name the new file, then the W (WRITE command) is used to write the new file to disk.

In practice, there is very little difference between loading a file from disk into memory by using the DEBUG NAME and LOAD commands or specifying the filename on the MS-DOS command line when executing the DEBUG program. Both methods of loading a file set up the BX and CX registers with the length of the file in bytes, both methods load the file at offset X'100' of the default segment (unless the LOAD command [start-address] parameter is used to override this default), and both methods set up the name of the loaded file for later use by the DEBUG program. This last fact will be helpful when you learn how to write out a block of memory to a disk file.

HALTING, PRINTING, AND ABORTING DEBUG COMMANDS

TRICK

You can use special keystroke combinations to halt, print, or abort the display and execution of any of the DEBUG commands while they are executing and displaying information on your screen. These features of the DEBUG program are similar to those available while executing many of the MS-DOS commands such as TYPE, DIR, and COMP.

The Ctrl-S or Ctrl-Num Lock keystroke combination halts the execution of a DEBUG command so that you can view the screen display without it scrolling. This feature is especially handy when the display for a command would scroll off the top of the screen before the command completes. Pressing any data key after the display has been halted with the Ctrl-S or Ctrl-Num Lock keystroke combinations allows the DEBUG program to continue with the execution of the command.

The Ctrl-P or Ctrl-PrtSc keystroke combination causes the display of any DEBUG command that is executing to be listed on your printer. If you do not have a printer or it is not *on-line* to your computer when the Ctrl-P or Ctrl-PrtSc keystroke combination is pressed, your computer may *hang,* ignore the keystroke combination, or display an error message.

Printing the results of a command can be very useful to get a listing of the file with the DUMP command, a list of addresses containing a certain data value with the SEARCH command, or a list of differences between two memory blocks with the COMPARE command.

Pressing the Ctrl-P or Ctrl-PrtSc keystroke combination a second time stops the screen display from being listed on your printer. Each time you press one of these keystroke combinations, MS-DOS *toggles* between printing the screen display on your printer and displaying data only on your screen. You will find it most useful to start output to the printer just before the command is entered, then stop output to the printer after the DEBUG program returns to the – prompt after the command has executed.

The Ctrl-C or Ctrl-Break keystroke combination causes the DEBUG program to abort the currently executing command before it has completed. The abort feature is most useful when you are only interested in the first few occurrences of a byte or string in a file, or when you see that the output for the command being executed will be much longer than you expected and want to repeat the command in order to print the entire display of the command using the Ctrl-PrtSc feature.

When using the DEBUG Program, another handy MS-DOS feature is the capability of printing the current contents of the screen. The Shift-PrtSc keystroke combination causes the current screen display to be listed on your printer.

MAKING DEBUG DO THE WORK OF LARGE FILE DISPLAY

The DEBUG program's DUMP command has a convenient default value for the starting address of the block of memory to be displayed when no [start-address] parameter is given. The default value supplied is the [segment:offset] of the last byte displayed by the previous DUMP command plus one. If no previous DUMP command has been issued, the default value for the [start-address] is offset X'100' for the current default segment.

These convenient defaults make it very easy to view a file that has been loaded at the default load address (offset X'100' for the current default segment). The first time you enter the DUMP command with no parameters the beginning of the file that has been loaded is displayed. Subsequent entries of the DUMP command with no parameters begin display of the file where the last DUMP command left off. Consequently, pressing D, Enter, D, Enter, D, Enter, etc., is a quick way to scan an entire file quickly and easily.

This method of alternately pressing two keys is so convenient that you can overlook easily a method that has the DEBUG program do *all* the work for you. Examine the contents of the CX register, then issue a DUMP command with a [start-address] of X'100' and a [length] parameter with the hexadecimal value in the CX register. This single DUMP command displays the *entire* contents of the file.

```
-R
AX=0000  BX=0000  CX=1CE8  DX=0000  SP=FFEE  BP=0000  SI=0000  DI=0000
DS=432B  ES=432B  SS=432B  CS=432B  IP=0100    NV UP DI PL NZ NA PO NC
432B:0100 C9            DB      C9
-D 100 L 1CE8
432B:0100  88 01 21 19 88 89 11 02-0D 08 20 98 96 82 54 12   ..!....... ...T.
       . . .

432B:1DE0  00 00 00 00 00 00 00 00                           ........
```

The Ctrl-S or Ctrl-Num Lock keystroke combination can be used to temporarily halt the continuous display of the file if required. If you find what you are looking for in the file and no longer want to continue the display, use the Ctrl-C or Ctrl-Break keystroke combination to abort the current DUMP command and return to the DEBUG – prompt.

CAUTION

FILES GIVEN SPECIAL TREATMENT BY THE DEBUG PROGRAM

Two types of files receive special treatment from the DEBUG program when they are loaded into memory. These files are *executable* and *hexadecimal load* files.

The DEBUG program identifies these files by their filename extensions, which are .EXE and .HEX respectively. When these file types are loaded by the DEBUG program, data conversions, data relocation, and other special processing is performed as the file is read from disk and placed in memory. The exact nature of these load time modifications is beyond the scope of this book. You only need to know that the "what you see is what you get" rule for the DEBUG program is no longer in effect. If you display parts of the file with the DEBUG DUMP command, you do not see the exact contents of the file as it exists on disk. Also, you are not able to write files with filename extensions of .EXE or .HEX because DEBUG does not support the conversions required to create these file types.

If you want to examine or modify files with a filename extension of .EXE or .HEX, rename the file with another extension, then use the DEBUG program as you would with any other file. When these files have been renamed and loaded into the DEBUG program, they are no longer executable because the required conversions have not been performed on them. However, you can modify the files and write them back to disk. When you have finished using the DEBUG program with the file, it should be renamed with the proper filename extension. Remember, when you use the DEBUG program with any file, first create a backup version of the file:

Before loading the file into DEBUG, create a new copy of the file instead of renaming it.

Another file type that receives special treatment by the DEBUG program is the *command* file, which is identified with a filename extension of .COM. The special treatment received by the command file is much more subtle: If the L (LOAD command) is used with a file that has a filename extension of .COM, the file is always loaded at offset X'100', and any [start-address] parameter given with the LOAD command is ignored. No warning message is displayed to indicate that the [start-address] parameter is ignored. The special treatment given to command files when they are loaded is seldom an inconvenience because normally you want to load files at offset X'100'. Occasionally, you may want to load a file at another offset so that you can load several files into memory at the same time.

Replacing .COM with another filename extension before using the DEBUG program, then after using DEBUG, renaming the file with its original name circumvents this [start-address] limitation for .COM files.

Modifying the Contents of a File Using DEBUG

Once a file has been loaded into memory from disk, DEBUG provides four commands that you can use to modify the file. These are the ASSEMBLE, ENTER, FILL, and MOVE commands. The ASSEMBLE command is covered in the trick box titled *Creating Assembler Language Programs with DEBUG*. The remaining commands are covered in the following three sections of this chapter.

One important thing to remember when you are modifying a file: You are only modifying the copy of the file that has been loaded into memory. If you make a mistake, don't panic. The copy of the file on disk has not been modified and won't be until you explicitly write the copy of the file in memory to disk. When you discover that you have made a mistake, correct it. If you are not sure what you have done or the mistake is too big to correct easily, reload the file being modified into memory using the DEBUG NAME and LOAD commands.

Normally, when you modify the contents of a file in memory, the intention is to save the modified version of the file on disk for later use. The section titled *Using the WRITE Command To Write a File to Disk* in this chapter explains how to save a file on disk.

Using the ENTER Command To Modify the Contents of a File

The DEBUG ENTER command has two *modes* of operation. You use the first mode to give a beginning offset where the entered data is to be placed in memory. You follow the beginning offset with a list of the data to be entered at the specified memory location. For example, the following command places hexadecimal values X'00' through X'0F' in memory beginning at offset X'100'.

```
-E 100 00 01 02 03 04 05 06 07 08 09 0a 0b 0c 0d 0e 0f
-D L 10
432B:0100  00 01 02 03 04 05 06 07-08 09 0A 0B 0C 0D 0E 0F   ................
```

The first parameter after the E (ENTER command) is the [start-address] where the data is to be placed. The remaining parameters are byte values that are to begin at the [start-address]. For the ENTER command to operate in this mode, at least one value in the list of values must be entered. The maximum number of values is determined by the restriction on DEBUG command line size, which cannot exceed 80 characters. After using any of the DEBUG commands that can alter memory, examine the memory locations using the D (DUMP command) to ensure that your modification has been performed correctly.

The byte values in the list of values must be separated by at least one space. Multiple spaces, tab characters, and commas are also allowed. However, using a single space is best. This command format is the most commonly used in the various computer magazines and texts, so becoming familiar with it is advantageous.

Remember that the byte values in the list must be hexadecimal: A 12 is interpreted as a hexadecimal 12 (decimal 18). The case of the hexadecimal digits A through F is not important when entering hexadecimal values. Consequently, the value 3F is interpreted the same as the value 3f. Leading zeros are not required for values less than hexadecimal 10; consequently, the value B is interpreted the same as the value 0B.

The list of values following the [start-address] for the ENTER command may also contain strings of ASCII characters. The characters to be entered are placed in double quote marks. This feature makes it convenient to enter printable characters interspersed with control characters. For example, the following ENTER command creates a short text file with three lines. Each line is followed by the hexadecimal values of the ASCII CR-LF control characters, and the entire file is followed by the hexadecimal value of the ASCII EOF (end-of-file) control character. The X'20' (32 decimal) bytes are displayed with the D (DUMP command) to show the results of the ENTER command.

```
-E 100 "1st line" 0d 0a "2nd line" 0d 0a "Last line" 0d 0a 1a
-D 100 L 20
432B:0100  31 73 74 20 6C 69 6E 65-0D 0A 32 6E 64 20 6C 69   1st line..2nd li
432B:0110  6E 65 0D 0A 4C 61 73 74-20 6C 69 6E 65 0D 0A 1A   ne..Last line...
```

Notice that the case of characters within the double quote marks *is* case sensitive. For example, the first occurrence of the letter L in "Last"line" is located at offset X'0114' and is represented by the hexadecimal value X'4C'. The second occurrence of the letter l in "Last line" is located at offset X'0119' and is represented by the hexadecimal value X'6C'. A quick check of the ASCII table in this book (see Table C.1, Appendix C) shows that these are the proper values for the upper- and lowercase ASCII representations of the letter *L*.

Writing files from memory to disk is covered subsequently in this chapter. For the moment, suppose that the file has been written to disk with the name TEMP.TXT. Here is what the file looks like when it is displayed on the screen using the MS-DOS TYPE command:

```
A>TYPE TEMP.TXT
1st line
2nd line
Last line
```

If you want to enter a string that contains a double quote mark, the string may begin and end with a single quote mark. Two consecutive double quote marks may also be used to indicate a single double quote within a string beginning and ending with a double quote mark. In other words, the following two strings are interpreted identically by the DEBUG program:

```
"The quote """To be or not to be?"""" is from Shakespeare's Hamlet"
```

```
'The quote "To be or not to be?" is from Shakespeare''s Hamlet'
```

The second mode for the E (ENTRY command) is initiated by

entering the E command with only a [start-address]. When no list of values to be entered is given, the DEBUG program displays the address and current value of the byte at the [start-address] and allows you to modify the byte value, skip to the next byte at the next address, return to the byte at the previous address, or return to the DEBUG prompt.

To modify the value, key in the one or two hexadecimal digits for the desired value of that memory location. Only one hexadecimal digit is required for values of less than X'10' (16 decimal). The leading zero is optional. Again, the case of the hexadecimal digits A through F is not significant. The Backspace key may be used to erase an incorrect digit and replace it with the correct value.

After modifying the value of a memory location, you can continue to display (and optionally modify) the byte at the next memory location, return to the DEBUG prompt line, or go back to display (and optionally modify) the byte at the previous memory location.

To *continue* in a forward direction, press the Space Bar. The value of the next byte is displayed and can be modified if you desire. After each eighth byte has been displayed (and possibly modified), the following line of the screen shows the current address and byte value. For screens in 40 column mode, the entry continues on the following line after each fourth byte.

To *return* to the DEBUG prompt line, press the Enter key. When your screen shows the – prompt, display the modified data to ensure that it is correct.

To *go back* to the previous memory location after modifying the current byte, press the – (minus) key. The display continues on the next line of the screen with the address of the previous byte in [segment:offset] format with the current value of the byte at that location in memory.

To skip the next memory location, return to the DEBUG prompt or return to the previous memory location *without modifying the displayed value for the current byte*, press the Space Bar, Enter key, or minus key without keying any hexadecimal digits.

The following example changes all occurrences of a lowercase l to an uppercase L using the Enter command. Notice that the Space Bar (abbreviated <SP>) is used to continue in a forward direction after a byte has been modified or to go forward when you are skipping modification of a byte. The DUMP command is used after the ENTER command to verify the results.

```
A>DEBUG TEMP.TXT
```

```
-E 100 "1st line" 0d 0a "2nd line" 0d 0a "Last line" 0d 0a 1a
-D 100 L 20
432B:0100  31 73 74 20 6C 69 6E 65-0D 0A 32 6E 64 20 6C 69   1st line..2nd li
432B:0110  6E 65 0D 0A 4C 61 73 74-20 6C 69 6E 65 0D 0A 1A   ne..Last line...
-E 104
432B:0104  6C.4c<SP>    69.<SP>      6E.<SP>      65.<SP>
432B:0108  0D.<SP>      0A.<SP>      32.<SP>      6E.<SP>
432B:010C  64.<SP>      20.<SP>      6C.4c<SP>    69.<SP>
432B:0110  6E.<SP>      65.<SP>      0D.<SP>      0A.<SP>
432B:1114  4C.<SP>      61.<SP>      73.<SP>      74.<SP>
432B:0118  20.<SP>      6C.<SP>      69.-
432B:0119  6C.4c<ENTER>
-D 100 L 20
432B:0100  31 73 74 20 4C 69 6E 65-0D 0A 32 6E 64 20 4C 69   1st Line..2nd Li
432B:0110  6E 65 0D 0A 4C 61 73 74-20 4C 69 6E 65 0D 0A 1A   ne..Last Line...
```

Assuming the file was written to disk, here is how the file appears when displayed with the MS-DOS TYPE command:

```
A>TYPE TEMP.TXT
1st Line
2nd Line
Last Line
```

Using the FILL Command To Modify the Contents of a File

Now that you are familiar with the Enter command, mastering the FILL command will be quite easy. The two formats for the FILL command are

```
-F [start-address] L [length] [data-list]
```

```
-F [start-address] [end-address] [data-list]
```

The FILL command fills a block of memory beginning at the location specified by the [start-address] parameter with the byte(s) given in the [data-list] parameter. The size of the block of memory is determined by the value of the [length] parameter or the calculation [end-address] minus [start-address] plus one.

If the [data-list] contains fewer bytes than the size of the memory block specified by the parameters, the [data-list] is used repeatedly until all of the designated memory locations are filled. If the [data-list] contains more bytes than required, the extra items in the [data-list] are ignored.

The [data-list] parameter must contain at least one byte of data. The maximum size of the [data-list] is limited by the size of the DEBUG command line.

As an example, the following FILL command fills 40 (hexadecimal) bytes beginning at offset 100 (hexadecimal) with binary zeros:

```
-F 100 L 40 00
-D 100 L 40
432B:0100  00 00 00 00 00 00 00 00-00 00 00 00 00 00 00 00   ................
432B:0110  00 00 00 00 00 00 00 00-00 00 00 00 00 00 00 00   ................
432B:0120  00 00 00 00 00 00 00 00-00 00 00 00 00 00 00 00   ................
432B:0130  00 00 00 00 00 00 00 00-00 00 00 00 00 00 00 00   ................
-
```

Using the MOVE Command To Modify the Contents of a File

The DEBUG MOVE command is used to move a block of memory from one location to another. A better name for the MOVE command would be COPY, because the original block of memory is unchanged after the move operation is performed (unless the source area and destination area overlap). The two formats for the MOVE command are

```
M [source-start-address] [source-end-address] [destination-address]
```

```
M [source-start-address] L [length] [destination-address]
```

The length of the block to be moved is determined by the value of the [length] parameter or the calculation [source-end-address] minus [source-start-address] plus one. The length of the destination block naturally must be identical to the size of the source block.

As an example, the following MOVE command copies a block of 18 (hexadecimal) bytes beginning at offset 100 (hexadecimal) to the memory location beginning at offset 120 (hexadecimal). A display of the source and destination memory areas is given to show the results of the MOVE command.

```
-F 100 L 20 01
-F 120 L 20 FF
-D 100 L 40
432B:0100  01 01 01 01 01 01 01 01-01 01 01 01 01 01 01 01    ................
432B:0110  01 01 01 01 01 01 01 01-01 01 01 01 01 01 01 01    ................
432B:0120  FF FF FF FF FF FF FF FF-FF FF FF FF FF FF FF FF    ................
432B:0130  FF FF FF FF FF FF FF FF-FF FF FF FF FF FF FF FF    ................
-M 100 L 18 120
-D 100 L 40
432B:0100  01 01 01 01 01 01 01 01-01 01 01 01 01 01 01 01    ................
432B:0110  01 01 01 01 01 01 01 01-01 01 01 01 01 01 01 01    ................
432B:0120  01 01 01 01 01 01 01 01-01 01 01 01 01 01 01 01    ................
432B:0130  01 01 01 01 01 01 01 01-FF FF FF FF FF FF FF FF    ................
```

Using the WRITE Command To Write a File to Disk

The DEBUG WRITE command has two different modes of operation for writing to the disk: file-oriented writes and sector-oriented writes. This section covers only the file-oriented mode of the WRITE command.

The file-oriented mode of the DEBUG WRITE command has a very simple format: Enter W with an optional [starting-address] parameter. If no [starting-address] parameter is given, the default is to write the memory block beginning at location X'100' in the default segment.

To properly write a file to disk, the DEBUG program needs more information than is given by the WRITE command parameters. Specifically, DEBUG needs to know how much data to write to the file and the name and location of the file.

The number of bytes of data written to the file is determined by the values in the BX and CX registers. Recall that these are the registers where the LOAD command places the size of a disk file when it is loaded into memory. This is a convenience when a file is loaded, modified, and written back to disk without changing the size of the file. As long as the values in the BX and CX registers have not been modified, you don't have to be concerned about setting up the proper values in the BX and CX registers in order to write out the correct number of bytes to a file (as long as the file size has not changed).

The name and disk drive of the file that the memory block is to be written to is determined by the parameter previously given, using the NAME command, to the DEBUG program. Again, recall that the NAME command is how you indicate to DEBUG the name of a file to be loaded using the LOAD command. This is a convenience when a file is loaded, modified, and written back to disk without changing the name of the file.

Notice the complementary way the LOAD and WRITE commands work together:

1. The LOAD command uses X'100' as the default [start-address] for the beginning location of the block of memory where the data from the file is loaded. The WRITE command uses X'100' as the default [start-address] for the beginning location of the block of memory written to the file.

2. The LOAD command places the size of the loaded file in bytes into the BX and CX registers. The WRITE command takes the value in the BX and CX registers as the length of the memory block in bytes to be written to the file.

3. The LOAD command loads from the file given by the [file-specification] parameter of the most recently issued NAME command. The WRITE command writes to the file given by the [file-specification] parameter of the most recently issued NAME command.

Consequently, the command sequence to read a file into memory and write it to disk is simple. First, the NAME command with a [file-specification] parameter must be used to identify the disk drive and filename of the file on which to be operated. Then a LOAD command is used to read the file from disk into memory. Finally a WRITE command with no parameters writes the file from memory to disk.

Earlier in this chapter, we loaded a file into memory by placing the name of the file to be loaded after the program name when we executed the DEBUG program. Loading a file using this method also places the size of the file in bytes into the BX and CX registers and sets up the name of the file for future use by the DEBUG program for later reloading or writing of the file.

You now have enough background information to go through a few examples of creating and changing files with the DEBUG program. The following three sections show step-by-step examples of creating a new file, modifying the contents of a file, and changing the name and size of a file.

Creating a New File with DEBUG

One of the simplest files, and one which often serves a useful purpose, is a file with a single byte, the ASCII form-feed (hexadecimal 'OC') character. When this file is redirected to the printer using the MS-DOS TYPE command, it directs most printers to go to the top of the next page. For example, if the file is named ASCIIFF.TXT, the following command causes a form feed.

```
A>TYPE ASCIIFF.TXT > PRN:
```

Putting the above command in a batch file named FF.BAT directs your printer to go to the top of the next page with only three keystrokes (ff Enter) from the MS-DOS command line. Creating the ASCIIFF.TXT file is something that cannot be done with some word processors because the form-feed character is one of the ASCII control characters. Here's how to create the file using the DEBUG program:

1. Execute the DEBUG program from the MS-DOS command line.

2. Use the NAME command to give the filename ASCIIFF.TXT.

3. Use the ENTER command to enter the form-feed character (hexadecimal 'OC') at memory location X'100'.

4. Check memory location X'100' to make certain the form-feed character is correct.

5. Use the REGISTER command with the name of the CX register as a parameter RCX. The current value of CX (X'0000') is displayed. Enter a 1 to modify the contents of the CX register.

6. Check the contents of the BX and CX registers using the REGISTER command with no parameters. The BX register should contain X'0000'. The CX register should contain X'0001'. (If no filename is specified on the MS-DOS command line when the

DEBUG program is executed, the default initial value for the BX and CX registers is zero.)

    7. Use the WRITE command to write the one byte file. The message `Writing 0001 bytes` is displayed by the DEBUG program.

    8. Use the QUIT command to exit the DEBUG program.

```
A>DEBUG
-N ASCIIFF.TXT
-E 100 0C
-D 100 L 1
432B:0100  0C
-RCX
CX 0000
:1
-R
AX=0000  BX=0000  CX=0001  DX=0000  SP=FFEE  BP=0000  SI=0000  DI=0000
DS=432B  ES=432B  SS=432B  CS=432B  IP=0100   NV UP DI PL NZ NA PO NC
432B:0100 0C00          OR      AL,00
-W
Writing 0001 bytes
-Q
```

If a message other than `Writing 0001 bytes` is displayed after the WRITE command is issued, the DEBUG program failed to write the file to disk properly. The most common errors are that the disk being written to is full or that the NAME command was not used properly to specify the disk drive and filename for the file. Forgetting to use the NAME command results in the not very helpful `No room in disk directory` error message for most versions of the DEBUG program. As you were warned at the beginning of this chapter, the DEBUG program is not known for being extremely user friendly.

One short cut you can take when creating a file is to specify the name of the file on the MS-DOS command line when executing the DEBUG program. The warning message `File not found` is displayed. Ignore the message. You already know that the file doesn't exist yet. When you start the DEBUG program this way, you can skip the second step in the previous example showing how the NAME command is used to tell DEBUG the name of the file to be created.

There is no limit to the number of files you can create during one execution of the DEBUG program (unless you create enough files to exceed the capacity of your disks). Repeat the previous steps two through seven for each file to be created. If the file size does not change, you don't need to change the values in the BX and CX registers. In addition to the ENTER command, you can use the FILL and MOVE commands also to modify the data in the file to be created.

When a file is written to disk using the DEBUG program, no check is made to determine whether an existing file is being overwritten. Because *no warning is given when overwriting a file*, you can easily lose the previous contents of a file and replace it with the new file. This is one of the reasons why backing up your disks frequently is stressed several times in this chapter.

Modifying a File with DEBUG

Suppose that one day you mention to a friend that you would like to print reports that have lines more than 80 characters long on your OKIDATA MICROLINE 82a printer. Your friend says, "Here's a program I wrote called OKSMALL.COM that sends the correct control code to your printer for smaller print." After using the program several times you begin to rely on it, but to return your printer to "normal" mode, you must turn your printer off, then on again.

You want to return the printer to normal mode by using a batch file that runs unattended. You call your programmer friend and explain the problem. Her reply is, "That's no problem. Call up your OKSMALL.COM file with DEBUG, change the byte at offset one from a one-dog to a one-easy, rename the file to OKNORMAL.COM, and write it out." Whew! That's no problem? Well, it shouldn't be if you've gotten this far in the chapter.

```
A>DEBUG OKSMALL.COM
-R
AX=0000  BX=0000  CX=0008  DX=0000  SP=FFFE  BP=0000  SI=0000  DI=0000
DS=434E  ES=434E  SS=434E  CS=434E  IP=0100   NV UP DI PL NZ NA PO NC
434E:0100 B21D          MOV     DL,1D
-D 100 L 8
434E:0100  B2 1D B4 05 CD 21 CD 20                        2.4.M!M
-E 101
434E:0101  1D.1E
-D 100 L 8
434E:0100  B2 1E B4 05 CD 21 CD 20                        2.4.M!M
-N OKNORMAL.COM
-W
Writing 0008 bytes
-Q
```

After you load the original program from the MS-DOS command line when executing the DEBUG program, use the REGISTER command to check the length of the file, out of curiosity, look at the contents of the file, enter the correct value at offset X'101', display the contents of the file again to verify the change, rename the file to be written, write the file, and quit the DEBUG program.

Only seven commands are required to complete the entire operation. If you care to eliminate the steps that validate what's being done (which we do *not* recommend), you could reduce the steps to four.

Changing the Size of a File with DEBUG

The next time you talk to your programmer friend, you mention that you're happy with your new program, but now you want to use your printer with the large print font. She tells you, "That's easy. Bring up the OKSMALL.COM file with DEBUG, load the OKNORMAL.COM program at X'106', which overlays the last two bytes of OKSMALL.COM, change the byte at offset X'107' to a one-fox, change the file size to hexadecimal easy, then save the new file as OKBIG.COM." The following screen shows how to perform this task, but first let's examine a small problem that arises when you use the DEBUG program to combine two .COM files.

The catch to this approach is that the DEBUG program does not allow a file with a filename extension of .COM to be loaded into memory at any offset other than the default load offset of X'100'. You can easily circumvent this problem: Rename the file with a different filename extension, use the DEBUG program to operate on the file, then rename the file to its original name after exiting the DEBUG program. Make a copy of the file before making modifications. When renaming files, choose a new filename that is easy to remember. One solution is to use a new filename with the three letters of the filename extension reversed, for example .BAT file extensions become .TAB. You can easily remember what the original filename should be when renaming the file to its original name. Of course, this doesn't work too well with filenames having extensions of .EXE, .TXT, .SYS, etc.

The restriction of the DEBUG program that always loads files with a filename extension of .COM at offset X'100' also points out how important it is to double check any work you do with DEBUG.

The DEBUG program loads .COM files at offset X'100' *without giving any indication that it has ignored the [start-address] parameter of the LOAD command.* Because no warning message is displayed, you could assume that the load has been performed correctly.

```
A>RENAME OKNORMAL.COM OKNORMAL.MOC


A>DEBUG OKSMALL.COM
-R
AX=0000  BX=0000  CX=0008  DX=0000  SP=FFFE  BP=0000  SI=0000  DI=0000
DS=434E  ES=434E  SS=434E  CS=434E  IP=0100    NV UP DI PL NZ NA PO NC
434E:0100 B21D          MOV     DL,1D
-D 100 L 8
434E:0100  B2 1D B4 05 CD 21 CD 20                        2.4.M!M
-N OKNORMAL.MOC
-L 106
-R
AX=0000  BX=0000  CX=0008  DX=0000  SP=FFFE  BP=0000  SI=0000  DI=0000
DS=434E  ES=434E  SS=434E  CS=434E  IP=0100    NV UP DI PL NZ NA PO NC
434E:0100 B21D          MOV     DL,1D
-RCX
CX 0008
:E
-R
AX=0000  BX=0000  CX=000E  DX=0000  SP=FFFE  BP=0000  SI=0000  DI=0000
DS=434E  ES=434E  SS=434E  CS=434E  IP=0100    NV UP DI PL NZ NA PO NC
434E:0100 B21D          MOV     DL,1D
-D 100 L 0E
434E:0100  B2 1D B4 05 CD 21 B2 1E-B4 05 CD 21 CD 20      2.4.M!2.4.M!M
-E 107 1F
-D 100 L 0E
434E:0100  B2 1D B4 05 CD 21 B2 1F-B4 05 CD 21 CD 20      2.4.M!2.4.M!M
-N OKBIG.COM
-W
Writing 000E bytes
-Q


A>RENAME OKNORMAL.MOC OKNORMAL.COM
```

REMOVING END-OF-FILE CHARACTERS FROM WORDSTAR FILES

Chapter 3 discussed the problems that can be created when the MS-DOS output data redirection feature is used to append the output of a program to a file created with WordStar or other programs that use the ASCII end-of-file character (hexadecimal '1A') to indicate the end of a file. Most MS-DOS programs use the byte count in the directory entry for a file to determine the length of a file and do not require the end-of-file character to be present. If the MS-DOS output data redirection feature is used to add data to the end of a file with end-of-file characters, the appended data appears to be "lost" when the file is viewed with any of several word processors, the MS-DOS TYPE command, and several other programs that deal with text files.

The DEBUG program can be used to replace these end-of-file characters with the ASCII SPace character so that the entire file may be accessed. Several programs are available commercially and in the public domain that read a file, delete the offending characters, and write a usable copy of the file. If you have one of these programs, use it rather than DEBUG, because all of them are faster, less prone to error, and can be used "unattended" within an MS-DOS batch command file. If you don't have one of these programs, here is an example that demonstrates how to use DEBUG to replace these characters.

First, load the file to be modified into memory by typing the filename after DEBUG on the MS-DOS command line. Use the DEBUG REGISTER command to determine the size of the file in bytes in the CX register. If the file is very large, the BX register has a nonzero value. See the *Breaking the 64K Barrier* trick box for additional information on dealing with large files.

Now, use the DEBUG SEARCH command with an offset of X'100', the value in the CX register as the length parameter, and '1A' as the search data parameter. This displays a list of all addresses where the end-of-file character exists in the file. The end-of-file characters normally appear in groups of up to 127 characters. Use the DEBUG FILL command to replace each group of end-of-file characters with the SPace character (hexadecimal '20'). The most convenient form of the FILL command to use is with the [start-address] [end-address] parameters, which avoids the necessity of performing a calculation to determine the length of the group of end-of-file characters to be replaced.

Repeating the SEARCH command with the same parameters finds all groups of end-of-file characters in the file. When no more groups remain, the SEARCH command returns to the DEBUG – prompt without displaying any addresses. The file can now be written to disk with the WRITE command. You don't have to change the file size in the BX and CX registers. You may have to use your word processor to delete any extra spaces that now occur at the beginning of each section of appended data.

The following example "straightens out" a memo file that had the output of the MS-DOS DIR command appended with the MS-DOS >> redirection feature. The MS-DOS TYPE command shows the before and after versions of the file.

```
C>WS MEMO
```

```
C>DIR A: >> MEMO


C>TYPE MEMO


John,
        Here's a floppy with the files you needed. A directory
listing of the disk follows:


C>DEBUG MEMO
-R
AX=0000  BX=0000  CX=0256  DX=0000  SP=FFEE  BP=0000  SI=0000  DI=0000
DS=432B  ES=432B  SS=432B  CS=432B  IP=0100    NV UP DI PL NZ NA PO NC
432B:0100 0D0A4A           OR       AX,4A0A
-S 100 L 256 1A
432B:0177
432B:0178
432B:0179
432B:017A
432B:017B
432B:017C
432B:017D
432B:017E
432B:017F
-F 177 17F 20
-S 100 L 256 1A
-W
Writing 0256 bytes
-Q


C>TYPE MEMO


John,
        Here's a floppy with the files you needed. A directory
listing of the disk follows:


Volume in drive A has no label
Directory of  A:\BOOK


CH2            66122   8-02-86    8:52a
CH3            74246   8-20-86    9:44p
CH3NOTES        4374   8-20-86   10:38p
CH5            26625   9-03-86    1:52p
CH5NOTES        4298   8-20-86   10:35p
CH7           115712   9-01-86   10:09a
CH7NOTES       11008   8-23-86    3:23p
```

The Built-In DEBUG Hexadecimal "Calculator"

The DEBUG program's HEXADECIMAL command is a rudimentary calculator that displays the sum and difference of two hexadecimal values. The two values are given as parameters to the HEXADECIMAL command.

```
A>DEBUG
-H 6789 ABCD
1356  BBBC
-Q

A>_
```

The calculator is limited to parameter values of four hexadecimal digits, and the output values are displayed with only four hexadecimal digits. If the sum of the inputs is greater than X'FFFF', the leading 1 is truncated. For example, X'FFFF' plus X'FFFF' is displayed as X'FFFE' rather than X'1FFFE'. When the second parameter is greater than the first, the difference is displayed in *two's complement notation* so that a difference of minus one is displayed as X'FFFF' rather than – 1. As unusual as this notation may appear, it is useful to programmers. Subtracting a larger number from a smaller number is not generally useful when using the DEBUG program only for manipulating files.

The fact that the sum and difference of numbers is not displayed in a straightforward manner sometimes makes it difficult to remember which is displayed first—the sum or the difference of the numbers. Using the HEXADECIMAL command with both parameters of 1 helps refresh your memory.

```
-H 1 1
02 00
-
```

The X'02' is obviously the sum. The X'00' is obviously the difference. Therefore, the sum is displayed first.

The limited capability of DEBUG's "built-in" calculator provides some help, but in general, if you have a memory-resident program that has a hexadecimal calculator, such as Sidekick, you will certainly find it much more useful and friendly than the DEBUG HEXADECIMAL command.

MASTER
TRICK

USING DATA REDIRECTION TO CREATE AND MODIFY FILES

The DEBUG program is normally used in an interactive manner: A command is entered from the keyboard, DEBUG displays the command's output on the screen, the next command is entered, and so on. This "normal" use of DEBUG is useful for many purposes. However, combining data redirection with the DEBUG program can add greatly to its usefulness. One of the advantages to this approach is that the DEBUG program can be executed unattended from within a batch file to create or modify a file. See Chapters 2 and 3 of this book for more information on using batch command files and data redirection with MS-DOS.

For example, suppose that you have an MS-DOS batch command file that creates on disk a report file that is confidential in nature. A small degree of data security is provided by replacing the first byte of the file with an end-of-file marker. This assumes that the first character in the file is of a "noncritical" nature, such as a few spaces to center the title of the report file. When the first character of a text file is an end-of-file marker, the remainder of the file cannot be accessed by many conventional text file programs, such as the MS-DOS TYPE and EDLIN commands, most word processors, etc. When the report file needs to be accessed, the first byte of the file can be changed to another character, such as a space. This modification can also be done in a batch file with the DEBUG program.

Although this simple procedure certainly does not provide extremely "tight" security (anyone with a knowledge of DEBUG can undo it), it can be surprisingly effective in preventing most attempts to access confidential data. It also has the advantages of not being very time-consuming and not requiring you to remember *encryption keys* to regain access to the data. See Chapter 14 for more information on data encryption and file security.

If the name of the file to be *secured* is PAYROLL.RPT, the following example shows how the DEBUG program would be used "interactively" to modify the file.

```
A>DEBUG PAYROLL.RPT
-E 100 1A
-W
Writing 2B3C bytes
-Q
```

To change the first byte of the PAYROLL.RPT file to an end-of-file character within a batch file, create a small text file that has the keystrokes which would be used interactively with DEBUG. The file could be created easily with most word processors. The following example shows how to create the file using the MS-DOS COPY command.

```
A>COPY CON: SECURE.INP
E 100 1A
W
Q
^Z
```

```
A>TYPE SECURE.INP
E 100 1A
W
Q
```

Now, all that is necessary is to add a line to the batch file that creates the PAYROLL.RPT file.

```
A>DEBUG PAYROLL.RPT < SECURE.INP > NUL:
```

The SECURE.INP file is redirected into the DEBUG program to perform the desired modification to the PAYROLL.RPT file. The output is redirected to the NUL: device so that it is not displayed on the screen while DEBUG is executing. Include an ECHO OFF command in the batch file before the DEBUG program executes so that no indication that DEBUG is executing appears on the screen.

To modify the file so that it can be used normally by another program, a similar procedure to the one used to secure a file could be applied to "unsecure" the file. A redirection input file named UNSECURE.INP could be created. It would be identical to the SECURE.INP file, except that the 1A would be replaced with the characters 20, which replace the ASCII end-of-file character in the report file with an ASCII SPace character.

Another convenient use of data redirection with the DEBUG program is to create a hexadecimal "dump" file of a file you want to look at in hexadecimal format. Suppose that you want to examine a database index file named INVY.NDX but think that it would be more convenient to use your word processor to look at an image of the file in the DEBUG DUMP command format than it would be to use DEBUG.

The first step is to execute the DEBUG program interactively in order to determine the size of the file in hexadecimal bytes.

```
A>DEBUG INVY.NDX
-R
AX=0000  BX=0000  CX=1A5E  DX=0000  SP=FFFE  BP=0000  SI=0000  DI=0000
DS=434E  ES=434E  SS=434E  CS=434E  IP=0100   NV UP DI PL NZ NA PO NC
```

```
434E:0100 B21D          MOV     DL,1D
-Q
```

Now, create a file that can be used for input redirection. That file will use the DEBUG DUMP command to display a formatted dump of the entire file. When the file is created, exit the DEBUG program.

```
A>COPY CON: TEMP.INP
D 100 L 1A5E
Q
^Z
```

Executing the DEBUG program with the input redirected from the TEMP.INP file and the output redirected to the INVYNDX.DMP file creates the desired "dump image" file.

```
A>DEBUG INVY.NDX < TEMP.INP > INVYNDX.DMP
```

The DEBUG program does not necessarily create "dump" files instantly. The light on your disk drive indicates whether the program is still executing. Always take care to include the Q (QUIT command) at the end of any text files created for redirection into the DEBUG program. This avoids the annoyance of having to restart your computer using the Ctrl-Alt-Del keystroke sequence and rerunning the DEBUG program to create the desired dump file.

Using input redirection files similar to the previous one to execute the DEBUG SEARCH, COMPARE, and UNASSEMBLE commands also can be useful. You can use the UNASSEMBLE command this way to recreate an assembly language source file for a .COM program for which you have lost the original source file. The source file created by this technique does not have the original comments or symbolic names that make the assembly program easy to read. However, it is better than having no source file at all.

Using the DEBUG SEARCH Command

The DEBUG program's SEARCH command is similar in format and operation to the FILL command. Instead of filling a block of memory with a byte or string of data specified with the [data-list] parameter, the block of memory is searched for occurrences of the byte or string.

The DEBUG program displays a list of the memory addresses that contain the specified [data-list].

One limitation that must be remembered when using the SEARCH command is that the letters in the [data-list] *are* case sensitive. The following example demonstrates the problem that this limitation can cause.

```
-S 100 L800 "Acme Trucking"
```

This SEARCH command does not find any occurrences of the string ACME Trucking in the specified memory block because the letters CME are *not* the same as cme to the DEBUG program SEARCH command. If you want to search for an ASCII string in a file and are not certain of the case of any letters in the string, you must search for *all* combinations of the string that might occur.

CREATING ASSEMBLER LANGUAGE PROGRAMS WITH DEBUG

The purpose of this trick box is not to turn you into an assembly language programmer. Entire books are available to accomplish that trick. However, you will often see short but useful programs in trade magazines that can be entered using the DEBUG program. If you've avoided creating these programs because of lack of familiarity with DEBUG and the ASSEMBLE command, the following examples are presented for you.

The important thing to remember when creating a program with the ASSEMBLE command is that if you make a mistake or get lost in the process, you do no harm by exiting DEBUG and starting over.

The first program is named FF.COM. Its purpose is to output an ASCII form-feed character to the printer. The program is 8 bytes long and consists of only four assembler language statements.

```
A>DEBUG FF.COM
File not found
-A 100
434A:0100 MOV DL,0C<ENTER>
434A:0102 MOV AH,05<ENTER>
434A:0104 INT 21<ENTER>
434A:0106 INT 20<ENTER>
434A:0108 <ENTER>
-RCX
CX 0000
:8
```

```
-U 100 L 8
434A:0100 B20C          MOV     DL,0C
434A:0102 B405          MOV     AH,05
434A:0104 CD21          INT     21
434A:0106 CD20          INT     20
-R
AX=0000  BX=0000  CX=0008  DX=0000  SP=FFFE  BP=0000  SI=0000  DI=0000
DS=434A  ES=434A  SS=434A  CS=434A  IP=0100    NV UP DI PL NZ NA PO NC
434A:0100 B20C          MOV     DL,0C
-W
Writing 0008 bytes
-Q
```

First, the DEBUG program is executed with the name of the file to be created on the MS-DOS command line. The File not found warning message can be ignored. Next, the following DEBUG commands are executed:

1. The A 100 command is issued to begin assembling at offset X'100'.

2. The four assembler language statements: MOV DL,0C, MOV AH,05, INT 21, and INT 20 are entered. After each assembler language statement is entered, DEBUG displays the address where the next statement is located in memory. When there are no more assembler language statements to be entered, the Enter key is pressed to indicate that DEBUG is to return to the normal - prompt.

3. The REGISTER command with the name of the CX register is used to display the contents of the CX register and modify it with the length of the program in bytes, which is 8.

4. The UNASSEMBLE and REGISTER commands are issued to verify that the assembler statements and placement of the file length in the CX register have been performed correctly.

5. The WRITE command is issued to write the file to disk.

6. The QUIT command is used to exit DEBUG.

As you can see, creating a program with the ASSEMBLE command is very similar to creating a text file. The only differences are that the filename must have an extension of .COM and the ASSEMBLE command, rather than the ENTER, FILL, or MOVE commands, is used to place the required data in memory.

The next example creates a program using a slightly different technique: The input required to create the program is supplied by an input data redirection file rather than from the keyboard. This program is named BEEP.COM and, when executed, causes a short beep tone to be generated. First, to create the file BEEP.COM file, the input file to be redirected into DEBUG is created.

```
A>COPY CON: BEEP.INP
N BEEP.COM
A 100
MOV   DL,07
MOV   AH,02
INT   21
INT   20


RCX
8
W
Q
^Z
```

It is important to include the blank line that follows the INT 20 assembler statement. The file BEEP.INP can now be redirected into the DEBUG program to create the BEEP.COM file.

```
A>DEBUG < BEEP.INP
-N BEEP.COM
-A 100
432B:0100 MOV       DL,07
432B:0102 MOV       AH,02
432B:0104 INT       21
432B:0106 INT       20
432B:0108
-RCX
CX 0000
:8
-W
Writing 0008 bytes
-Q
```

Notice how nice it is to sit back and watch as the DEBUG program does all the work. The contents of the file may be verified by using the DEBUG program to unassemble the program and check its length.

```
A>DEBUG BEEP.COM
-R
AX=0000  BX=0000  CX=0008  DX=0000  SP=FFFE  BP=0000  SI=0000  DI=0000
DS=434A  ES=434A  SS=434A  CS=434A  IP=0100   NV UP DI PL NZ NA PO NC
434A:0100 B207          MOV       DL,07
-U 100 L 8
434A:0100 B207          MOV       DL,07
434A:0102 B402          MOV       AH,02
434A:0104 CD21          INT       21
434A:0106 CD20          INT       20
-Q
```

Using the DEBUG COMPARE Command

The DEBUG program's COMPARE command is used to compare the contents of two blocks of memory. The formats for the command are

```
C [start-address1] [end-address1] [start-address2]
```

```
C [start-address1] [length] [start-address2]
```

Both blocks of memory must be of the same length, so the size and ending address of the second block is determined by the size of the first block. Any differences between the two blocks of memory are displayed in the form:

```
addr1  byte1  byte2  addr2
```

The first two entries on each line indicate the address and value of the byte at that address for bytes in the first block of memory that do not have the same value as the corresponding byte in the second block. The second two entries on each line indicate the value and address of the byte at that address for the byte in the second block of memory. Each occurrence of bytes that do not have matching values are displayed on a new line. All addresses are in the *segment:offset* format. If no differences between the two blocks of memory are found, no special message is given, and DEBUG returns to the – prompt.

MASTER TRICK

BREAKING THE 64K BARRIER

This trick box describes how to access memory outside the current default segment supplied by the DEBUG program. First, a description of the *segmented architecture* of the IBM PC is presented, followed by examples that use addresses with the [segment] notation.

The IBM PC and its close compatibles, which are the most common computer systems on which the MS-DOS operating system is used, can directly access one megabyte of memory. One megabyte is equivalent to 1,048,576 decimal or 100000 hexadecimal bytes. An *address* is a numerical value that indicates the location of a given byte in memory. It would be convenient if these addresses were numbers ranging from X'00000' through

X'FFFFF'. Unfortunately, due to the segmented architecture of the INTEL 8088/8086 family of central processing unit (CPU) chips used in the IBM PC XT and AT series of personal computers, the addressing scheme is not that simple. Addresses for the IBM PC are in the form *segment:offset*, where the values for a segment and an offset may be in the range from X'0000' through X'FFFF'.

A *segment* is a block of X'10000' bytes of memory. Each byte within the segment can be addressed with an *offset* in the range X'0000' through X'FFFF'. Each segment is aligned on a 16 (decimal) byte boundary, so that segment X'0000' consists of bytes X'0000' through X'FFFF', segment X'0001' consists of bytes X'0010' through X'1000F', segment X'0002' consists of bytes X'0020' through X'1001F', etc. Consequently, there is a considerable amount of overlap between segments. For example, the last 32,520 (decimal) bytes of the 32,536 bytes in segment zero are the first 32,520 bytes in segment one.

The first byte in segment one is referenced (pointed to) with the address 0001:0000. The same byte is also pointed to with the address 0000:0010. In fact, any byte in memory may be referenced with 4096 (decimal) unique [segment:offset] combinations. Adding X'10' to the offset portion of an address and subtracting X'1' from the segment portion yields an equivalent address. Conversely, subtracting X'10' from the offset of an address and adding X'1' to the segment portion of the address also yields an equivalent address.

These *synonyms* for addresses mean that there is more than one way to derive an address in order to examine the byte at offset X'500' in a file. The most straightforward method is to add X'500' to the offset of the address where the file was loaded in memory. For example, if the file was loaded into memory at address 3A40:0100, the byte at offset X'500' is at memory address 3A40:0600. Adding X'50' to the segment portion of the address also yields an equivalent address so that the addresses 3A90:0100 and 3A40:0600 reference the same memory location.

When a file larger than 64K bytes (65,536 decimal bytes) is loaded into memory with the DEBUG program, referencing the 65,537th decimal byte of the file would require adding X'10000' to the offset of the address where the file was loaded into memory. If the file was loaded into memory at 3A40:0100, the address required to reference the 65,537th byte would be 3A40:10100. Because an offset cannot be greater than X'FFFF', the address 3A40:10100 is not valid. However, the same byte may be referenced by adding X'1000' to the segment of the address. Therefore, 4A40:0100 is a valid address that references the 65,537th byte of the file.

Working with memory addresses in the [segment:offset] format is not as convenient as the more straightforward *offset* only format. However, examining and modifying files larger than 64K bytes becomes easier with practice.

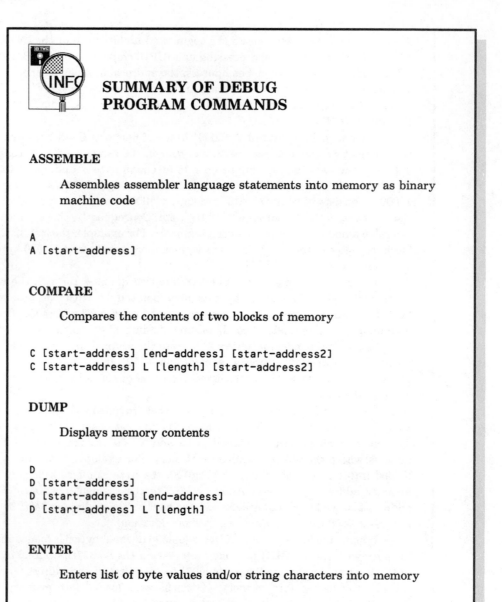

SUMMARY OF DEBUG PROGRAM COMMANDS

ASSEMBLE

Assembles assembler language statements into memory as binary machine code

```
A
A [start-address]
```

COMPARE

Compares the contents of two blocks of memory

```
C [start-address] [end-address] [start-address2]
C [start-address] L [length] [start-address2]
```

DUMP

Displays memory contents

```
D
D [start-address]
D [start-address] [end-address]
D [start-address] L [length]
```

ENTER

Enters list of byte values and/or string characters into memory

```
E [start-address] [data-list]
```

Displays and, if desired, changes memory contents

```
E [start-address]
```

FILL

Fills block of memory with list of byte values and/or string characters

```
F [start-address] [end-address] [data-list]
F [start-address] L [length] [data-list]
```

GO

Begins program execution

```
G
G=[start-address]
G=[breakpoint(s)]
G=[start-address] [breakpoint(s)]
```

HEXADECIMAL

Displays the sum and difference of two hexadecimal numbers

```
H [number1] [number2]
```

INPUT

Reads and displays a byte from a port

```
I [port-address]
```

LOAD

Loads a file into memory

```
L
L [start-address]
```

Loads sector(s) into memory

```
L [drive] [sector-number] [sector-count]
L [start-address] [drive] [sector-number] [sector-count]
```

MOVE

Copies a block of data from one memory location to another

```
M [start-address] [end-address] [start-address2]
M [start-address] L [length] [start-address2]
```

NAME

Names a file

```
N [filespec]
```

Names a parameter list

```
N [parameter-list]
```

OUTPUT

Sends a byte value to a port

```
O [port-address] [byte]
```

QUIT

Exits the DEBUG program

```
Q
```

REGISTER

Displays the contents of registers and status flags

```
R
```

Displays and, if desired, allows modification to the contents of a register

```
R [register-name]
```

Displays and changes, if desired, the status flags

```
RF
```

SEARCH

Searches a block of memory for a list of byte values and/or string characters

```
S [start-address] [end-address] [data-list]
S [start-address] L [length] [data-list]
```

TRACE

Executes one machine instruction

```
T
T=[start-address]
```

Executes a number of machine instructions

```
T [number]
T=[start-address] [number]
```

UNASSEMBLE

Unassembles binary machine code into assembly language
statements

```
U
U [start-address]
U [start-address] [end-address]
U [start-address] L [length]
```

WRITE

Writes a file to disk

```
W
W [start-address]
```

Writes to sector(s) on disk

```
W [drive] [sector-number] [number-count]
W [start-address] [drive] [sector-number] [number-count]
```

Summary

This chapter has presented an extensive tutorial for the MS-DOS
DEBUG program. The orientation of the chapter has not been how to
debug programs with DEBUG, but rather how to use the DEBUG
program to manipulate files by taking advantage of its low-level access
method of dealing with files. Several trick boxes presented additional
functions that can be performed using the DEBUG program, including how to use the ASSEMBLE command to create small program

files that are presented in the popular computing magazines. This is an excellent way to obtain small but useful programs for your computer system at no cost. The next chapter, *Obtaining and Using Free and Low-Cost Software*, describes an easy way to obtain useful larger programs for your system.

Obtaining and Using Free and Low-Cost Software

Chapter 8

One of the many advantages afforded to MS-DOS users is the availability of software. Although selecting the right program for your needs from such a variety is often confusing and frustrating, the very fact of there being so many options is what usually attracts microcomputer users to the MS-DOS operating system in the first place. On the other hand, most of the commercial programs available provide solutions to "big" problems, such as word processing or database management, but rarely provide the "little" solutions to things that MS-DOS and its commands are incapable of handling.

Two categories of free and low-cost MS-DOS software that are often overlooked are *public domain* and *user-supported* software. This chapter summarizes some public domain and user-supported programs that the authors have often found indispensable.

Public domain programs are programs written by people who, for one reason or another, have decided not to market the programs commercially and instead have donated them to the public. These programs then change hands and are distributed by the public, usually without any direct costs involved. The "public" in this case refers to those people who know what public domain programs are and where to find them. User-supported programs, sometimes called "Freeware" or "Shareware," also are distributed through public domain channels, under the premise that if the user finds the program useful, he or she is requested to make a reasonable donation to the author. In many cases, user-supported programs are good enough to be marketed commercially, but because of the costs involved, the author decided to use low-cost methods of distribution.

It is unfortunate that in the busy world we live in, many people do not take advantage of this resource. Public domain and user-supported programs are often ignored either because users are suspicious of the software's quality or because they simply don't have the time to hassle with it. Indeed, sifting through hundreds of programs with little or no documentation can be time-consuming. But very often, all it takes is a few hours to go through the programs and extract those you think might be useful or, at least, interesting. You'll be surprised at what you find. Frequently, programs can be found that solve a problem that's been nagging you for a long time. If you haven't the time or desire to write the program, or you haven't been able to find a commercial program that does the trick, the chances are quite good that you can find just what you've been looking for in the public domain. Why spend lots of time developing a program to solve a problem when others have probably already done it and have donated their program to the public domain?

Because literally thousands of public-domain and user-supported programs are available for MS-DOS, the programs described in this chapter represent a very small percentage of the programs available.

Public Domain Software

Public domain programs, as explained previously, are programs donated to the public for anyone to use free of charge. One reason for their lack of use is that many people don't know how to obtain them. You can obtain public domain programs in four basic ways.

1. By accessing one of the many electronic bulletin board systems nationwide that contain MS-DOS programs and using a modem to download the files you want.

2. By joining a user group that deals specifically with the MS-DOS operating system and copying the files you want from its library of public domain programs.

3. By buying or renting disks from a large library of public domain and user-supported software. An organization that maintains a large library of MS-DOS and IBM PC public domain programs is called the *PC Special Interest Group* (or PC-SIG). A

good way to find what's available is to obtain the PC-SIG library catalog, which describes over 500 floppy disks containing public domain and user-supported programs. Many of the PC-SIG library programs can also be found on bulletin board systems and user group libraries. See Appendix B for more information about PC-SIG and other similar organizations.

4. By copying the files from friends who have encountered useful programs during their searches through the various public domain sources.

If you find yourself really "getting into" public domain programs, you'll probably be obtaining the programs from two or more of the sources listed previously. For example, you can obtain the PC-SIG library catalog, then use it as a guide to determine what files to look for when communicating with bulletin board systems.

Using Public Domain Programs in Business Environments

Certain ethical questions about the use of public domain programs need to be addressed. Because public domain programs are meant to be free to anyone (with the occasional exception of a nominal fee for the magnetic media the programs come on), some shady areas can be entered into when the programs are used in a business environment. Although everyone may use the programs for their own use, it is considered highly unethical to resell a public domain program with a company's product or to include it as part of a commercial package as an added "free" feature. This doesn't mean that business users mustn't use public domain programs for their own use. But people should be extremely careful when they "give" programs to their customers: It must be 100 percent understood that the programs given away are completely free of charge and that they are in no way being used for promotion or marketing of a commercial product. Public domain programs should never be given away to promote or advertise a commercial product without express permission from the author. Furthermore, it must be completely clear to customers obtaining these programs that they are public domain and that they must never be sold to anyone. They can only be given away free of charge.

"User-Supported" Software

Another category of software is called *user-supported*, also known occasionally as *freeware* or *shareware*. User-supported programs are initially distributed free of charge through public domain distribution channels. Usually in the documentation accompanying the programs, however, is a statement to the effect that if you find the program useful, a suggested "donation" or fee be paid to the program's originators, generally in the range of $10 to $40. In some cases, the originators of the programs specify a "registration fee" that's required if the programs are going to be used in a commercial environment, whereas individual users may use the programs for noncommercial purposes as if they were public domain programs. No one is legally responsible for paying the fees or donations, but, needless to say, *everyone* is responsible on ethical grounds if they use the programs extensively and get good use out of them.

One of the big advantages that user-supported programs have over commercial software, apart from lower cost, is that user-supported programs provide the user with the opportunity to try the programs before paying for them. The way user-supported programs are distributed and the way their authors recover their costs are based strictly on the honor system. In many cases, potential users of user-supported software are enticed into paying with the promise that they'll be registered users entitled to receive the "official" documentation and free software updates (via mail) for a predetermined period of time. In this time of software piracy, copy protection, and general unethical (and illegal) use of software, user-supported software is a welcome and pleasant alternative to the generally overpriced commercial software with which we're continually faced.

The remainder of this chapter consists of brief descriptions of public domain and user-supported programs that the authors have found useful. Many of the programs provide solutions to the "little" problems encountered in the MS-DOS operating system. To many users, these little problems can turn into big problems, representing facilities that Microsoft Corporation (the manufacturer of MS-DOS), IBM Corporation, and the various companies that implement versions of MS-DOS for their machines "forgot" to include, such as displaying and modifying file attributes, renaming subdirectories, recovering erased files, enhancing subdirectory path searching, and enhancing the operation of batch files. Depending on your needs, many other utilities with varying degrees of usefulness are available.

Useful File- and Directory-Related Programs

The following information boxes describe a variety of file-related programs, which are public domain or user supported. "File related" refers to programs entered at the MS-DOS prompt that in one way or another manipulate files, providing functions such as displaying sorted directories, changing file attributes, dealing with subdirectories, and so on.

Advanced Directory Programs

Are you frequently frustrated at not being able to get the DIR command to display your directory the way you want despite using all the options, such as /W, and including the SORT filter? Several "super directory" programs are available in the public domain that go beyond the capabilities of DIR. SDIR.COM Version 2.41 is one of them: It displays the directory in two sorted columns, pausing at each full screen, and includes columns showing each file's size and time-date stamp. In addition to showing the remaining space on the disk, as does DIR, SDIR also displays the total size of all files displayed, which DIR does not do! Knowing the total size of all the files displayed is useful if you need to copy all the files to a disk with limited free space and you want to verify that they'll all fit. SDIR is also capable of displaying any attributes assigned to files: the *hidden, read-only, system*, and *archive* attributes. The following is a summary of the SDIR command and how it is used.

SDIR PROGRAM

PROGRAM: SDIR.COM (or SDIR24.COM; might be archived with source code and documentation in SDIR24.ARC or SDIR24.LBR)

CATEGORY: Public domain

AUTHOR: John F. Ratti

SYSTEM REQUIREMENTS: MS-DOS Version 2.00 or higher

SYNTAX: SDIR [filespec] [/options]
    default [filespec] is *.* (default drive) sorted by [filename.ext],
    without screen erase, and pauses at each full screen

OPTIONS: */A—List hidden files
    */E—Clear screen before displaying directory
    */P—Don't pause when screen is full
    /X—Sort by extension
    /S—Sort by size
    /D—Sort by date and time
    /N—Do not sort: use original order

    * = Option may be combined with other options

An alternate super-directory program to SDIR Version 2.41, is SDIR50.COM. It is very similar to SDIR.COM except that it is capable of storing the directory in a buffer so that you can use the PgUp and PgDn keys to scroll back and forth while the program is active. The following is a brief overview of the program.

SDIR50 PROGRAM

PROGRAM: SDIR50.COM (or D.COM; might be archived with documentation in SDIR50.ARC or SDIR50.LBR)

CATEGORY: User supported

AUTHOR: W. Lawrence Hatt

SYSTEM REQUIREMENTS: IBM PC or close compatible MS-DOS Version 2.00 or higher 128K RAM for "Command Mode"

SYNTAX: SDIR [filespec] [/options]

    default [filespec] is *.* (default drive) sorted by filename.ext

OPTIONS: /A—List hidden files
    /C—Single-column commented directory
    /X—Sort by extension
    /S—Sort by size

/D—Sort by date-time

/N—Do not sort, original order

Note: The /C option creates a file called SDIR.$$$ containing comments typed about the files displayed.

COMMANDS: PgDn scrolls down through directory

PgUp scrolls up through directory

Esc terminates program and exits to MS-DOS

/ key activates "command mode" with the following commands:

COPY   Copy files between drives and subdirectories

DEL   Delete selected files?

LOOK   Examine contents of any ASCII or WordStar text file

R   Change the read-only attribute status

A   Change the archive attribute status

GO   Execute any .COM, .EXE, or .BAS file

Moving Files

When trying to "move" files to another disk or directory, no doubt you've often gone through the tedious task of copying each file, then deleting it? The MOVE.COM command makes this task considerably easier. When you specify the correct parameter, MOVE copies the files you specify, then automatically deletes the original files. The following is a summary of how it is used.

MOVE PROGRAM

PROGRAM: MOVE.COM (might be archived with documentation in MOVE.ARC or MOVE.LBR)

CATEGORY: Public domain

AUTHOR: Lewis Haupt

SYSTEM REQUIREMENTS: MS-DOS Version 2.00 or higher

SYNTAX: MOVE [filespec] [target directory] [/options]

[filespec] includes drive, directory path, and filename. * and ? wildcards are permitted. The [target directory] includes the drive and directory path.

OPTIONS: Each option is entered preceded either with a / or –. Options are

Erase—Erase each file after it is copied

Yes—Cause automatic Yes responses to each query

Terse—Suppress display of version message and instructions

An option may be abbreviated to its first character (for example, /Erase may be entered as /E, /Yes as /Y, etc.).

USING MOVE: If no options are specified with the MOVE command, it prompts you for each file, in response to which you enter Yes or No to specify whether a file is to be copied. None of the files are deleted. When prompted to copy a file, you may press the Esc key to cancel the MOVE command at that point. If you use the /Yes option, yes answers are entered automatically for you at each file's prompt. Only when the /Erase option is used are the files deleted after they've been copied. The /Yes and /Erase options can be used together to completely automate the operation of the MOVE command.

Locating Files in a Directory Tree Structure

Once a hard disk has been set up with a complex directory tree structure and many files have been stored all over the disk, a time comes when we want to locate a particular file but don't want to spend the time searching manually through each subdirectory. Other times, we may want to search for all files with a certain extension and find out in which subdirectories each is located. A very useful program called WHEREIS.COM solves these problems. WHEREIS.COM searches through all directories on the current drive for the [filespec] specified. The [filespec] in this case can be a full filename with extension. The * wildcard can be used to substitute for the filename or extension. Each time WHEREIS.COM locates a file matching the [filespec] description, it displays the full directory path of the directory in which the file is stored, including the full filename and extension. A faster version of WHEREIS.COM is called WHEREIS2.COM.

WHEREIS PROGRAM

PROGRAM: WHEREIS.COM (or WHEREIS2.COM; might be archived with documentation in a file called WHEREIS.ARC, WHEREIS2.ARC, WHEREIS.LBR, or WHEREIS2.LBR)

CATEGORY: Public domain

AUTHOR: John Socha

SYSTEM REQUIREMENTS: MS-DOS Version 2.00 or higher

SYNTAX: WHEREIS [filespec]

[filespec] is any filename with or without extension. The * wildcard may be used. A drive name and directory path must not be used.

OPTIONS: None

USING WHEREIS: The WHEREIS command may be entered within a subdirectory, and it searches the entire disk. Note, however, that WHEREIS searches only the current drive. A drive name other than the default must not be specified. Note also that the * wildcard may not replace a partial filename or extension (that is, combined with other characters). This wildcard may only replace other characters. For example, WHEREIS *.DAT or WHEREIS FINDME.* are valid, whereas WHEREIS ALL*.DR* is not.

An alternative to the WHEREIS.COM and WHEREIS2.COM programs is called FINDIT.COM. FINDIT.COM is faster than both versions of WHEREIS and makes better use of the wildcard characters. Additionally, a drive name other than the default can be used with FINDIT to cause the search to be made on a specified drive.

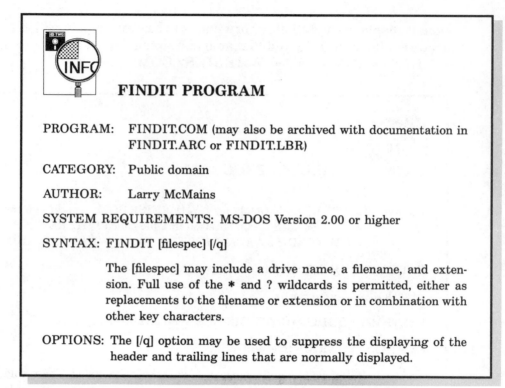

FINDIT PROGRAM

PROGRAM: FINDIT.COM (may also be archived with documentation in FINDIT.ARC or FINDIT.LBR)

CATEGORY: Public domain

AUTHOR: Larry McMains

SYSTEM REQUIREMENTS: MS-DOS Version 2.00 or higher

SYNTAX: FINDIT [filespec] [/q]

> The [filespec] may include a drive name, a filename, and extension. Full use of the * and ? wildcards is permitted, either as replacements to the filename or extension or in combination with other key characters.

OPTIONS: The [/q] option may be used to suppress the displaying of the header and trailing lines that are normally displayed.

Changing File Attributes

Before the introduction of MS-DOS Version 3.00, no command was provided with MS-DOS to deal with the file attributes archive, read-only, hidden, and system. Not only could the attributes not be changed, but they could not even be detected unless nonstandard programs were used. In MS-DOS Version 3.00 and higher versions, the ATTRIB command is provided to change the read-only and archive attributes. However, ATTRIB is not capable of changing the hidden and system attributes. Additionally, none of the MS-DOS versions provide a "standard" way of displaying a directory so that file attributes are also displayed, including those with the hidden and system attributes assigned. Fortunately, a few programs are available that are capable of displaying and changing file attributes. The two "super directory" programs SDIR24 and SDIR50 described previously are capable, when using certain options, of displaying all files in a directory, including hidden files, along with any attributes assigned. Another very useful public domain program called ALTER.COM is capable of actually *changing* file attributes.

There are many instances where you may want to change a file's attributes. One example might be to set the read-only attribute on important files to prevent them from being inadvertently erased. You also may want to disable the hidden attribute on certain files so that they can be copied to another disk or to access them for some other purpose. If you use the MS-DOS BACKUP and RESTORE commands extensively, you may want to, on occasion, change the archive attribute status of files. Whatever the reason, the ALTER command can be very useful regardless of the version of the MS-DOS you're presently using.

ALTER PROGRAM

PROGRAM: ALTER.COM (may also be archived with documentation in ALTER.ARC or ALTER.LBR)

CATEGORY: Public domain

AUTHOR: T. A. Davis

SYSTEM REQUIREMENTS: MS-DOS Version 2.00 or higher

SYNTAX: ALTER [filespec] [/options]
                        or
              ALTER [directory path] [/options]

The [filespec] may consist of the drive, directory path, filename, and extension. Note that wildcards may not be used. The [directory path] consists of only the drive and the directory path.)

OPTIONS: /V—Make ALTER function interactively, causing the current attributes set for the file to be displayed, and prompting you for new attribute settings

/N—Cause all attributes of the file or subdirectory, except the archive attribute, to be removed

/R—Set the file's read-only attribute

/A—Remove the file's archive attribute

/B—Set the file's archive attribute

/H—Set the hidden attribute of a file or subdirectory

/S—Set the file's system attribute

USING ALTER: In addition to changing the attributes of files, you can also make a subdirectory "secret" by setting its hidden attribute. A secret subdirectory can still be accessed as normal, but it isn't displayed in a directory listing when you use the DIR command. However, secret subdirectories are still displayed when you use the SDIR24 or SDIR50 public domain programs with the /D option. Note also that the secrecy of hidden subdirectories should not be depended on too much because the DIR command is capable of displaying the *contents* of a subdirectory if the subdirectory's name is specified with the command.

Changing the Date and Time Stamps of Files

If you frequently rely on the date and time stamps of files for information as to when a file was created or last modified, you will find it useful to be able to change the information when you need to. The user-supported program REDATE is just such a program. You can use it to change the time and date stamps of newly created or edited files that have erroneous stamps due to the system clock being incorrectly set. Or you can use it to set the same time and date on a group of files that are to be copied to a floppy disk for a customer or for distribution.

REDATE PROGRAM

PROGRAM: REDATE.COM (includes REDATE.HLP and REDATE.DOC. All three files may be archived in REDATE.ARC or REDATE.LBR)

CATEGORY: User supported

AUTHOR: Thomas Tuerke

SYSTEM REQUIREMENTS: Runs under any version of MS-DOS

SYNTAX: REDATE [/option] [filespec]

OPTIONS: /SUMMARY—Display information on how to use REDATE

/NONE—Remove any date and time (set all zeros)

/LIST—Set the file's date and time to that currently set in the system

/QUIET—Same as /LIST but without displaying any information

Comparing the Contents of Two Subdirectories

If you extensively use tree-structured directories, you may want to go beyond the simple comparison of two files and compare the contents of two directories. The public domain program DIRCOMP.COM can be used for this purpose.

DIRCOMP PROGRAM

PROGRAM: DIRCOMP.COM

CATEGORY: Public domain

AUTHOR: Pingching Lee (Corona Data Systems)

SYSTEM REQUIREMENTS: MS-DOS Version 2.00 or higher

SYNTAX: DIRCOMP [1st directory path] [2nd directory path]

OPTIONS: None

USING DIRCOMP: To use DIRCOMP, follow the command with the directory pathnames of the two subdirectories that you wish to compare. DIRCOMP subsequently displays information about which files existing in both subdirectories are the same and which are not.

Making Subdirectories Secret

If you are dealing with many sensitive or confidential files, one method you can use to make them difficult to find is to place the files into "secret" subdirectories. Secret subdirectories do not show in the directory listing displayed by DIR command or other directory command. The following describes three public domain programs for making, changing, and removing secret subdirectories.

MDSECRET, CDSECRET, AND RDSECRET PROGRAMS

PROGRAMS: MDSECRET.COM, CDSECRET.COM, RDSECRET.COM

CATEGORY: Public domain

AUTHOR: Unknown

SYSTEM REQUIREMENTS: MS-DOS Version 2.0 or above

SYNTAX: Command is entered with no parameters. Subdirectory name is entered in response to prompt that is displayed subsequently.

OPTIONS: None

USING MDSECRET, RDSECRET, AND RDSECRET:
These three programs are analogous to the standard MS-DOS MD (MKDIR), CD (CHDIR), and RD (RMDIR) commands, except that the subdirectory name is entered in response to a prompt that is subsequently displayed instead of being entered on the command line. Because the existence of secret subdirectories cannot be verified by using normal MS-DOS commands, don't forget a secret subdirectory's name.

Excluding Files from Wildcard File Specifications

Have you ever wanted to specify exceptions to wildcard file operations? Many times, it would be easier to say, "copy all files except these" rather than individually copying several files when you'd like *most* but not all files copied. The following very useful utility solves this problem.

NO PROGRAM

PROGRAM: NO.COM

CATEGORY: Public domain

AUTHOR: Charles Petzold (published in *PC Magazine,* Vol. 5, No. 9 (May 13, 1986)

SYSTEM REQUIREMENTS: MS-DOS Version 2.0 and above

SYNTAX: NO [file] [other command]
NO [file1] NO [file2] .... [other command]
NO [files (wildcards)] [other command]

OPTIONS: None

USING NO: The NO command provides a way to specify file exclusions from the operation of any other MS-DOS command. For example, if you wanted to copy all files except those ending in .BAK, you would enter NO *.BAK COPY *.* B:/V. If you wanted to copy all files except those ending .BAK and .BKP, the NO command can be used several times on the command line before the regular command, such as NO *.BAK NO *.BKP COPY *.* B:/V. Note, however, that any path or drive name you specify with the regular command also *must* be included with all occurrences of NO on the command line. For example, if you wish to copy from C:\UTILS, and you wanted certain files excluded, you would enter NO C:\UTILS*.BAK NO C:\UTILS*.DOC COPY C:\UTILS*.* C:\TEMP/V.

Globally Affecting All Directories with a Command

Sometimes it would be useful to have an MS-DOS command globally affect all subdirectories on disk, although this is a potentially dangerous affect. The following shows how you can accomplish this.

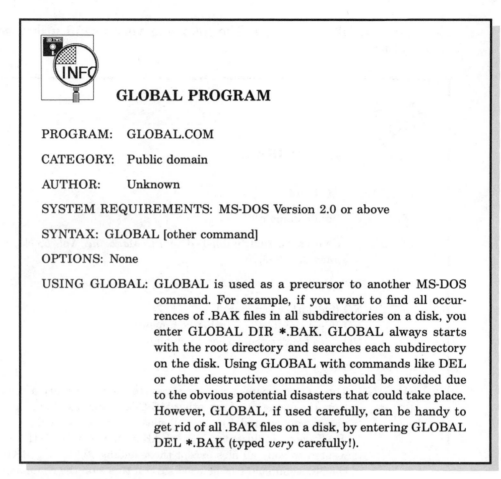

GLOBAL PROGRAM

PROGRAM: GLOBAL.COM

CATEGORY: Public domain

AUTHOR: Unknown

SYSTEM REQUIREMENTS: MS-DOS Version 2.0 or above

SYNTAX: GLOBAL [other command]

OPTIONS: None

USING GLOBAL: GLOBAL is used as a precursor to another MS-DOS command. For example, if you want to find all occurrences of .BAK files in all subdirectories on a disk, you enter GLOBAL DIR *.BAK. GLOBAL always starts with the root directory and searches each subdirectory on the disk. Using GLOBAL with commands like DEL or other destructive commands should be avoided due to the obvious potential disasters that could take place. However, GLOBAL, if used carefully, can be handy to get rid of all .BAK files on a disk, by entering GLOBAL DEL *.BAK (typed *very* carefully!).

Cutting Down on the Amount of Space Occupied by Files

The following programs can be used to make files smaller, a process commonly referred to as "squeezing" files. Squeezing files is useful if you have several files you don't use a lot but want stored on a particular disk for later use. Files that are squeezed are reduced in size anywhere between 1 percent and over 50 percent, depending on the efficiency of the squeezing program and the type of file being squeezed. Program (.COM and .EXE) files normally are not reduced in size as much as data files with a lot of repeating characters or text files. Additionally, squeezed program files cannot be run, and squeezed text files cannot be viewed, until they are "unsqueezed." The ability to squeeze files is also very useful if you're transferring files over a modem to another computer, and you want to cut down on the transfer time and phone connection costs.

SQ AND USQ PROGRAMS

PROGRAMS: SQ.COM and USQ.COM

CATEGORY: Public domain

AUTHOR: Unknown

SYSTEM REQUIREMENTS: Most versions of SQ.COM and USQ.COM work under all versions of MS-DOS

SYNTAX: SQ [filename]
        USQ [filename]

OPTIONS: None

USING SQ AND USQ:

To squeeze a file, enter SQ followed by the name of the file. SQ analyzes the file, then writes to the disk a squeezed version of the file. The name of the squeezed file is the same as the original file, except Q is substituted for the middle character of the file's extension (or type). If the original file doesn't have an extension, SQ gives the squeezed file the extension .Q, and the original file is not deleted. For example, if you wanted to squeeze the file CHAPTER1.TXT, the resulting squeezed file would be called CHAPTER1.TQT. To unsqueeze a file, use the USQ command, followed by the complete name of the squeezed file. For example, to unsqueeze the file VERSES.TQT, enter USQ VERSES.TQT. When a file is squeezed with SQ, the original name of the file is stored in the resulting squeezed file so that when USQ is used to unsqueeze the file again, the original filename is restored. Several versions of SQ and USQ have been in the public domain. Although most versions of USQ are compatible with the various versions of SQ, don't always assume compatibility. If you've obtained a given version of SQ, make sure you have a compatible version of USQ as well.

Archiving Several Files into One File

In addition to the file squeezers described previously, several utilities are available that can place several files into a single archive file for later retrieval. The most popular programs available through public domain channels are LU (librarian utility) and ARC (archiver). The main difference between these two programs is that LU places the files intact into the archive file, whereas ARC squeezes the files in the process. Knowing about these two programs is especially important if you do a lot of communicating with electronic bulletin board systems (BBS) over your modem. Many of the downloadable files contained in these BBS systems were previously archived either using LU (files with the extension .LBR) or ARC (files with the extension .ARC). You need to obtain both these archiving programs if you download archive-type files. Most BBS systems have LU and ARC available for downloading to your system.

LU (OR LU87) PROGRAM

PROGRAM: LU.EXE (or LU87.EXE)

CATEGORY: Public domain

AUTHOR: Tom Jennings and Paul Homchick

SYSTEM REQUIREMENTS: No special requirements

SYNTAX: LU –[action] [archive-file] [first-file] ....[last-file]

OPTIONS: for –[action]

    t or l List of files in LBR file
    a   Extract all files from the LBR file
    e   Extract file(s) from LBR file
    u   Add to or create LBR file (wildcards ok)
    d   Delete a file from LBR file
    r   Reorganize the LBR file
    s   Stamp LBR file with directory update date

USING LU: Several files can be archived into a single file by entering LU followed by a hyphen (–) and a single character that indicates the action you want performed, the name of the archive file (no need for an extension because .LBR is assumed), then all the files you want included in the archive (each interspersed with a space). The files archived by LU are stored intact in the archive file and are not squeezed. However, you can archive files previously squeezed with SQ (described previously).

ARC PROGRAM

PROGRAM: ARC.EXE

CATEGORY: User supported (fee required for commercial use)

AUTHOR: System Enhancement Associates

SYSTEM REQUIREMENTS: No special requirements

SYNTAX: ARC [action] [archive-file] [first-file] ... [last-file]

OPTIONS: for [action]

a	Add files to archive
m	Move files to archive
u	Update files in archive
f	Freshen files in archive
d	Delete files from archive
x or e	Extract files from archive
r	Run files from archive
p	Copy files from archive to standard output
l	List files in archive
v	Verbose listing of files in archive
t	Test archive integrity
c	Convert entry to new packing method

The following actions may be used to alter how the above actions work with [action]:

b	Retain backup copy of archive
s	Suppress compression (store only)
w	Suppress warning messages
n	Suppress notes and comments
g	Encode or decode archive entry

USING ARC: Many users of MS-DOS systems find ARC one of the most useful utilities they've ever encountered. One reason is because ARC is extremely efficient in the way it archives files into one file. It not only places many files into a single file, but also squeezes them in the process, automatically selecting one of three squeezing methods according to the nature of the file data encountered by ARC. ARC is usually more efficient at file squeezing than other programs, such as SQ. Files are squeezed on average by about 30 percent, with individual files sometimes squeezed by as much as 90 percent. When files are archived using ARC, one of the following squeezing methods is used for each file:

1. No compression—the file is stored as is. Either the file is too small or complex to be compressed or an explicit action was specified with the command that prevented file compression.

2. Repeated-character compression—repeated sequences of the same byte value are collapsed into a three-byte code sequence.

3. Huffman squeezing—the file is compressed into variable length bit strings, similar to the method used by the SQ programs.

4. Dynamic Lempel-Zev compression—the file is stored as a series of variable size bit codes that represent character strings and are created "on the fly."

It is not uncommon to see users who use ARC extensively to archive seldom-used files on a hard disk, nor is it uncommon to see 20Mb hard disks that have 30Mb to 35Mb of file data, much of which is archived. ARC is the type of program that once you start using it, you'll never stop. It is highly recommended for any MS-DOS machine.

Useful Disk-Related Programs

The following describes several programs that deal with disks in general, as opposed to specifically with files.

EFFIC PROGRAM

PROGRAM: EFFIC.COM

CATEGORY: Public domain

AUTHOR: Unknown

SYSTEM REQUIREMENTS: MS-DOS Version 2.0 or above

SYNTAX: EFFIC –[options] [>result file]

OPTIONS: –S [Drive:Path] Start in the specified drive and directory

–R	Search recursively, down all subdirectories found
–Q	Quiet mode: report only noncontiguous files
–A	Automatic mode: analyzes entire default drive quietly
–?	Display help message

USING EFFIC: EFFIC measures the storage efficiency of any group of files on any floppy or hard disk supported by MS-DOS. It returns a list of files with the number of clusters used, the number of noncontiguous clusters, and a measure of the efficiency of storage as it will affect read/write performance. If all clusters are contiguous, the efficiency is rated as 100 percent. Otherwise, the efficiency is downgraded by the percentage of clusters that are noncontiguous.

If no options are specified, the files in the current drive and directory are analyzed, and a report listing all files found is written to the standard output. You can redirect the output of EFFIC to an output file using the MS-DOS output redirection symbol >.

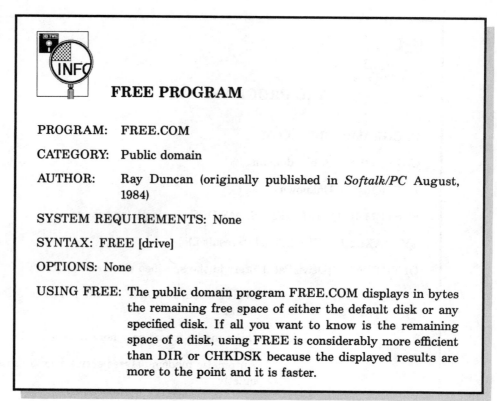

FREE PROGRAM

PROGRAM: FREE.COM

CATEGORY: Public domain

AUTHOR: Ray Duncan (originally published in *Softalk/PC* August, 1984)

SYSTEM REQUIREMENTS: None

SYNTAX: FREE [drive]

OPTIONS: None

USING FREE: The public domain program FREE.COM displays in bytes the remaining free space of either the default disk or any specified disk. If all you want to know is the remaining space of a disk, using FREE is considerably more efficient than DIR or CHKDSK because the displayed results are more to the point and it is faster.

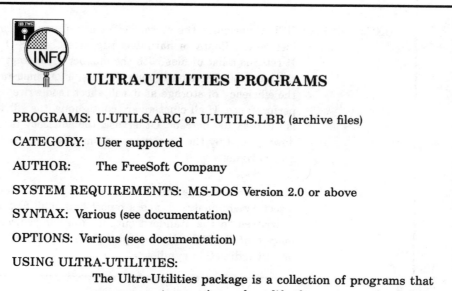

ULTRA-UTILITIES PROGRAMS

PROGRAMS: U-UTILS.ARC or U-UTILS.LBR (archive files)

CATEGORY: User supported

AUTHOR: The FreeSoft Company

SYSTEM REQUIREMENTS: MS-DOS Version 2.0 or above

SYNTAX: Various (see documentation)

OPTIONS: Various (see documentation)

USING ULTRA-UTILITIES:

The Ultra-Utilities package is a collection of programs that you can use to examine and modify the contents of a disk as well as "unerase" files. It is similar to the Norton Utilities commercial package. Look for a file called U-UTILS.ARC in the PC-SIG library or on bulletin boards. U-UTILS.ARC is an archive file that contains all the pertinent Ultra-Utilities files, including some other neat features. Ultra-Utilities is a user-supported program, so if you find the program useful and end up using it frequently, it's worth "registering" it with the originators by sending a small fee. If you've registered the program, you are entitled to receive free updates directly from the originators.

Batch-File-Related Programs

The following programs are designed for use within batch files. They all greatly enhance MS-DOS's batch capabilities by performing functions not supported under MS-DOS, such as displaying prompts for yes/no answers or text input for decision-making within batch files.

QUERY PROGRAM

PROGRAM: QUERY.COM

CATEGORY: Public domain

AUTHOR: Warren Craycroft

SYSTEM REQUIREMENTS: None

SYNTAX: QUERY [prompt] followed by one or more [errorlevel] checks on the next line, as follows:

IF NOT ERRORLEVEL 1 [command] (true if N pressed)
IF NOT ERRORLEVEL 2 [command] (true if Y pressed)
IF NOT ERRORLEVEL 3 [command] (true if Esc pressed)

OPTIONS: See above

USING QUERY: The statement QUERY followed with any text for the prompt is inserted in a batch file at the place where you want execution of the batch file to stop, display the prompt, then continue when the appropriate key is pressed. Depending on the key that you press in response to the prompt, QUERY sets an MS-DOS [errorlevel], which can be checked with the IF ERRORLEVEL or IF NOT ERRORLEVEL batch commands. The [errorlevel]s checked are as follows:

1. If N is pressed, QUERY sets [errorlevel] at 0.

2. If Y is pressed, QUERY sets [errorlevel] at 1

3. If Esc is pressed, QUERY sets [errorlevel] at 2

Because of the way MS-DOS interprets the IF ER-RORLEVEL command, check for input to QUERY in the following ways:

1. Always check for the N keypress first, in the format IF NOT ERRORLEVEL 1 [command], because [command] executes only if [errorlevel] is *less* than 1. If you use the statement IF ERRORLEVEL 0 [command] (which seems more logical at first), [command] executes if [errorlevel] is *equal to or greater than* 0, not yielding very efficient input checking!

2. On the next line of the batch file, check for the Y keypress with the statement IF NOT ERRORLEVEL 2 [command] so that [command] executes only if [errorlevel] is 1 (less than 2, but not 0 because 0 was checked for in the previous line).

3. On the third line, check for the Esc keypress with the statement IF NOT ERRORLEVEL 3 [command], so that [command] is executed only if [errorlevel] is 2, following the same logic used in the previous line.

If any key other than N, Y, or Esc is pressed, QUERY sounds a short beep and the prompt is redisplayed. As shown, QUERY is a very useful command for simple yes /no decision-making within batch files.

ANSWER PROGRAM

PROGRAM: ANSWER.COM

CATEGORY: Public domain

AUTHOR: Frank Schweiger

SYSTEM REQUIREMENTS: MS-DOS Version 2.0 or above

SYNTAX: ANSWER [text prompt]

OPTIONS: None

USING ANSWER: Have you ever wanted to ask a question and get an answer that you could use in a batch file? This program is the ANSWER. For example, if you need to ask for a directory and program name in a batch file, ANSWER does it. The ANSWER command is used within batch files by including the statement ANSWER at the point where you want the batch file to pause and ask for input. Optionally, the ANSWER statement can be followed on the same line by text that is displayed as a prompt when ANSWER executes. The text you enter in response to ANSWER is placed in the variable [ANSWER] in the MS-DOS *environment*. Then you can use the text assigned the variable ANSWER by using %ANSWER% statements within the batch file, much like the way %1, %2, etc., are used. Refer to Chapter 2 for more information about using batch files and to Chapter 13 for information on the MS-DOS environment.

BEEP PROGRAM

PROGRAM: BEEP.COM

CATEGORY: Public domain

AUTHOR: Unknown

SYSTEM REQUIREMENTS: None

SYNTAX: BEEP

OPTIONS: None

USING BEEP: Produces a 1000 Hz beep for 0.1 second at the point in the batch file where the statement BEEP occurs

REBEEP PROGRAM

PROGRAM: REBEEP.COM

CATEGORY: Public domain

AUTHOR: Martin Kelinsky (Published in *PC World*, October, 1984, and modified by Ken Goosens).

SYSTEM REQUIREMENTS: None

SYNTAX: REBEEP

OPTIONS: None

USING REBEEP: Causes a batch file to pause and generates continuous short double-beeps at the line in the batch file where the statement REBEEP occurs. REBEEP also displays a message indicating that the user must press any key to continue. REBEEP is roughly equivalent to a looping beep routine with the MS-DOS PAUSE command. This program is useful if you want walk away from your computer while it is running a long batch file, but wish to be informed once the file is completed or at some point requiring your supervision in the batch file.

Converting Files between Different Word Processors

The following programs were designed to help deal with various file formats generated by different word processing programs.

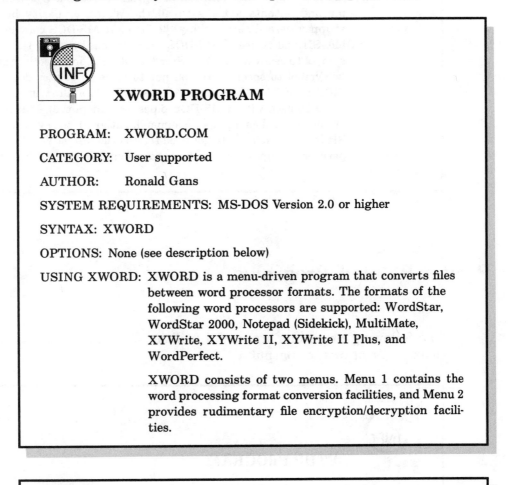

XWORD PROGRAM

PROGRAM: XWORD.COM

CATEGORY: User supported

AUTHOR: Ronald Gans

SYSTEM REQUIREMENTS: MS-DOS Version 2.0 or higher

SYNTAX: XWORD

OPTIONS: None (see description below)

USING XWORD: XWORD is a menu-driven program that converts files between word processor formats. The formats of the following word processors are supported: WordStar, WordStar 2000, Notepad (Sidekick), MultiMate, XYWrite, XYWrite II, XYWrite II Plus, and WordPerfect.

XWORD consists of two menus. Menu 1 contains the word processing format conversion facilities, and Menu 2 provides rudimentary file encryption/decryption facilities.

SH PROGRAM

PROGRAM: SH.COM

CATEGORY: Public domain

AUTHOR: Phil Suematsu

SYSTEM REQUIREMENTS: MS-DOS Version 2.0 or higher

SYNTAX: SH<[WordStar-file] >[output-file]

OPTIONS: None

USING SH: SH is a simple filter command program. It reads a WordStar file and outputs a file with all the WordStar parity bits stripped (zeroed out), making the file more MS-DOS compatible. SH makes use of MS-DOS's redirection, by using the < symbol to redirect the WordStar file into SH, followed by the > symbol to specify SH's output to a file or printer device (LPT1:, LPT2:, PRN:, etc.). Although SH is a filter, it *must* *never* be used within MS-DOS pipes (see Chapter 3). It must always be used as a proper command. Although the syntax of SH is a little strange to get used to, it is the fastest WordStar parity-bit stripper the authors have found in the public domain.

Printer-Related Programs

The following programs are useful utilities to enhance the control of printers or of printer output.

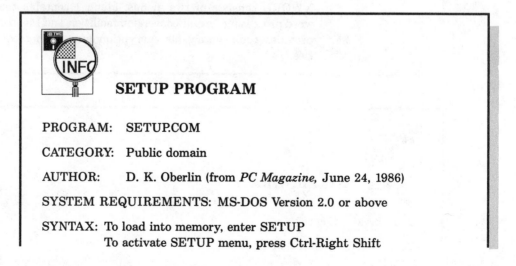

SETUP PROGRAM

PROGRAM: SETUP.COM

CATEGORY: Public domain

AUTHOR: D. K. Oberlin (from *PC Magazine,* June 24, 1986)

SYSTEM REQUIREMENTS: MS-DOS Version 2.0 or above

SYNTAX: To load into memory, enter SETUP
              To activate SETUP menu, press Ctrl-Right Shift

OPTIONS: None

USING SETUP: A memory-resident program that allows calling at any time a menu of 10 printer options, setting the desired option(s), then returning to your application program. SETUP is set up for Epson FX- and RX-series printers connected to LPT1. For modifications, see file SETUP.ASC and the original article. Pressing Ctrl-Right Shift activates the selection window. Use Options on the menu to set the printer to the following modes: draft, emphasized, italics, bold, double-width, condensed, and others.

SPOOLD PROGRAM

PROGRAM: SPOOLD.COM

CATEGORY: Public domain

AUTHOR: Unknown

SYSTEM REQUIREMENTS: MS-DOS Version 2.0 or higher

SYNTAX: To load into memory, and redirect printer output to a file, enter SPOOLD [output file]

To disable printer redirection to output file, and restore normal printer output, enter SPOOLD

OPTIONS: None

USING SPOOLD: The SPOOLD program allows you to redirect output normally sent to a parallel printer to a disk file. This might be useful if you plan to later send the file over a modem to another computer for printing, or for including printer-output examples in documents. SPOOLD is invoked by entering SPOOLD [output-file], where [output-file] is the file into which the print data is to be placed. The file need not exist, but if it does, it is deleted and recreated. Once SPOOLD has been invoked for the first time the message SPOOLD INSTALLED is displayed, leaving the program memory resident. Output directed to the printer is directed to the file until an error occurs or the disk containing the file becomes full (in this case an error message is displayed and the file is closed).

At any time, you can stop the spooling process and redirect printer output to the printer by typing SPOOLD with no filename. SPOOLD may be restarted again as described previously (but the permanent part remains resident even when it has been disabled).

System-Related Programs

The following programs do not fit in any obvious category, and therefore are referred to as *system utilities*.

STAT PROGRAM

PROGRAM: STAT.COM

CATEGORY: Public domain

AUTHOR: Unknown

SYSTEM REQUIREMENTS: MS-DOS Version 2.0 or higher

SYNTAX: STAT [drive]

OPTIONS: None

USING STAT: STAT is an easy-to-use program that displays various system statistics on the screen. Included in the statistics are

Memory—planar memory, total memory, free memory, and free-memory addresses

Equipment—number of parallel ports, serial ports, floppy drives, and game adapters

Keyboard buffer—character capacity with start
and end memory addresses

Video—initial mode (CGA, monochrome, etc.), current
mode, attribute at cursor, buffer offset, video page, cursor
mode, 6845 mode, and 6085 palette

MS-DOS and ROM BIOS Versions

Ctrl-C (Break) and verify (VERIFY) status

Disk parameters—on time, off time, settling time, bytes
per second, sectors per track.

Environment settings—first few lines of the environment

SLOW AND NOSLOW PROGRAMS

PROGRAMS: SLOW.COM and NOSLOW.COM

CATEGORY: Public domain

AUTHOR: John Bridges

SYSTEM REQUIREMENTS: MS-DOS Version 2.0 or higher

SYNTAX: To slow down system, enter SLOW
            To speed up system, enter NOSLOW

OPTIONS: None

USING SLOW AND NOSLOW:

Two useful programs for computers that run at speeds
above 4.77 MHz, and especially useful for IBM AT and
compatible systems running at 6 and 8 MHz or higher.
Some programs developed when the IBM PC was first introduced make use of hardware timing, and sometimes therefore won't work on systems that run faster than 4.77 MHz
8088. SLOW is a memory-resident program and is initially
loaded and run by entering SLOW with no parameters. To
disable slow function, run the NOSLOW program.

Memory-Related Programs

CORELOOK PROGRAM

PROGRAM: CORELOOK.COM

CATEGORY: Public domain

AUTHOR: B. Soucie

SYSTEM REQUIREMENTS: None

SYNTAX: CORELOOK

OPTIONS: None

USING CORELOOK: CORELOOK is a full-screen program that you use to examine any portion of memory in your system. Good help information is also displayed, which shows how to move around in memory.

MEM PROGRAM

PROGRAM: MEM.COM

CATEGORY: Public domain

AUTHOR: Unknown

SYSTEM REQUIREMENTS: None

SYNTAX: MEM

OPTIONS: None

USING MEM: MEM is a simple and fast program that displays the total amount of memory in your system, including amount of free memory and its beginning and ending addresses. This is a very nice alternative to using CHKDSK when all you want to see are memory statistics. The following shows typical output from the MEM command.

```
    Total memory = 655360  <-Actual count of RAM bytes
     High memory = 655360  <-Last address available for program loading
      Low memory = 349664  <-First address available for program loading)
Available memory = 305696  <-High-low
```

MINFO PROGRAM

PROGRAM: MINFO.COM

CATEGORY: Public domain

AUTHOR: Unknown

SYSTEM REQUIREMENTS: MS-DOS Version 2.0 or higher

SYNTAX: MINFO

OPTIONS: None

USING MINFO: MINFO displays a map of how memory is being used. Under MS-DOS Version 3.0 and higher, the names of all memory-resident programs are displayed, including the pathnames from where the programs were originally loaded. In versions of MS-DOS below 3.0 (but above 1.X), the names and originate-paths of memory-resident programs are not included. The beginning address of each program is listed. The following shows a sample output from MINFO.

```
ID Block Paras (Size)  Owner
M  0825  0B4C  46272  0008 DOS
M  1372  00C0   3072  1373 SHELL (permanent)
M  1433  003E    992  1373 SHELL (permanent)
M  1472  0003     48  0000 DOS (unallocated)
M  1476  0032    800  14AA C:\UTILS\REF\REFWATCH.COM
M  14A9  0578  22400  14AA C:\UTILS\REF\REFWATCH.COM
M  1A22  0032    800  1A56 C:\SYSTEM\STARTUP\SPATH\SPATH.COM
M  1A55  0047   1136  1A56 C:\SYSTEM\STARTUP\SPATH\SPATH.COM
M  1A9D  0032    800  1AD1 C:\SYSTEM\STARTUP\MOUSE\MSMOUSE.COM
M  1AD0  010F   4336  1AD1 C:\SYSTEM\STARTUP\MOUSE\MSMOUSE.COM
M  1BE0  0032    800  1C14 C:\UTILS\KEYBOARD\KEY\KEY.COM
```

```
M   1C13   0E29    58000   1C14  C:\UTILS\KEYBOARD\KEY\KEY.COM
M   2A3D   0031      784   2A70  C:\WP\LIGHT\LIGHT.COM
M   2A6F   0FDA    64928   2A70  C:\WP\LIGHT\LIGHT.COM
M   3A4A   0032      800   3A7E  C:\UTILS\MISC\SK\SK.COM
M   3A7D   1AAF   109296   3A7E  C:\UTILS\MISC\SK\SK.COM
M   552D   0030      768   555F  D:\1\MINFO.EXE
M   555E   0238     9088   555F  D:\1\MINFO.EXE
Z   5797   4868   296576   0000  DOS (unallocated)
```

MARK, FMARK, AND RELEASE PROGRAMS

PROGRAMS: MARK.COM, FMARK.COM, and RELEASE.COM

CATEGORY: Public domain

AUTHOR: Kim Kokkonen

SYSTEM REQUIREMENTS: MS-DOS Version 2.0 or higher

SYNTAX: To mark memory, enter MARK

To mark memory and specify marking information to a file, enter FMARK [drive:path:filename]

To clear all memory above the MARK or FMARK in memory, enter RELEASE for MARK, or RELEASE [drive:path:filename] for FMARK.

OPTIONS: None

USING MARK, FMARK, AND RELEASE:

MARK.COM and RELEASE.COM are used to remove memory-resident programs from memory, without the usual problems of creating holes or leaving interrupts dangling. The two programs are used as follows:

1. Run MARK.COM before installing any memory-resident program that you may wish to deinstall later. This marks the current position in memory and stores the MS-DOS interrupt vector table (all interrupts from 0 to FFH).

2. Install in the normal way whatever memory-resident programs that you want to use.

3. When you want to deinstall all memory-resident programs above the last MARK, run RELEASE.COM. This releases all the memory above (and including) the last MARK and restores all interrupt vectors taken over by the memory resident programs.

MARK and RELEASE can be "stacked" as many times as desired. RELEASE releases the memory above the last MARK call. MARK uses about 1600 bytes of memory each time it is called. This 1600 byte region is released when a RELEASE is done. MARK memory usage is dominated by the copies of the MS-DOS interrupt vector table (interrupts 0 through FFH) and the copy of the EMS page map (blocks 0 through 31 only) that MARK keeps when it goes resident.

MARK and RELEASE can optionally be called with a single command line parameter:

    MARK [MarkName]
    RELEASE [MarkName]

In this way a particular mark is given a name. Calling RELEASE with the same name releases all memory above and including the mark of that name and also releases any intermediate marks in the process. If no mark of the proper name is found, RELEASE halts with a warning. A RELEASE call with no [MarkName] specified releases the last MARK, whether or not that MARK was named.

The [MarkName] can be any text string up to 126 characters in length. It may not contain embedded blanks or tabs. Case (upper or lower) is not important when matching MarkNames.

[MarkName] supports an additional feature. If the MarkName begins with ! (exclamation point), the mark is called a "protected mark." That mark can be released *only* by an exact match to its name (including the exclamation point). A protected mark is *not* released with an "unnamed" RELEASE. Any named or unnamed RELEASE stops without releasing any blocks if it encounters a protected mark that it does not match exactly.

As of version 2.0, a new form of marking, called a *file mark,* is also supported. The new mark has the advantage that it uses only about 150 bytes of memory rather than the 1600 of MARK.

The new mark is placed with the command

FMARK [drive:path\filename]

The bulk of the vector table and the EMS page map are stored in the file that you specify on the command line rather than in memory. Note that a command line parameter is *required* in this case. Otherwise FMARK halts with an error. The file created by FMARK is between 1000 and 2000 bytes in size, depending on usage of expanded memory.

If you might switch drives or directories after using FMARK, specify a complete pathname when FMARK is initially called. To avoid confusion, you may want to keep the FMARK files in the root directory, or in a separate directory defined just for this purpose.

The RELEASE program has been upgraded so that it can release either an in-memory mark (placed by MARK.COM) or a file mark (placed by FMARK.COM). Use of RELEASE with in-memory marks is the same as before. To use RELEASE with file marks, call it with the name of the mark file on the command line:

RELEASE [drive:path\filename]

Note that in this case the filename must be specified on the command line, and that only a file mark exactly matching the command line is released. If the specified mark file is not found, RELEASE halts with an error message. When the memory is released, the mark file is also deleted from the disk.

There is no direct equivalent of protected marks for FMARK. If an unnamed RELEASE finds an in-memory mark below a file mark, the file mark is released in the process of the unnamed release. In this case, the mark file is not deleted from disk.

Communications Programs

The following is a sampling of utilities that can make life easier when using your computer for communicating with other computers via modem.

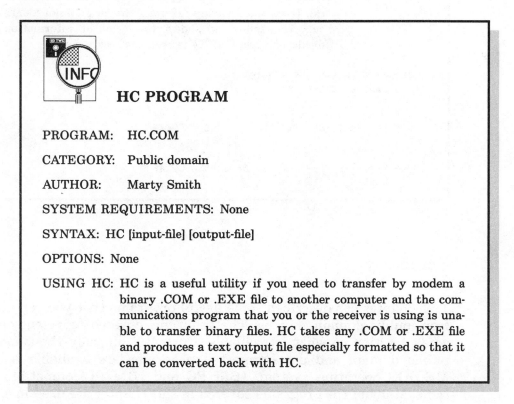

HC PROGRAM

PROGRAM: HC.COM

CATEGORY: Public domain

AUTHOR: Marty Smith

SYSTEM REQUIREMENTS: None

SYNTAX: HC [input-file] [output-file]

OPTIONS: None

USING HC: HC is a useful utility if you need to transfer by modem a binary .COM or .EXE file to another computer and the communications program that you or the receiver is using is unable to transfer binary files. HC takes any .COM or .EXE file and produces a text output file especially formatted so that it can be converted back with HC.

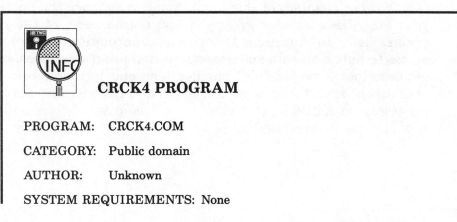

CRCK4 PROGRAM

PROGRAM: CRCK4.COM

CATEGORY: Public domain

AUTHOR: Unknown

SYSTEM REQUIREMENTS: None

SYNTAX: CRCK4 [filename]

OPTIONS: None

USING CRCK4: CRCK4 is used to produce a cyclic-redundancy check (CRC) of any file. This function is useful if you wish to verify a file that was transferred over a modem. If the users at both ends run CRCK4 on the same file and the resulting CRC numbers are the same, the files are identical. If the numbers are different, the files are not identical. The following shows the type of information displayed when CRCK4 is used to check a file.

```
CRCK ver 4.2B (MS DOS VERSION )
CTL-S pauses, CTL-C aborts


--> FILE:  OUTLINE .TXT          CRC = 09 AE


  ----------------------> SUM OF CRCS = 09 AE
        DONE
```

Summary

This chapter has described some useful programs that you can obtain from public domain sources. The programs covered represent only a small fraction of what is available. Currently, literally thousands of public domain and user-supported programs are available for the MS-DOS operating system, IBM PC and IBM PC-compatible systems. Many of the programs covered in this chapter are used in examples in other chapters of this book. You can enhance the operation of your MS-DOS computer greatly if you obtain some of the key programs. Refer to Appendix B for more information on how to gain access to public domain and user-supported programs. The next chapter describes how MS-DOS handles files and is therefore a natural "next step" from the information covered in this chapter. Many of the programs described in this chapter will help you better understand how files are manipulated by MS-DOS.

Secrets of Files   Chapter 9

T his chapter deals with the characteristics of files and how they are handled by MS-DOS and various types of application programs. With regular use of MS-DOS, we normally don't have to concern ourselves with the characteristics of files beyond filenames, extensions, and file sizes. The information about files that we need on a daily basis can be derived by displaying the directory with the DIR command. However, what should we do when we need more information, such as the status of a file that's been damaged, erased, or lost? And what can we do to correct file problems? The answers to these questions, as well as many others, are in this chapter, which explores how MS-DOS manages files and how some commands and application programs deal with files.

Secrets of MS-DOS Disk Formats

When the MS-DOS FORMAT command is used to format a floppy or hard disk, the command divides the disk into *tracks* and *sectors*. A sector is used by MS-DOS as a unit of storage. Each sector has a unique number. All sectors on a disk are allocated for specific MS-DOS uses into four major sections: the boot area, file allocation table (FAT) area, directory area, and data storage area.

Figure 9-1 shows a theoretical diagram of a disk's appearance and how sectors are allocated for different uses by MS-DOS.

As shown in Figure 9-1, a disk formatted under MS-DOS is divided into a set of concentric rings called *tracks,* and each track is

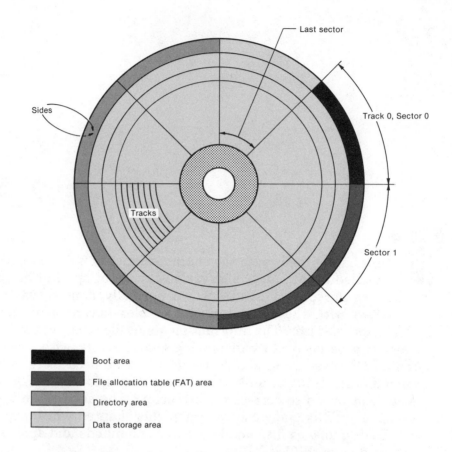

Figure 9-1.   A Disk's Physical Structure

divided into several sectors. The first few sectors on a disk are not used for the storage of file data. Rather, they are used for *controlling* how files are stored on the disk. Table 9-1 shows how the different MS-DOS disk formats make use of these sectors. Note the column titled *Reference Code*. The reference code is used throughout this chapter to identify the various formats supported for 3½-inch, 5¼-inch, and 8-inch floppy disks.

The reference codes used in Table 9-1 are abbreviations of disk formats. Based on the information shown in this table, the following explains the logic behind the abbreviations.

1.   3DQ9 = 3½-inch, double-sided, quad-density (80 tracks), 9-sectors-per-track micro floppy disk.

2.   5SS8 = 5¼-inch, single-sided, single-density, 8-sectors-per-track mini floppy disk

3. 5DS8 = same as 5SS8, but double-sided.

4. 5SD9 = 5¼-inch, single-sided, double-density, 9-sectors-per-track mini floppy disk.

5. 5DD9 = same as 5SD9, but double-sided.

6. 5DQ15 = 5¼-inch, double-sided, quad-density (80 tracks), 15-sectors-per-track, high capacity mini floppy disk.

7. 8SS26 = 8-inch, single-sided, single-density, 26-sectors-per-track standard floppy disk.

8. 8DD8 = 8-inch, double-sided, double-density, 8-sectors-per-track standard floppy disk.

9. XT10M = 5¼-inch, IBM XT 10M fixed hard disk.

10. AT20M = 5¼-inch, IBM AT 20M fixed hard disk.

These ten disk formats represent the majority of the standards supported by MS-DOS. The last two, XT10M and AT20M, represent the standard hard (fixed) disks installed in IBM XT and IBM AT systems, respectively. Many other types of hard disks can be added to the IBM PC series and compatible systems, but most of them adhere to the original IBM 10M or 20M format. The reference to 8-inch floppy disks as *standard* refers to the term given to them over the years (even

Table 9-1. General Characteristics of MS-DOS Disk Formats

Reference Code	Size	Sides	Tracks per Side	Sectors per Track	Total Sectors	Bytes per Sector	Total Capacity (Bytes)	Boot Sectors	FAT Sectors	Directory Sectors	Data Sectors	Data Capacity (Bytes)
	General Characteristics							Sector Usage				
3DQ9	3.5	2	80	9	1,440	512	737,280	1	10	7	1,422	728,064
5SS8	5.25	1	40	8	320	512	163,840	1	2	4	313	160,256
5DS8	5.25	2	40	8	640	512	327,680	1	2	7	630	322,560
5SD9	5.25	1	40	9	360	512	184,320	1	4	4	351	179,712
5DD9	5.25	2	40	9	720	512	368,640	1	4	7	708	362,496
5DQ15	5.25	2	80	15	2,400	512	1,228,800	1	14	14	2,371	1,213,952
8SS26	8	1	77	26	2,002	128	256,256	1	6	17	1,972	252,416
8DD8	8	2	77	8	1,232	1,024	1,261,568	1	2	6	1,221	1,250,304
XT10M	5.25	4	305	17	20,740	512	10,618,880	1	16	32	20,691	10,593,792
AT20M	5.25	4	614	17	41,752	512	21,377,024	1	82	32	41,636	21,317,632

before MS-DOS was created) to easily distinguish them from the smaller 5¼-inch mini floppy disks, or the even smaller 3½-inch micro floppy disks.

The following paragraphs explain the mechanics behind formats of disks that are formatted under MS-DOS.

Control Sectors and Data Sectors

As explained previously, the first few sectors on a disk are used to *control* how files are stored on the disk. All sectors after these control sectors are used for the actual storage of file data and are called *data sectors*. The following paragraphs describe in more detail how each area of a disk is used by MS-DOS and explain the purpose of each "control" sector.

The Boot Record

Side 0, track 0, sector 0 of every disk formatted under MS-DOS contains the *boot record*. The boot record includes a short program that is used when the system is booted to instruct the ROM BIOS where to look for the MS-DOS boot files, and if present, load them, then transfer control to MS-DOS. In addition to this short program, the boot sector also contains information regarding the version of MS-DOS originally used to format the disk, the names of the boot files, and some basic error messages in case things don't go quite right.

Not only is the MS-DOS version stored in the boot record, but also the *implementation* of MS-DOS. For example, if the disk was formatted using IBM DOS Version 3.2, you would find "IBM 3.2" in the boot record. If COMPAQ MS-DOS Version 3.1 was used, you'd find a message at the end of the boot record that reads "COMPAQ 1983,84,85." The following trick shows how you can look at the contents of the boot sector by using DEBUG within a batch file.

EXAMINING THE CONTENTS
OF THE BOOT RECORD

The following listing shows the contents of a batch file called READBOOT.BAT that can be used to examine the contents of the boot record on any disk originally formatted under MS-DOS. Create the batch file exactly as shown, then run it. It uses DEBUG to read the boot sector of the specified disk, temporarily stores the information in a file, then displays the file to the screen.

```
ECHO off
ECHO                     READ AND DISPLAY BOOT RECORD
ECHO ^H
SET DRV=ERROR
IF (%1)==(a) set DRV=0
IF (%1)==(A) set DRV=0
IF (%1)==(b) set DRV=1
IF (%1)==(B) set DRV=1
IF (%1)==(c) set DRV=2
IF (%1)==(C) set DRV=2
IF (%DRV%)==(ERROR) goto :ERR1
REM
ECHO l 0100 %DRV% 0 1 >temp.inp
ECHO d 0100 02FF >>temp.inp
ECHO q >>temp.inp
DEBUG <temp.inp >bootrec.out
TYPE bootrec.out ¦ MORE
DEL temp.inp >nul:
GOTO :END
:ERR1
ECHO ^H
ECHO ERROR: Illegal drive.
ECHO        Syntax: READBOOT drv
ECHO        where "drv" is drive A, B, or C (without the colon!).
ECHO ^H
:END
SET DRV=
```

Note that READBOOT.BAT shown in the listing is capable of reading the boot sector from Drives A, B, or C. Adding more drives is a simple matter of expanding the set of IF statements at the beginning of the file. The following shows an example of what can be displayed when READBOOT.BAT is used.

```
-l 0100 0 0 1
-d 0100 02FF
5942:0100  EB 21 90 49 42 4D 20 20-33 2E 31 00 02 01 01 00   .!.IBM  3.1.....
5942:0110  02 E0 00 60 09 F9 07 00-0F 00 02 00 00 00 00 00   ...'............
5942:0120  00 00 00 C4 5C 08 33 ED-B8 C0 07 8E D8 33 C9 0A   ....\.3......3..
5942:0130  D2 79 0E 89 1E 1E 00 8C-06 20 00 88 16 22 00 B1   .y....... ..."..
```

```
5942:0140   02 8E C5 8E D5 BC 00 7C-51 FC 1E 36 C5 36 78 00   .......|Q..6.6x.
5942:0150   BF 23 7C B9 0B 00 F3 A4-1F 88 0E 2C 00 A0 18 00   .#|........,....
5942:0160   A2 27 00 BF 78 00 B8 23-7C AB 91 AB A1 16 00 D1   .'..x..#|.......
5942:0170   E0 40 E8 80 00 E8 86 00-BB 00 05 53 B0 01 E8 AB   .@.........S....
5942:0180   00 5F BE 73 01 B9 0B 00-90 F3 A6 75 62 83 C7 15   ._.s.......ub...
5942:0190   B1 0B 90 90 F3 A6 75 57-26 8B 47 1C 99 8B 0E 0B   ......uW&.G.....
5942:01A0   00 03 C1 48 F7 F1 80 3E-71 01 60 75 02 B0 14 96   ...H...>q.`u....
5942:01B0   A1 11 00 B1 04 D3 E8 E8-3B 00 FF 36 1E 00 C4 1E   .......;..6.....
5942:01C0   6F 01 E8 39 00 E8 64 00-2B F0 76 0D E8 26 00 52   o..9..d.+.v..&.R
5942:01D0   F7 26 0B 00 03 D8 5A EB-E9 CD 11 B9 02 00 D3 E0   .&....Z.........
5942:01E0   80 E4 03 74 04 FE C4 8A-CC 5B 58 FF 2E 6F 01 BE   ...t.....[X..o..
5942:01F0   89 01 EB 55 90 01 06 1E-00 11 2E 20 00 C3 A1 18   ...U....... ....
5942:0200   00 F6 26 1A 00 91 A1 1E-00 8B 16 20 00 F7 F1 92   ..&........ ....
5942:0210   8B 0E 18 00 F6 F1 2A CC-91 FE C5 86 E9 D0 CE D0   ......*.........
5942:0220   CE 0A F1 86 F2 87 CA 8A-16 22 00 C3 98 BF 05 00   .........".....
5942:0230   50 B4 02 CD 13 72 02 58-C3 80 FC 11 74 F9 33 C0   P....r.X....t.3.
5942:0240   CD 13 4F 58 75 EA BE D3-01 E8 1D 00 BE A9 01 E8   ..OXu...........
5942:0250   17 00 33 C0 CD 16 36 C7-06 72 04 34 12 EA 00 00   ..3...6..r.4....
-- MORE --
5942:0260   FF FF B4 0E BB 07 00 CD-10 AC 3C 24 75 F4 C3 00   ..........<$u...
5942:0270   00 70 00 49 42 4D 42 49-4F 20 20 43 4F 4D 49 42   .p.IBMBIO  COMIB
5942:0280   4D 44 4F 53 20 20 43 4F-4D 0A 0D 4E 6F 6E 2D 53   MDOS  COM..Non-S
5942:0290   79 73 74 65 6D 20 64 69-73 6B 20 6F 72 20 64 69   ystem disk or di
5942:02A0   73 6B 20 65 72 72 6F 72-24 0A 0D 52 65 70 6C 61   sk error$..Repla
5942:02B0   63 65 20 61 6E 64 20 73-74 72 69 6B 65 20 61 6E   ce and strike an
5942:02C0   79 20 6B 65 79 20 77 68-65 6E 20 72 65 61 64 79   y key when ready
5942:02D0   0A 0D 24 0A 0D 44 69 73-6B 20 62 6F 6F 74 20 66   ..$..Disk boot f
5942:02E0   61 69 6C 75 72 65 24 43-6F 70 72 2E 20 43 4F 4D   ailure$Copr. COM
5942:02F0   50 41 51 20 31 39 38 33-2C 38 34 2C 38 35 55 AA   PAQ 1983,84,85U.
-q
```

The File Allocation Table

Following the boot record are several sectors reserved for the storage of the *file allocation table* (or *FAT,* as it is usually called). The FAT provides a map of the disk, keyed to filenames in the directory. The FAT is made up of what are called *FAT entries,* and each entry corresponds to specific *clusters* on the disk. Depending on the format of the disk, a cluster consists of one or a set of data sectors. FAT entries include information concerning which clusters are presently in use, which clusters are marked as bad and therefore are unusable, and which ones are free to be used for new file data. Table 9-2 shows the relationship between data sectors and clusters on the various MS-DOS-formatted disks.

Table 9-2.   Data Sectors and Clusters
on MS-DOS-Formatted Disks

Reference Code	Size	Data Sectors	Bytes per Sector	Sectors per Cluster	Bytes per Cluster	Total Clusters	Data Capacity (Bytes)
3DQ9	3.5	1,422	512	2	1,024	711	728,064
5SS8	5.25	313	512	1	512	313	160,256
5DS8	5.25	630	512	2	1,024	315	322,560
5SD9	5.25	351	512	1	512	351	179,712
5DD9	5.25	708	512	2	1,024	354	362,496
5DQ15	5.25	2,371	512	1	512	2,371	1,213,952
8SS26	8	1,972	128	4	512	493	252,416
8DD8	8	1,221	1,024	1	1,024	1,221	1,250,304
XT10M	5.25	20,691	512	8	4,096	2,586	10,593,792
AT20M	5.25	41,636	512	4	2,048	10,409	21,317,632

The FAT consists of a series of *linked lists*. Each cluster is assigned a FAT entry: FAT entry 2 corresponds to Cluster 2, FAT entry 3 corresponds to Cluster 3, and so on. The contents of a FAT entry normally consist of the number of the next cluster occupied by a file and its corresponding FAT entry. The last cluster occupied by a file has, in its corresponding FAT entry, an end-of-file marker. If, while a disk is being formatted, a cluster is found to be unusable, MS-DOS marks the cluster as "bad" by placing a special value in its corresponding FAT entry. Table 9-3 shows the different values that can be placed in FAT entries.

Table 9-3.   FAT Entry Values Controlling File Allocation

FAT Entry Hex Value	Meaning
000	Cluster is unused and available for new file storage
FF0 through FF6	Reserved cluster (not available for normal file storage)
FF7	Cluster is marked as bad by MS-DOS and is not used for file storage
FF8 through FFF	Last cluster occupied by a file
XXX	Any other value indicates a cluster number in the chain defining how a file is stored

Cluster Numbering

Although most items MS-DOS deals with, such as disk tracks and sectors, begin with the number 0, the first data cluster on a disk is always numbered 2. (See Table 9-4.) The reason is because the first two FAT entries, FAT entries 0 and 1, are not used for the regular mapping of the data clusters. Instead, FAT entry 0 is used to contain a code that identifies the format of the disk, and FAT entry 1 is used simply as a buffer or dividing line between FAT entry 0 and FAT entry 2.

Table 9-4. Cluster Numbering on MS-DOS-Formatted Disks

Reference Code	Size	Data Sectors	Sectors per Cluster	Total Clusters	Cluster-Number Range
3DQ9	3.5	1,422	2	711	2 to 712
5SS8	5.25	313	1	313	2 to 314
5DS8	5.25	630	2	315	2 to 316
5SD9	5.25	351	1	351	2 to 352
5DD9	5.25	708	2	354	2 to 355
5DQ15	5.25	2,371	1	2,371	2 to 2,372
8SS26	8	1,972	4	493	2 to 494
8DD8	8	1,221	1	1,221	2 to 1,222
XT10M	5.25	20,691	8	2,586	2 to 2,587
AT20M	5.25	41,636	4	10,409	2 to 10,410

Disk Format Identification Codes

When MS-DOS first reads a disk, it reads the format code to determine how the rest of the disk should be read. Table 9-5 shows the identification codes for the different disk formats.

Interpreting the Contents of FAT Entries

The way in which information is stored in FAT entries is not as straightforward as one would expect. Because a great number of clusters often need mapping, as much information as possible must be fitted into the FAT sectors. Unraveling the contents of FAT entries is beyond the scope of this book. Refer to other references on the subject that describe the FAT in greater detail. A recommended book is *MS-DOS Developer's Guide* (Sams #22409).

Table 9-5.   Disk Type Values in FAT Entry 0

FAT Entry 0 (Hex Value)	Type of Disk and Format
FF8	Hard (fixed) disk (IBM PC, XT, and AT with MS-DOS 2.0 and higher versions)
FF9	5DQ15 (MS-DOS Version 3.0 and higher) or 3DQ9 (MS-DOS Version 3.2 and higher)
FFC*	5SD9 (MS-DOS Version 2.0 and higher)
FFD*	5DD9 (MS-DOS Version 2.0 and higher)
FFE*	5SS8 (MS-DOS Version 1.0 and higher) or 8SS26 or 8DD8 (MS-DOS Version 2.0 and higher, and normally only supported with device drivers [see Chapter 13])
FFF*	5DS8 (MS-DOS Version 1.1 and higher)

*Many nonstandard forms of disk storage are available for MS-DOS systems that cannot be handled directly by the ROM BIOS of an IBM PC XT, AT, or compatible system, and therefore require special software so that they operate correctly. In many cases, nonstandard disks, such as 8-inch floppy disks and BERNOULLI BOX cartridges, use the same format codes shown in Table 9-5 as originally defined for standard 5¼-inch floppy disks. Through the special software accompanying these types of disk drive hardware, the codes, and consequently the formats, are correctly interpreted. To obtain more information on the formats of nonstandard disks, refer to the manufacturer's documentation.

The Directory Sectors

The directory sectors store the directory information for all files on the disk. When you issue the DIR command, the information displayed is obtained directly from the directory sectors and nowhere else on the disk. Regardless of the MS-DOS disk format, each directory sector contains space for 16 directory entries. Because a sector is always 512 bytes long, we can deduce easily that each directory entry is 32 bytes in length. The total number of directory entries permitted for the entire disk depends on how many directory sectors are defined. For example, single-sided 40-track floppy disks have a total of 64 directory entries, whereas double-sided 40-track floppy disks have a total of 112 directory entries and double-sided 80-track (high capacity) floppy disks have a total of 224 directory entries. For most hard disks, the total number of directory entries depends on how the disk is formatted. In the case of the IBM PC and some compatible systems, the total number of directory entries depends on the size of the MS-DOS partition created when the disk is first formatted. The total number of directory entries determines the maximum number of files that can be stored on the disk.

The information contained in a directory entry is divided into six components, as shown in Table 9-6.

Table 9-6.   Components of a Directory Entry

Field	Offset	Description	Size	Format
1	0	1st character of filename or file status	1	ASCII character
2	1	Rest of file's name	7	ASCII characters
3	8	File type or extension	3	ASCII characters
4	11	Attribute	1	Bit coded
5	12	Reserved	10	Unused (zeros)
6	22	Time stamp	2	Word, coded
7	24	Date stamp	2	Word, coded
8	26	Starting cluster and FAT entry	2	Word
9	28	File size	4	Integer

Filename, File Type, and File Status

The filename and type consist of 11 bytes, each byte representing an ASCII character and the name of the file to which the directory entry corresponds. In MS-DOS versions 2.0 and above, the filename in a directory entry always refers to a file in the *root* directory. Because *subdirectory* names are treated as files by MS-DOS, they also have their own entries in the directory sectors. A subdirectory name, however, contains information in its directory entry that is slightly different from normal files.

Root Directory Entries and Subdirectories

Under MS-DOS versions 2.0 and above, the maximum number of files or directory entries that a floppy disk can accommodate (64, 112, and 224) correspond only to the root directory. Because all files stored in a subdirectory have directory entries in the subdirectory "file" itself, there effectively is no limit to the number of files that can be stored on a disk within the space provided by the particular type of disk and format.

File Status and Erased Files

When a file is erased, two things happen to the disk. The first item affected is the first character of the filename in the directory entry. As shown in Table 9-6, the first byte in a directory entry can either indicate the file's status or represent the first ASCII character of the file's name. If a directory entry has not been used since the disk was last formatted, this first byte is always set to 00, and the rest of the directory entry is filled with the hexadecimal value of F6. In this way, MS-DOS only needs to read the first byte of a directory entry to determine whether it can be used. When a file is created, the first byte is changed to represent the first character of the file's name. When the file is erased later, the first byte is changed to a hexadecimal value of E5. The rest of the information in the erased file's directory entry is left intact. Therefore, when you examine the disk's sectors for the information on the erased file's directory entry, this value is your first clue that the desired directory entry has been found.

The second clue, of course, is the presentation of the rest of the file's name and type in ASCII format. But the first character, which is set to hex E5, tells us that the directory entry represents an erased file. The first character is set to this value so that MS-DOS knows that should the directory entry be needed, it is free to be overwritten with new file information.

File Attribute

The *attribute* byte contains information about the file's storage attributes. Attributes indicate how MS-DOS treats the file. Table 9-7 shows the definitions of each attribute and the respective hexadecimal values that can be stored in the attribute byte. Each bit in the byte defines a specific attribute and is set to 1 when the attribute is assigned to the file.

Read-Only Status   The file cannot be erased by normal means. (That is, using DEL, ERASE, or built-in functions of many application programs do not erase a read-only file.)

Hidden Status   The file is excluded from normal directory searches, such as the DIR command.

System Status   This attribute is normally required for boot files, such as the IBMBIO.COM and IBMDOS.COM files, used by IBM

DOS in the IBM PC series and compatible systems. The system attribute is almost always used in conjunction with the hidden attribute.

Table 9-7.   File Attribute Definitions

Bit 7 6 5 4 3 2 1 0	Value DEC	HEX	Attribute
. . . . 1	1	01	Read-only
. . . . . . 1 .	2	02	Hidden
. . . . . 1 . .	4	04	System
. . . . 1 . . .	8	08	Volume label
. . . 1	16	10	Subdirectory
. . 1	32	20	Archive
. 1	64	40	Not defined (unused)
1	128	80	Not defined (unused)

Volume Label   This attribute indicates that the directory entry contains a volume label (DOS 2.0 and above only). Apart from the name of the volume label in the filename and type fields, the rest of the entry contains no useful information.

Subdirectory Entry Status   An attribute indicating that the directory entry pertains to a "file" which, in turn, contains directory-entry information for the files in the subdirectory itself.

Archive Status   An attribute that is set when the file has been opened and closed. It is used by some hard disk backup and restore utilities.

Notice that a file can have more than one attribute. For example, if a file is assigned the read-only (hex 01) and hidden (hex 02) attributes, the resulting value in the attribute byte is the sum of both attribute values—hex 03. Normally, you don't have to be concerned with what attributes are assigned to a file unless you need to do something to the file that conflicts with its attribute status. For example, if you needed to examine a file that has the hidden attribute, you would have difficulty doing so until the attribute is removed, unless you're using an application program that's capable of ignoring the attribute. In some cases, however, file attributes are essential. For example, a file that contains the directory information for subdirectories must have the subdirectory attribute set, otherwise MS-DOS incorrectly interprets the portion of the disk pertaining to the subdirectory.

Time Stamp

The time stamp field contains a two-byte value that marks the time that the file was created or last changed. It's used in conjunction with the date stamp field. The two fields can be read as a single four-byte number. The value can be compared with the values in other directory entries using greater-than, less-than, or equal values. The time stamp, by itself, is read as a number built out of the hours, minutes, and seconds, using the following formula:

$$\text{Time} = (\text{hour} \times 2{,}048) + (\text{minutes} \times 32) + (\text{seconds} \times 0.5)$$

The hour is always in the 24-hour format, with a value ranging from 0 to 23. Because the field is one bit too short to accommodate all of the seconds, they are stored in units of 2 seconds from 0 to 29. For example, 16 seconds would be represented by 8. The time of 10:15:24 would be converted to and stored as 20972.

Date Stamp

The date stamp field, like the time stamp field, contains a two-byte value that marks the date the file was created or last changed. As mentioned previously, both the date stamp and the time stamp can be used in conjunction so that the two fields can be read as a single four-byte number. The date stamp, by itself, is read as a number built out of the year, month, and day, using the following formula:

$$\text{Date} = ((\text{year} - 1980) \times 512) + (\text{month} \times 64) + \text{day}$$

Notice in the previous formula that the year becomes compressed by having 1980 subtracted from it. As a result, the year 1987 would be converted to a value of 7. Using the previous formula, a date such as July 3, 1987 is converted to the value of 4035, as follows:

$$(1987 - 1980) = 7 \rightarrow 7 \times 512 = \quad 3584 \text{ (year)}$$
$$7 \times 64 = \quad 448 \text{ (month)}$$
$$+ \quad 3 \text{ (day)}$$
$$\overline{\quad 4035 \quad}$$

Although the highest year supported by this scheme is 2108, MS-DOS only supports 2099.

Starting Cluster

A starting cluster is a 2-byte, 16-digit, binary number that represents the first section of the disk occupied by the file. This section of the disk is referred to as a *cluster*, explained previously in the discussion on the file allocation table sectors. The starting cluster is the initial "pointer" to the file's first data cluster as well as to subsequent pointers in the FAT sectors. Once MS-DOS reads this initial pointer in the directory entry, it proceeds to read the rest of the pointers to the file's data clusters in the FAT sectors.

File Size

A file's size is represented by a four-byte binary number, which many MS-DOS commands, including the DIR command, use to extract and display the file's size in bytes. The file's size should always be equal to or slightly less than the total sum of bytes in all the clusters occupied by a file. Because the size of a cluster can range from 512 bytes to 4,096 bytes (or higher), it is usual to find that the last cluster occupied by a file is only partially full. The file size field in a directory entry can therefore be used to extract an exact byte count of the file.

Changing a File's Attributes

Until MS-DOS Version 3.0 was released, no official program was available to deal with file attributes at the MS-DOS command prompt level. The name of the command used to accomplish this task is called ATTRIB. The ATTRIB command is capable of changing the read-only attribute status of files. (In MS-DOS Version 3.2, ATTRIB is also capable of changing the archive attribute.) Unfortunately, that is the only thing it can do. It cannot change the hidden attribute or the system attribute. However, the incongruity of having a command called ATTRIB that can only change one of eight attributes doesn't need to be great issue if you can obtain one of several public domain and commercial programs that do a better job. Chapter 8 provides descriptions of some of the public domain programs that handle file attributes.

Several commercial programs are also available. These programs provide as a feature the ability to change file attributes. For example, the XTREE program, designed to provide a usable display of a system's directory tree structure, is capable of displaying and changing the system, hidden, read-only, and archive attributes. It wouldn't make much sense to change the subdirectory attribute because that would have disastrous effects. The subdirectory attribute instructs the DIR command to display the DIR next to subdirectory names in a directory listing).

Many may ask, "Why would one want to ever change the system attribute?" Normally, one wouldn't. In some cases, however, it may be necessary. For example, if you format a floppy disk so that the system boot files are copied to the disk making it a "boot" disk, then decide that you want to make it a "data" disk without reformatting the disk, how would you eliminate the system files? What if you wanted to turn "system" files into normal files so that they could be copied, renamed, and examined? Using a utility to remove the system attribute from a file allows you treat that file like any other file.

Recovering Damaged Files

Understanding how a disk is laid out under MS-DOS can be very useful if a file or a part of a disk appears to be damaged. Fortunately, MS-DOS provides several functions that not only call attention to damaged parts of a disk, but also allow you to recover data that is otherwise inaccessible. When faced with file storage problems or defective disks, MS-DOS automatically isolates the part of the disk with the problem when it attempts to access it. Although MS-DOS does not necessarily tell you exactly what has happened, you probably will get an error message indicating that the part of the disk you wanted to read from cannot be accessed properly. The following information boxes explain how the RECOVER and CHKDSK commands can be used to restore damaged or lost data.

USING THE RECOVER COMMAND TO RESTORE DAMAGED FILES

If you repeatedly get disk sector errors when you attempt to access a file, the file in question quite possibly is occupying one or more damaged sectors. Copying the file may not alleviate the problem because the COPY command may not be able to read the rest of the file beyond the bad sectors. The RECOVER command can be of immense help in this type of situation because its purpose is to extract as much data pertaining to the file as it can, leaving gaps in between that originally pertained to the bad sectors. The RECOVER command makes as much of a copy of the file as it can and writes the data out to new sectors. In the process, RECOVER marks any bad data clusters it encounters in the file allocation table so that they are prevented from being used in the future. Note that RECOVER may not recover all of the file. If you're recovering a text file, you should go through the file with a text editor or word processor and determine if and where data has been lost.

USING CHKDSK TO RECOVER LOST FILES OR PARTS OF FILES

If through the use of the DIR command, you find that the directory listing does not contain files that you know should be there, use the CHKDSK command, initially without any parameters. You probably will get a message stating that a certain number of clusters is lost on the disk. This is a good sign. It indicates that you can use the CHKDSK command again, accompanied by the /F parameter. This causes CHKDSK to read all "lost" clusters and store them in one or more files. For every sequential set of lost clusters CHKDSK encounters, the data contained in them is copied to a file. The first file CHKDSK creates is called FILE0000.CHK. If a gap is found between two sets of lost clusters, CHKDSK copies the contents of the second set of clusters into a second file, called FILE0001.CHK. CHKDSK continues to recover the lost clusters in this manner until all lost clusters are found and deallocated. Sometimes CHKDSK cannot recover all the lost data in one pass because the disk has insufficient room left to write the new files. If this occurs, be sure to copy the recovered (.CHK) files to another disk, delete the old copies, then run CHKDSK again until no more "lost clusters" messages are displayed.

If the recovered data in the files created by CHKDSK corresponds to text files, you can open the file with a text editor or word processor and sort the information. If, however, the recovered data corresponds to files that are not in a readable text format (such as object code or machine code), you'll have to use DEBUG or some other utility to look at the information and sort it out. In either case, do not be surprised if a small part of the data is missing. The part of the disk on which the data was stored may have been so badly damaged that it can't be read. Most of the time, data that isn't recoverable is in increments of 512 or 4,046 bytes (or more bytes), depending on the format of the disk (one 512-byte sector in one cluster for single-sided floppies, two 512-byte sectors in one cluster for double-sided floppies, or four to eight 512-byte sectors in many hard disks). The reason MS-DOS will not recover this data is that the cluster(s) in question already are isolated in the corresponding FAT entries, and each entry contains a value of FF7 that indicates the clusters are bad and that no program is to use them under any circumstances. You could try to read these clusters with DEBUG, but the clusters may be so badly damaged that even DEBUG won't be able to read them.

Recovering Erased Files

As explained earlier in this chapter in references to directory entries and the file allocation table, you can unerase an erased file under certain conditions. When the ERASE or DEL commands are used to erase a file, two things happen to the disk:

1. The first character of the file's name in the directory entry is changed to a hexadecimal value of E5.

2. All the file allocation table entries pertaining to the clusters occupied by the file are zeroed out, meaning that the data clusters are now available for new data storage.

Everything else is left intact, including the remaining information in the file's directory entry and contents of the file's data clusters themselves. However, this only remains the case until new file data is written to the disk. As long as you don't write any new file data to the disk after inadvertently erasing a file, you should be able to recover the file. The actual technical details as to how to go about unerasing a file are beyond the scope of this book. However, several excellent programs are available both commercially and in the public domain that can do the job as well as it can be done. Some of the more popular programs available for unerasing files are Norton Utilities, Ultra-Utilities (user supported), MACE Utilities, and UNDEL (public domain).

In most cases, the aforementioned programs are able to recover an erased file without any problems as long as you haven't written any new information to the disk since the file was deleted. However, the logic used by these programs to trace through the file allocation table and match zeroed-out entries with data clusters is usually sequential. This can pose a problem if the file you deleted is on a hard disk that has seen a significant amount of activity over several months. When files are copied, erased, written, and moved a lot on a hard disk, the data tends to become fragmented, often resulting in complex interweaving file allocation chains. Having a hard disk in this state can make the job of recovering an erased file extremely difficult for any program because there are only three things that a program can go by when recovering an erased file: the file status in the first position of the directory entry, the number of the first cluster occupied by the file, and the file's size. All the program can do beyond this information is to look at a sequence of file allocation table entries that are zeroed out until a sufficient number of entries/clusters have been examined that match the file's size. There's never a guarantee that the file allocation table entries examined all pertain to the correct clusters. It's guess work!

How can one avoid allowing a hard disk to become fragmented over extensive use? There are two ways to, on a periodic basis, correct the fragmentation effect. One is to perform a complete backup of the hard disk, reformat the hard disk, then restore all the backed up files to the hard disk. Another method, which is a lot safer and more efficient, and therefore highly recommended, is to use a *disk optimizer* program, such as Disk Optimizer from SoftLogic Solutions. Optimizing your hard disk with a disk optimizer program on a regular basis can help streamline file allocation on the disk, making the potential success of subsequent erased-file recoveries significantly greater. Having a hard disk optimized on a regular basis during extensive use also significantly speeds up the disk's response time.

Secrets of File Formats

Quite a bit is covered in Chapter 5, *Secrets of MS-DOS commands,* and Chapter 7, *Discovering Secrets: A Debugger Tutorial,* on the different types of command-type files (.COM, .EXE, and .BAT) and how they're treated by MS-DOS and DEBUG. However, other types of files deserve some attention due to the way they are interpreted sometimes by MS-DOS and its commands. The following paragraphs describe how *ASCII files* are treated by MS-DOS.

ASCII Files

Some text files are of a special type known as ASCII text files, or *DOS text files*. Like all files stored on disk, the contents of ASCII files are stored as a series of bytes, each of which normally has a value between 0 and 127. Each byte represents its equivalent character in the ASCII code. The codes contained in ASCII files include lower- and uppercase letters, numbers, punctuation marks, and special symbols such as &, /, ¦, %. Sometimes, control characters are included in ASCII files, which although part of the ASCII code system, are not normally visible when viewing a file on the screen. Appendix C provides a table showing the complete ASCII code system.

The control characters Ctrl-J (ASCII 10), Ctrl-M (ASCII 13), and Ctrl-Z (ASCII 26) have special significance in ASCII files. In all ASCII files, each line of text is terminated by a *newline*—a combination of a carriage return and line feed, represented by Ctrl-M and Ctrl-J, respectively. Ctrl-Z is often used as an end-of-file marker. Normally, when MS-DOS encounters a Ctrl-Z in a file, it does not display anything in the file past that point.

It is interesting to note that although MS-DOS normally recognizes the presence of a Ctrl-Z in a file, it never actually uses it to mark the end of the file because a file's exact size in bytes is always calculated and stored in the file's directory entry. Why does MS-DOS bother with the detection of the Ctrl-Z character? The reason is an historical one. What could be called the ancestor of MS-DOS, or at least a prior generation, is the CP/M operating system. CP/M always used Ctrl-Z marker as the end of file so that it didn't have to calculate a file's exact size. As a result, many application programs originally developed for use under CP/M also used Ctrl-Z extensively. When those applications were converted for use under MS-DOS, they didn't lose this little attention to detail. As a result, many MS-DOS commands, such as COPY, often detect the presence of Ctrl-Z. Probably the most notable example of an application originally developed for use under CP/M, and now in extensive use under MS-DOS, is the WordStar word processor from MicroPro International Corporation.

Although the ASCII code range is officially between 0 and 127, the IBM Personal Computer series and compatible systems use, in addition to standard ASCII codes, what sometimes is called *IBM Extended ASCII*. The IBM extended ASCII system extends the range of codes or characters from 128 to 255. The tables in Appendix C show both the standard ASCII code system and the IBM extended

ASCII system. Although a byte consists of eight bits, the standard ASCII system was originally designed so that none of the characters would use more than the lower seven bits of the byte, leaving the eighth (most significant) bit free to be optionally used as a parity bit for those computers and programs that perform parity checking on ASCII characters. Because parity checking on ASCII bytes is rarely used in modern microcomputers in the storage of files, IBM decided to make use of the eighth bit in ASCII bytes to create a whole new set of characters that can be used in conjunction with the standard ASCII characters.

Although the availability of new extended ASCII characters has proven very useful in a lot of applications, it also has caused problems with certain older application programs, most notably the WordStar word processor. If you use WordStar, or have used it in the past, you undoubtedly have noticed that when WordStar files are TYPEd to the screen, the file doesn't look at all what it should look like. IBM extended ASCII characters are displayed where standard ASCII characters should be. The reason this occurs is because WordStar uses the eighth bit of each ASCII byte for other purposes. The eighth bit is used to distinguish hard carriage returns (normal) from soft carriage returns needed for formatted paragraphs. Other characters are also affected in this way by WordStar, such as spaces and hyphens. So when the file is TYPEd to the screen, the TYPE command interprets all ASCII characters with the eighth bit set as IBM extended ASCII characters and displays them as such.

Several public domain utilities are available (see Chapter 8), which can be used to strip (zero) out the eighth bit of every byte in a Word-Star file. When a file is processed in this manner, none of the actual text is damaged, but the file is no longer a WordStar-formatted file.

If you use WordStar on an extensive basis, refer to Chapter 8 for more information on programs that can convert WordStar files to non-WordStar files when needed.

Summary

This chapter has provided an overview of some of the more critical aspects of files and how files are handled by MS-DOS. In addition to the basics of how disks are formatted and laid out under MS-DOS, topics such as file recovery, file types, and disk optimization are potentially important in almost all aspects of using MS-DOS. If you find yourself in a difficult situation where a significant amount of work has been lost due to damaged, erased, or lost files, refer to this chapter and carefully pursue the recovery methods mentioned. The next chapter covers various types of application programs that are used in the MS-DOS environment.

Secrets of Add-On Software

Chapter 10

One of the consequences of the MS-DOS operating system being in common use for some time is that many software manufacturers are trying constantly to develop new and innovative ideas for application programs. Because so many application programs are available for users of MS-DOS, particularly users of the IBM Personal Computer series and compatible systems, software manufacturers no longer are satisfied with the status quo but are desirous of creating new products for which no competition exists. One of the drawbacks of this situation is that many of the applications have become so fancy that they overtax the MS-DOS environment for which they're intended, or at least they overtax the particular environments that we've set up for ourselves.

This chapter deals with some aspects of add-on software, with the intention of shedding some light on how best to use applications within your system's general environment and how to avoid conflicts between different applications. There are basically two types of applications that potentially conflict with our existing applications. The first type corresponds to the commonly named *desktop applications* or *pop-up utilities,* so called because entire programs usually reside in memory at all times and are activated by special keyboard key sequences. The second type refers to *do-all* applications, often referred to as *integrated* or *operating environment* programs. These programs usually take up as much memory as they can get when they are run and replace the standard MS-DOS interface to the system.

Having pop-up utilities and operating environment programs on your system can be both good and bad, depending on your point of view and what you are trying to do with your system in general. The problem with memory-resident utilities is that it is impossible to find one program that does everything for everyone. As a result, it is no longer uncommon to see several memory-resident programs loaded at once in a system, which can cause conflicts among themselves and with other application programs.

Desktop Accessories

The popularity of desktop accessories, or memory-resident programs, has skyrocketed. When Sidekick from Borland International was introduced in the early 1980s, it changed the applications market.

Problem #1: Having Enough Memory

Ever since Sidekick, memory-resident programs for applications have multiplied. With the current proliferation of memory-resident software, no MS-DOS system has enough memory to load a version of each available application. Although you probably wouldn't want to load one of every application anyway, the problem persists if you want to load a selection of applications, such as a multipurpose program like Sidekick, a keyboard enhancer, a printer buffer, a spelling checker, and so on. Even if you're able to load into memory all the applications you want, your system may not have enough memory left to run nonresident applications. Figure 10-1 shows what a memory map of a system loaded with several "typical" memory-resident programs looks like.

As shown in Figure 10-1, all memory resident programs are loaded after MS-DOS, and therefore are considered to be *above* MS-DOS. So the first memory-resident program loaded is *below* the second, the second below the third, and so on. All remaining free memory lies above the last memory-resident program, which is where non-memory-resident application programs are run. Once a non-memory-resident application finishes execution, all memory above the last memory-resident program is freed for the next application program.

Problem #2: Programs Conflicting with One Another

Another problem with memory-resident programs is that they are a *special* type of application because they're designed to have a certain

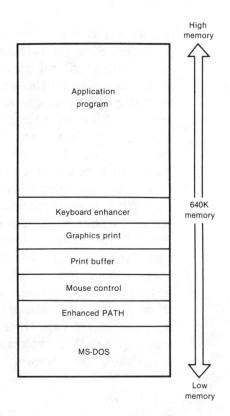

Figure 10-1. Memory Map of System with Several Typical Memory-Resident Programs Loaded

amount of control over the system at all times, even when other application programs are running. They use a special programming function introduced in MS-DOS Version 2.0, called *Terminate and Stay Resident* (often abbreviated to TSR), as opposed to the normal *Terminate* (but not stay resident) function that most application programs used. In addition to the TSR function, memory-resident programs also contain what are called *interrupt vector trappers*.

Even if you don't want to study *interrupts*, you should know that almost all activity between an application program, MS-DOS, and the ROM BIOS is accomplished through the execution of various interrupts. Each interrupt is listed in a vector table with the "go to" addresses of the routines that are to be executed when an interrupt occurs.

Most memory-resident programs intercept certain interrupt vectors. For example, each time you press a key on the keyboard, a specific interrupt occurs, and the vector associated with that interrupt transfers control over the addressed routine that then interprets and does something with the key being pressed. This lasts until another interrupt occurs.

What many memory-resident programs do is intercept one or

more interrupt vectors that have to do with the keyboard. For example, when Sidekick is loaded, pressing the Alt and Ctrl keys simultaneously activates and displays the main menu on the screen over any other text also on the screen. You are normally able to activate Sidekick regardless of the application program currently running, so in order for Sidekick to know whether or not it is to be activated, it must intercept the keyboard interrupt, scan for the codes associated with the Alt and Ctrl key, and, if found, activate itself. If the codes are not found, Sidekick hands over the characters to the ROM BIOS routine that handles keyboard input.

What possibly could be the problem with a scheme of interrupt vector "stealing" used in a program like Sidekick? Well, one problem is that if you want to load several memory-resident programs at one time, and they all have special key sequences that activate them once they've been loaded, conflicts can arise. If all memory-resident programs steal the keyboard interrupt, who has priority? What happens if two different memory-resident programs use the same key sequences to activate themselves? These are the kind of problems that memory-resident programs can cause in a system, and trying to resolve them can often be very difficult.

Problem #3: Removing Memory-Resident Programs from Memory

Another common problem is that once you have the right number of memory-resident programs loaded in memory and working without conflicts with one another, how can you remove them from memory without rebooting the system? You may want a particular program resident except when you need to run a large application program. Some memory-resident programs have "unload" features, but they usually don't work right. The following paragraphs and tricks explain how you can solve these problems.

The Solutions

How can you solve memory-resident program problems? The first problem of running out of memory has an obvious solution: Restrict yourself to only as many programs as can be resident in memory at one time while still having enough left over to run your normal application programs.

DETERMINING WHETHER YOU HAVE ENOUGH MEMORY FOR YOUR MEMORY-RESIDENT PROGRAMS

Determining whether you have enough memory available for the memory-resident programs that you wish to use depends on how well documented the memory-resident programs are, along with a little help from some of the public domain utilities mentioned in Chapter 8. The first step is to obtain the MINFO program as described in Chapter 8. MINFO displays a map of memory, shows how much memory MS-DOS and all other programs currently resident occupy, and how much free space is available. Run MINFO first to familiarize yourself with what it displays and to get an idea of how much free memory you have to work with. Next, read the documentation accompanying the memory-resident software and look for any references to the amount of space occupied by each program. Then, you have to experiment by loading each program and determining how the system performs. Load the first program, then run MINFO to check the status of occupied and free memory. Load the next program, run MINFO again, and so on, until you've loaded all of the programs or at least all of the programs that you can safely fit into memory.

AVOIDING CONFLICTS BETWEEN MEMORY-RESIDENT PROGRAMS

To avoid conflicts between memory-resident programs, carefully read the software's accompanying documentation and determine whether it recommends any particular placement in memory when the program is loaded. Generally, a software developer indicates whether a program should be loaded before or after particular types of memory-resident programs, should be loaded last, or has no particular placement rules.

Generally, if a program's documentation indicates that no special memory-placement requirements are applicable, more than likely it is true. However, such a program is rare. General rules apply to virtually all circumstances: You can determine the approximate order in which memory-resident programs should be loaded by organizing the programs into *categories*.

The following shows the order in which categories of programs should be loaded.

Loaded first: Keyboard enhancer/macro programs

Loaded next: Printer buffers/spoolers and other types of programs that don't require any particular order of placement

Loaded last: Most multifunction pop-up utilities (like Sidekick) and other programs with documentation that stresses being loaded last

Those programs that generally should be loaded first, such as keyboard enhancers or macro programs, operate better with both other memory-resident programs and non-memory-resident application programs if they are loaded *before* other programs. With programs that apparently don't have any particular loading order, be cautious because occasionally they have some exotic routine that conflicts with other memory-resident programs.

Often, the real problems occur with those programs that are supposed to be loaded last (according to the accompanying documentation): What do you do if you have two or more programs that you want to use at the same time, both of which "must be loaded last"? The answer: Experiment to find out which one really should be last, then hope for the best! More than likely, you'll find that two or more "last-load" programs simply will not work together, so you'll have to decide on using one or the other.

Finding out the right order in which memory-resident programs should be loaded is accomplished by first following the advice of the program's developer, then experimenting with varied ordering to see which works best for your system. Once you've established the correct order for loading all the programs, you may find that adding automatic and optional loading capabilities to your AUTOEXEC.BAT file gets all those programs into memory without problems, or optionally, loading some of the programs according to how much memory you want free for other purposes.

The following example shows how you can add the necessary lines to your AUTOEXEC.BAT file to provide the capability of automatically or optionally loading several memory-resident programs when your system is booted. Note that a public-domain program called QUERY is used in the batch file to display a prompt in response to which a yes (Y) or no (N) can be entered. QUERY is described in more detail in Chapter 8.)

```
       .
       .
(other statements at beginning of AUTOEXEC.BAT file)
       .
       .
REM Set default status for autoloading TSR programs:
   SET TSRAUTO=Y
```

```
      SET TSRMARK=N
      SET REF=Y
      SET SL=N
      SET SMPTH=Y
      SET MSMSE=Y
      SET NOKEY=N
      SET GRFTBL=N
      SET GRPHCS=N
      SET PRNT=N
      SET STEPSON=N
      SET TM=N
      SET CUB=N
      SET KEY=Y
      SET LIGHT=Y
      SET SK=Y
REM
REM QUESTIONS:
:Q2
   CLS
   ECHO If you answer Y to the following prompt, each of the
   ECHO following memory-resident programs, shown with "Y" next
   ECHO to it, is automatically loaded (in the order shown).

   ECHO -----------------------------------
   ECHO |     |                | Auto       |
   ECHO |Order|    Program     | Load?      |
   ECHO |=====|================|============|
   ECHO | 1   | REFEREE        | %REF%          |
   ECHO | 2   | SIDELINE       | %SL%            |
   ECHO | 3   | SMARTPATH      | %SMPTH%          |
   ECHO | 4   | MSMOUSE        | %MSMSE%          |
   ECHO | 5   | NOKEY          | %NOKEY%          |
   ECHO | 6   | GRAFTABL       | %GRFTBL%          |
   ECHO | 7   | GRAPHICS       | %GRPHCS%          |
   ECHO | 8   | SETEPSON       | %STEPSON%           |
   ECHO | 9   | PRINT          | %PRNT%         |
   ECHO | 10  | TIMEMASTER     | %TM%         |
   ECHO | 11  | CUBITR         | %CUB%          |
   ECHO | 12  | SUPERKEY       | %KEY%          |
   ECHO | 13  | TURBO LIGHT.|  %LIGHT%           |
   ECHO | 14  | SIDEKICK       | %SK%         |
   ECHO -----------------------------------
   ECHO If you answer N, you'll be asked whether
   ECHO each program is to be loaded.
   ECHO ^H
   ECHO Do you want programs autoloaded
   QUERY as shown in the above table? (Y/N):
   IF not errorlevel 1 SET TSRAUTO=N
   ECHO ^H
   ECHO Do you want the beginning of memory MARKed
   ECHO (after DOS but before REFEREE) so that all
   QUERY memory can be cleared later with RELEASE? (Y/N):
   IF not errorlevel 1 SET TSRMARK=N
   IF errorlevel 1 SET TSRMARK=Y
   IF (%TSRAUTO%)==(Y) goto QEND
```

```
:TSRQS
  CLS
  QUERY Do you want Referee loaded (Y/N)?
  IF not errorlevel 2 SET REF=Y
  IF not errorlevel 1 SET REF=N
  IF (%REF%)==(N) goto :TSRQS2
  ECHO ^H
  QUERY Do you want Sideline (for Referee) loaded (Y/N)?
  IF not errorlevel 2 SET SL=Y
  IF not errorlevel 1 SET SL=N
:TSRQS2
  ECHO ^H
  QUERY Do you want SmartPath loaded (Y/N)?
  IF not errorlevel 2 SET SMPTH=Y
  IF not errorlevel 1 SET SMPTH=N
  ECHO ^H
  QUERY Do you want the MSMOUSE driver loaded (Y/N)?
  IF not errorlevel 2 SET MSMSE=Y
  IF not errorlevel 1 SET MSMSE=N
  ECHO ^H
  QUERY Do you want NOKEY loaded (Y/N)?
  IF not errorlevel 2 SET NOKEY=Y
  IF not errorlevel 1 SET NOKEY=N
  ECHO ^H
  QUERY Do you want GRAFTABL.COM loaded (Y/N)?
  IF not errorlevel 2 SET GRFTBL=Y
  IF not errorlevel 1 SET GRFTBL=N
  ECHO ^H
  QUERY Do you want GRAPHICS.COM loaded (Y/N)?
  IF not errorlevel 2 SET GRPHCS=Y
  IF not errorlevel 1 SET GRPHCS=N
  ECHO ^H
  QUERY Do you want SETUP.COM loaded (Y/N)?
  IF not errorlevel 2 SET STEPSON=Y
  IF not errorlevel 1 SET STEPSON=N
  ECHO ^H
  QUERY Do you want PRINT.COM loaded (Y/N)?
  IF not errorlevel 2 SET PRNT=Y
  IF not errorlevel 1 SET PRNT=N
  ECHO ^H
  QUERY Do you want TIMEMASTER loaded (Y/N)?
  IF not errorlevel 2 SET TM=Y
  IF not errorlevel 1 SET TM=N
  ECHO ^H
  QUERY Do you want memory-resident CUBIT (CUBITR) loaded (Y/N)?
  IF not errorlevel 2 SET CUB=Y
  IF not errorlevel 1 SET CUB=N
  ECHO ^H
  QUERY Do you want SUPERKEY loaded (Y/N)?
  IF not errorlevel 2 SET KEY=Y
  IF not errorlevel 1 SET KEY=N
  ECHO ^H
  QUERY Do you want TURBO LIGHTNING loaded (Y/N)?
  IF not errorlevel 2 SET LIGHT=Y
  IF not errorlevel 1 SET LIGHT=N
```

```
    ECHO ^H
    QUERY Do you want SIDEKICK loaded (Y/N)?
    IF not errorlevel 2 SET SK=Y
    IF not errorlevel 1 SET SK=N
:QEND
        .
        .

        .
    (other batch file statements)
        .
        .

REM
REM LOAD MEMORY-RESIDENT PROGRAMS
REM NOTE: Do *not* change the following order
REM         for loading memory-resident programs!
  CLS
  ECHO Loading memory-resident programs.
  REM
  REM Make sure TSRMARKS directory was created on RAMdisk D:
  REM
  REM Load memory-resident programs
  IF (%TSRMARK%)==(Y) FMARK d:\tsrmarks\start.mrk
  REM
  IF (%REF%)==(Y) CD c:\utils\ref
  IF (%REF%)==(Y) REFWATCH
  REM
  IF (%SL%)==(Y) CD c:\utils\ref
  IF (%SL%)==(Y) SIDELINE /G
  REM
  IF (%SMPTH%)==(Y) CD c:\system\startup\spath
  IF (%SMPTH%)==(Y) SPATH c:\;c:\ws;c:\SC4
  REM
  IF (%MSMSE%)==(Y) CD c:\system\startup\mouse
  IF (%MSMSE%)==(Y) MSMOUSE /1
  REM
  IF (%NOKEY%)==(Y) CD c:\utils\disk\copy2pc
  IF (%NOKEY%)==(Y) NOKEY
  REM
  IF (%GRFTBL%)==(Y) c:\system\GRAFTABL
  REM
  IF (%GRPHCS%)==(Y) c:\system\GRAPHICS GRAPHICS /R
  REM
  IF (%STEPSON%)==(Y) CD c:\utils\printer
  IF (%STEPSON%)==(Y) SETUP
  REM
  IF (%PRNT%)==(Y) PRINT /D:PRN /B:512 /U:1 /M:2 /S:8 /Q:10
  REM
  IF (%TM%)==(Y) CD c:\utils\2
  IF (%TM%)==(Y) TM f/cd=of/
  REM
  IF (%CUB%)==(Y) CD c:\utils\2
  IF (%CUB%)==(Y) CUBITR
  REM
  IF (%KEY%)==(Y) CD c:\utils\keyboard\key
  IF (%KEY%)==(Y) KEY /OT+10
```

```
  REM
  IF (%LIGHT%)==(Y) CD c:\wp\light
  IF (%LIGHT%)==(Y) LIGHT
  REM
  IF (%SK%)==(Y) CD c:\utils\misc\sk
  IF (%SK%)==(Y) SK
:TSREND
  CD c:\
.
.
(other batch file statements)
.
.
REM
REM STATUS REPORTS
  CLS
  VER
  ECHO ^H
  ECHO Memory-resident programs:
SET      REFMSG= ^H
SET   SMPTHMSG= ^H
SET   MSMSEMSG= ^H
SET   NOKEYMSG= ^H
SET  GRFTBLMSG= ^H
SET  GRPHCSMSG= ^H
SET     STEPMSG= ^H
SET     PRNTMSG= ^H
SET       TMMSG= ^H
SET      CUBMSG= ^H
SET      KEYMSG= ^H
SET    LIGHTMSG= ^H
SET       SKMSG= ^H
IF (%REF%)==(Y)        SET      REFMSG=Referee,
IF (%SL%)==(Y)         SET     SIDEMSG=Sideline,
IF (%SMPTH%)==(Y)      SET   SMPTHMSG=SmartPath,
IF (%MSMSE%)==(Y)      SET   MSMSEMSG=MSMOUSE,
IF (%NOKEY%)==(Y)      SET   NOKEYMSG=Nokey,
IF (%GRFTBL%)==(Y)     SET GRFTBLMSG=GRAFTABL,
IF (%GRPHCS%)==(Y)     SET GRPHCSMSG=GRAPHICS,
IF (%STEPSON%)==(Y)    SET     STEPMSG=SETUP,
IF (%PRNT%)==(Y)       SET     PRNTMSG=PRINT,
IF (%TM%)==(Y)         SET       TMMSG=TimeMaster,
IF (%CUB%)==(Y)        SET      CUBMSG=Cubit,
IF (%KEY%)==(Y)        SET      KEYMSG=Superkey,
IF (%LIGHT%)==(Y)      SET   LIGHTMSG=Turbo Lightning,
IF (%SK%)==(Y)         SET       SKMSG=Sidekick,
ECHO %REFMSG%%SIDEMSG%%SMPTHMSG%%MSMSEMSG%
ECHO %NOKEYMSG%%GRFTBLMSG%%GRPHCSMSG%
ECHO %STEPMSG%%PRNTMSG%%TMMSG%%CUBMSG%
ECHO %KEYMSG%%LIGHTMSG%%SKMSG% -- end.
ECHO ^H
.
.
(rest of batch file)
.
```

```
.
REM
 :CLR_VAR
  REM CLEAR OUT UNNECESSARY ENVIRONMENT VARIABLES
  SET TSRAUTO=
  SET REFMSG=
  SET SIDEMSG=
  SET SMPTHMSG=
  SET MSMSEMSG=
  SET NOKEYMSG=
  SET GRFTBLMSG=
  SET GRPHCSMSG=
  SET STEPMSG=
  SET PRNTMSG=
  SET TMMSG=
  SET CUBMSG=
  SET KEYMSG=
  SET LIGHTMSG=
  SET SKMSG=
```

Notice in the above listing that several environment variables are defined toward the beginning of the batch file. These initial settings establish the defaults as to whether each program is loaded automatically. If you enter Y in response to the "autoload" menu, only those programs with Y next to them are loaded automatically. If you answer N in response to the menu, you are asked whether each program is to be loaded. Note that the above example is extracted from the AUTOEXEC.BAT file in one of the author's machines, so the programs listed and the order in which they're loaded is real.

MANAGING YOUR MEMORY-RESIDENT PROGRAMS: ACTIVATION, DEACTIVATION, AND REMOVAL FROM MEMORY

One type of application program that you may consider adding to your system is a *memory resident program manager* (abbreviated as TSR manager in this chapter). Several commercial and public domain utilities can help in the management of memory-resident programs. The main reason one would want to use a TSR manager is to have the ability to *remove* memory resident programs from memory without having to reset the system. The following is a list of TSR manager programs available commercially and in the public domain.

1. MARK, FMARK, and RELEASE (TSR.ARC): These three programs were developed by TurboPower Software and are available in

the public domain (which means they're free). They are not as fancy or sophisticated as some of the other TSR managers but are capable of freeing memory quite effectively. MARK and FMARK are TSR programs themselves, one or more of which can be loaded to mark positions in memory. The RELEASE program frees all memory above and including the last MARK or FMARK loaded. Unfortunately, it is difficult to automate the process of freeing memory with RELEASE using a batch file because RELEASE also destroys the portion of the currently executing batch file in memory before it reaches completion. However, if you don't mind manually clearing memory, these utilities can be very handy additions to your system. See Chapter 8 for more information on these and other public domain programs.

2. PopDrop: PopDrop is a utility from Infostructures that combines the functions of marking and releasing memory. Although not much more sophisticated than MARK and RELEASE, it is an inexpensive way to add a TSR manager to your system.

3. Referee: Referee, available from Persoft, Inc., is probably the most sophisticated TSR manager available. It is a memory-resident program that is loaded before all the other memory-resident programs that you want managed. It is capable of disabling and reenabling memory-resident programs or optionally removing them completely. Referee is normally accessed by entering REFEREE without parameters if you want to access the menu or with parameters to direct commands to Referee without invoking the menu. Referee is accompanied by another program called SIDELINE, which is another memory-resident program that can be loaded optionally after Referee. Sideline provides "hot-key" access to Referee, so Referee's menu can be displayed at any time while running another application by pressing a special key sequence. One of the biggest advantages of Referee is that you can use the REFEREE command accompanied by parameters within batch files without affecting the operation of the batch file. Referee is a highly recommended program.

4. Resident: Available from Information Software, Resident is a slightly different type of program in that it not only manages memory-resident programs but also is able to take normal nonresident applications and make them memory-resident. Resident takes care of providing hot-key access to those programs that it makes resident. One of the advantages of Resident is that because it must be used to actually load programs into memory, if they are to be memory resident, it has a better "handle" on how to remove the programs from memory without hurting other resident applications.

5. Software Carousel: Available from SoftLogic Solutions, Inc., Software Carousel is more of a memory-management program than a TSR manager. It is designed to divide all of free memory (above MS-DOS and any previously loaded TSR programs) into partitions, each of which can

be accessed by simple keystrokes. Although Software Carousel is by no means a multitasking program, it does provide you with the capability of having several application programs loaded at the same time, each in its own memory partition. Both normal applications and memory-resident programs can be loaded into these partitions.

Software Carousel also can make use of *expanded* memory (memory installed above the normal 640K) and treat it as if it were normal memory. Software Carousel is also a TSR manager because it is capable of removing memory-resident programs loaded into its partitions. However, Software Carousel cannot affect any memory-resident programs loaded before Software Carousel was invoked. Software Carousel provides an interesting approach to memory management.

Operating Environments

Another type of application program becoming increasingly popular is the operating environment. An operating environment is a sophisticated program containing many types of applications. Examples of operating environments are Microsoft Windows from Microsoft Corporation, TopView from IBM, and DESQVIEW from QuarterDeck Systems. These programs are called *operating environments* because although they don't replace MS-DOS, they do replace many of its functions as well as its "user-interface." In effect, they behave as if they were operating systems. Operating environments have several advantages and disadvantages. On the advantageous side, many operating environments add multitasking capabilities to the system as well as easy-to-use, common interfaces with the user. Both TopView and DESQVIEW make extensive use of menus, filling the screen with a substantial amount of information at once, and windowing capabilities, allowing you to run and view several application programs simultaneously. Both TopView and DESQVIEW rely on the use of normal ASCII and IBM Extended ASCII characters. Microsoft Windows, on the other hand, uses a bit-mapped interface (graphics) to display windows and icons (much like the Apple Macintosh computer), requiring the use of graphics cards and displays.

Of the disadvantages of operating environment programs, probably the most significant is the amount of memory they require to operate. Although some programs, such as Microsoft Windows, are capable of using portions of a disk as *virtual memory*, they still grab as much memory as they can get. Although these types of programs can provide new and exciting ways of using your computer, they effectively invalidate many aspects of the configuration you had before, such as memory-resident programs. Although some memory-resident programs are usable with operating environments, some of the larger programs, such as Sidekick, take up too much room to justify their use.

Of all the operating environments available today, Microsoft Windows seems to be gaining the most in popularity. With the increased popularity of these programs, we can hope that many application program developers will work toward making their programs more compatible with these operating environments.

File Searchers

With the extensive use of hard disks and directory trees, the MS-DOS search path facility established with the PATH command has become increasingly important in various ways to virtually all MS-DOS users. Although the path created by the PATH command and placed in MS-DOS' environment works well for searching all .COM, .EXE, and .BAT commands entered at the command line, it does not solve some problems encountered with some application programs. Many application programs developed before MS-DOS Version 2.0 was released (the version under which the PATH command was introduced) were not designed with complex multidisk-directory paths in mind. Thus, when we store these types of programs in specific subdirectories on a disk, MS-DOS's PATH command allows the program to be run when we enter its name on the command line, but the program itself is unable to locate its own data files unless the directory in which they're stored is the *current* (default) one.

The Inability of MS-DOS To Search for "Overlay" Files

A classic example of this type of application is the WordStar word processor. The WordStar program, in its basic form, consists of three files: WS.COM, WSOVLY1.OVR, and WSMSGS.OVR. The two .OVR files are called *overlay* files because they contain various parts of the WordStar program that are referenced by WS.COM as it needs them, temporarily overlaying parts of the program in memory. WordStar was designed this way because when it was first introduced under the CP/M operating system (MS-DOS's ancestor) for 8-bit (Intel 8080-based) systems, it had to be able to run using less than 64K of memory. When WordStar was converted to run under MS-DOS and 16-bit machines, its basic structure changed very little. Because CP/M does not support complex tree-structured directories, and rarely is used in systems with more than two floppy disk drives, having WordStar structured the way it is isn't much of a problem. When running Word-Star under MS-DOS Version 2.0 or above in a system with a hard disk, however, problems can arise. If WordStar is executed via the established PATH, and the directory in which the WordStar files are stored is different than the one you currently have active at the time, the program runs, but you get error messages stating that it "can't find its overlay files," thereby rendering WordStar useless.

A facility to search for overlay-type files, similar to the way PATH is used to search for commands, does not exist within MS-DOS. If application programs do not have the search facility built into them, using them in hard disk environments is less than flexible. Many users want to be able to use older application programs, such as WordStar, because they've been using them for years and want to be compatible with their extensive set of text files as well as with other users. What can you do to enable WordStar and other older programs to work smoothly in today's common MS-DOS environments?

The Solution: Adding Extended Path Facilities

Fortunately, the limitations of MS-DOS's PATH facility were not ignored. Several companies have developed add-on memory-resident programs, that, in effect, extend the capabilities of the PATH setting. These third-party programs, referred to in this chapter as *file searchers,* permit you to specify an additional path specifically for the searching of overlay files, independent of and without interfering with MS-DOS's PATH setting. The following box describes some of the file searcher programs available today and explains how some of them are implemented.

ADDING FILE SEARCHERS TO YOUR MS-DOS SYSTEM

Several file searcher programs are available, most of which are commercial and one of which is in the public domain. You may have seen some of these programs advertised or listed somewhere, but usually there is little indication as to what these programs do unless you already know what you're looking for. File searcher programs available are SmartPath (commercial), FilePath (commercial), EasyPath (commercial), and DPATH (public domain).

The following listing shows how you might add the SmartPath file searcher to your system by adding the right statements to your AUTOEXEC.BAT file. The name of SmartPath's program file is SPATH.COM.

```
.
.
(first part of AUTOEXEC.BAT)
.
.
REM
REM ENVIRONMENT PATH SETTINGS
   SET PATH_1=c:\;
   SET PATH_2=c:\sys;c:\bat;c:\utils;
   SET PATH_3=c:\ws;c:\sc4;c:\dbase;c:\comm;
REM
REM ACTUAL PATH SETTINGS
   PATH %PATH_1%%PATH_2%%PATH_3%
   SPATH %PATH_3%%PATH_1%
.
.
(rest of AUTOEXEC.BAT)
.
.
```

The previous example shows how you can first assign path strings to *dummy* variables in the environment, then use those variables to make the actual path assignments both for the MS-DOS PATH command and for SmartPath. Why not assign the paths directly to the commands? The logic behind setting up the paths as shown in the previous example is to keep a record in the environment of what the original path settings were after the system was booted. If you change the PATH or SmartPath settings at any time after booting the system, you can revert easily to the original settings by running a short batch file that reassigns the PATH_1, PATH_2, and PATH_3 environment variables to PATH and SPATH as they are were assigned on boot up.

The following listing shows a slightly different approach to installing a file searcher. The public domain DPATH program has the capability of referencing a specific environment variable for its path string.

```
       .
       .
(first part of AUTOEXEC.BAT)
       .
       .
REM
REM ENVIRONMENT PATH SETTINGS
   SET PATH_1=c:\;
   SET PATH_2=c:\sys;c:\bat;c:\utils;
   SET PATH_2=c:\ws;c:\sc4;c:\dbase;c:\comm;
   SET EP=%PATH_2%%PATH_1%
REM
REM ACTUAL PATH SETTINGS
   PATH %PATH_1%%PATH_2%%PATH_3%
   DPATH

       .
   (rest of AUTOEXEC.BAT)
       .
       .
```

The previous listing shows a variation on how the paths can be set up in the AUTOEXEC.BAT file. The DPATH file searcher program, by default, references the environment variable [EP] unless instructed otherwise. The beauty of this method is that you can change the EP variable at any time without ever having to remove DPATH from memory and reloading it again.

The other file searcher programs are used the same way with only slight variations. The authors have found that SmartPath is the most efficient at finding different kinds of overlay files, but if all you want the file searcher for is WordStar, any of them work just fine.

RAM Disks

Do you ever get tired of waiting for your floppy disk or hard disk drive to finish copying a lot of files? Or maybe you use a word processing program that slows down considerably due to the constant shuffling of data between memory and the disk as files being edited get beyond a certain size. One solution is the addition of a *RAM disk*. A RAM disk is a program that reserves a certain amount of memory to make it appear to MS-DOS as if it were real disk. The biggest advantage of RAM disks is that they are fast! RAM disks operate almost as fast as any other data being moved in and out of memory, "almost" meaning that the speed of the RAM disk is a little slower than regular memory because the RAM disk control program must emulate a real disk, with file allocation table (FAT) sectors, directory sectors, and data sectors and clusters. (See Chapter 9 for more information on disks and disk sectors.)

Advantages and Disadvantages

As mentioned, one of the advantages of RAM disks is that they operate about as fast as one can conceive of a disk drive operating. Unfortunately, speed is about the only advantage worth considering when taking into account the disadvantages. The main disadvantage is that RAM disks lose their contents when the system is turned off. Losing RAMS disks' contents due to power loss is the most critical disadvantage because the potential of losing hours or even days of work is great if you don't have the RAM disk files backed up on a hardware disk.

CAUTION

THE CAREFUL USE OF RAM DISKS

When using RAM disks, always make sure that

    1. copies of all files copied to a RAM disk remain on a hardware disk as backups.

    2. you regularly back up changed files in the RAM disk to a hardware disk, minimizing to minutes worth the amount of potential data loss.

    Note that you can lose the contents of a RAM disk not only to an out-and-out power loss, but also if for some reason the system halts (no response from screen and keyboard), forcing you to turn power off then on again to reboot the system. The importance of backing up a RAM disk *often* cannot be overstressed!

Another disadvantage of RAM disks (or at least a potential one) is the amount of available memory in your system. Many RAM disks can be configured to your specifications when they are first created, but others have limited or no configurability. If your system has a limited amount of memory (say 256K versus 640K) and/or you need to use a lot of the memory for application programs and memory-resident utilities, trying to fit a reasonably sized RAM disk in the remaining memory is difficult. Those RAM disks that have limited or no configurability usually emulate an MS-DOS floppy disk format (see Chapter 9), so the RAM disk can range in size from 160K to 360K. This can be quite a big chunk of your memory, even if you have 640K. Those RAM disks that are configurable may allow you to establish variations of MS-DOS floppy disk formats, such as being able to specify the number of tracks, sectors per track, bytes per sector, directory entries, and so on. Configurable RAM disk programs often allow you to configure RAM disks as small as 64K or as large as you can fit into memory (with enough left over for application programs of course)!

Memory-Resident versus Device Driver RAM Disks

Some RAM disk programs are regular memory-resident programs that can be loaded from the MS-DOS command prompt, whereas others are *device drivers* that must be loaded when the system is booted, using the information in the CONFIG.SYS file (see Chapter 13 for more information on the start-up process). By following the information covered earlier in this chapter on memory-resident programs, you sometimes can remove from memory a RAM disk that is controlled by a memory-resident program. A possible approach is writing a batch utility that automatically backs up a RAM disk to a hardware disk, then removes it from memory to allow more memory for other applications. However, the problems pointed out previously on memory management and the removal of memory-resident programs should be taken into account. As a general rule, if you plan to use a RAM disk, set it up so that it's a relatively permanent part of your configuration and work under the assumption that the memory occupied by the RAM disk is never available for anything other than the RAM disk.

Although the best thing to do if you want to change the configuration of a memory-resident RAM disk is to reboot the system, you definitely have to reboot the system if you're using a RAM disk controlled by a device driver. If you're reconfiguring a device-driver

RAM disk, make sure you change the contents of the CONFIG.SYS file *before* you reboot the system.

CAUTION

ENSURING THAT YOU CAN STILL BOOT THE SYSTEM

When reconfiguring RAM disks that are controlled by device drivers on a system that normally boots off a hard disk, always make sure that you are also able to boot off a floppy disk. This is to ensure that you are still able to boot the system in case the RAM disk configuration in the CONFIG.SYS file on the hard disk does not allow the system to boot properly.

Using Conventional or Expanded Memory for RAM Disks

Most RAM disk programs are obtained only through the purchase of a multifunction or memory add-on card for IBM PC and compatible systems. Although most RAM disk programs work in *conventional* memory (within the 640K range), all memory and multifunction add-on cards that allow the use of expanded memory also include RAM disk programs that make use of expanded memory. Expanded memory is memory that exists outside of the 640K range, accessed by MS-DOS via a special device driver program. For more information on add-on boards and expanded memory, refer to Chapter 11. The advantage of RAM disk programs that use expanded memory rather than conventional memory is that they are fully configurable and use very little conventional memory for the device driver control program itself. Most expanded memory RAM disk programs can be configured from as small as 128K to as large as 8Mb according to how much expanded memory you have installed or want to use.

Increasing the Speed of Accessing Commands in Your System

A RAM disk can also be used to speed the accessing of external commands in your system. By copying the most commonly used command and program files to a subdirectory in the RAM disk and including the RAM disk's drive name and subdirectory in the PATH, the command searches are sped up considerably. The following shows how you can add the necessary statements to your AUTOEXEC.BAT file so that on bootup, the files are automatically copied to the RAM disk. Incidentally, the nice thing about this scheme is that as long as the files are copied from a hardware drive, you never have to worry about losing the files during a power loss.

AUTOMATICALLY COPYING PROGRAM FILES TO THE RAM DISK AFTER BOOTUP

TRICK

The following listing shows how you can have several program and command files automatically copied to a RAM disk after the system has booted. The statements in the listing should be included toward the beginning of the AUTOEXEC.BAT file so that the access speed of the later batch-file commands is improved. All kinds of files can be added, including word processing, spreadsheet calculator, and various utility program files. If you're a WordStar user, you'll find that its performance increases dramatically if you copy both the program file and the overlay files. If you're a Turbo Lightning user, you definitely want to copy the big dictionary file to the RAM disk to maximize Turbo Lightning's thoroughness in checking spelling.

```
     .
     .
     .
(initial statements)
     .
REM
REM INITIAL RAMDISK SUBDIRECTORY SETUP
   MD d:\1
   MD d:\temp
REM INITIAL ENVIRONMENT SETTINGS
   PROMPT $P$G
   SET TMP=d:\temp
   SET TEMP=d:\temp
   SET MAINPATH=d:\1;c:\;c:\system;c:\bat;c:\utils\2
   SET SMRTPATH=d:\1;c:\calc\sc4;c:\database\reflex;c:\comm\xtalk;c:\
.. (other environment variable) ..

REM
REM PATH SETTINGS
   PATH %MAINPATH%
   SPATH %SMRTPATH%
REM
REM COPY UTILITIES TO RAMDISK
```

```
      ECHO Copying WordStar to Drive D:
      COPY c:\wp\ws\ws*.com d:\1/v >NUL:
      COPY c:\wp\ws\*.ovr d:\1/v >NUL:
      ECHO Copying Turbo Lightning's complete dictionary to Drive D:
      COPY c:\wp\light\disk.dic d:\1/v >nul:
      ECHO Copying miscellaneous utilities to Drive D:
      COPY c:\system\1\*.* d:\1/v >NUL:
      COPY c:\bat\1\*.* d:\1/v >NUL:
      COPY c:\utils\1\*.* d:\1/v >NUL:
REM
.
.
.

(rest of AUTOEXEC.BAT file)
.
.
.
```

In the previous example, note that in some cases special subdirectories were created on Drive C to store all the files that are to be copied to the RAM disk. Being able to use wildcards to copy many files at once without repeatedly specifying the COPY command significantly speeds the copying process.

The Importance of Backing Up the RAM Disk

The larger you make your RAM disk (especially if you're using expanded memory), the more likely you are to use it to modify several large files. Thus, regularly backing up the RAM disk becomes crucial. The following box shows how you can create a batch file that loads your favorite word processor, then automatically backs up the text file just edited to a hardware drive.

MASTER TRACK

AUTOMATICALLY BACKING UP YOUR RAM DISK TEST FILES TO A HARDWARE DRIVE AFTER THEY'VE BEEN EDITED

The following batch file is designed to execute a word processor, keep a record of the file being edited, and back up the edited file to a hardware drive. This particular example uses the WordStar word processor (WS.COM). The batch file thus could be named WSX.BAT.

This file's use is simple: WSX can be entered without any parameters to cause display of a prompt, in response to which you enter the file to be edited, or you can enter WSX [filename] where [filename] is the file to be edited. In either case, WordStar is loaded quickly, and you can use it as you normally would. Once you fully exit WordStar, control is returned to the batch file, whereupon you are prompted as to whether or not the file is to be backed up. The path to which the backup is to be made is automatically determined by the edited file's name. Once the backup has been made, WSX.BAT loops back and asks whether you want to edit the same file again. If you want to edit a new file, answer *no*, and the "new file" prompt is displayed. The batch file keeps looping in this manner until you explicitly instruct it to exit. Note that the following example makes use of two public-domain programs ANSWER and QUERY (covered in more detail in Chapter 8).

```
:BEGIN
  SET HARD_DRV=c:\files\writing
  IF (%1)==() GOTO :NOFILE
  SET FILE1=%1
  IF not exist %FILE1% GOTO :NEWFILE
  SET RET_LABEL=:EDIT
  GOTO :SORT
:EDIT
  SET ENTRY=Y
  WS %FILE1%
  GOTO :BACKUP
:NOFILE
  IF (%ENTRY%)==(Y) SET RET_LABEL=:SO
  IF (%ENTRY%)==(Y) GOTO :AGAIN
  ECHO Enter one of the following files or create a new one.
  ECHO Press Enter for no file.
  SDIR
  ANSWER Enter file name to edit:
  IF (%ANSWER%)==() GOTO :END
  SET FILE1=%ANSWER%
  SET RET_LABEL=:SO
  GOTO :SORT
:SO
  IF not exist %FILE1% GOTO :NEWFILE
  GOTO :EDIT
:AGAIN
  ECHO ^H
  QUERY Do you wish to edit to %FILE1% again? (Y/N):
     REM if N pressed, set ENTRY=N
  IF not errorlevel 1 SET ENTRY=N
     REM if Esc pressed, goto END
  IF errorlevel 2 goto :END
     REM otherwise, continue
  IF (%ENTRY%)==(N) GOTO :NOFILE
  GOTO %RET_LABEL%
:NEWFILE
  ECHO The file specified (%FILE1%) does not exist.
  QUERY Do you wish to create it? (Y/N):
```

```
      REM if N is pressed, then goto NOFILE
  IF not errorlevel 1 GOTO :NOFILE
      REM otherwise, continue
  SET RET_LABEL=:EDIT
  GOTO :SORT
:BACKUP
  IF not exist %FILE1% GOTO :NOFILE
  SDIR %FILE1%
  ECHO Do you want to copy (back up) %FILE1%
  ECHO to the following drive/path:
  ECHO ^H
  ECHO %HARD_DRV%%BAKDIR%
  ECHO ^H
  QUERY (Y/N):
  IF not errorlevel 1 GOTO :NOFILE
  IF errorlevel 2 GOTO :END
  ECHO Copying %FILE1% to %HARD_DRV%%BAKDIR%
  COPY %FILE1% %HARD_DRV%%BAKDIR% >nul:
  ECHO Done!
  SET ANSWER=
  GOTO :NOFILE
:SORT
  SET BAKDIR=
  IF (%FILE1%)==(article1.txt) SET BAKDIR=\ARTICLES\ARTICLE1
  IF (%FILE1%)==(article2.txt) SET BAKDIR=\ARTICLES\ARTICLE2
  IF (%FILE1%)==(book1c01.txt) SET BAKDIR=\BOOKS\BOOK1
  IF (%FILE1%)==(book1c02.txt) SET BAKDIR=\BOOKS\BOOK1
  IF (%FILE1%)==(book1c03.txt) SET BAKDIR=\BOOKS\BOOK1
  IF (%FILE1%)==(book2c01.txt) SET BAKDIR=\BOOKS\BOOK2
  IF (%FILE1%)==(book2c02.txt) SET BAKDIR=\BOOKS\BOOK2
  IF (%FILE1%)==(book2c03.txt) SET BAKDIR=\BOOKS\BOOK2
  GOTO %RET_LABEL%
:END
  SET HARD_DRV=
  SET BAKDIR=
  SET ANSWER=
  SET FILE1=
  SET RET_LABEL=
  SET ENTRY=
```

Summary

This chapter has described several popular application programs that can be added to your MS-DOS environment to make using your machine more effective and pleasant. Information also has been included on things to watch for when adding certain types of applications to your systems, particularly any type of memory-resident program. Although not all programs mentioned in this chapter will be used by everyone, they provide good examples of how your system's internal memory can be used very quickly, and the consequences of having several programs loaded simultaneously that conflict with each other or other applications that are subsequently loaded.

Additionally, information was presented on the effects of some operating environments that tend to take control of memory from MS-DOS, sometimes causing various types of problems. Even if you presently don't (or don't plan to) use any of the programs mentioned in this chapter, refer to this chapter to learn about some of the things to watch out for when using extensive amounts of memory or when accessing unusual devices.

Secrets of Add-On Boards

Chapter 11

Because of the immense popularity of the MS-DOS operating system on the IBM family of personal computers, this chapter deals solely with systems and products that are destined for the IBM PC XT and AT family, IBM clones, and IBM compatibles.

System Basics

If you are happy with your existing computer and never plan to add any new boards, you probably don't *need* to read this chapter. However, if you are not one of that blessed group, this chapter is for you.

One difficulty with building your own computer from available system components, or adding new plug-in cards to your existing computer without making other changes, is that not all components work with all other components. The flip side of this problem is that some components which appear to be incompatible or function incorrectly may actually be fine, once you know how to set them up properly. After all, manufacturers are notorious for not telling you everything that you need to know or to watch out for. This chapter is intended to help when you're confronted with these difficulties. The most important trick contained within these pages is *knowledge!*

What this chapter does is tell you about the most common pitfalls you may encounter when you put together or add to a system and how to avoid or work around these problems. In the process, some features that you may not be aware of are mentioned. For those readers who have a board in hand and are anxious to install it, the section on *Memory Space, I/O Space, and Interrupts* is particularly applicable.

Some Necessary Definitions

This chapter begins with the notice that only true IBM systems, clones, and compatibles are covered within. That list itself is quite a mouthful, so it is often convenient, as we have done here, to collect the entire range of products under the single name of *MS-DOS PCs* (remembering as we do so that we are leaving out quite a number of personal computer systems that run MS-DOS, but don't use the IBM architecture). The first pitfall encountered by the novice user is the use of the term *compatible*. You see, compatible means different things to different people.

Compatibility comes in three flavors. First, there are the true IBM products. These items, stamped with the IBM logo, set the standard for *functional* compliance. Unfortunately, they also tend to be more expensive, give less performance, and take up more space than other available products. However, when the emphasis is on having a brand name product, the best known name in personal computers is still *IBM*.

The second level of compatibility consists of the IBM *clones*. These systems are designed to be as close copies of IBM designs as can be legally achieved. Sometimes the distinction is so narrow that only lawyers can tell the difference. However, one aspect usually differentiates the clone from the IBM: The clone performs better. So why doesn't everyone buy clones? These items are often sold by mail order, and you just might end up dealing with a fly-by-night company. Even assuming that the equipment arrives in working order (usually a safe bet), most mail order companies do not have a reputation for extensive support after the sale.

The last level of compatibility consists of those boards and systems that are known simply as *compatibles*. Products in this class promise the same functional operation as IBM products, but they use different methods to meet that goal. Companies that make compatibles, such as COMPAQ and Leading Edge, combine the virtues of a well known firm with the enhanced performance required to compete against IBM. Unlike clones that attempt to duplicate an IBM product exactly (usually including IBM's bugs as well), a compatible product often strives for *software compatibility*. As a result, not all IBM and compatible products work together.

At the hardware level, the MS-DOS PCs (IBM machines, their clones, and IBM compatibles) all belong to a single group of *bus compatible* machines. Bus compatible means that you can plug a board intended for an IBM system into a clone or compatible system and reasonably expect that it will work correctly. In more technical terms, bus compatible means that the board follows a standard definition of what contacts are used for what purposes, which voltage levels are used for signals, the physical dimensions of the board, and to a lesser extent, what timing parameters the board requires and what timing specifications it adheres to.

However, this does not mean that choosing bus compatible boards is all that is required to assure a proper hardware configuration. Even if a board is bus compatible, there may be other reasons that it won't work with your existing system. To find out why, we look at a typical MS-DOS PC to see what is inside.

The Motherboard

The heart of any MS-DOS PC is the *motherboard*. That's usually the large printed circuit board at the bottom of the system enclosure. The motherboard contains the main processor chip, some system memory, and the keyboard, power supply, and expansion slot connectors. One other item found on the motherboard that is of utmost importance is the BIOS ROM. This device contains a program that tells the system how to get started when the power is turned on and how to use the devices once the system is running.

The three basic types of PC motherboards are designated by the type of IBM machine that they resemble. Earliest were the IBM PC motherboards, designed around the 8088 processor. Their most visible feature is that they have only five connectors for expansion boards. Less visible, but more important, is that the original IBM PC motherboards can only contain a maximum of 64K of RAM memory.

As the prices of semiconductor (RAM) memory prices decreased and hard disk storage units' popularity burgeoned, the IBM XT was introduced. The XT added a hard disk unit, the XT's motherboard was modified to support up to 256K of memory, and the number of board connectors was increased to eight. The processor chip, the 4.77 MHz Intel 8088, was unchanged.

Finally, as the market clamored for more performance, the IBM AT was designed. It uses the newer and more powerful 80286 processor. Unlike the 8088, which internally is a 16 data bit processor using an 8-bit external data bus, the 80286 required a 16-bit external data bus. So, coincident with the change in processor, the bus on the IBM

AT was expanded to 16 bits. This required a different type connector. Rather than make obsolete all the previous products in one fell swoop, IBM decided to implement the bus and connectors so as to allow the use of the older style PC XT boards in the AT, but only in five of the eight slots.

When IBM introduced a new model, development did not stop on the old models. Later revisions of both the PC and XT models were released. These revisions included increasing the PC's memory to 256K and the XT's memory to 640K. Three versions of the IBM AT motherboard were released. The first revision expanded memory capacity to 640K. The latest revision increased the AT's processor speed from 6 MHz to 8 MHz. (The IBM XT 286, which is basically a 6 MHz AT in an XT-type enclosure is also available.)

In addition to the changes IBM has introduced, the compatible and clone manufacturers have made modifications, producing motherboards with higher speed processors and varying amounts of memory. Because the characteristics of motherboards aren't easily changed, you might think that an owner of an older system is left with a pink elephant. Luckily, in the computer market, where there's a will, there's a way. Thoughtful manufacturers, well aware of the large number of older systems, now provide upgrades that change PCs into XTs, add memory to the motherboards, and even allow higher processor speeds.

Adding Memory to the Motherboard

With board space at a premium, and software requiring more and more memory (Microsoft's C compiler, for example, requires a *minimum* of 256K), increasing the storage capacity of the IBM PC- and XT-style motherboards is becoming increasingly popular. (The AT-style motherboards already come equipped to handle from 512K to 1M.) A number of after-market kits are available to assist in this endeavor and are usually quite simple to install. The first step in changing your system is to determine your existing configuration.

Table 11-1 shows the common motherboard configurations available in 1986, and what can be done to improve the situation. Some types of motherboards may be upgraded simply by changing a few chips. Other upgrades require some soldering and other hardware work. For those who don't feel up to doing the "cuts and patches," some of the better computer service stores often do the work at a nominal cost.

Table 11-1.   Motherboard Memory Configurations

Mother -board	Standard Configuration					After Mod.	Soldering Required?
	Bank 0	Bank 1	Bank 2	Bank 3	Total		
PC-1	16K	16K	16K	16K	64K	640K	Yes
PC-2	64K	64K	64K	64K	256K	640K	Yes
XT-1	64K	64K	64K	64K	256K	640K	No
XT-2	256K	256K	64K	64K	640K	Not required	
AT-1	128K	128K	128K	128K	512K	Not available	
AT-2	64K	64K	256K	256K	640K	Not required	

One distributor of upgrade kits is ARISTO Computer Services (listed in Appendix B), which even has a network of associated dealers who can do the necessary work. Upgrade kits are available from them for IBM PC, IBM XT, close clones, and early COMPAQ models.

DON'T FRY YOURSELF!

When you open a computer, make sure the computer is turned off. Better yet, unplug the computer from the power source. The inside of a computer is not as unfriendly as, for example, a television, but nasty electrical shocks are possible. In addition, operating on a computer with the power on can damage expensive components. You should leave "power-on" troubleshooting to professionals unless you are experienced in electronics.

DETERMINING YOUR COMPUTER'S MEMORY CONFIGURATION

You can determine the memory configuration of your computer. *First, turn the power off and unplug your system.* Open the system enclosure and look for a group of similar chips laid out as 4 rows of 9 chips. On an IBM-type motherboard, these chips are located on the right front corner of the board. The chips themselves are about ¼″ wide and about 1″ long (6.3mm by 19.2mm is the industry standard). On the top of each chip, two rows of numbers are printed. One is the batch designation (when and where it was made), and the other is the part number, which contains the information you're after.

The part number can be identified by a trailing hyphen and number. Examples of the number are MB8264A-15 and D41256C-15. The two or three digits before the hyphen should be 16, 64, or 256, indicating that the chip holds 16K, 64K or 256K *bits*. The size of each memory bank (9 chips) is the same as the number on the chip: 16K, 64K or 256K. The number after the hyphen gives the response time of the memory chip in *tenths of nanoseconds*. (A nanosecond is one billionth of a second and is abbreviated as *ns*.) Common speeds for personal computer memories are 10 (100ns RAMs), 12 (120ns RAMs), 15 (150ns RAMs), and 20 (200ns RAMs).

The memory banks on an IBM-type motherboard are normally numbered from back to front, starting at zero, and they must be filled with memory starting at bank zero. Rows of sockets without chips are always the higher numbered banks. Eight chips in each bank are required to make a byte. (Eight 64-Kbit chips hold 64K.) The ninth chip in a memory bank provides *parity,* a method of detecting errors in the memory.

To find the total memory contained on the motherboard, add the sizes of each memory bank. You can compare this number with Table 11-1 to determine what type of system you have.

This method of reading the part number to find the memory size should only be applied to motherboard memory where each chip is known to be one bit wide. For example, the eight MB81464-12 chips used on Paradise Auto-Switch EGA cards appear to be 64 Kbit chips but are actually 64K by 4 bits, which yields a total of 256 Kbits. In these cases, only the manufacturer's part specification tells for sure, and that information is usually obtained from the semiconductor manufacturer's catalog or specification sheets.

Processor Speed Upgrades

The basic throughput of the system is mostly determined by the speed at which the central processing unit (CPU) executes instructions. (IBM PCs, XTs, and lookalikes nearly always use an Intel 8088 processor, whereas the IBM AT and its imitators use the Intel 80286.) For any system, the processor's throughput is a function of its internal efficiency and the clock speed at which it is run. Although not much can be done individually to change efficiency, a processor running at a higher clock rate does execute instructions faster.

Crystal Oscillators   The clock rate on any system is determined by a *crystal oscillator.* This is a little silvery "can," about ½" square and

⅛″ high, with two leads coming out of it. Stamped on the top is the crystal frequency in megahertz (MHz). The form is 14.31318, 24.00, or similar. In a PC- or XT-type system, that number is *three times* the frequency used by the processor. The PC XT standard is a 4.77 MHz processor, which requires a 14.31318 MHz crystal. In the case of AT-type systems, the crystal's frequency is only twice that of the processor's frequency. The 6 MHz IBM AT uses a 12.00 MHz crystal.

Because changing the crystal changes the processing speed, changing one part would seem to result in a big improvement. The obstacle is that with computer parts, as with cars, faster parts cost more money. With this in mind, systems are built with the least expensive parts that can do the job. For example, an IBM XT system is designed for operation at 4.77 MHz. The 8088 processor won't "cut it" over 5.0 MHz. The 200ns RAM memory chips can't "take it" over 5.0 MHz. Even worse, some of the soldered support chips may impose limitations to higher speed operations.

This isn't to say that changing the crystal won't increase the speed, just that it's a job for an experienced computer technician, who can advise you whether your system is suitable for such an upgrade.

The NEC V Series of Processors   Although changing the crystal frequency of your system can give you increased performance, don't take this step lightly. Although most of us shy away from extensive hardware modifications, this doesn't necessarily "leave us out in the cold" regarding processor *throughput* improvements. Increased performance can be achieved not only by increasing the system clock frequency, but also by making the processor use the existing clock more efficiently.

Just as Zilog introduced the enhanced-performance Z80 to compete against the Intel 8080, Nippon Electric Company (NEC) has developed two processors that not only execute 8088 code, but do it faster with the same clock frequency and offer extra instructions as well. These products, the V20 (replacing the 8088) and the V30 (replacing the 8086), are touted as offering as much as a 25 percent throughput improvement. Although this percentage is true for some kinds of programs, a more typical figure seems to be about 10 to 15 percent overall improvement.

Buying a NEC V20 isn't just valuable for gaining speed. The V series also offers compatibility with the older 8080 series instruction set, allowing users to run most older programs intended for the CP/M operating system. Of course, a software package is required to provide the services of the CP/M system. For the old-timers whose taste runs more to the Z80, rumor has it that NEC plans to release the V25 and V35 processors that supposedly will provide compatibility with the esteemed Z80.

Another advantage of the V20 and V30 chips is that they consume less power and run cooler. Many users of the V-series chips have reported that overheating problems previously experienced in their systems don't occur once the new chip is installed.

The "down side": Although the NEC V20 is for most purposes a pin for pin replacement of the Intel 8088, the V20 apparently won't work in some systems. Most sources seem to agree that although nearly all true IBM machines and close clones can accept the V20, the results when used in compatibles is mixed. Still, the majority seem to accept the chip. At an average cost of about $20, it doesn't seem a bad gamble.

Before rushing out to buy a new crystal or processor, you should know that another, maybe better, way to increase system throughput is *accelerator cards*. These plug-in cards, often containing their own memory, can boost your system's performance without the hassles of resocketing chips, cutting circuit traces, and soldering. Accelerator cards are covered in their own section under *Product Guide* in this chapter.

If That's Not Enough

When either the cost or difficulty of a processor upgrade isn't worth it, or the resulting performance increase isn't good enough, one other option is available. Replace the entire motherboard! This really isn't as difficult as it seems. All the work of replacing the motherboard is mechanical disassembly and reassembly. Nearly all after-market motherboard kits come with complete instructions on removing drives, disconnecting the power supply, and removing the board. Reverse the steps to install the new board and reassemble the system.

Motherboard replacements often offer features that the originals never had, such as the ability to change processor speeds, increased memory space, pins for a true hardware reset line, and more. The prices range from about $125 for a dual-speed (4.77 MHz and 8 MHz) XT motherboard to about $500 for an 8 MHz AT motherboard, so they can be great deals for the performance-minded user who doesn't mind spending an evening getting into the machine.

Note that although these boards usually come with processor chip and ROM BIOS, they don't normally include memory chips. Bought separately, the chips are just plugged in. *Ground yourself while doing the work to prevent static damage.*

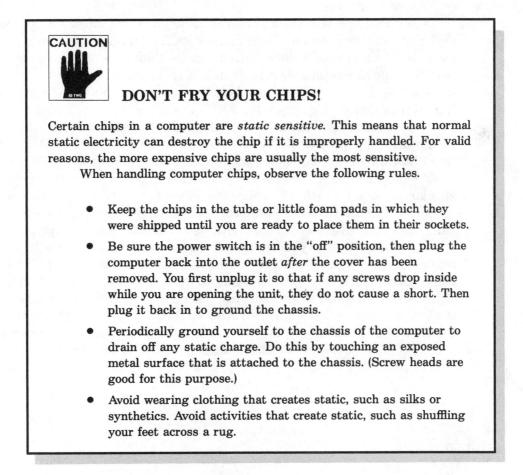

CAUTION

DON'T FRY YOUR CHIPS!

Certain chips in a computer are *static sensitive.* This means that normal static electricity can destroy the chip if it is improperly handled. For valid reasons, the more expensive chips are usually the most sensitive.

When handling computer chips, observe the following rules.

- Keep the chips in the tube or little foam pads in which they were shipped until you are ready to place them in their sockets.

- Be sure the power switch is in the "off" position, then plug the computer back into the outlet *after* the cover has been removed. You first unplug it so that if any screws drop inside while you are opening the unit, they do not cause a short. Then plug it back in to ground the chassis.

- Periodically ground yourself to the chassis of the computer to drain off any static charge. Do this by touching an exposed metal surface that is attached to the chassis. (Screw heads are good for this purpose.)

- Avoid wearing clothing that creates static, such as silks or synthetics. Avoid activities that create static, such as shuffling your feet across a rug.

Incompatibilities Due to Speed

We've been approaching the subject of speed and memory increases as if they were unconditionally desirable. Although this is true of memory increases where more memory can't hurt you (unless you get into *memory conflicts,* explained in the next section on *Memory Space, I/O Space, and Interrupts*), even successful speed increases can have nasty side effects. In the early days of creating applications programs for the IBM series, some software developers decided to squeeze the last ounce of performance from existing hardware by making use of idiosyncrasies and timing characteristics of the hardware. What this means in plain English is that although programs like the early Visi-Calc run fine on the standard IBM PC or XT, they don't work so well on "souped up" versions.

To solve speed compatibility problems, most high speed clones and compatibles have an "IBM compatibility" mode. The funny part is that this mode usually does nothing more than slow down the system to IBM performance levels. Look for this feature on systems, motherboards, and add-in boards. It can be invaluable when products fail to function at high speeds.

"Supercharged" clones aren't the only systems susceptible to the incompatibility problem. Prospective owners of AT and AT-clone systems should be aware that some PC XT software will *never* run on their system, and XT users may occasionally (but rarely) experience similar problems with PC software. Sometimes there are just basic incompatibilities between some software designer's myopic view of the world and the ever expanding options available from computer hardware. Luckily, these types of problems are usually confined to games (which always seem to make more hardware assumptions). If you're really addicted to some vital piece of software, make sure it runs on the system that you're considering before you sign the check. Ask the dealer for a presales demonstration. If the dealer won't do it, find another dealer. After all, it's your money. Sometimes it helps to take your favorite software to the dealer and try it out on the machine you're planning to buy.

Board Basics

The motherboard of an IBM-type system supplies the basic memory, the processor, and the keyboard interface. Functionally, that results in a computer that can accept and process commands, but can't store, transfer, or display data. These functions are provided by the boards that are plugged into the system's *expansion slots*.

The name *expansion slots* is somewhat of a misnomer because these slots are required for more than just expansion. Maybe it is for this reason that IBM calls these slots *I/O channels*. At the very minimum, a mass storage interface (hard or floppy disk) and display interface is required. Before going into individual board types, let's review the parameters that apply to the selection and installation of a board.

Physical Space

If you are thinking of adding another card to your system, the first thing that you must resolve is whether your system has enough room inside to hold another board. These boards are plugged into the motherboard connectors. The number of slots for a particular motherboard and their characteristics are shown in Table 11-2.

Table 11-2.   Physical Characteristics for Expansion Slots

Motherboard Type	Number of Slots	Card[1] Dimensions	Slot[2] Spacing	Connector Type[3]
PC	5	13.12″ x 4.0″	1.0″	62 pin
XT	6	13.12″ x 4.0″	13/16″	62 pin
	2	5.0″ x 4.0″		
XT Clone[4]	7	13.12″ x 4.0″	13/16″	62 pin
	1	6.0″ x 4.0″		
AT	6	13.12″ x 4.8″	13/16″	62 & 36 pin
	2	13.12″ x 4.8″		62 pin
COMPAQ 286	2	13.12″ x 4.8″	13/16″	62 & 36 pin
Portable	2	13.12″ x 4.8″	13/16″	62 pin
	1	6.0″ x 4.8″	13/16″	62 pin

All dimensions are +/−1/8″
[1] Board height does not include the connector (see Figure 11-1).
[2] Manufacturers recommend 1/4″ space between adjacent cards.
[3] PC XT-type 62-pin connector is 8-bit only. AT-type connectors consist of an 8-bit, 62-pin connector *and* an additional 8-bit, 36-pin connector.
[4] Common clone configuration—not all systems are the same.

The most important difference shown in Table 11-2 is the difference that exists between a PC XT-style card and an AT-style card. An AT-type card has an extra edge connector that is used for the extra bits of data and address that the AT supports. (This is how the AT provides for 16-bit data accesses. The ability to read two bytes at a time means that the AT can read and write to memory twice as fast as a PC or XT, both of which can access only one byte per bus cycle.)

The presence of the extra connector on an AT-style card means that an AT card cannot be installed in a PC or XT chassis. Cards intended for the AT may be used only in an AT. What about the other way around? As it turns out, many but not all cards developed for the PC XT can be successfully installed in an AT. Two conditions can prevent use of a PC XT card in an AT. The physical condition is that some PC XT cards gain additional board space by having the board descend below the level of the connector (the area marked in dotted lines in Figure 11-1). If this proves to be the case with a given board, it still can be plugged into the XT-only slots of the AT, which lack the second connector, but only if there's sufficient clearance with the chips on the motherboard. The second reason that PC XT cards fail in an AT system is speed. The difference between the 4.77 MHz clock rate in the PC and the 6.00 MHz rate in the AT can be too much for some boards. If you aren't sure about the board, ask first.

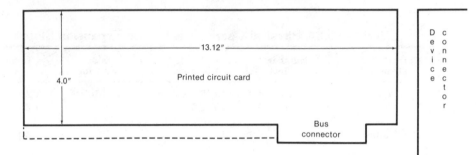

Figure 11-1.   IBM PC XT-Style Card Physical Layout

Not all the slots in a chassis can take a standard size board. In nearly all PC XT systems (and clones) the rightmost slot, and sometimes two righthand slots, are partially blocked by the presence of a storage device in the left *drive bay,* such as a floppy disk drive, a hard disk, or a tape drive. (The name *drive bay* is derived from the use of *bay* as an enclosed place to park something, such as a "hanger bay" for airplanes.) Sometimes there appears to be enough room to squeeze a card into one of the short slots, but this *must not be done!* There must be enough clearance between a card and a device to prevent physical contact, which can cause *shorting* (a short circuit) on the board. Close inspection usually reveals that a full-length board would indeed contact the side of the drive.

However, these blocked slots are not wasted. With increasing miniaturization of circuits, many functions that normally occupied an entire card now can be found on what are called *half-slot cards,* which are usually less than 6″ long. Some examples of half-slot cards available as of this writing are display controllers, internal modems, serial port and parallel port interface cards (required for interfacing to printers, external modems, "mouse" devices, etc.), memory cards, and much more. These types of cards are ideal for use in a short slot, which saves the longer slots for those cards that require them.

Assuming that you have determined that a slot exists for a prospective card and that the slot is long enough, are you ready to plug the card in and go? Unfortunately, no. One other physical space requirement is the thickness of the card. Although many cards are only as thick as the chips on the board, some cards use what are known as *daughter cards* or *piggy-back cards*. These are smaller cards that plug onto the main card, allowing additional features and/or memory to be added to an existing card without using another connector. Boards actually exist that use up to two layers of daughter cards (one on each side of the main card), which achieves the astonishing thickness of nearly 1⅛″. Such cards rarely fit next to adjacent cards.

On the original IBM PC and its clones, there is one inch between adjacent cards. With the advent of the IBM XT, 8 slots were squeezed into the same space as the previous 5 slots of the IBM PC, which decreases the slot spacing to about ¾″ between cards. Although sufficient even for most boards that use daughter cards, some older boards can cause problems when used in the XT chassis. The only way to be sure is to check your particular configuration.

Drive Bay Space

The areas in a system enclosure where the drives are installed are known in the trade as the *drive bays*. In the IBM PC and XT there are two bays, each about 5.8″ wide by 3.2″ high by about 8″ in depth. Devices designed to fit these bays are called *five and a quarter inch drives* because the media used in them is usually a disk 5¼″ across. A storage device that matches the drive bay dimensions is known as a *full-height* drive because it uses all 3.2″ of height. As the need grew to pack more performance into the same space, *half-height* drives were developed. These units are the same width and depth, but only about 1.6″ high, which allows two of them to be stacked into the space of a full-height drive. Available also are a few third-height drives, which allow the installation of three drives in a full-height bay. The IBM AT computer also has two drive bays, but each bay is 50 percent higher than those in the PC XT chassis, allowing up to six half-height units to be installed.

Today, you can find floppy disk drives, hard disk drives, and tape storage devices in the half-height format. Because these devices are often of newer design than their larger cousins, they are usually more reliable and require less power, which makes them an intelligent choice for a new or expanded system.

An alternative format that is becoming increasingly popular with the compact models is the 3½-inch drive. These drives are smaller still, usually requiring even less power. The IBM laptop PC uses 3½-inch drives, and these drives are now available as options for other IBM personal computer models. Support for the new 3½-inch format was officially introduced with MS-DOS Version 3.2, so if you add 3½-inch drives to your PC and you want to ensure that you're using the format endorsed by Microsoft and IBM, you need to upgrade to MS-DOS Version 3.2 or higher. Almost all laptop computers running MS-DOS use 3½-inch drives, but not all of them adhere to the format used in MS-DOS Version 3.2.

Installing a drive can be a very simple matter and requires only a few minutes if you have the proper materials. However, some things that you need to be aware of are

- Mounting hardware (screws, cables, plates, etc.) is not included with the drive unless the vendor explicitly states that it is supplied.

- Not all drives use the same kind of mounting screws. For example, TEAC floppy disk drives have different screw threads than most other types.

- Where standard screws can be used, their length varies. For example, the standard screws from an IBM drive fit the screw holes in the popular Seagate ST-225 hard disk drive, but they are too long. Unless trimmed to size, they can puncture the case and damage the drive when fully tightened!

- If you are installing two half-height drives in a bay, you need a special mounting plate. Although you can pay up to $5 for this piece of tin, you can probably make your own, using Figure 11-2 and the actual dimensions from your drives as guidelines.

- If you are installing two drives in place of one, you need a Y connector for the power cables to your drives. This item can usually be purchased from a computer supply or electronics supply store.

- Depending on the type of drive controller, you may need a different data and control cable to add a second drive. If you're not sure, ask the vendor for advice. Usually the cables are *keyed* so that they can be put on the connector in only one position. If this is not the case, note that most cables have a colored stripe on one side, denoting the *pin one* position. If you're not sure which side is pin one, ask! Putting a cable on backward can badly damage the drive or controller.

- Another helpful tool when installing two drives in a single bay is a file for removing some of the plastic faceplate. For some reason, the faceplates on half-height drives tend to be somewhat oversized and require adjustment. *Take care not to get dust or chips into the drive.*

- *Work with the power off and the computer unplugged.*

By following directions, almost anyone can install a second drive. Take your time, have patience, and if you get into trouble, ask someone. Better to take an extra day than see expensive equipment go "up in smoke."

Power Problems

Another factor to take into account when adding boards or peripherals (including storage devices) to your system is the power consumption of the device. A power supply can provide only a finite amount of power. If this amount is exceeded, your system may fail to work or, worse, suffer permanent damage. Understanding the power distribution system of your computer can help prevent overloading.

To begin, the typical PC XT or AT power supply produces four different voltages, plus and minus five volts (+5V DC and −5V DC), and plus and minus twelve volts (+12V DC and −12V DC). These voltages

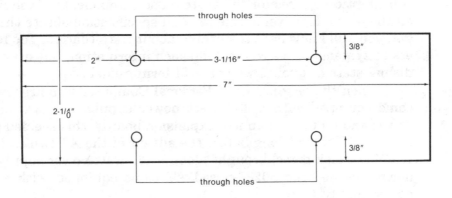

Figure 11-2.   Half-Height Mounting Plate

are distributed to the rest of the system through four PC XT or five AT connectors. Two six-pin connectors are used to supply power to the motherboard, and the remaining two or three four-pin connectors are used for the +5V and +12V supplies to the drives. To complete the distribution, all four voltages are bused out from the motherboard to the card connectors into which add-on boards are plugged.

In turn, each of the boards or devices installed in the system draws on one or more of the voltages supplied to it. The task at hand is to make sure that no combination of boards or devices draws more power than the power supply can provide. First, we'll consider the ideal method.

Each of the individual lines from the power supply can supply a particular current load, expressed in units of *amperes* (abbreviated as A, and commonly referred to as *amps*). Each of the cards or devices draws a particular load, also expressed in amperes. All that is required is to make sure that the amps drawn on any line do not exceed the amps provided.

For example, if the four-pin drive connectors that supply power to the storage devices are each rated at 2.8A on the +12V line and 1.8A on the +5V line, that connector can supply power to any drive or combination of drives (if half-height drives are considered) that doesn't require more than the rating. Amperage is additive, so two floppy disk drives that each require 1.0A of +12V and 0.5A of +5V require a total of 2.0A on the +12V and 1.0A on the +5V, still remaining under the maximum supply capacity of that connector and power supply. Exceeding power capacity cannot only damage components or the power supply, but it can also melt wires and cause fires.

So much for the ideal. What is the actual situation? If there was ever a big unknown in personal computers, it is the power supply and consumption figures for the system and components. Even if you read all the manuals, advertisements, and specification sheets that you can get, you still know next to nothing about the situation. Too few suppliers of systems or boards include such information, but even with this dismal state of affairs, we can still form guidelines.

When the original IBM Personal Computer was first released, it came equipped with a 63.5-watt power supply. For two floppy disk drives and no more than five expansion boards, this seemed sufficient. However, it wasn't long before the advent of the XT (which included a 10M hard disk drive) brought along a 130-watt power supply. Further down the line, the 80286-based AT came equipped with a 200-watt power supply.

One can only assume that this continual increase in power capacity is related to some real need. However, casual observers who focus on the expanding use of CMOS components might also conclude that power supplies would get smaller because CMOS components require less power and yield higher degrees of circuit integration, thus reducing the number of chips required on a board. Is the need for bigger and bigger power supplies all hype? It's hard to know for certain. In certain cases, hard disk drives have been successfully added to original IBM PC systems (with their 63.5-watt power supplies). On the other hand, some people have added so many boards to their systems that their power supplies simply shut down. (Shutting down is the proper—noncatastrophic—response to overloading.)

Among all these conflicting claims, where does the truth lie? In most cases, it seems that 63.5 watts is insufficient for a fully loaded system, especially if a hard disk drive is installed. (See Table 11-3.) However, it is very rare to hear of a system failure due to overloading a 130- or 150-watt power supply. The rule of thumb: Buy as big a power supply as you can afford that still fits inside your system and hope for the best. Until manufacturers see fit to inform us clearly of the power requirements of their products, it will be very difficult to calculate the actual amount of power required. Note that although the 200-watt power supply used in the AT is physically too big to fit in a PC or XT system, PC XT power supplies rated higher than 150 watts may be available in the near future.

Table 11-3. Approximate Power Supply and Consumption Examples

Power Supply Type	Max Current (amps) @			
	+5V	−5V	+12V	−12V
63.5-watt power supply	7.0	0.3	2.0	0.25
130.0-watt power supply	15.0	0.3	4.2	0.25
200.0-watt power supply	19.8	0.3	7.3	0.30

Current Requirements (amps) for device type	Normal		Max	
	+5V	+12V	+5V	+12V
5¼″ full-height disk drive	0.6	0.9	Not avail.	
10M full-height fixed disk	0.7	1.8	1.0	4.5

Device/Board	Power Consumed
Motherboard	~ 10 to 15 watts
Floppy disk drive	~ 12 to 15 watts
Hard disk drive	~ 10 to 20 watts
Disk controller card	~ 5 watts
Video display card	~ 6 watts
Memory card (1M)	~ 5 watts
Accelerator card	~ 7 to 13 watts

Table 11-3 reflects the power supply and consumption figures for some typical power supplies, boards, and components gleaned from what little information is available. These numbers may or may not relate to other boards or components and are only meant as a rough indication.

Memory Space, I/O Space, and Interrupts

For a board to be of use to the system, the system must be able to communicate with it. The three methods that can be used for communication between a board and a system are as follows:

1. Shared memory, where the board and the system communicate by reading and writing a common memory space.

2. Input/output memory called *I/O ports*, another type of memory addressing that is accessed with the special 8088 instructions IN and OUT. These should not be confused with *communications ports*, such as COM1 and LPT1.

3. *Interrupts*, which are a means for a board to signal the main processor that something just happened or that the board requires service. Interrupts are used in conjunction with either shared memory or I/O ports.

When a board is assigned a memory range or group of I/O ports, it has *exclusive* rights to those addresses. Therefore, no more than one board in a system may use the same I/O ports. The reason for this is that where two boards share the same addresses, they would both start talking at the same time when the system tries to communicate with them. The system would be unable to tell which board was responding and each board could be receiving commands intended for the other. Not only is this confusing to the system and the boards, it is potentially damaging.

To ensure that each board and device has an exclusive means of communications, the memory and I/O addresses in the system are allocated to certain functions. A chart of what addresses are used for what functions is called a *map*, and although there is some flexibility in assigning functions, there is also a standard.

The Memory Map

The heart of any computer is its CPU. In a PC or XT computer, this is an Intel 8088, which has 20 *address lines* with the capability to reference 2^{20} bytes of memory. In more common terms, the Intel 8088 has the ability to address 1,048,575 bytes of data, more often called 1 megabyte. This memory is often viewed as 16 groups of 65,536 bytes apiece, called *segments*. In computer terminology, 1,024 bytes are known as one kilobyte (K), so each segment can be said to be 64K long. Figure 11-3 shows this information in a visual form. The addresses shown in Figure 11-3 are given in the hexadecimal number system, which we use in this chapter for memory addresses.

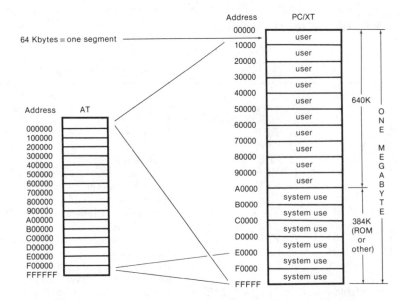

Figure 11-3.   Relationship of PC XT to AT Memory

As Figure 11-3 indicates, the memory addressable by the PC or XT is only a fraction of the memory that may be used by AT-type computers, such as the IBM AT and COMPAQ 286. AT systems use the Intel 80286 or 80386 CPUs, which have 24 address lines rather than 20. As a result, they can address 2^{24} bytes or 16Mb of memory!

Unfortunately, because of the IBM architecture, MS-DOS is only able to use 640K of memory for the programs and system. (XENIX, another operating system for AT-type computers, is able to access directly the additional memory, but that is another story.) However, the additional 15Mb of memory space in an AT need not go to waste.

Called *Extended Memory,* memory installed in this space can be configured as RAM disk drives or bank-switched memory. The section *Add-On Memory* later in this chapter goes into more detail on this subject.

Our concern lies mostly with MS-DOS' use of the first megabyte of address space. Under the IBM standard, the first ten segments of this memory are made available for general use. This is where MS-PC DOS and the applications programs reside. The remaining six segments are reserved for use by the ROM BIOS, various device drivers contained within the BIOS, and for communicating with other boards in the system. Table 11-4 goes into more detail, explaining the various reserved areas. Not all of the areas indicated in Table 11-4 are necessarily in use in a particular system, nor are the areas indicated as *available* necessarily free. The table simply shows the areas reserved by some of the more common boards.

Table 11-4. **PC XT and AT Memory Map**

Address		Range	Length	Use[1]
00000	-	9FFFF	640K	User memory for DOS and programs
A0000	-	AFFFF	64K	EGA graphics mode
B0000	-	B3FFF	16K	MDA
B4000	-	B7FFF	16K	—available—
B8000	-	BBFFF	16K	CGA and EGA character memory
BC000	-	BFFFF	16K	EGA character memory
C0000	-	C7FFF	16K	EGA BIOS
C8000	-	CBFFF	16K	Fixed disk adapter and BIOS
CC000	-	DFFFF	80K	—available—
E0000	-	EFFFF	64K	Reserved for system ROM BIOS[2]
F0000	-	FFFFF	64K	Reserved for system ROM BIOS[3]
100000	-	FDFFFF	15M	Extended memory available with 80286 and 80386 protected mode[2]
FE0000	-	FFFFFF	128K	"Shadow" of system ROM[2]

[1] BIOS = Basic input output system
CGA = Color graphics adapter
EGA = Enhanced graphics adapter
MDA = Monochrome display adapter
[2] Applies only to AT
[3] Use varies by computer type

From an examination of Table 11-4, it would appear that not much room is left for expansion cards. However, a given system is unlikely to have all of the indicated areas in use. To make the task of installing boards that occupy memory address space easier, most such boards have the capability of being configured to one of many addresses within the "system" range (A0000 to EFFFF). This configuration is accomplished though *jumpers* (small plugs or wires that fit over pins on the board) or through *DIP switches* (switches that resemble a standard "Dual In-Line Package" IC chip). Even if the area of memory reserved for expansion boards is completely used, an add-on board may sometimes be configured to occupy memory normally used for user programs (addresses below 9FFFF). If the latter method proves necessary, note that it restricts the amount of memory available for user programs.

Once a place in memory has been found for a new board, the software that uses the board usually must be configured for that particular address. This is frequently accomplished by running an installation program supplied with the board or by setting up a configuration file. In some cases, the software may not support all the addresses that the board can occupy. Using the board at a nonsupported address may require programming.

When you consider the purchase of a new board, be sure to ask the salesperson about software that uses the board and if that software is configurable. Buying a board that can be installed but has no software available to use it can be as bad as buying a board that cannot be installed at all.

One recommendation for those configuring their own systems is to write down the memory areas used by all the boards currently in their system. Knowing this information can put you in a better position to evaluate whether or not a new board will coexist peacefully in your system. By knowing such details, you can purchase boards through discount houses with greater confidence and cut through all the "hype" that the more unscrupulous salesmen may attempt to use. Once again, be sure to ask about software that can access the board at the particular addresses at which you will install it.

The I/O Map

Of equal or greater importance when configuring boards for a system is the board's use of I/O ports. An I/O port is a special type of memory that exists in parallel with the system's normal memory. Unlike normal memory, ports are used exclusively for communicating with devices and boards within the system. Like normal memory, only a limited number of ports are available within the system. Care must be taken to avoid having more that one device attempt to use the same port address.

Although the 8088 CPU supports over 65,000 discrete port addresses, the IBM design reduces the number of usable ports to 1,024. (There are some exceptions to this limit, one of which is the expanded memory boards described in the section on *Add-On Memory*.) Table 11-5 shows typical port usage in PC XT- and AT-type computers.

Table 11-5. I/O Port Assignment for PC XT and AT Computers

Port Usage for PC XT	I/O Address	Port Usage for AT
DMA controller	000 - 01F	DMA controller #1
Interrupt controller	020 - 03F	Interrupt controller #1
Timer	040 - 05F	Timer
PPI (system config.)	060 - 063	
	060 - 06F	Keyboard
Reserved	070 - 07F	Real time clock
DMA page register	080 - 09F	DMA page register
NMI Mask register	0A0 - 0AF	
	0A0 - 0BF	Interrupt controller #2
Reserved	0B0 - 0FF	
	0C0 - 0DF	DMA controller #2
	0F0 - 0FF	Math coprocessor
Unusable	100 - 1FF	
	1F0 - 1F8	Fixed disk
Game I/O	200 - 20F	Game I/O
Expansion unit	210 - 217	
Multifunction card[2]	218 - 21F	Multifunction card[2]
Reserved	220 - 24F	
Parallel port 2	278 - 27F	Parallel port 2
Clock calendar[2]	2C0 - 2DF	Clock calendar[2]
Serial port 4[2]	2E0 - 2E7	
Serial port 3 or 4[2]	2E8 - 2EF	
Reserved	2F0 - 2F7	
Serial port 2	2F8 - 2FF	Serial port 2
Prototype card	300 - 31F	Prototype card
Fixed disk	320 - 32F	
	360 - 36F	Reserved
Parallel port 1	378 - 37F	Parallel port 1
SDLC, bisync 2	380 - 38F	SDLC, bisync 2
SDLC, bisync 2	3A0 - 3AF	SDLC, bisync 2
MDA & printer adapter	3B0 - 3BF	MDA & printer adapter
Enhanced graphics adapter	3C0 - 3CF	Enhanced graphics adapter
Color graphics adapter	3D0 - 3DF	Color graphics adapter
Reserved	3E0 - 3E7	
Serial port 3[2]	3E8 - 3EF	
Disk controller	3F0 - 3F7	Disk controller
Serial port 1	3F8 - 3FF	Serial port 1

[1] In IBM PC and IBM XT computers, the entire range of ports from 0 through 1FF is reserved for the system.
[2] Use of port for this function is common, but not standard.

Most boards that use I/O ports may be configured to use one block of ports chosen from a range of ports. This enables the user to position the board conveniently and retain use of existing boards. As with memory address selection, I/O port addresses are most often selected with jumpers or DIP switches on the board itself.

In addition to the reserved system ports in the low range, the ports most likely to be in use in an existing system are those required for the standard devices: the floppy and fixed disk drives, serial ports one and two (COM1 and COM2), parallel port one (usually LPT1), and the display adapter ports. Because MS-PC-DOS contains built-in support for these devices, their port assignments are fixed and unlikely to cause trouble. For nonstandard devices, the key to a successful installation is to choose port addresses that are unused and known to the software that will be used with the device. (See the trick box *Getting the Most from the System COM Ports.*)

Interrupt Lines

Although I/O ports are used to control the boards and to transfer data to and from them, they require that the system CPU initiate all interactions. This method of operation is called *polled* operation because the system must poll the ports to determine when the board requires service.

Although simple, polling is slow and can result in some important events being missed altogether. For these reasons, MS-DOS PCs are equipped with the capability of using *interrupts*. An interrupt is used when a device requires immediate attention. The device puts a signal onto its interrupt request (IRQ) line, which in turn causes the processor to stop what it is doing and check to see what the device wants. The processor knows which device to check because each IRQ line is associated with its own *interrupt vector* in the CPU. Each interrupt vector points to its own separate program, called an *interrupt service routine* (ISR). Figure 11-4 shows the chain of events for a keyboard interrupt.

Interrupt request lines are allocated even more strictly than memory addresses or I/O ports. Table assignments of IRQ lines in both PC XT- and AT-type computers.

From Table 11-6, it is apparent that the AT-type systems support nearly twice as many interrupts as the PC XT-type systems. For the most part, AT systems continue to support the original PC XT assignments, with the exceptions of IRQ lines 2 and 5.

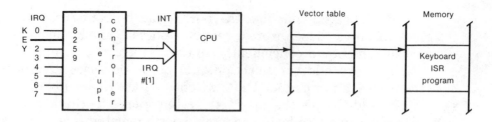

Figure 11-4. Keyboard Interrupt Processing

Table 11-6. Interrupt Request Lines

IRQ Lines Available on XT and AT Systems			
IRQ Number	**INT Vector**	**Used By**	**Assigned Function**
0	08	System	System timer
1	09	System	Keyboard
2	0A	XT card	XT: unallocated, marked *reserved* AT: Not available
3	0B	XT card	Serial port 2
4	0C	XT card	Serial port 1
5	0D	XT card	XT: fixed disk AT: 2nd parallel port
6	0E	XT card	Disk controller
7	0F	XT card	Parallel port 1
IRQ Lines Available Only on AT Systems			
IRQ Number	**INT Vector**	**Used By**	**Assigned Function**
8	70	AT system	Real-time clock interrupt
9	71	XT card	Replaces IRQ 2 in AT systems
10	72	AT card	Unallocated, marked *reserved*
11	73	AT card	Unallocated, marked *reserved*
12	74	AT card	Unallocated, marked *reserved*
13	75	AT system	Coprocessor
14	76	AT card	Fixed disk controller
15	77	AT card	Reserved

INTERRUPT LINE NUMBER 2 ON THE IBM PC XT AND AT

To add a second interrupt controller chip to the AT computer, one of the existing IRQ lines was used as the input from the second chip. IRQ 2 was taken for this purpose. As a result IRQ2 is not available on the IBM AT or on AT-style computers such as the COMPAQ 286.

To maintain compatibility, the IRQ 2 line on the XT connector in an AT system was attached to IRQ 9 and is "redirected" in software from vector 71 to vector 0A. Most software that works with IRQ 2 will continue to work as before, but some programs may experience difficulty.

MODEM OPERATION TRICK #1

One common problem encountered when first installing a modem is that the modem control program can send information to the modem, but no information can be read from the modem. This circumstance sometimes occurs when the modem port has been configured for the wrong interrupt request line. Check to make sure that the modem port is on the right line and that no other ports are connected to the wrong line.

This problem appears more frequently with modems because although most software ignores the interrupt capability, many modem control programs depend on interrupts to indicate that data has been received from the modem.

INTERRUPT CONTENTION

In spite of the fact that the IRQ lines are clearly assigned, contention problems do arise. For example, it has been reported that in order to use the Tiny Turbo 286 accelerator card from Orchid Systems, the printer port (parallel port) must be disconnected from IRQ 7. However, because very few programs make use of printer interrupts, disconnecting the printer from IRQ 7 should not affect their operation.

In light of this, when installation of a new board appears to cause a problem with system operation, check for contention problems among I/O ports. If the problem persists after I/O port contention has been resolved, check for contention on interrupt request lines. If such contention exists, disconnect one of the devices from the IRQ line by removing the jumper or setting the controlling DIP switch. Chances are that none of the software uses the IRQ line anyway, and operation can continue normally. *Do not resort to hardware cuts and patches unless you're sure that IRQ contention*

> *is the problem, that removing the IRQ connection will fix the problem, and*
> *that future changes to your configuration won't be affected.*

GETTING THE MOST FROM THE
SYSTEM COM PORTS

Most of the newer cards that use serial ports can be configured to use one of
up to four port addresses: COM1, COM2, and what are called *COM3* and
COM4. By using COM3 or COM4 for special applications, COM1 and COM2
can be saved for other uses that *must* use COM1 or COM2. MS-DOS doesn't
support anything but COM1 and COM2, so no system modifications are
required when you use COM3 or COM4. The only necessity is to make sure
no other device is using those ports and to find software that can use the
extended ports.

Even though there is no standard for COM3 or COM4, there is quite a
bit of overlap among the different configurations. For example, the popular
Crosstalk XVI communications program can be used with modems connected to COM1, COM2, COM3, or COM4, using port base addresses of
3F8, 2F8, 3E8, and 2E8. The MCT-MIO multifunction board also supports
COM1 through COM4 at port addresses 3F8, 2F8, 2E8, and 2E0. By setting
the MCT-MIO port to COM3 (at 2E8) and Crosstalk to COM4 (2E8), you can
use a modem without giving up COM1 or COM2.

One other item must be configured. Crosstalk *does* depend upon the
board being able to signal that it has data ready to be read. Because Crosstalk "thinks" it is using COM4, it expects IRQ4 to be connected to that
port. To achieve this, the MCT-MIO board must be set to use IRQ4, not
IRQ3, which is normally used for COM3.

This example also points out that the important factors are the port
addresses and IRQ lines in use, not the name given to a configuration by a
particular manufacturer.

Speed Issues Revisited

Another question that must be considered when investigating compatibility is "Can it run at my system's speed?" Some of the more com-

mon processor (and thus bus) speeds are 4.77 and 8.0 MHz for PCs, XTs, and compatibles, and either 6.0, 8.0, or 10.0 MHz for the ATs and compatibles. Although nearly everything runs at 4.77 MHz, problems can occur when running some products at a higher speed.

One example of this problem is with the National Semiconductor MM58167A real-time, clock-calendar chip found on many multifunction cards. Unfortunately, this particular chip doesn't behave well at speeds of 8 MHz or higher. A number of solutions are available. One is not to buy a board using that chip. Another is to not use the clock-calendar function. A third solution is available on speed selectable systems: Slow the system down to access the chip. Note also that AT and compatible systems running at 6 MHz or greater rarely can be slowed down to the 4.77 MHz speed at which the standard PC's or XT's processor runs, sometimes causing compatibility problems for some applications.

CHANGING PROCESSOR SPEED IN SOFTWARE FOR SPEED SELECTABLE SYSTEMS

Many clone and compatible systems have the ability to run at either of two speeds. Speed selection is normally accomplished through a special key sequence, but can often be done from software as well.

For speed selectable PC and XT systems using the ERSO DTK BIOS, the speed can be changed by setting or clearing bit 2 in the I/O control word located at I/O port address 61 (hex). An example sequence for fast speed is

```
IN   AL,61
OR   AL,04
OUT  61,AL
```

An example sequence for slow speed is

```
IN   AL,61
AND  AL,FB
OUT  61,AL
```

To create programs to switch the processor's speed, enter the following lines into the file ERSO.INP *exactly as shown*, including the blank lines. Then type DEBUG <ERSO.INP at the command line, and DEBUG automatically creates the programs FAST88.COM and SLOW88.COM.

```
r cx
8
n fast88.com
a 100
IN    AL,61
OR    AL,04
OUT   61,AL
INT   20

w
n slow88.com
a 100
IN    AL,61
AND   AL,FB
OUT   61,AL
INT   20

w
q
```

The COMPAQ Deskpro 286 and COMPAQ Portable 286, two speed-selectable, AT-compatible systems can have their CPU speeds changed between 6 MHz and 8 MHz using BIOS interrupts. An example of its fast speed switch sequence is

```
MOV   AX,F001
INT   16
```

An example of its slow speed switch sequence is

```
MOV   AX,F000
INT   16
```

To create the programs to switch the COMPAQ's processor speed, enter the following lines into a file called COMPAQ.INP *exactly as shown*, including the blank lines. Then type DEBUG <COMPAQ.INP at the command line, and DEBUG automatically creates the programs CPQFAST.COM and CPQSLOW.COM.

```
r cx
7
n cpqfast.com
a 100
MOV   AX,F001
INT   16
INT   20
```

```
w
n cpqslow.com
a 100
MOV   AX,F000
INT   16
INT   20

w
q
```

Even if you have a speed selectable system that isn't shown above, you can probably find information in the reference manual on how to change the speed from software.

When difficulties are encountered with particular boards or programs running on speed selectable systems, try the program or board at the slower speed. If speed turns out to be the culprit, a program may be run to slow the system before using the speed sensitive program or device. The entire sequence of slowing the system, running the program, and speeding the system can be put into a batch file. This idea proves to be an ideal solution for the problem of using the National Semiconductor MM58167A clock-calendar chip on an ERSO DTK speed selectable system.

Support and Price—An Opinion

A great deal of controversy surrounds the choice of buying computer products from discount houses that offer little support or from "full-service" dealers that charge more but supposedly offer better after-sale support. The price versus support trade-off is also cited when considering purchase of a brand name product over an import imitation. If the issue were as simple as stated, the decision should go to the dealers and companies offering better support. Unfortunately, the choices aren't so clear.

Experience seems to show that the discount houses do not offer substantial support, but the counter argument is that neither do many of the full-service dealers. Except in the most trivial cases, these dealers are often unable to answer customer questions or resolve compatibility issues. Discount houses are pictured as indifferent to the requirements of the customer, but the high pressure sales techniques of full-service dealers can turn this into an advantage. Not uncommonly, full-service dealers, whose large sales staffs must be paid for by commissions, push expensive and poorly planned solutions on unwary customers. The "solutions" are often based on what the dealer happens to have in stock at the time. Salespersons rarely inform the inexperienced user of solutions that the store can't provide.

In the realm of manufacturers' choices, the trade-offs are different, but the results are much the same. The largest, best known manufacturers present a good facade of support, but their products are often inferior in both price and performance. Smaller companies may not trade on the New York Stock Exchange, but in their need to differentiate themselves from the pack, they are forced to offer more performance for less "buck." The other reason given for going with a brand name product is compatibility. This is definitely a double edged sword. The larger companies don't always get where they are through building a better mousetrap. Sometimes they got where they are through building a better customer trap, locking the customer into a proprietary architecture that prevents migration while forcing the customer to undergo the painful process of continual upgrades just to stay even.

It has been suggested that the customer can either spend more money to have someone configure their system for them or spend the time to learn how to do it themselves. Until computer dealers purge themselves of those who believe that a computer is just a high priced stereo or vacuum cleaner, having a salesperson configure a system is not always an option. If you are reading this book you already know more than the average salesperson.

What can customers do to protect themselves? Spend the time to learn what's a good deal and what's a bad deal. Demand better documentation from the manufacturers and better support from dealers of all kinds. Reward those sales and manufacturing organizations that provide the types of product, service, and documentation that you deserve. Don't base decisions solely on any single item. In a phrase, force the evolution of the computer industry into the competitive, high quality market that it is supposed to be.

CONFIGURATION CHECKLIST

The following items should be considered when planning a purchase of computer equipment:

- Physical:

    Boards: Is the board a full-length board or shorter? If
    shorter, how short? Does the board descend below
    connector height? Does the board use a daughter
    card? If so, how wide is the board with a daughter
    card added? Does the board require another
    connector slot for cable attachments?

    Devices: Is the device external, full-height internal, or half-
    height internal? Does it require special mounting
    hardware? If so, is that hardware included with
    the purchase? Does the device require any special
    data or power cables? If so, are the cables
    included in the purchase?

- Power: How much power does the board or device draw? Has
  anyone else used it in the same type of chassis with the same
  type of power supply?

- Speed: At what speeds does the board or device run? Has it
  been tested at those speeds? Were any problems encountered?

- Memory, I/O, and Interrupt Usage: What memory space and/or
  I/O ports does the board require? What addresses can it be
  configured to use? Does the board or device use IRQ lines? If
  so, what IRQ lines can it be configured to use?

- Software: Does the software support the planned configuration?
  Can the software be configured for the addresses, I/O ports,
  and IRQ lines that the board uses?

- Documentation: What type of documentation comes with the
  product? Does it cover configuration and use? If possible, try
  to see the documentation before you purchase.

- Support: Who can answer configuration and technical questions
  and help resolve problems? Try to get that person's phone
  number at the time of purchase.

- Other Problems: Are there any other compatibility problems
  that the sales or technical representative is aware of?

- Warranty and Return Policy: How long is the warranty, and
  what are its terms? If the board fails to work because of
  incompatibility, can it be returned for a refund?

- Price: Shop around. Call for quotes. Board and device prices
  can vary by as much as 50 percent of retail cost.

Product Guide

This section deals with specific products. No attempt is made to comprehensively survey the current market. Instead, we included those products that we find interesting or feel could present unique problems. In some places, we include personal observations and evaluations. This isn't to say that these are the best products available, only the ones that we are impressed by. Our opinions may be more experienced, but not necessarily better.

Add-On Memory

Add-On memory has always been an important item for MS-DOS PC users. In the early days, when PCs had only 64K on the motherboard, plug-in cards containing extra memory were required before any substantial programs could be run. Configuration of these types of cards essentially involves setting the starting address of the memory on the card to coincide with end of memory in the system. For example, if an existing system has 256K of memory its last memory address is 3FFFF. The starting address of an add-on memory card then is set to 40000.

CAUTION

USING ADD-ON MEMORY IN AN EXPANSION CHASSIS

Add-On memory cards usually don't function well in an expansion chassis and should be used in the main chassis only.

The fact that the majority of systems today already support 640K on the motherboard hasn't slowed the sales of memory cards. The emphasis today is on *expanded memory*. Unlike extended memory (the memory space above 1M on AT-type systems), expanded memory can be used in any system.

Expanded memory cards contain up to 2M of internal memory. To access this memory, small pieces of it (16K at a time) are mapped into the address space of the system. This process of mapping sections of a larger memory into a smaller one is called *bank switching.* Each 16K piece of memory is called a *page,* and the area of the system that receives the page is called a *page frame.* The number and locations of the page frames within the system vary with the type of expanded memory board used and the existing configuration of the system.

At this time, two standards exist for expanded memory cards. The original Expanded Memory Specification standard is backed by Lotus, Intel, and Microsoft and thus is called the LIM EMS standard. The second standard is the Enhanced EMS standard, sometimes called the AQA standard after its supporters: AST, Quadram, and Ashton-Tate. The configurations available with both these standards are shown in Figure 11-5.

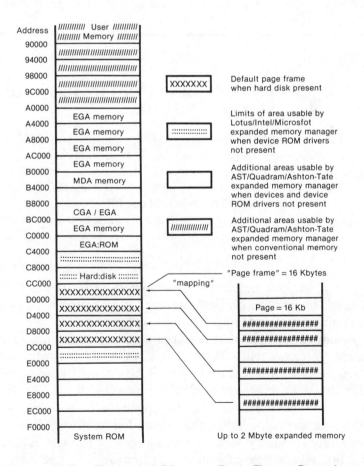

Figure 11-5. Expanded Memory Page Frame Locations

As Figure 11-5 shows, the Enhanced EMS type boards can be configured to use a broader range of system addresses, including all of the areas usable by the LIM-type boards. What Figure 11-5 does not show is that although LIM boards support four pages of expanded memory (64K mapped from a maximum of 2Mb), the Enhanced EMS boards can map up to 64 pages (1Mb mapped from a maximum of 2Mb). Use of all 64 pages on the Enhanced EMS board is impossible because some memory must be maintained for bootup, the ROM BIOS, and display memory. Because the Enhanced EMS board is a superset of the LIM board, it is considered upwardly compatible and should be capable of supporting all software written for the LIM standard.

The expanded memory pages that are currently mapped into the page frames are selected through the use of I/O ports. These ports are configurable over a wide range of addresses, so you shouldn't have any problems finding a home for the board in your system.

I/O PORT DECODING BY EXPANDED MEMORY BOARDS

Both the EMS and Enhanced EMS expanded memory boards utilize I/O ports more efficiently than most other boards. By decoding 12 I/O address lines rather than the normal 10, these boards are capable of squeezing four I/O ports into one. Therefore, although IBM states that the I/O address space is from 0 to 3FF, these boards use I/O addresses 02[x]8, 42[x]8, 82[x]8, and C2[x]8 (where [x] is configurable for each board in the system).

Up to four expanded memory boards of 2Mb apiece can be installed, but although that increases the number of pages available, all of them still must map into the same page frames.

Because none of this extra memory is normally within MS-DOS' range, you may ask, "What it is good for?" A common use of expanded memory is as a RAM disk, which functions like a much faster physical disk drive. (You also lose all the contents of a RAM disk if you turn off the power without saving the contents to a physical disk.) A *device driver* is supplied with the expanded memory board to manage the expanded memory and provide support for the RAM disk. However, the big advantage of expanded memory is that now that a standard exists for the hardware, software developers are producing programs such as Lotus 1-2-3 and Microsoft Windows to use the extra storage and speed capabilities.

USING EXPANDED MEMORY AS *EXTENDED MEMORY*

Most expanded memory boards for the AT can be configured also as extended memory. Should the user decide someday to switch to an operating system like XENIX that can use all the AT's memory, the investment in the expanded memory card is not wasted.

Storage Devices and Controllers

The two most popular forms of storage devices for MS-DOS PCs are floppy disks and hard (or fixed) disks. Floppy disks for the IBM PC can usually store 360K at 9 sectors per track. The IBM AT introduced the "high-capacity" floppy, which is capable of storing 1.2M at 15 sectors per track. Although there is definitely a physical difference in the floppy disk drives themselves, some controllers can support both types of drive. Consult the manual to find out if you can connect a different type of drive to your controller.

   If you change the type of floppy drive connected to your system, you will probably need to install a different device driver to handle the different format. (You may be able to get by with a patch as explained in the following box *Changing Floppy Disk Parameters*, but unless you know a lot about floppy device drivers, consult a professional.) If you add a floppy drive of the same format, you most probably will only have to change the switch settings on your motherboard. Refer to your system documentation for the correct switch settings to control the number of floppy drives in the system.

   Adding a hard disk to your system is easier. Beginning with the IBM PC-2, support for hard disks is contained in the system BIOS. When a hard disk controller is installed in a PC-2 or XT system, the system recognizes the existence of the controller and includes it in the system device tables. When the system is booted without a floppy disk in the primary drive, the BIOS looks on the hard disk for the MS-DOS system and proceeds to boot it if it is found. (See Chapter 12 for more information on setting up a hard disk.)

The procedures for selecting the type of disk vary from controller to controller, but note that the standard IBM hard disk controller for the IBM XT does not support hard disk drives over 10M in capacity.

FORMATTING HARD DISKS WITH A WESTERN DIGITAL CONTROLLER

One of the most popular combinations for add-on mass storage is the Western Digital WD1002S-WX2 hard disk adapter board coupled with the Seagate ST-225 half-height 20M hard disk. One of the great advantages of the Western Digital controller is that the routines required to physically format the disk are contained in the ROM BIOS on the board. If you need to perform a physical reformat on the hard disk, follow these steps:

- Insert a disk containing DEBUG into drive A.
- Invoke DEBUG and type g C800:5.
- Follow the instructions.

CHANGING FLOPPY DISK PARAMETERS

Sometimes the floppy disk parameters stored in the BIOS don't match the actual drives in use. Signs of this occurring are frequent errors from the drive or excessive noise when the drive is in operation. If the source of these problems is a parameter mismatch, the following trick can help set things straight.

Interrupt vector 1E (hex) contains the address of the floppy disk parameter block (FDPB). Under PC DOS versions 2.0, 2.1, 3.0, and 3.1, this address is 0:522 (segment 0, offset 522). The contents of the FDPB are as shown in Table 11-7. (Example values match the DEBUG sequence shown in this table.)

Table 11-7. Floppy Disk Parameter Block

Offset	Function	Configurable	Example
0	Step rate[1] & head unload time	yes	DF
1	Head load time		02
2	Motor on delay		25
3	Number of bytes per sector		02
4	Last sector number		09
5	Gap length		2A
6	Data track length		FF
7	Format gap length		50
8	Format byte		F6
9	Head settle time	yes	0F
A	Motor start time	yes	02

[1] Step rate values: FF = 1 ms, EF = 2 ms, DF = 3 ms, CF = 4 ms, etc.

If the drive is stepping from track to track too fast, errors result. If the step rate is too slow, the drive sounds like a bad transmission. The first task is to find out what the existing parameters are by running DEBUG and entering the following commands:

```
C>DEBUG
-d 0:78 l 4                          ← get address of
                                       FDPB
0000:0070      22 05 00 00           ← most likely
                                       response
-d 0:522 l a                         ← get FDPB
                                       default values
0000:0520      DF 02 25 02 09 2A FF 50 F6 0F 02
-q                                   ← quit for now
```

The address 0:522 is found from reading the first series of four bytes *backward*. If the four numbers are different than what is shown, use them as the address of the FDPB.

The best way to find the correct value for the disk parameters is to change the existing values one step at a time and try the changes. Most problems can be fixed by changing only the step rate parameter. You can try new parameters by using the program DISKFIX.COM. Enter the following commands into the file called DISKFIX.INP *exactly as shown*, including the blank line. Remember to include your own values for the three parameters in hexadecimal. Then enter DEBUG<DISKFIX.INP at the command line, and DEBUG automatically creates the file DISKFIX.COM.

```
n diskfix.com
a 100
XOR  AX,AX
MOV  DS,AX
LDS  SI,[0078]
```

```
MOV   BYTE PTR [SI], your step rate here
MOV   BYTE PTR [SI+9], your head settle time here
MOV   BYTE PTR [SI+A], your motor start time here
INT   13
INT   20

r cx
17
w
q
```

Run DISKFIX, then use TYPE or some other command to read a file from the floppy disk. If the problem is worse, change the parameter the other way and try again. Keep going until you fix the problem or until you're so far off the original parameters that it seems a parameter mismatch can't be the source of the problem.

If you have fixed the problem, edit your AUTOEXEC.BAT file to run DISKFIX every time you boot, and you won't have any more problems with the drive.

If you're interested in how this program works: DISKFIX reads the address of the FDPB from vector 1E (hex address 78). Then it alters the values in the FDPB, calls INT 13 with the AH register still equal to zero to install the parameters. DISKFIX terminates via INT 20.

There have been other developments in mass storage besides the move to half-height drives. One has been the packaging of fixed disk drives on a card. Designed to offer fixed disk storage to those with full drive bays, these cards mount a slim 3½-inch fixed disk drive and controller on one full-length card, which has lower power consumption than a separate controller and drive combination. Although supposedly some can fit into one PC size slot, all the current offerings take two slots in an XT or AT.

Another recent innovation in storage technology is *run length limited* (RLL) encoding. Using a different method of writing on a disk than the industry standard MFM encoding, RLL encoded disks can store about 50 percent more data on the same disk. The 30M Seagate ST-238, for example, is really an RLL-encoded 20M Seagate ST-225. (RLL disks are standard MFM disks that have been screened for higher quality.) Current disk controllers support only one format or the other, so systems that already contain an MFM mode controller require an additional controller. For users who have not added a hard disk to their systems yet, RLL encoding gives a 50 percent increase in storage without an increase in space. This may be the way to go.

Multifunction Cards

The half decade since the introduction of the IBM PC has seen a quiet revolution in the nature of "standard" peripheral interfaces. The first designs were bulky and usually contained only one function per board. Current designs have taken advantage of VLSI (very large scale integration) chips and new construction techniques to pack an amazing array of functions on a single card.

If one is patient and willing to search the back pages of computer oriented publications, one can find boards that support nearly any desired combination of functions. Some examples of the combinations of functions available on one board are

- Conventional, expanded, or nonvolatile memory; serial, parallel, and game ports; clock-calendar
- Floppy disk controller; serial, parallel, and game ports; clock-calendar
- Display controller; serial, parallel, and game ports; clock-calendar
- Display controller, accelerator card (Orchid)

The profusion of serial and parallel ports that come packaged on multifunction cards allows the owner of a full system to add the functions of a new card by replacing an existing interface card, thereby not losing any interface ports. In this way, expanded memory, for example, can be added by replacing an *asynchronous* (serial) interface card with a new expanded memory card that also supports a serial port.

However, although originally intended as an advantage for slot-conscious buyers, the profusion of ports and clock-calendar chips can leave a newer owner wondering what to do with all the extra functions that came along for the ride. One clock is surely enough. The simplest solution is not to use them. Nearly all cards allow the user to disable any particular function through on-board DIP switches or jumpers. When disabled, the function doesn't use any I/O ports, reducing the chance of a conflict.

Of course, if space can be found in the I/O map, the extra functions can always be used. Three or four serial ports in a system is not uncommon today, although MS-DOS does not support anything beyond COM2. Even those programs that support extended ports rarely go beyond COM4. However, if the need for extra serial ports manifests itself, support may arise for even more ports.

The abundance of choices makes the job of planning a system more serious because extra functions can be added with a variety of boards. The reasonable approach is to attempt to buy only what's necessary while recognizing that the presence of an extra port or clock is no reason to turn down an exceptional deal.

TRICK　　　**MODEM OPERATION TRICK #2**

Some modems require that commands be sent to them in 8-bit mode and thus default to 8-bit mode when started. However, not all remote systems use 8 bits of data when sending and receiving data. If you call a remote system and start receiving "garbage" when the connection is established, you may have a mismatch between your system's settings and the remote system's settings.

Try using 7-bit mode and see whether the problem clears up. Similar problems can occur also with speed, parity, and stop bit mismatches. If you don't know the remote system's settings try using different parameters.

Display Adapters and Monitors

One of the most confusing choices presented to those who build or enhance their systems is that of what type of display to use. The various options are the MDA (monochrome display adapter), CGA (color graphics adapter), Hercules Standard, Plantronics Standard, EGA (enhanced graphics adapter), and PGC (professional graphics controller). And those are only the standards!

Each of the different standards offers different advantages: price, resolution, and performance. Your decision has to depend on the type of work that you want to do and what your pocketbook can bear. Remember that each type of controller also uses different resources. Refer to Tables 11-4 and 11-5 for information on the memory addresses and I/O ports utilized by some of the standards.

If you find too difficult the choice of what type of display adapter to use, there is good news. You may not have to choose at all. There are now display adapters available that support five of the six standards: MDA, CGA, EGA, Hercules, and Plantronics. Mostly based on a radical new chip set from Chips and Technologies, these boards are available from a variety of manufacturers and can be set to emulate any of the five modes. If you still can't decide what mode to emulate, Paradise offers the Auto-Switch EGA, a display adapter that can automatically determine the proper mode from the type of access, then switch to that mode.

Most of the new multimode display adapters are half-slot cards and include the full 256K of display memory that is supported by the EGA standard. Honestly, the price and performance of these boards is so good, that it is hard to understand why anyone would want one of the older cards. (An older card is usually a full-slot board, contains only 64K of standard display memory and supports only one display mode.)

The other issue to be confronted is the choice of the display monitor. There are many manufacturers with many different types of monitors at all types of performance and price levels. Two that we consider worthy of special consideration are the NEC MultiSync and the SONY Multiscan. Unlike the majority of monitors that work with one type of display adapter, these monitors can function with a wide variety of adapters (MDA, CGA, EGA, Plantronics, and Hercules). The trade-off for increased compatibility is that the MultiSync and Multiscan monitors cost more. Of the two, the SONY Multiscan has the better screen definition.

New high-resolution computer monitors are expected to appear in 1987. These monitors also may be used with video cassette recorders and standard television receivers. This may be an option worth considering.

Accelerator Cards

One of the big hopes for owners of older systems is the relatively recent introduction of accelerator cards. Plugging in an accelerator card holds the promise of AT-like performance and more for a PC or XT system. This feat is accomplished by including a high speed processor on the board, usually the 8.00 MHz Intel 80286. However, not all accelerator cards work the same way.

The most basic type of accelerator card is a simple replacement processor. The user removes the 8088 CPU from the motherboard and plugs a cable from the accelerator card into the empty 8088 socket. The system now has a higher speed CPU. Cards with more features can have *cache* memories to avoid repeated disk accesses. Some have sockets reserved for the 80287 math coprocessor.

Some cards, like the Orchid Tiny Turbo, provide space for resocketing the 8088 CPU on the accelerator card. Then, the user is given the option of switching between the slower 8088 and the higher speed processor. The reason for allowing either processor to be used is to provide a "compatibility mode" for those programs and devices that cannot operate at the higher speed.

The most advanced accelerator cards, such as the Orchid Turbo 286e and Phoenix Pfaster 286, have a complete system on a board with optional features, such as an 80287 math coprocessor and up to 2M of RAM memory usable as LIM expanded memory. CPU performance is greatly increased by the on-board memory, and system performance is enhanced through the use of the motherboard memory as a disk cache. In return, the cards with more features cost about four times as much (twice as much when purchased through discount houses).

Each type has its advantages and disadvantages. The simplest cards cost the least but do not offer the compatibility feature of 8088 operation.

All of the cards that require removal of the motherboard CPU limit speed selectable systems. The resocketed 8088 is often driven by a 4.77 MHz crystal on the accelerator card, which effectively disables the motherboard's 8.00 MHz "turbo" mode. This loss can be endured if the original board is not equipped with an 8087 math coprocessor. When the accelerator card is in 286 mode, it is unable to make use of an 8087 math coprocessor. That leaves the user with three choices: Use 8088 mode with the coprocessor at 4.77 MHz, use the 286 mode without the coprocessor at 8 MHz, or buy the 80287 math coprocessor for maximum performance, and cost.

The most advanced accelerator cards offer the best compatibility. Because the high-speed system is contained entirely on the accelerator card, removal of the motherboard's 8088 CPU is not required. When the accelerator card is disabled, no "hooks" are left in the system, which returns the system to its "virgin" state.

Even these advanced accelerator boards can sometimes present a problem. Because they operate as a self-contained system on a board, their access to the motherboard memory is limited, which in turn limits the accelerator card's ability to access additional LIM expanded memory cards. This difficulty can be overcome with special software drivers, but the user may prefer to buy an accelerator card that uses the host system's memory directly, including existing expanded memory cards.

The nice thing about accelerator cards is that if this year's offerings aren't fast enough, wait a bit and something faster is bound to come along. The current "king of the hill" is the PC-elevATor 286 from Applied Reasoning. Running a 12.5 MHz 80286, this board offers something approaching a performance increase of eight times that of the standard PC XT.

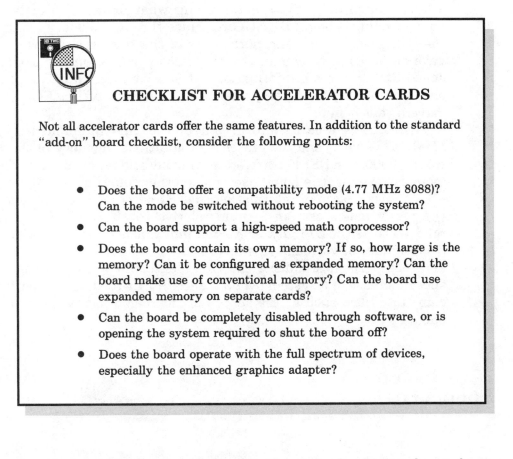

CHECKLIST FOR ACCELERATOR CARDS

Not all accelerator cards offer the same features. In addition to the standard "add-on" board checklist, consider the following points:

- Does the board offer a compatibility mode (4.77 MHz 8088)? Can the mode be switched without rebooting the system?

- Can the board support a high-speed math coprocessor?

- Does the board contain its own memory? If so, how large is the memory? Can it be configured as expanded memory? Can the board make use of conventional memory? Can the board use expanded memory on separate cards?

- Can the board be completely disabled through software, or is opening the system required to shut the board off?

- Does the board operate with the full spectrum of devices, especially the enhanced graphics adapter?

Because accelerator cards can offer up to five times the performance of an XT, they are worthwhile investments for "power users" who often find themselves waiting for their computers to finish tasks. The market in these cards is evolving rapidly, so prospective buyers should check recent computer publications for the latest evaluations and recommendations.

BIOS Signatures—How To Find Out What's Out There

When an MS-DOS PC system boots, it must be able to locate the ROM device drivers for installed devices such as the EGA and hard disk controller. It does this by looking for the two bytes 55 and AA at the start of a memory page (16K pieces). This pattern is called a *BIOS signature*. When the system finds that pattern, it installs the device's driver.

Although one way of determining what drivers are installed in your machine is using DEBUG to cruise through memory looking for the BIOS signature mark, purchasers of the Norton Utilities package have an easier way. One of the programs provided in the package is called SI (for system information). If you have this program, run SI and it informs you of the presence and location of the ROM device drivers that it finds.

SI also is able to inform you of the amount of memory that MS-DOS is using and the presence of additional memory in the range from A0000 to EFFFF. SI refers to this additional memory as display memory, even if it is being used for another function.

Another piece of information that SI can give you is an index of the performance of your system relative to an IBM PC. Variously referred to as the *SI index* or *Norton index*, it is often used to rate the performance of various systems or accelerator cards. Although useful as a comparison standard, the SI index cannot tell you the actual speed increase of a system over a standard PC. Too many other factors come into play, such as the speeds of the memories, peripherals, and disks.

Summary

Having read this chapter, you should feel confident of your ability to intelligently plan, purchase, and install anything from a system to a single board. The best advice that we can give is to follow these simple steps:

- Consider what features or functions you want.

- Look around and don't be pressured into a sale. *You know better than the salesperson what you want!*

- Ask whatever questions are called for and get decent documentation.

- Read the documentation, and put your new system together. It's easier than you may think.

Given a little time (and sorry to say, a fair amount of money), you *can* have the system that you've dreamed about. Happy computing!

Secrets of Add-On Mass Storage

Chapter 12

T his chapter concentrates on one of the areas of most interest to users of personal computers: adding disk and tape drives to existing systems to increase their permanent storage capacity. After some background on the issues of why and when you should consider adding such capability to your MS-DOS computer, we explore the purchase decision itself. Then we discuss some installation and interface considerations. Finally, we talk about how to make effective and efficient use of add-on mass storage, including the all-important issue of data security through backup procedures.

Why and When Add More Storage?

There are a great many reasons why you might consider obtaining add-on mass storage beyond your system's current capabilities. The mere fact that you are running out of room on your present hard disk or are getting "floppy elbow" from making numerous tedious floppy disk swaps during some applications might be sufficient justification for the decision.

Essentially, there are three major categories of reasons for considering adding mass storage: capacity, convenience and speed. Let's take a brief look at each in turn.

More Capacity Required

Some applications and environments require more storage capacity than you may have now. Many of the more recently introduced relational database managers, for example, require a hard disk with at least one or two megabytes free. Any program that comes with more than two or three floppy disks and requires more than two disks to be used to run it is, of course, a strong hint that a hard disk is needed.

In some cases, it isn't the application itself that cries out for additional mass storage capacity but your use of storage. For example, the person who uses a word processor to write letters, memos, and short reports is far less likely to need additional storage capacity than a professional writer who works on book-length manuscripts that run to hundreds or even thousands of typed pages in a single project.

Convenience: Access and Saving Time

Probably the most common reason for purchasing add-on mass storage for a desktop PC is convenience. It may be possible to run a program on a system containing only floppy disk drives, but running it there might require such incessant disk-swapping that it simply isn't practical.

Alternatively, the need for additional mass storage may arise from the fact that you are not a single-program user. If you use a word processor, a spreadsheet, a database manager, a telecommunications program, and a few utilities, you might find yourself spending a lot of time trying to find the right disk for the program you want to run or the data you want to store or retrieve. That's true even if you are relatively organized. If you are like most of us, rummaging around on an already cluttered desk for the right disk can make you unproductive, to say nothing of your frustration.

Faster Program Load and Data Retrieval

If you've been around the microcomputer industry as a user for many years, you may recall the early days of microcomputers when "mass storage" consisted of a punched paper tape that took as long as a half an hour to load a small BASIC program. When audio cassette interfaces became available, those of us who were involved in the industry thought heaven had come to earth. Within a few months of using cassettes, though, we were ready for the next step: floppy disks. When we'd used them for a while, we got tired of waiting even the several seconds it took to load a program.

This progressive impatience with the machine and its capability of retrieving programs and data from its mass storage area is another major reason for considering add-on mass storage for your PC. If you find yourself spending what seems to be a lot of time waiting for the computer to load something from or save something to a floppy disk, you're probably ready for a hard disk.

It's Not for Everyone

Even if you fit into one of these categories, you shouldn't run right out and start deciding which hard disk drive to buy. You should be aware of the disadvantages to add-on mass storage.

For one thing, you'll find that you are more dependent on your particular machine than you might like to become. If you are running all of your programs from floppy disks, you can throw a few floppies into a briefcase, head for the office or a friend's house, and run the programs without giving the process a lot of thought. But the instant you add a hard disk or other mass storage capacity to your PC, you are more dependent on its availability.

Not only does this mean that moving your programs from your home to your office and other locations becomes a process that requires more planning and thought, but you are also in far more difficulty if your system should "decide" to experience a malfunction. When your computer is "down," and you're using floppies for everything, obtaining access to another machine isn't too difficult, and the time lost can be fairly minimal. However, if all you're working on is locked in the hard disk in the machine that just went out the door to the repair shop, you can find yourself in a really difficult situation! (Of course, we recommend that you keep all your information— programs and data—backed up from the hard disk to more secure media. We discuss the options for this later in the chapter. That doesn't alter the fact that you may find yourself with data that exceeds floppy capacity or programs that really require a hard disk to operate.)

A second drawback to mass storage is embodied in what we like to call the *Fibber McGee Phenomenon*. (If you're too young to remember the radio show, ask someone older about it.) The principle: Junk expands to fill the amount of space available. You buy a 10M hard disk and think you'll never need more capacity. In two weeks, you get a "disk full" error trying to save a file, and you start tearing your hair out.

The principle is simply this: When you're using floppies, you tend to be far more careful about data organization and what you save versus what you throw out because the cost of the additional floppies is a visible, ongoing one. The hard disk, however, sits there inside your PC humming away, and you find that you allow it to accumulate a lot of stuff that you don't need any more. The availability of large mass storage capacity can lead to sloppy system management.

Finally, the effective use and management of a mass storage subsystem requires an investment of time on your part. You must spend time evaluating the alternatives available to you, making the right purchasing decision for your system and needs, possibly installing the device, and most importantly, learning how to use it effectively. There isn't much to learning about floppy disks. The same cannot be said of hard disk subsystems, tape drives, and other means of mass storage that we discuss in this chapter.

Alternatives Available

Assuming that you've read all these caveats and are ready nevertheless to purchase add-on mass storage, what are your major options?

Essentially, you can choose from among hard disk systems, tape drives, additional floppy drives, removable-media cartridge systems or for some limited applications, optical disks (also called *CD-ROM*, for compact disk read only memory).

Hard disk subsystems can be further divided into three categories depending on their physical connection to the PC: external drives, internal or chassis-mounted systems, and plug-in boards with integrated hard disks.

Tape drives, for the most part, are significant only as backup devices (which we discuss later in this chapter).

A PC or XT system can accommodate up to four ½-height floppy disk drives. This capability permits you to add almost 1Mb of additional mass storage to your system at relatively low cost. But with the price of hard disks declining (see the section in this chapter called *Cost per Megabyte*), adding more floppy drives may not make economic sense.

JUMPER SETTINGS FOR MULTIPLE FLOPPIES

If you are planning to add another floppy disk drive to your system, there are several things to keep in mind. First of all, almost all disk drive controllers have jumpers that are used to determine whether more than one disk drive is connected. In most cases, a second disk drive has some of the strands of its flat-ribbon cable twisted once (reversed), which is a signal to the controller that it is the second drive. If, however, the cable does not have this set of wires twisted, you must set the *drive-select* jumper appropriately on the controller card.

There's another thing to check when adding a second drive: Each drive should have a *resistor pack* (a dual in-line (DIP) connector with resistors). The resistor pack is always installed in the *last* drive connected to the controller. Thus, if you started out with one disk drive, it should contain the resistor pack. When adding a second drive, the resistor pack must be removed from the first drive and installed in the second (or last) drive.

Removable-media systems using cartridges are gaining in popularity in the months before this book is published and such devices should be considered, particularly in situations where data transportability is an issue.

Optical disks are, for the moment at least, read-only, which means they have no use as storage places for your data and programs. You can, however, relieve your traditional mass storage device of a considerable load by storing programs or data with permanence on CD-ROMs. This frees your hard disk to handle dynamic data. As optical disk, or CD-ROM, technology develops over the next few years and the *write-once, read-many* (WORM) archival disks become more available and popular, followed by the read-write version, these devices will have to be considered as viable storage options in many PC systems.

Purchasing Considerations

There are nearly as many factors to take into account when shopping for add-on mass storage as there are when buying a personal computer in the first place. The following summarizes some of the most important criteria.

Crucial

Adequate capacity
Compatibility—system
Compatibility—programs
Power requirements
Backup Capability

Important

Manufacturer support
Serviceability
Ability to boot from medium
Documentation

Tie Breakers

Physical size
Cost per megabyte
Speed

Adequate Capacity

Determining how much additional mass storage you need is not an easy task. Most programs on the market don't give any clue as to how much storage capacity you should plan on for the data they create. (Accounting packages tend to be an exception to this rule for some reason.) Word processing storage is a bit simpler.

TRICK

CALCULATING WORD PROCESSING STORAGE DEMANDS

You can determine fairly easily and accurately how much storage capacity you need for word processing documents. Figure that a single page of double-spaced text with margins of ½ inch to one inch on all four sides occupies about 2,000 characters (bytes) of storage.

Don't forget to take into account backup copies of the document that may be automatically created by your word processor. Automatic backups can double the expected storage capacity and have undesirable surprise side effects.

If you use one program far more frequently and for far more applications and documents than any other on your system, you probably can get some idea of how much storage capacity is needed for its data by examining a few of the applications you've created with it. Then with some judicious calculation and planning, you can probably anticipate what storage you need in order to accommodate documents for that application.

ALLOWING FOR EXPANSION AND ERROR IN CAPACITY CALCULATIONS

When you figure the total capacity required for your applications, including program storage, data storage, and system requirements, multiply the result by 1.5 to give yourself plenty of additional safety margin. This 50 percent rule has come in handy for many people when faced with the "how much is enough?" decision. One reason for this rule is that most files are short, causing a half-cluster per file on average to be wasted.

Compatibility Issues

Determining the degree to which any add-on mass storage device is compatible with your existing system and software is not usually too difficult but it is extremely important. If a particular device is advertised in its technical literature as being compatible with DOS 2.X and higher, for example, and you are using DOS 3.2, you might want to check with the manufacturer or have your dealer do so before buying it.

Most add-on mass storage for the PC works with any program, but if you are using programs that are sensitive to disk drive timing (for example, speech compression or analog-to-digital, real-time data gathering), you might have to do some more technical investigation before making a purchasing decision.

Power Requirements

A hard disk requires a fair amount of power to operate and power is crucial to it. Most PCs and compatibles have 65-watt power supplies, whereas most XTs and compatibles feature 135-watt power supplies.

Be sure to check the power required by any mass storage device that you are considering adding to your system. Again, if the device needs external power or if you have to purchase a new or replacement power supply, the documentation for the mass storage system should tell you so, but double check to be sure.

Support and Serviceability

Support and serviceability go hand in hand. If the manufacturer is a reputable, established company with dealer and sales outlets easily accessible to you and if it has a good reputation, serviceability is not as major an issue. If on the other hand, you've shopped for price and have purchased a unit that may or may not be supported well by its maker, be sure that proper documentation is available so that you can either service it yourself or take it to a knowledgeable computer repair technician who might not know that particular system well.

Bootability

In any PC or compatible with a hard disk subsystem, you can usually boot either from the primary floppy drive (drive A if it hasn't been reconfigured) or from the primary hard disk (usually drive C). If you are presently running a floppy-only system and are considering adding mass storage, be sure that your first add-on device allows you to boot from it. The convenience you'll experience will reward you many times over for taking the time to ensure that this is the case.

If on the other hand, you are adding mass storage to an existing system that already has a hard disk from which you can boot, bootability on the next add-on device is almost certainly not an issue.

Cost Per Megabyte

Like almost everything else in the microcomputer industry, the cost of add-on mass storage has steadily declined since it was first introduced. As we were writing this book, the price per megabyte of hard disk systems was in the $50-75 range, depending on what type of system you bought and how large its capacity. The cost per megabyte goes down as the total capacity goes up. This means that adding a 20M hard disk to your system is not twice as expensive as adding a 10M hard disk.

Although it is seldom wise to shop only on the basis of price, if you have found two or more competing mass storage systems that seem equal on all other counts, determine the price per megabyte. You'll probably find that it doesn't vary much from one system to another. If it does, it can become a major factor in the purchase decision. Hard disks aren't yet inexpensive.

TRICK

CAPACITY = FORMATTED CAPACITY

Be sure that when you are evaluating capacity needs and cost per megabyte, you use the add-on mass storage device's formatted capacity. Usually, for example, a 20M hard disk refers to its capacity before it is formatted to contain data. Formatting can reduce the capacity by a few percentage points, but we've seen some systems where the difference between unformatted and formatted capacity was significant.

External Add-On Hard Disks

With this general information, you are prepared to take a look at some of the specific issues involved in installing, interfacing, and using the various types of add-on mass storage. We'll start with external hard disk drives, then move, in order, to internal hard disk systems, added floppy drives, BERNOULLI (and other) boxes, and optical disks.

Connection Considerations

All of the external hard disk drive systems that we know about require the installation of a printed circuit board inside the PC. None operate over built-in serial or parallel data ports as is the case with hard disks for other kinds of computer systems. This means that you have to be concerned with the usual range of factors when installing any kind of plug-in PC board:

- Ensuring that you have enough of the right length slots available to run the new hardware with your existing board set-up
- Checking power considerations to ensure that enough power will be available through the PC and the board to run the newly connected external drive or that power is separately available to the drive. (Note that virtually all external drives incorporate separate power supplies, making them at once more expensive than chassis-mounted or board-based drives and less of a problem in terms of their power consumption from the system viewpoint.)
- Resolving memory address conflicts

We have more to say about address conflicts later in the chapter. You should also refer to the material in Chapter 11, *Secrets of Add-On Boards,* for general data on plug-in board considerations. You should also know that some external disk drives require two slots for their controller card, typically because the board is too thick to permit another board to be inserted into an adjacent slot.

Relative Speed

Disk drive speed is measured in average access time, which in turn is measured in milliseconds. (A millisecond is a thousandth of a second.) Early in the history of external disk drives, these units were often perceptibly slower than their chassis-mounted counterparts, but this difference has all but disappeared. Almost all hard disks, whether chassis-mounted or external, have average access times in the 28-30 ms range, though some range as high as 35 or 40 ms.

Availability

At the time this is written, at least a dozen companies are offering external hard disk systems for the PC. These systems range in capacity from 10M to as much as 160M. (We have more to say later about these high-capacity drives and how MS-DOS deals with them.)

Advantage: Decentralization

The primary advantage of external hard disk drive systems is their decentralization from the computer system. If your computer breaks down and must be repaired, you can remove the PC board from your system and plug it, and the hard disk it controls, into a different computer with no loss of data or programs.

Internal, Chassis-Mounted Hard Disks

By far, the most commonly used hard disk systems are those that are mounted inside the chassis of the PC, occupying one of the floppy slots on a PC or in the eighth area of an XT, which is reserved for incorporation of a hard disk drive.

Connection/Interface Considerations

Every disk drive, floppy or hard, must connect to the PC via a controller card. Many hard disk controller cards are available on the market and many of them "drive" any of several hard disk systems. Most often, though, you will buy your hard disk and its controller card at the same time, probably from the same manufacturer.

There is very little to be concerned about, beyond the usual plug-in board issues, when installing a chassis-mounted hard disk drive subsystem. Assuming you've ensured compatibility and dealt with the power requirements issue as outlined earlier in this chapter, the interface is fairly straightforward.

**MULTIPLE INTERNAL HARD DISKS:
RISKY AND DIFFICULT**

Many hard disk controller cards are designed so that they can support two (sometimes up to four) hard disks at one time. We do not recommend that you install additional hard disks if you can avoid it unless you know for sure that the disk controller you're using supports more than one drive. If your hard disk controller doesn't support more drives, trade up to a larger capacity drive or add an external hard disk drive that doesn't conflict with your internal hard disk.

DOS pathing, directory location, and general disk management issues become more complex with a second hard disk drive system in your computer.

Adding Floppy Capacity

Most PCs come equipped with two floppy disk drives. If you have an XT or compatible with two floppy drives in it, the system has space for the addition of a hard disk drive. If you have a good reason for doing so, you can add two more floppies to an XT-compatible system and install them in the space reserved for the hard disk. You will not, of course, be able then to add a hard disk to the system unless you choose a single half-height floppy and a half-height hard disk system.

Higher Density Floppies

One way to increase the capacity of your system without buying any additional drives is to buy a controller card that permits your existing drives to store more on a floppy. A number of manufacturers, including Rana Systems, Inc., offer such products.

Rana's product permits you to put as much as 2.5Mb of data on a single quad-density, double-sided disk.

LEAVE YOURSELF ONE "STANDARD" DRIVE!

If you decide to increase the capacity of your system with a super density disk controller card, be sure to leave yourself at least one standard floppy drive configuration. In all likelihood, you will not be able to boot from a super dense floppy, and programs you buy on disk generally are not compatible with that format either.

You should also note that the disks for such special controller densities are more expensive than ordinary floppy disks, although they are not proportionally costlier.

BERNOULLI and Other Boxes

A separate class of add-on mass storage is typified by the BERNOULLI BOX from Iomega. Because these boxes are nonstandard and in many ways unique, we treat them separately here. The generic term for these products is "cartridge disks." They combine the speed and reliability of hard disk technology with the convenience of removable media.

A BERNOULLI BOX, or any of its approximately half-dozen competitors, generally consists of a standalone, external unit that connects to your PC via a plug-in circuit board. It has two cartridge slots, each of which typically holds 10 or 20Mb of data on a cartridge. The advantage is in the cartridge, which can be removed and transported much like a floppy disk. (Although it is obviously larger than a 5¼-inch floppy disk, it is not too large to fit into an ordinary briefcase.)

Advantages of Disk Cartridges

All disk cartridge products have the advantages of convenience, virtually automatic backup, unlimited total storage capacity, data security, and system reliability.

Convenience

Switching from one operating system to another—for example, from UNIX to MS-DOS, as is often done by today's microcomputer power users —or between large applications programs on a disk cartridge system is as straightforward as swapping one or both cartridges from the external box for one or two others. In this respect, the cartridges have the convenience of a floppy disk—with multiple megabytes of capacity.

Backup Nearly Automatic

Each cartridge in a disk cartridge system virtually *is* a backup. Because it can be removed from the system and stored in a safe place, it is arguable that a second copy is not necessary. For the extra cautious, however, backing up one cartridge to another is quite simple (akin to copying a floppy to another floppy) and requires very little technical know-how, unlike hard disk backup, which is the subject of an entire section of this chapter.

Unlimited Capacity

Exactly like floppies, disk cartridges offer the user unlimited capacity—in limited-size segments. The difference, of course, is that on a floppy-based system, the segment is typically less than half a megabyte, whereas with a disk cartridge, the segment can be 10, 20, or more megabytes.

The disk cartridges, although more expensive than floppies, are not as expensive as whole new disk subsystems and make for relatively economical ways of storing large amounts of data for later use.

Data Security

The removability of the medium has another advantage: data security. Any power user who wants to can eventually get at all the data on your built-in or external hard disk, no matter what you do to encode, encrypt, password-protect, or otherwise lock it away. However, if you have the information with you, in your briefcase, as opposed to resident in the machine or connected to it at all times, it's a different matter.

System Reliability

Disk cartridges have built a well deserved reputation for ruggedness. They are intended to be removed, carried around in briefcases, filed in ordinary cabinets, and even knocked around a bit. They are less prone to damage and consequent data loss than floppies or most hard disk systems. (Although the hard disk systems in many transportable and laptop computers are becoming more reliable all the time.)

Disadvantages of Disk Cartridges

This is not to say that disk cartridges are the ultimate solution to add-on mass storage needs. There are a number of disadvantages to this technology as well: price per megabyte, nonstandardness, and nonbootability (for virtually all compatibles).

Price per Megabyte

These removable medium systems tend to be more expensive—on the order of five to seven times more expensive—than their hard disk system counterparts. This is a high premium to pay for the added convenience and other advantages outlined previously, but if those advantages are important to your system needs, it may be worth it.

Nonstandardness

Whether you buy an Iomega BERNOULLI BOX or one of their competitors', in each case you are dealing with nonstandard media formats, nonstandard directory approaches, and nonstandard interface requirements. Because each box is available only from one supplier, you are solely dependent on that manufacturer. This is almost always viewed by experienced computer users as an uncomfortable if not dangerous situation.

Nonbootability

Iomega's BERNOULLI BOX is available with a variety of controller cards, of which there are two basic types: bootable and nonbootable. A third type of controller can be configured to be either bootable or nonbootable. If you're installing a BERNOULLI BOX subsystem as your first hard disk, you should consider obtaining the controller card that is capable of booting (fixed or selectable). If on the other hand, you're adding the BERNOULLI BOX to a system that already contains a bootable hard disk, you should get either the nonbooting controller card or the boot-selectable controller card.

Backup: The Important Issue

The more information and programs you have stored on a hard disk or other add-on mass storage device and the more important that information is to you, the more significant the issue of backup becomes. In this section, we look at when and why to back up data from a hard disk, how to do it, alternative methods and approaches, and some software that assists you with this process.

We assume that you do not have a BERNOULLI BOX or any similar removable mass storage medium, including floppy drives, as your primary or only add-on mass storage.

CAUTION

HOW YOU DO IT IS LESS IMPORTANT THAN THAT YOU DO IT!

At the outset of this discussion, we want to make painfully clear something that may already be painfully clear to you. Whether you choose one of the many methods we discuss in this section or find other alternatives you like, we can't overemphasize the importance of data backup. We strongly recommend that you back up your complete hard disk system once when you first get it configured in its final form, again completely any time you change it radically, and at least weekly for all data that has changed since the last update. If you do significant work on a major project during the day, back up the project's data even if you just did a total backup an hour ago. The cost of the backup medium and the time to perform a backup is never greater than the cost of replacing the data if it's lost through a power failure, system crash, theft, or inadvertent deletion.

HOW BAD WOULD IT BE IF I DIDN'T BACK UP TODAY?

One of the more useful public-domain programs we've encountered in the area of disk backup is a little gem called BACKSTAT. Like other such programs (see Chapter 8), this program is obtainable free from CompuServe and many other public bulletin board systems. The program searches through your entire hard disk, subdirectory by subdirectory, and shows you a list of all the files that have had their contents changed since the last time you backed up your disk. The program runs quickly and is quite helpful, showing the subdirectories in inverse video or contrasting colors. It doesn't do anything with these files, but it does let you know how many you'd lose if the system crashed right now and you hadn't backed up your data.

IBM's "Answer" to Backup Needs

With any IBM or compatible system, you receive an MS-DOS utility called, appropriately enough, BACKUP. It has a companion product, RESTORE. These programs, as is obvious from their names, are designed to place information from your hard disk (although it can be used with floppies, it seldom is) to one or more floppy disks and to retrieve that information later should it be needed.

This BACKUP/RESTORE utility combination is marginally adequate in the view of most experienced PC users. It is "better than nothing" but many preferable solutions are available both in the public domain and from commercial software suppliers.

Key problems with IBM's solution are speed, ease of use, and reliability.

Speed Problems

Backing up a 10M hard disk using IBM's BACKUP utility can require as much as 45 minutes to an hour. This compares somewhat unfavorably with the capability of backing up 20Mb in five to 15 minutes using other techniques.

Ease of Use

In the view of most experienced users, BACKUP and RESTORE are two of the more difficult to use and poorly documented programs in the IBM DOS arsenal. A number of options to BACKUP are available to the user for telling the system which files to back up, how to treat any existing data on the floppies being used as backup media, and how to handle subdirectories.

The RESTORE process is not much more straightforward. To begin with, you can't use the COPY or similar command to move a file from a floppy created with the BACKUP utility into the hard disk. You must use RESTORE, which is cumbersome at best. In addition, the system does not maintain a directory of which floppy contains which programs and you have no easy way of knowing (especially because some files overlap from one disk to another). Therefore, restoring a backed up file can take an inordinate amount of time and disk-swapping.

THERE *IS* HOPE FOR RESTORE

Users of IBM's BACKUP/RESTORE routines want to be able to restore files from disks created with the BACKUP routine without having the system go through all of the disks. A public domain program called UNDO.BAS, written in BASIC, permits you to accomplish this task. The program, created by Rich Schinnell of Rockville, MD, is available on CompuServe and on most public domain software bulletin board systems in the country. (See Chapter 8 for details on obtaining free and low-cost software.)

Another program that assists in the process of recovering files originally stored with the MS-DOS BACKUP command is called HEADERSTRIP, written by Conrad ("Connie") Kageyama, one of the best-known PC gurus in the country. Also in the public domain, Kageyama's program works basically the same as UNDO.BAS, but it runs more quickly. Both programs operate on the principle that when BACKUP writes your file to the disk, it appends to the front of the file contents a 128-byte header that tells DOS where to put the file when it is RESTOREd. This is fine unless you don't want to or cannot use RESTORE to recover the file. These programs strip the header and make the file directly usable by the MS-DOS COPY command.

Reliability

Users have consistently reported problems with the BACKUP and RESTORE utilities overlooking files, failing to check that the file is stored correctly on the floppy, and causing other data reliability problems.

It has reached the point where most experienced DOS users prefer to use software other than IBM's provided programs to back up data from and restore it to their hard disk subsystems.

Other Backup/Restore Software

Fortunately, there is a great deal of software, both in the public domain and commercially available, that overcomes all the problems with IBM's built-in programs. Space limitations do not permit us to examine all of the available alternatives, but we discuss briefly some of the solutions that are in fairly widespread use.

Commercial Products

Almost certainly the best-known and most widely used hard disk backup routine available commercially is FASTBACK from Fifth Generation Systems of Seal Beach, California. This program, which earns high marks from veteran PC users, makes it possible to back up in about eight minutes a 10Mb hard disk full of data and programs. In addition, the program includes some sophisticated error detection and correction logic that makes the backup copies of the disks usable even if they are damaged.

Some of the MS-DOS directory tools discussed in Chapter 4 also enable you to look at the attributes of a file, determine from that examination whether the file needs to be backed up, then mark the file for copying to an archive disk. In this sense, they are good supplements to or replacements for the DOS BACKUP routine.

There are other products similar to FASTBACK but none that we know of has built the faithful following of professional MS-DOS users that this one has.

Public Domain Programs

Numerous MS-DOS users have noted the problems with the MS-DOS approach to BACKUP and RESTORE over the years and have developed other solutions. Four of these which have attained some degree of renown are: Backup Companion, IBU (incremental backup utility), DOWNLOAD, and FBR (file backup and restore). We look briefly at each of these public-domain alternatives to BACKUP.

Backup Companion:	We've found a frequent use for this program. It copies any files on your hard disk that have been created or modified today (on the system date) to a floppy disk. It is smart enough to look on the floppy for a file with the same name, extension, date, and time and, if it finds one, skips that backup. This makes it feasible to back up files regularly, even more often than daily, in minimum time. The program is by Mitchell D. Miller of Cumming, Georgia.
Download:	A kind of BACKUP "clone" with one big difference: The files it stores on the floppy disk are immediately usable because it does not store a header with each file. It permits the same kind of subdirectory and wild card usage as the BACKUP command, with a few exceptions, and it runs quickly. This program has been around quite a while and was contributed to the public domain by Pseudonym Software of Pasadena, California.
FBR:	A program that is quite similar to BACKUP with two important exceptions. First, it can only handle one directory or

subdirectory at a time, but it permits you to define in a list up to 30 file specifications for files to be backed up. This gives you much more flexibility than BACKUP. Second, it has an ingenious little switch feature that lets you specify that you are using two floppy drives for backup. If you set this switch, all backup processing continues while you switch floppies. This can represent a time saving of 10 to 15 percent in itself. The program was contributed to the public domain by Vernon D. Buerg of Daly City, California.

IBU (Incremental
Backup Utility):   This program has a great many useful options including the ability to exempt from backup certain files from a selected list based on your file criteria, automatic deletion of files as they are backed up (be careful!), and displaying the amount of space left on both the hard disk and the target backup disk. This program is shareware produced by Mike Hodapp of Louisville, KY, who asks a $20 suggested donation if the program is used.

Backup Hardware Options and Decisions

The software options discussed in the preceding section are used primarily, although not exclusively, for backing up a hard disk's contents to one or more floppy disks. In reality, the contents of a hard disk can be backed up to any of several possible target media: removable media (including disk cartridges), other hard disks, magnetic tape, and video cassettes.

Backing up data to the first two of these types of media—removable cartridges or plug-in hard disks and other hard disks that are fixed in the system or external to it—involves basically the same software and approaches as backing up data to a floppy disk. These were described in the previous section and are not dealt with again here.

Backup to magnetic and video tape is given more attention in the next few paragraphs.

Magnetic Tape

High-speed magnetic tape backup has become a major factor in the PC mass storage market in the past year or so. Magnetic tape backup units with tape cartridges capable of holding up to as much as 60Mb each are available from dozens of manufacturers.

Some hard disk drive subsystems come with integrated tape backup systems. Some magnetic tape units are external and some are mounted inside the PC.

MAG TAPE NOT FOR ALL USERS

Magnetic tape is still relatively expensive as a means of backing up computer data. When compared with storing data on floppy disks, even by the simple expedient of storing a file twice, once on the hard disk and once on a floppy, as the file is being created and edited, it can be seen as prohibitively expensive.

This means of mass storage backup is probably only economical for people with large capacity disk drives (in excess of 20M) who need to back up data frequently.

Video Cassettes for Computer Data?

One of the most intriguing ideas for computer storage backup has come in the past year or so from a small handful of companies who see the ubiquitous video cassette recorder (VCR) as an ideal means for storing precious computer information. Several companies have announced products that handle data backup via an ordinary VCR. One of these is Alpha Microsystems of Santa Ana, California. Their VIDE-OTRAX product consists of a printed circuit board that plugs into your PC, cables, and an optional VCR that you can obtain from the company. (You can use any standard VCR for the storage, however.

The VIDEOTRAX recorder has one major advantage: It has control of record/playback and other motor functions built into a special plug accessible to the plug-in board, which greatly automates the backup and restore process.)

Backing up 10M of hard disk storage takes about 15 minutes using the VIDEOTRAX system.

Interfacing Considerations

Given that you've decided to buy a hard disk system and that you've grappled with and solved the backup issues involved in implementing that decision, you need to be aware of some interfacing and installation considerations as you proceed. Some of these involve the efficient organization and use of tree-structured directories (discussed in detail in Chapter 4). Others concern MS-DOS' inherent storage addressing limits and the assignment of disk drive designations.

Beyond 32 Megabytes

MS-DOS places an inherent limit of 32M on a single "volume" or "logical disk." If you are not planning to extend beyond this limit, feel free to skip the following discussion.

Going beyond this 32M limit—which is in fact an addressing limitation of MS-DOS—can be accomplished in one of two ways:

1. Partitioning the hard disk into multiple logical drives
2. Patching MS-DOS to overcome the limit

Disk Partitioning

A physical disk consists of one or more "platters" that are the specially coated surfaces on which magnetically recorded data is stored. Regardless of how many or how few platters a given hard disk drive has, it can be set up so that the system "believes" it is more than one disk drive. In other words, it is possible to differentiate between a *physical* disk drive and the *logical* drive(s) of which it is composed.

For example, by partitioning a 60M hard disk into two 30M logical disks with different drive designators, you can store 60M of hard disk-based information inside the PC.

Partitioning of a disk is usually carried out with a nonstandard program provided with some implementations of MS-DOS. The MS-DOS FDISK command can create up to four partitions on a hard disk, although only one of them usually is the MS-DOS partition. Most people use partitioning to permit their PCs to run more than one operating system, setting aside part of the disk for UCSD p-System or UNIX, for example.

DOS Patching

You patch MS-DOS in such a way that it overcomes the 32M limit.

CAUTION

PATCHING MS-DOS CAN LEAD TO INCOMPATIBILITY

You should always proceed with caution when patching MS-DOS because a mistake can render your system useless. Always work on a backup copy of your system, not on the working copy or the master. If you ignore this warning, you might find that some or all of your programs no longer work on your system.

Assigning Disk Drive Designations

As you know, the disk drives on your PC are addressed by their single-letter names. Generally, the floppy disk is drive A, a second floppy if there is one is drive B, and the hard disk is drive C. If you have one floppy drive and a hard disk, the floppy is both drive A and drive B and the hard disk is still drive C.

If you partition the hard disk into two logical drives, they are addressed as C and D. (It is possible, using a special program supplied with some implementations of MS-DOS, to partition the hard disk into up to four segments, addressed respectively as C, D, E, and F.)

MS-DOS automatically assigns these disk names when you use the partitioning program to set up your partitions. You have no control over this operation, nor can you easily modify drive designations once they have been assigned by the system.

Add-On Storage Under DOS Version 3.x

Under DOS 3.x, as with DOS 2.1 and later, the system automatically assigns drive name designators: A and B are the floppy drive(s), C through F are the valid names for hard disk drives and G through Z can be used for virtual disks. You can cause a call to any directory on any logical drive to be rerouted to any other logical drive by means of the ASSIGN command.

The ASSIGN command looks like this:

```
ASSIGN A=C B=C
```

with as many arguments as needed. Each argument consists of two currently valid drive designators separated by an equal sign.

TRICKING PROGRAMS THAT USE FLOPPIES

One of the most frequent uses of the ASSIGN command in DOS 2.1 is to force DOS to look on the hard disk for any I/O requests and instructions received that would normally address the floppy drives, A or B. Thus,

```
ASSIGN A=C B=C
```

has the effect of telling DOS, "If you get a request to look on either Drive A or Drive B for something, look in Drive C instead."

Several programs let you copy them to the hard disk but keep looking at Drive A for a data file or some kind of information that enables the program to run correctly. This makes it impossible for those programs to run entirely from the hard disk.

CAUTION

WHEN *NOT* TO USE ASSIGN

You must be careful when you use the ASSIGN command. Some MS-DOS commands—most notably BACKUP and PRINT—must know which disk drive is intended for file I/O because they handle file access at a level below that where ASSIGN operates. Having ASSIGN in effect rerouting file I/O requests while BACKUP or PRINT is active can be quite dangerous to your data.

Be aware also that FORMAT, DISKCOPY, and DISKCOMP ignore any special drive designations made with the ASSIGN command and use the proper logical drive.

LASTDRIVE Parameter Usage

Under MS-DOS 3.x, there is a special command called LASTDRIVE. Its purpose is to inform MS-DOS of the highest drive letter name used by the system so that the system can reject any call to a drive with a higher letter name as referring to a nonexistent device. The command looks like this:

```
LASTDRIVE=N
```

where *N* can be replaced by any letter A through Z. This command is placed in the CONFIG.SYS file. If no LASTDRIVE command appears in the CONFIG.SYS file, the system assumes the highest valid drive name is E. If you have two floppy drives, have configured your hard disk to be four logical drives, and are using two virtual disks, you would use this command:

```
LASTDRIVE=H
```

Making Effective Use of Mass Storage

With the add-on mass storage safely snuggled into your PC's working environment and at home with MS-DOS, the last two subjects to which we turn our attention are making effective use of this new-found capacity and safety considerations. Effective use of the hard disk typically divides into two areas of interest: disk speed optimization and file accessibility.

Speeding Up a Disk

There are at least three ways to speed the rate at which your hard disk retrieves and saves files. There are plug-in boards that are variously billed as *turbo* and *booster* boards. Typically, these products, which are discussed in greater detail in Chapter 11, either use a separate processor to control the disk and thus relieve your system's CPU of the task, or they use a technique called *caching* to store in high-speed memory the programs and data for which you are likely to have the most immediate need instead of keeping them only on the disk. Some of these products use both techniques.

Another way to coax more speed from a hard disk on a PC or XT is with software that uses various techniques to accelerate the rate of access. One of the most effective in the view of power users is a public domain utility called FASTDISK. This program reduces the head settle time on your drives to 2ms and prevents the system from always moving the read head back to Track 0 after an access. (The utility may have no effect on a PC compatible because it is really designed to address a problem that exists on IBM systems due to a design change made by the company in MS-DOS 2.1.)

Disk Optimizers

The final category of disk speed enhancers is known generically as *disk optimizers*. These programs restructure data on your hard disk and should be used with great caution.

Noncontiguous Files on the Disk

When you create and edit files on your hard disk—or on your floppy disk, for that matter—and enlarge them beyond the size they were when they started out in life, MS-DOS takes pieces of the file and places them in areas on the disk where space is available. These areas are not necessarily contiguous to one another or to the original file location. To retrieve a file then, MS-DOS must take the following steps:

1. Find the starting point of the file from information stored on its directory tracks.

2. Read as much of the file as is stored contiguously starting at that location.

3. Obtain from the file information the address of the next place on the disk where part of the file is found.

4. Move the read head of the disk to the new address and retrieve the next segment of information.

Obviously, MS-DOS repeats steps 3 and 4 as many times as necessary. If you are using a spreadsheet or database program that creates large files and if these files are frequently updated, the disk drive can be doing a great deal of extra work to retrieve the data when you need it.

Disk optimizing programs make all—or virtually all—files contiguous, thereby making it much more efficient for MS-DOS to retrieve information contained in them. These programs do this by relocating data so that all the parts of a given file are located physically adjacent to one another on the disk.

Two Available Programs

At least two programs are available that handle disk optimization as outlined. The first is commercially available from SoftLogic Solutions in Manchester, NH, and is called *Disk Optimizer*. The other is a public domain program called *DOG*. Long-time PC users say there is virtually no difference between the programs' capabilities except in terms of options provided at run-time. Both seem to have a good reputation for improving disk speed in file-intensive application situations.

Safety Consideration

Our discussion of add-on mass storage would not be complete without this final tip.

TRICK   **PARK THOSE HEADS!**

Most commercially available hard disk systems include with their complement of system software a program called variously PARK, SIT, SAFETY, or another similar title. These programs have one purpose: Move the read /write heads of the disk drive out of the way of the recording surface itself before turning off the machine.

It is virtually impossible to overly stress the importance of this step. When the power to your PC is turned on or off, a "power spike" can be generated through the system. If this spike is transmitted to the read/write head of your disk drive, data on the disk surface may be damaged. These programs take the read/write head out of harm's way so that if such a spike occurs and is transmitted to the read/write head, your hard disk-based data is not affected.

If your hard disk didn't come equipped with such a program, check out the public domain software called PARKALL or PARKER. Both reportedly work with any disk that runs correctly under MS-DOS.

Summary

In this chapter, we have taken a look at the issue of add-on mass storage: whether you need it, what options are available, how to back up data once it's on a hard disk, some special installation and interface issues, and how to make effective use of a hard disk subsystem. Some of what you can do to make your use of the hard disk and other portions of the system effective involves configuring your system for maximum performance. That is the subject of Chapter 13.

Secrets of System Configuration

Chapter **13**

T his chapter deals with secrets and tricks related to configuring the MS-DOS operating system. Although several aspects of MS-DOS configuration relate to both standard and special hardware installed in a system, the information presented in this chapter deals with the software side of configuration.

The MS-DOS Configuration Process

Configuring MS-DOS for a particular computer can be accomplished in several ways, ranging from modifying the MS-DOS operating system, and its basic input/output system (BIOS), to more accessible methods, such as modifying special files that are read by MS-DOS when it is booted. The MS-DOS configuration process described in this chapter deals with the more accessible methods of configuration. The MS-DOS configuration process is divided into two basic parts:

1. Configuration relating specifically to MS-DOS
2. Configuration relating to how applications are used with MS-DOS

The two parts correspond roughly to two files that MS-DOS reads when it is booted: the CONFIG.SYS file and the AUTOEXEC.BAT file. The use of these two files was introduced with MS-DOS Version 2.00 and their potential capabilities were enhanced with later versions. Where does this leave MS-DOS Versions 1.00 and 1.10? The answer is that versions of MS-DOS prior to 2.00 do not have any easy means of configuration by the user other than to modify MS-DOS's boot files and its BIOS (bootable from disk or stored in a ROM [read-only memory]), which is not a task to be undertaken lightly. For this reason, this chapter deals only with MS-DOS Versions 2.00 through 3.20.

MS-DOS Bootup Overview

The MS-DOS bootup process is accomplished in three basic stages. After initial powerup or reset, the first stage consists of hardware initialization normally controlled by a program stored in ROM. In the IBM Personal Computer series and all close compatibles, this ROM routine contains the BIOS, commonly referred to as the *ROM BIOS*. The ROM BIOS contains software routines needed to control all standard hardware and performs such tasks as checking the integrity of the system's internal RAM memory, the status of the keyboard, the monitor, and other similar tasks.

After the ROM BIOS has completed its checks, the bootup process begins the second stage of the MS-DOS boot procedure by executing a routine that checks the disk drives for the MS-DOS operating system files. If it finds the MS-DOS files on the boot disk (normally a floppy disk drive designated as drive A), it loads the MS-DOS operating system and transfers control to it. In systems equipped with a hard disk, the ROM BIOS checks the hard disk (normally drive C) if the MS-DOS boot files were not found on a disk in drive A (or a disk wasn't inserted in drive A). Once the MS-DOS boot files have been loaded into memory, MS-DOS takes control of the system, although it always interacts with the ROM BIOS.

The third stage of the MS-DOS boot process begins after MS-DOS has been successfully loaded into memory and has been given control over the system. MS-DOS subsequently checks the disk from which it was originally loaded for a file called CONFIG.SYS. The CONFIG.SYS file is a text file created by the user that contains special parameters used to establish certain aspects of MS-DOS's behavior while it is controlling the system. After all the parameters in the CONFIG.SYS file have been read and accepted by MS-DOS, the system checks for a file called AUTOEXEC.BAT. If it is found, MS-DOS reads the file's contents and executes all its parameters. The AUTOEXEC.BAT file is the same as any other MS-DOS batch file, except that it is automatically executed by MS-DOS during the boot process. Both CONFIG.SYS and AUTOEXEC.BAT are optional: If either file is not found by MS-DOS on the boot disk during the boot process, MS-DOS loads normally and the MS-DOS prompt is displayed on the screen. The following paragraphs describe the CONFIG.SYS and AUTOEXEC.BAT files in more detail and explain how you can use them to configure MS-DOS.

The CONFIG.SYS File

The purpose of the CONFIG.SYS file is to provide you with the means of specifying how MS-DOS operates and how it relates to your system's hardware. When nonstandard hardware is added to a system, such as extended memory cards, external hard disks, special graphics cards, and so on, special software routines are needed so that the added hardware can be accessed correctly by MS-DOS. Because modifying the ROM BIOS is impractical, the CONFIG.SYS file can be used to specify the loading of certain types of software programs to control special hardware. These types of programs are called *device drivers*. When they are loaded by MS-DOS, they behave in much the same manner as the routines in the ROM BIOS, except that they reside in . RAM memory alongside MS-DOS. A device driver is specified in the CONFIG.SYS file with the command

```
DEVICE=[filespec]
```

where [filespec] is the name of the device driver program file and the drive and path indicating where the file is stored. You can tell MS-DOS to load any number of device drivers by including a series of lines in the CONFIG.SYS file each containing DEVICE= commands.

The AUTOEXEC.BAT File

The AUTOEXEC.BAT file provides a considerably more sophisticated method of customizing the configuration of your system. Although the commands used in the CONFIG.SYS file cannot be used in the AUTOEXEC.BAT file, the batch facilities afforded you via the

AUTOEXEC.BAT file make it considerably easier for you to configure your system. Not only can you automatically execute MS-DOS commands and load memory-resident programs with AUTOEXEC.BAT, but you can also pause the batch file with queries to determine what you want the batch file to do next. As discussed in Chapter 8, several programs are available that add this flexibility to batch files. (Two programs in the public domain discussed in Chapter 2 are QUERY.COM, and ANSWER.COM. See also the section later in this chapter called *Specifying Options Requiring User Input* for a description of the use of these files and other public domain programs in AUTOEXEC.BAT files.) Combined with the use of *environment* variables, using these query commands can allow you to structure your AUTOEXEC.BAT file in a *modular* format.

The following paragraphs describe in more detail how you can modify the CONFIG.SYS and AUTOEXEC.BAT files to enhance your system's configuration.

Creating the CONFIG.SYS File

Although many of the commands that can be placed in the CONFIG.SYS file are described in the MS-DOS technical manual, it is often unclear exactly what purpose each serves and what parameters should be given to each. Furthermore, some of the parameters associated with CONFIG.SYS commands are not fully described or are not described at all. Because of the vague information currently available for CONFIG.SYS commands, the following paragraphs are presented to help clarify how the commands are used and what parameters should and can be assigned to them.

Table 13-1 provides a list of the commands that can be placed in the CONFIG.SYS file in versions of MS-DOS up to 3.20. Note that not all commands are available in all versions of MS-DOS. Other commands have different parameter ranges between MS-DOS versions, as shown in Table 13-1.

Most of the commands can be used in any configuration situation, although some of them need to be used only in certain situations, such as when your computer is attached to a local area network. The following paragraphs describe each command in more detail and explain how to determine the right kind of parameters for your configuration needs.

Table 13-1.   List of CONFIG.SYS Commands

Command	Parameters	MS-DOS Version 2.X	MS-DOS Version 3.X	MS-DOS Version 3.2
BREAK=	ON or OFF (Default = OFF)		yes	
BUFFERS=	1 through 99 (default = 2 (IBM PC XT) or 3 (IBM AT))			
FILES=	5 through 255 (default = 8)			
DEVICE=	[filespec] (no default)			
SWITCHAR=	/ or [-] (default = /)	yes	no	
SHELL=	[d:][path][filespec] (default = COMMAND.COM) NOTE: See text for parameters.	yes	improved	
COUNTRY=	[country code] (default = 001), (USA)	no	yes	
LASTDRIVE=	A through Z (default = E)			
FCBS=	[x,y] ([x] = 1 through 255; [y] = 0 through 255) (default = 4,0)			
STACKS=	[n,s] ([n] = 8 through 64; [s] = 32 through 512) (default = 9,128)	no		yes

Using the BREAK Command

The BREAK command is used to establish MS-DOS' response to the Ctrl-Break key combination when it is pressed. If BREAK=OFF is inserted in CONFIG.SYS (which is the default setting if the BREAK= command isn't used), MS-DOS responds to a Ctrl-Break command only during screen, keyboard, serial port, or printer input/output operations. If the BREAK=ON is inserted in CONFIG.SYS (which the equivalent of entering the BREAK ON command at the MS-DOS prompt or within a batch file), MS-DOS responds to a Ctrl-Break command during all input/output operations, including disk accesses.

Why doesn't MS-DOS have the break function turned on all the time? The reason is that when the break function is turned on, MS-DOS must work extra hard during disk access operations because it constantly checks to see whether the Ctrl-Break command has been entered. Additionally, issuing the Ctrl-Break command while the break function is turned on can cause unpredictable results if you have certain types of programs running, such as word processor or spreadsheet programs. Indeed, some programs actually turn off the break function while they are running to avoid problems.

In some configurations, you are likely to discover that even though you have the BREAK=ON command entered on one of the first lines in the CONFIG.SYS file, issuing the BREAK command at the MS-DOS prompt once the system booted showed the break function to be turned off. This occurs if you are using the CONFIG.SYS DEVICE= command to load one or more device driver programs that automatically turn off the break function once they are loaded. If it is important that you always have the break function turned on after MS-DOS has been loaded, follow the advice described in the following trick.

ENSURING THAT BREAK IS TURNED *ON* AFTER MS-DOS IS LOADED

If you are not loading device drivers with the CONFIG.SYS DEVICE= command, having the command BREAK=ON as the first line your CONFIG.SYS file is normally adequate to ensure that the break function remains turned on. However, if device drivers *are* loaded, place the BREAK=ON command on the first line of the CONFIG.SYS file, then again on the last line. Setting CONFIG.SYS in this way ensures that the use of the Ctrl-Break command works while the CONFIG.SYS file is being processed and until it is canceled by the loading of the device driver, then the break function is turned on again once all lines in the CONFIG.SYS file have been processed.

If you find that repeating the BREAK=ON command in the CONFIG.SYS file still doesn't work, a program probably is being loaded by the AUTOEXEC.BAT file that also automatically turns off the break function. To correct this problem, insert the command BREAK ON (with or without the = sign) at the end of the AUTOEXEC.BAT file. Please read the following caution on the use of the break function.

THE PRO'S AND CON'S OF TURNING BREAK *ON*

Caution should be exercised when turning on the break function with either the BREAK=ON command in the CONFIG.SYS file or the BREAK ON at the MS-DOS prompt or within a batch file. Some programs, such as word processors, database managers, and spreadsheet calculators, react in unexpected ways when the Ctrl-Break command is entered while the break function is turned on. Although using the Ctrl-Break command with the break function turned on is sometimes the only way you can terminate a program without resetting the system, accidentally issuing the Ctrl-Break command could cause the program to terminate such that you could lose data that you created or changed. Turn off the break function when you use programs with which you're familiar and that can be terminated normally (via an "exit" or "quit" command). Turn on the break function only when using a new program with which you are not familiar or that is known not to have a normal termination command, then turn the break function back off when the MS-DOS prompt is redisplayed. If you need to have the break function turned on only for some programs, create a batch file that executes the program with the BREAK ON command at the beginning of the file and the BREAK OFF command at the end of the file.

Using the BUFFERS Command

The BUFFERS= command is used to establish the number of *disk buffers* that are to be reserved for use by MS-DOS and application programs. A disk buffer is an area of memory reserved for the temporary storage of disk data during disk access operations. Many application programs, including MS-DOS commands such as COPY and DISKCOPY, require a certain amount of disk buffer space in memory. Generally, MS-DOS processes intensive disk operations faster when the number of disk buffers is increased but slows down again when there are too many disk buffers. The CONFIG.SYS BUFFERS= command is used to set the number of disk buffers. If the BUFFERS= command is not used, the default number of buffers is set to 2 in IBM PCs and IBM XTs or to 3 in IBM ATs. For many application programs, however, this default value is simply too low. Generally, setting the number of buffers to 16 is adequate, although some programs require more, sometimes as many as 64.

In most machines (such as the IBM PC, IBM XT, and compatible systems), setting the number of buffers to a value greater than 20 or 30 slows the system down just as if there were too few disk buffers. However, setting the number of buffers above 30 (such as 64) in "faster" machines (such as the IBM AT and compatible systems) does not cause an appreciable slowdown. Therefore, if you're using an IBM PC, IBM XT, or compatible system (with an 8088 microprocessor), the BUFFERS command should be set anywhere between 10 and 20, unless a greater value is required by certain programs. If you're using an IBM AT or compatible system (with an 80286 microprocessor) or a system equipped with an 8 MHz (or higher) 8088 or 8086 microprocessor, you can set the number of buffers above 30, up to 64 or more.

Note that each disk buffer defined by the BUFFER command takes up 528 bytes of memory. If your system is equipped with plenty of memory, the number of disk buffers you define shouldn't be of great concern. However, if your system is not equipped with a lot of memory or if you need most of the memory to load memory-resident programs, you should determine carefully the optimum number of disk buffers for your needs. It makes no sense to define more disk buffers than you're really going to use. Note that the 528 bytes taken up by a disk buffer is slightly greater than half a kilobyte, so you can easily determine memory usage by thinking that for every two disk buffers which you define, a little more than 1K of memory is used.

Using the FILES Command

The CONFIG.SYS FILES= command is used to adjust the total number of files that can be opened at any given time in the system. If the FILES command is not used, a default of eight files is established. MS-DOS automatically opens five files for each process that is loaded, so the default of eight files is adequate for most environments. These five files represent the following:

1. Standard input (the keyboard part of CON:)
2. Standard output (the monitor part of CON:)
3. Standard error (the handling of errors such as ERRORLEVEL in batch files)
4. Standard printer (PRN:, LPT1:, LPT2:, or LPT3:)
5. Standard auxiliary device (COM1: or COM2:)

Some application programs, however, require a higher number of files to be opened. If after loading an application program, an error message is displayed that indicates an insufficient number of files, use the FILES= command to increase the number of files that can be opened at any given time. Note that an individual program cannot have more than 20 files open simultaneously. Increasing the number of files to 10 or even 20 is adequate for most circumstances. Some programs may require a higher number, such as some database manager programs or local area network interface programs, increasing the number of files up to 100. Note that for each additional file specified above the default of 8, 48 bytes of memory is reserved.

Using the DEVICE Command

The CONFIG.SYS DEVICE= command is crucial to configuring your system for use with different types of hardware devices because it is the only means by which special device driver programs can be loaded into memory. As discussed at the beginning of this chapter, device drivers are special types of programs needed to control nonstandard hardware devices installed in your system that aren't supported by the routines in the ROM BIOS (or memory-resident BIOS in some systems). Because modifying the BIOS, whether it is in ROM or is memory resident, is impractical and ill-advised, the DEVICE= command is a facility provided to solve configuration problems involving the addition of nonstandard hardware, such as external hard disks, input devices (mouse, graphics tablet, etc.), special memory cards, and so on.

Unless you're adventurous and you like to write your own device drivers, any hardware added to your system that requires special software support should be accompanied by the appropriate device driver program. A device driver is loaded by placing the following command in your CONFIG.SYS file.

```
DEVICE=[d:][path][filespec]
```

The parameters indicate where the device driver file is stored and the file's name, where [d:] is the disk drive, [path] is the full directory path, and [filespec] is the name of the file, including the extension. Note that if the device driver's extension is omitted, MS-DOS automatically assumes the default extension .SYS. However, the device driver can have any extension as long as it is specified when assigning the filename to the DEVICE= command.

As with many MS-DOS commands, some device drivers are (or can be) accompanied by parameters that are meaningful only to the device driver. When device driver parameters are specified on the line containing the DEVICE= command, MS-DOS automatically passes the parameters to the device driver once it has been loaded. Otherwise, MS-DOS ignores these parameters.

Any number of device drivers can be loaded into memory by

specifying the appropriate number of DEVICE= commands in the CONFIG.SYS file. Generally, the lines containing the DEVICE= command should be listed in the order in which you want the device drivers loaded.

Some special device drivers are also provided with the MS-DOS operating system. In MS-DOS Version 2.00 and above, the device driver ANSI.SYS is provided to add certain features to the standard output device (the monitor screen) as well as the standard input device (the keyboard). The features provided by the ANSI.SYS device driver are discussed in Chapter 6. In MS-DOS Version 3.00 and above, another device driver was introduced called VDISK.SYS. When loaded, VDISK.SYS creates and "drives" a RAM disk with format and size characteristics established by parameters. Although the loading of device drivers is fairly straightforward, creating one from scratch is another matter. Writing a device driver requires a good understanding of assembly language and high-level language programming, the internals of MS-DOS, and the hardware for which the device driver is intended. Although writing a device driver is beyond the scope of this book, some excellent reference books available on the subject are listed in the bibliography.

Using the SHELL Command

The CONFIG.SYS SHELL= command is used to specify which *shell* to load while MS-DOS is being booted. The default shell, also called the *command interpreter,* is the file called COMMAND.COM. You can use the SHELL= command to specify a different file or to indicate a drive and directory other than the root directory from which MS-DOS was loaded. Under MS-DOS Version 3.00 and above, you can also specify the size of the environment as well as cause or prevent the execution of the AUTOEXEC.BAT file after MS-DOS has completed processing the CONFIG.SYS file. The following paragraphs describe in more detail how to use the SHELL= command.

Using SHELL To Specify How the Shell Is Loaded

The CONFIG.SYS SHELL command can be used not only to indicate from where the file COMMAND.COM is to be loaded, but also to specify a different shell. The default loading of the standard MS-DOS shell (COMMAND.COM), if the SHELL command is not used, is equivalent to the command SHELL=A:\COMMAND.COM if booting from floppy disk drive A, or SHELL=C:\COMMAND.COM if booting from hard disk drive C. In most cases, you don't have to change the default setting. However, if you have more than one shell (either as a modified copy of COMMAND.COM or a completely different shell file), you must use the SHELL command to inform MS-DOS what file to use and where it is located.

Using SHELL To Set COMSPEC

The SHELL command also provides another useful function: When it is executed, the parameter COMSPEC stored in the environment is given the parameters that you specify with the SHELL command. The COMSPEC parameter is needed because part of COMMAND.COM resident in memory is overwritten when an application program is loaded. When an application program terminates, the portion of COMMAND.COM previously overwritten (called the *transient* portion) needs to be reloaded from disk, so MS-DOS reads the COMSPEC setting to determine where COMMAND.COM is stored. Therefore, if you insert the command SHELL=C:\COMMAND.COM in your CONFIG.SYS file, displaying the contents of the environment (using the SET command) reveals COMSPEC=C:\COMMAND.COM.

The SHELL command does not work properly under versions of MS-DOS prior to 3.00. The following trick shows how the problem can be fixed.

**FIXING THE COMSPEC PROBLEM
IN MS-DOS VERSION 2**

TRICK

Because the SHELL command does not operate correctly under versions of MS-DOS prior to 3.00, its use is discouraged. However, if you need to specify the location from which MS-DOS reloads the transient portion of COMMAND.COM, you can use the SET command to assign the correct parameters to the COMSPEC parameter in the environment. Although setting the COMSPEC parameter with SET places the correct parameters in the environment, MS-DOS is not properly informed of the change. To solve the problem, you need to use the public domain program COMSPEC4 described in Chapter 8. For example, if you wanted to inform MS-DOS that the transient portion of COMMAND.COM is to be reloaded from a directory called DOS in a RAM disk designated as drive D:, you need to insert the following in your AUTOEXEC.BAT file.

```
.
.
.
COMSPEC4 D:\DOS\COMMAND.COM
SET COMSPEC=D:\DOS\COMMAND.COM
.
.
```

These commands show how the COMSPEC problem is fixed. By first executing the COMSPEC4 command, MS-DOS is informed properly as to the location from which the transient portion of MS-DOS is to be reloaded. By subsequently executing the SET COMSPEC= command with exactly the same parameters as were specified with the COMSPEC4 command, the correct parameters are placed in the environment for later reference by MS-DOS. If you use these two commands in an AUTOEXEC.BAT file, you are effectively informing MS-DOS of the location of COMMAND.COM for subsequent reloads even though the initial loading of COMMAND.COM during boot time is from a completely different drive and directory.

Special SHELL Command Features in MS-DOS Version 3

Many of the problems encountered with the SHELL command and the COMSPEC parameter were fixed in MS-DOS Version 3.00. Under MS-DOS Version 3.00 and above, you can use the SHELL command exactly as documented. Additionally, you don't need to run the COMSPEC4 program. Some new parameters were added to the SHELL command in MS-DOS Version 3.00 that are described in the following paragraphs. The correct syntax for the SHELL command is as follows:

```
SHELL=[d:][path][filespec] [d:][path] [/P] [E:][size]
```

The [d:][path][filespec] is the disk drive, full directory path, and filename of the shell to be loaded. The default is A:\COMMAND.COM if booting from floppy drive A, or C:\COMMAND.COM if booting from hard disk drive C. The second [d:][path] is the drive name and full directory path from which MS-DOS is to reload the transient portion of the shell when needed. The default is A:\ if booting from floppy drive A or C:\ if booting from hard disk drive C. The /P and /E:[size] parameters are described in the following paragraphs.

Enabling or Disabling Execution of AUTOEXEC.BAT   The /P parameter (default) is used to enable the execution of the AUTO-EXEC.BAT file once processing of the CONFIG.SYS file has completed and COMMAND.COM has been fully loaded into memory. This parameter is actually a parameter to COMMAND.COM, not to the SHELL command. If you want to prevent the execution of the AUTOEXEC.BAT file, use the parameter /D (for "don't execute") rather than /P. When /D is used, the MS-DOS DATE and TIME commands are executed automatically after processing of the CON-FIG.SYS file has completed, just as if no AUTOEXEC.BAT file were present. Yet a third parameter can be used instead: /F, which causes the error message Abort, Retry, Ignore to be displayed instead of executing the AUTOEXEC.BAT file. What is the purpose of the /F parameter? Why anyone would want to use it is unclear. If you experiment a little, maybe you'll find a use for it.

Expanding the Environment Size   Following the /P, /D or /F parameter, you can optionally include the /E:[size] parameter to establish the size of the environment. Under MS-DOS Versions 3.00 and 3.10, the value assigned to /E:[size] is the number of *paragraphs* (16-byte portions) of memory to be reserved for the environment. The number of paragraphs of memory reserved for the environment ranges from 10 (160 bytes) to 62 (992 bytes). The default number of paragraphs is 10. If you use environment variables extensively with batch files, you'll probably want to maximize the size of the environment to 62 paragraphs.

Under MS-DOS Version 3.20, the size of the environment specified with the /E: parameter is specified in terms of absolute bytes rather than paragraphs. If you want to set the size of the environment to 1K (1,024 bytes), the parameter /E:1024 is used. The size of the environment under MS-DOS Version 3.20 can range from 160 to 16384 (16K) bytes. The default value is 160 bytes. Setting the size of the environment to 1,024 bytes (1K) should normally be sufficient for most configurations.

CAUTION

TELLING MS-DOS TO RELOAD COMMAND.COM FROM A DIFFERENT LOCATION IS NOT ALWAYS EFFECTIVE

Despite the powerful effects of the CONFIG.SYS SHELL= command and the environment COMSPEC parameter, you shouldn't expect the settings

---

for reloading the transient portion of COMMAND.COM to work all the time. Some application programs use COMMAND.COM for certain purposes while they are running, and not all of them read the SHELL= and COMSPEC settings. Many of these application programs always search for COMMAND.COM exactly by name and always in the drive and directory from which MS-DOS was initially loaded. If you use such programs, you may find using SHELL and COMSPEC to specify parameters other than the default has no affect.

Using the SWITCHAR Command (MS-DOS Version 2 Only)

Under MS-DOS Versions 2.00 and 2.10, the CONFIG.SYS SWITCHAR command is provided so that you can change the character used to specify options or *switches* to MS-DOS commands. The default value is the / character. For example, if you want the DIR command to display a directory in two-column format, the command is followed by the /W switch. In the MS-DOS operating system, the / character is traditionally used for switches, as is the case in older operating systems such as CP/M. However, other operating systems, such as UNIX for example, use the – character instead, making it confusing for users who frequently move from operating system to operating system. If you're used to using a character other than / for switches, you can use the SWITCHAR command to change it.

Overcoming the Absence of SWITCHCHAR in MS-DOS Version 3

With the introduction of MS-DOS Version 3.00, the SWITCHAR command was removed from the operating system. Why? Probably because it was a little-used command due to the fact that many application programs forced the use of / regardless of the SWITCHAR setting. There may be other reasons, too. However, if you're an ardent SWITCHAR fan, you can implement its function with an MS-DOS command shown in the following trick.

ADDING THE SWITCHAR FUNCTION TO MS-DOS VERSION 3.00 AND HIGHER

The text in the following listing shows the contents of the file called SWITCHAR.INP. You can use it in conjunction with the DEBUG command to create a program called SWITCHAR.COM.

```
n switchar.com
a
MOV DL,2F
CMP BYTE PTR [0080],00
JZ   010D
MOV DL,[0082]
MOV [0131],DL
MOV AX,3701
INT 21
MOV DX,0122
MOV AH,09
INT 21
MOV AX,4C00
INT 21
DB  'SWITCHCHAR = ',AF,' / ',AE,0D,0A,'$'

rcx
37
w
q
```

To create the program SWITCHAR.COM, simply enter DEBUG <SWITCHAR.INP in response to the MS-DOS prompt. Once the MS-DOS prompt is redisplayed, you can begin using the SWITCHAR program. If SWITCHAR is entered by itself, it sets the switch character to the default character /. To change the switch character to another character, simply enter SWITCHAR followed by the character you want to use.

Using the LASTDRIVE Command

The CONFIG.SYS LASTDRIVE command is used in MS-DOS Version 3.00 and above to inform MS-DOS of the number of drives it is to recognize. MS-DOS is capable of using up to 26 drives (A through Z), some of which are physical drives (hardware installed in the system) and others that are virtual drives established with the SUBST command. The default last drive is E, but you can use the LASTDRIVE command to set the last drive to Z (LASTDRIVE=Z), thereby enabling the use of all drives between A and Z.

To wrap up our discussion on using the CONFIG.SYS commands to configure the system, an example of a completed CONFIG.SYS file is shown in the following listing.

```
BREAK=ON
COUNTRY=001
LASTDRIVE=Z
BUFFERS=64
FILES=20
SHELL=C:\COMMAND.COM C:\ /P /E:1024
DEVICE=C:\SYSTEM\ANSI.SYS
DEVICE=C:\SYSTEM\VDISK.SYS 256 512 64
```

Creating the AUTOEXEC.BAT File

The AUTOEXEC.BAT file provides a way to further define your system's configuration beyond the capabilities of the CONFIG.SYS file. Because the AUTOEXEC.BAT file, unlike CONFIG.SYS, makes full use of all of MS-DOS's batch facilities, many potential variations in the way your system starts are provided.

Specifying Options Requiring User Input

As mentioned earlier in this chapter, the two public domain programs QUERY.COM and ANSWER.COM can be used in the AUTOEXEC.BAT file to present queries that ask for your instructions as to what the AUTOEXEC.BAT file should do next. The first program presents a prompt in response to which you can enter yes or no answers. Based on what you enter, the program sets an error condition that can be detected with the IF ERRORLEVEL [x] or IF NOT ERROR LEVEL [x], where [x] is the error level you want to check. Based on the error level condition, you can execute a command or branch to another location in the batch file. If you want your AUTOEXEC.BAT file to execute certain commands according to your system's configuration, you can use the QUERY.COM commands so that you can be prompted to make a decision when the system is powered up or reset. For example, if you sometimes have an expanded memory card installed in your system that normally has a RAM disk assigned to it, you could use QUERY.COM to pause and ask for your input before copying any files to the RAM disk or before loading a program that makes use of the extra memory. Having AUTOEXEC.BAT ask for input in this manner can prevent certain routines in the batch file from executing that otherwise would fail due to an incorrect hardware configuration.

An alternative to the QUERY.COM command is the ANSWER.COM command. The ANSWER.COM program provides a different approach: You can enter any text in response to the prompt it displays. The text that you enter in response to its prompt is saved in the environment assigned to the variable ANSWER. For example, if you had the following lines in your batch file and in response to the prompt you entered `Hello`, ANSWER.COM would assign the variable ANSWER to `Hello` just as if you entered the DOS command sequence SET ANSWER=Hello.

```
A>ANSWER Enter some text:
Enter some text: Hello

A>
```

By entering the SET command without any parameters, the contents of the environment is displayed and the text assigned to ANSWER also is displayed. You can use environment variables much like replaceable parameters in batch files. Placing the % on either side of the variable name, DOS automatically replaces the variable name with the text that's assigned to it in the environment. So if you wanted to check the contents of the ANSWER variable, you could use the batch command `if (%ANSWER%)==(Hello) goto OK` to automatically branch to the OK label or take some other action if ANSWER was not assigned the text `Hello`. Each time the ANSWER.COM program is used, it reassigns the ANSWER variable with whatever new text you specify. Therefore, if you want to save any text previously entered, you have to assign a new variable with the text currently assigned to ANSWER.

Because any kind of text can be entered in response to a prompt generated by ANSWER.COM, you can use it for many more purposes. For example, you can use ANSWER.COM to prompt you to enter a number. Then, you can check what was entered and in the process, determine what are "legal" entries for the prompt. For example, the following listing shows how you can implement ANSWER.COM to accept only specific numbers as input.

```
:AGAIN
ANSWER Enter any number between 1 and 5 (0 to exit):
if (%ANSWER%)==(0) goto END
if (%ANSWER%)==(1) goto OK
if (%ANSWER%)==(2) goto OK
if (%ANSWER%)==(3) goto OK
if (%ANSWER%)==(4) goto OK
if (%ANSWER%)==(5) goto OK
ECHO The entry "%ANSWER%" does not fall within
ECHO the range of 1 through 5.
goto AGAIN
:OK
ECHO The number "%ANSWER%" falls within the range of 1 through 5.
:END
```

Loading Memory-Resident Programs

By using the QUERY.COM command and environment variables, you can modularize your AUTOEXEC.BAT file so that it is easy to maintain. For example, if you have a collection of memory-resident programs that you normally want loaded, but you want to be given the choice after MS-DOS is booted to load some or none of them, you can set up your AUTOEXEC.BAT file so that no matter which memory-resident programs you specify to be loaded, they are always loaded in a specific order. The following listing shows how this can be accomplished.

```
REM
REM INITIAL ENVIRONMENT SETTINGS
  SET MSMSE=Y
  SET PRNT=Y
  SET GRFTBL=N
  SET GRPHCS=N
  SET SK=Y
:Q1
  ECHO *
  ECHO If you answer Y to the following prompt, each of the
  ECHO following memory-resident programs will be automatically
  ECHO loaded (in the order shown).
  ECHO
  ECHO ----------------------------------------------
  ECHO | ORDER |    PROGRAM     | AUTOLOAD? |
  ECHO |=======|================|===========|
  ECHO |   1   |    MSMOUSE     | %MSMSE%   |
```

```
   ECHO |   2   |   PRINT      | %PRNT%          |
   ECHO |   3   |   GRAFTABL   | %GRFTBL%        |
   ECHO |   4   |   GRAPHICS   | %GRPHCS%        |
   ECHO |   5   |   SIDEKICK   | %SK%          |
   ECHO  ----------------------------------
   ECHO If you answer N, you'll be asked whether each
   ECHO program is to be loaded.
   ECHO *
   ECHO Do you want programs autoloaded as
   QUERY shown in the above table? (Y/N)
   IF not errorlevel 1 goto TSRQS
   GOTO Q3
:TSRQS
   ECHO *
   QUERY Do you want the MSMOUSE driver loaded (Y/N)?
   IF not errorlevel 1 SET MSMSE=N
   ECHO *
   QUERY Do you want PRINT.COM loaded (Y/N)?
   IF not errorlevel 1 SET PRNT=N
   ECHO *
   QUERY Do you want GRAFTABL.COM loaded (Y/N)?
   IF not errorlevel 1 SET GRFTBL=N
   ECHO *
   QUERY Do you want GRAPHICS.COM loaded (Y/N)?
   IF not errorlevel 1 SET GRPHCS=N
   ECHO *
   QUERY Do you want SIDEKICK loaded (Y/N)?
   IF not errorlevel 1 SET SK=N
REM
REM LOAD MEMORY-RESIDENT PROGRAMS
REM NOTE: Do *not* change the order in which memory-resident
REM       programs are loaded!
   CLS
   ECHO Loading memory-resident programs.
   REM
   IF (%MSMSE%)==(Y) CD c:\system\startup\mouse
   IF (%MSMSE%)==(Y) MSMOUSE /1 >nul:
   REM
   IF (%PRNT%)==(Y) PRINT /D:PRN /B:512 /U:1 /M:2 /S:8 /Q:5
   REM
   IF (%GRFTBL%)==(Y) c:\system\GRAFTABL >NUL:
   IF (%GRPHCS%)==(Y) c:\system\GRAPHICS GRAPHICS /R >NUL:
   REM
   IF (%SK%)==(Y) CD c:\utils\misc\sk
   IF (%SK%)==(Y) SK
   CD c:\
```

The portion of the AUTOEXEC.BAT file shown is divided into three modules:

1. Define environment variables to determine which memory-resident programs should default to automatic loading.

2. Display current automatic loading defaults. Ask if programs are to be loaded as shown in table, and if not, query for the loading of each individual program.

3. Load each program that has its corresponding environment variable assigned to Y.

The advantage of structuring your AUTOEXEC.BAT file as shown is that if you want to change the defaults, all you need to change are the environment assignments in the first module and nothing else.

Fixing Problems in COMMAND.COM

The part of the MS-DOS operating system that contains internal commands such as DIR and COPY and the routines for handing batch files is in the file called COMMAND.COM. This file is often referred to as the shell or command interpreter because it is responsible for displaying the MS-DOS prompt as well as processing any text you enter in response to the prompt. In addition to the processing of batch files, COMMAND.COM also contains all the "batch" commands, such as ECHO, GOTO, FOR, IF, and so on.

Unfortunately, as is usually the case with computer software, COMMAND.COM does not provide all the functions we might like. Additionally, COMMAND.COM does not handle some functions the same way in various versions of MS-DOS. For example, in versions of MS-DOS prior to 3.00, COMMAND.COM has an undocumented feature (not mentioned in the technical manual) whereby you can insert the ECHO command in a batch file followed by two spaces to cause a blank line to be displayed. However, in MS-DOS Versions 3.00 up to 3.20, the command ECHO followed by two spaces causes the annoying echo status message to be displayed (ECHO is off or ECHO is on).

There are various ways to fix this problem, one of which involves modifying all your batch files and another one involving the modification of the COMMAND.COM file itself. But the COMMAND.COM file has other potential problems that require subtle modifications to the way you write your batch files or that require rather involved changes to the COMMAND.COM file itself. The following tricks identify some potential problems and show how you can solve them. Where possible, alternatives to modifying the COMMAND.COM file are described, such as tricks in the way batch files are written. Note also that changes to the COMMAND.COM file (called "patches") are rarely the same between MS-DOS versions, so it is very important that you first identify the version of MS-DOS that you're running before making any changes.

Displaying Blank Lines in Batch Files

One of the many problems in learning how to use MS-DOS and its commands and facilities is that you quickly discover that not all functions are clearly described in the documentation. Another problem is that some commands in MS-DOS are never described at all! This is particularly the case with MS-DOS's batch facility.

Under MS-DOS Versions 2.00 and 2.10, someone discovered that the ECHO command followed by two spaces displays a blank line. Whether this feature was intentionally implemented is unknown. It was certainly not documented anywhere in MS-DOS's documentation. Before MS-DOS Version 3.00 was released, the people who knew about this feature used it as a solution to their problem. Then, along came MS-DOS Version 3.00, and it was discovered that this useful little feature was removed entirely, leading everyone back to square one.

The following trick shows how you can cause blank lines to be displayed in batch files regardless of the version of MS-DOS being used.

TRICK

USING THE ECHO COMMAND TO DISPLAY BLANK LINES IN BATCH FILES

To cause blank lines to be displayed with the ECHO command in all versions of MS-DOS, follow the ECHO command with a space and an ASCII Back-Space character. The BackSpace character (normally shown as ^H) can be generated in many types of word processors and text editors by using the Ctrl-Backspace or Ctrl-H command. While in WordStar, for example, you can insert an ASCII BackSpace character in the text by first issuing the Ctrl-P command followed by the H key.

Preventing the Display of ECHO OFF in AUTOEXEC.BAT and All Batch Files

Another annoying aspect of using MS-DOS batch files is that when the ECHO OFF command is used at the beginning of a batch file, the command itself is always displayed before "echoing" is turned off. One solution is to immediately follow the ECHO OFF command with the CLS command to clear the screen quickly. However, how do you fix the problem if you don't want the screen to be cleared each time a batch file is run? The following trick shows how you can solve this problem.

TRICK

PREVENTING THE DISPLAY OF ECHO OFF AT THE BEGINNING OF BATCH FILES

To implement this trick, you must have the ANSI.SYS device driver loaded (using the DEVICE= command in the CONFIG.SYS file). Then create a file called NOECHO.FIX with the contents shown in the following listing. Note that all occurrences of ^[in the file (highlighted for emphasis) represent one character, the ASCII ESCape character. The ESCape character can be generated using most word processors and text editors. For example, in Word-Star, an ASCII ESCape character can be inserted in the text by using the Ctrl-P command, immediately followed by pressing the Esc key.

```
ECHO off
ECHO ^[[s^[[1A^[[K^[[u
```

This NOECHO.FIX file can be used as an "include" file whenever you create a new batch file or modify an existing one. When a batch file containing the contents of NOECHO.FIX is executed, the escape sequences on the second line cause the cursor to move to the beginning of the previous line, erase all text to the end of the line, then move the cursor back down one line.

Other Useful Tricks

You can do many things to improve the MS-DOS boot process. A number of them involve programs and batch procedures that you can create, whereas other improvements require modifications to the MS-DOS boot files.

Displaying Time and Date without the Prompts

One of the nice features of MS-DOS is its capability of maintaining an internal clock that can be accessed at any time. The correct date and time are loaded into this internal clock at boot time by either the user manually entering the data or by means of a special program that gets the data from a battery-clock circuit installed in the system. MS-DOS provides the built-in commands DATE and TIME so that you can both see and set the current date and time. However, we often want to simply *see* the date and time without having to press the Enter key to bypass the prompts that are displayed asking for the new date and time. Unfortunately, no parameters are provided with the DATE and TIME commands to bypass these prompts. The following trick shows a batch file you can create that solves this problem.

DISPLAYING TIME AND DATE WITHOUT PROMPTS USING TIMEDATE.BAT

The TIMEDATE.BAT batch command provides the function of displaying both the date and time without the annoying prompts. Although a program can display the date and time in considerably more efficient ways, TIME-DATE.BAT is the easiest to implement. Before creating TIMEDATE.BAT, however, a small file called CRLF.INP must be created. The CRLF.INP file contains a single blank line (one carriage return and one line feed), and is created:

```
A>copy con: crlf.inp
                              ← make sure this blank line is here
Ctrl-Z


A>
```

The CRLF.INP file produces the equivalent of pressing the Enter key. It redirects this equivalent to the DATE and TIME commands when they are executed, so their respective prompts are ignored. The contents of the TIMEDATE.BAT batch command is shown in the following listing.

```
REM Insert the contents of NOECHO.FIX in place of this line.
REM
DATE <crlf.inp
TIME <crlf.inp
```

To run TIMEDATE.BAT, simply enter TIMEDATE at the MS-DOS prompt. First the current date, then the current time is displayed. The prompts asking you to enter the current date and time are also displayed but essentially ignored because the CRLF.INP file directs the equivalent of pressing the Enter key in response to each prompt. Although TIME-DATE.BAT, as shown in this listing, is the quickest and easiest way to accomplish the task at hand, the batch file can be enhanced so that the date and time are displayed without the prompts. The enhanced TIME-DATE.BAT is shown in the following listing.

```
REM Insert the contents of NOECHO.FIX in place of this line.
REM
DATE <crlf.inp >date.txt
TIME <crlf.inp >time.txt
ANSWER <date.txt >nul:
SET CURRDATE=%ANSWER%
ANSWER <time.txt >nul:
SET CURRTIME=%ANSWER%
SET ANSWER=
ECHO %CURRDATE%
ECHO %CURRTIME%
DEL date.txt >nul:
DEL time.txt >nul:
SET CURRDATE=
SET CURRTIME=
```

The prompts normally displayed by DATE and TIME in the enhanced TIMEDATE.BAT are ignored because we use the public-domain AN-SWER.COM command in the file. When the DATE.TXT and TIME.TXT files are redirected as input to ANSWER.COM, only the first line of text (the line we want displayed) is accepted by ANSWER.COM because it can only handle single-line inputs. Note that the enhanced TIMEDATE.BAT makes extensive use of input/output redirection and a certain amount of disk accessing. You may find it rather slow if you're using a floppy disk drive, but its performance should be acceptable if you're using a hard disk and even better with a RAM disk.

If you want the "timedate" function in your AUTOEXEC.BAT file, copy the contents of TIMEDATE.BAT into the location in your AUTOEXEC.BAT file where you want the date and time to be displayed.

Rebooting the System Using an MS-DOS Command

There may be times when you would like to reboot the system by executing a command instead of pressing the Ctrl-Alt-Del key sequence or turning the power off and then on again. The reasons for wanting to reboot the system in this manner vary from system to system according to how they are used. For example, you may want to cause the system to automatically reboot after a user failed a security check during the initial boot sequence. Or you may be experimenting with the loading of various memory-resident programs so that you want a quick and automatic method of rebooting the system from a batch file. Whatever the reason, rebooting the system from the MS-DOS command line can be accomplished very easily as shown in the following trick.

REBOOTING THE SYSTEM FROM MS-DOS WITH REBOOT1.COM

Creating REBOOT1.COM is a very short and simple process as shown in the following. As in all of this book's examples, enter only the highlighted text.

```
A>debug
-n reboot1.com
-a 100
XXXX:0100 mov ax,0040
XXXX:0103 push ax
XXXX:0104 pop es
XXXX:0105 es:
XXXX:0106 mov word ptr [0072], 1234
XXXX:010C jmp ffff:0000
XXXX:0111
-rcx
cx 0000
:11
-w
-q

A>
```

The simplicity of REBOOT1.COM is demonstrated by how it is created using DEBUG. When the program is executed, a jump to the reset routine at memory location FFFF:0000 in the ROM BIOS occurs. This is the routine in the ROM BIOS that is executed when the Ctrl-Alt-Del key sequence is pressed. The next free location displayed by DEBUG after the instructions have been entered is XXXX:0111, so we know that the instructions occupied at offset locations 0100 through 010C, yield a total of 17 (11 hexadecimal) bytes—a short program indeed. To execute REBOOT1.COM, enter REBOOT1 at the MS-DOS prompt. It's that simple. The effect of REBOOT1.COM is the same as the Ctrl-Alt-Del key sequence.

USING OTHER METHODS OF REBOOTING THE SYSTEM FROM MS-DOS

The reboot method used in REBOOT1.COM is not necessarily the shortest or most efficient way to reset the system. For example, a two-byte program could be created using the instruction INT 19 to execute BIOS interrupt 19. It reboots the system even more quickly than REBOOT1.COM could. However, such a program does not work properly if you have installed certain types of device drivers (such as that used for an expanded memory card) or memory-resident programs (such as Sidekick) that take control of interrupt 19. Therefore, the instructions used in REBOOT1.COM provide a much safer method of rebooting the system. Beware of commercial or public domain rebooting programs that use the INT 19 method.

DON'T MAKE REBOOTING YOUR SYSTEM *TOO* EASY

The sheer simplicity of the REBOOT1.COM command also makes it dangerous. It is strongly advised that REBOOT1.COM be executed only by using a batch file that displays precautionary prompts which prevent you from accidentally rebooting the system. The batch file REBOOT.BAT shown in the following listing displays two prompts before executing the REBOOT1.COM command. If N is entered in response to any of the prompts, the batch file terminates and REBOOT1.COM does not execute. Note that REBOOT.BAT makes use of two public-domain utilities: BEEP.COM and QUERY.COM (see Chapter 8 for more information on these commands).

```
REM Insert the contents of NOECHO.FIX in place of this line.
REM
REM This procedure reboots system.
REM Check for immediate reboot parameter.
IF (%1)==(g)  goto DO_IT
IF (%1)==(go) goto DO_IT
IF (%1)==(gO) goto DO_IT
IF (%1)==(G)  goto DO_IT
IF (%1)==(Go) goto DO_IT
IF (%1)==(GO) goto DO_IT
REM otherwise check first:
ECHO                          CAUTION
ECHO
ECHO About to reboot the system.
ECHO
ECHO Make sure that you've saved all of your memory-resident data.
ECHO
ECHO Answer N (no) if you haven't yet saved the data,
ECHO or Y (yes) to go ahead and reboot the system.
ECHO
BEEP
ECHO
ECHO Are you sure you want to
QUERY reboot the system right now? (Y/N):
IF not errorlevel 1 goto END
ECHO
QUERY Are you absolutely certain? (Y/N):
IF not errorlevel 1 goto END
:DO_IT
REBOOT1
:END
```

This REBOOT.BAT file can also be executed so that the system is
rebooted without any precautionary prompts. When REBOOT is entered,
followed by go or g, the batch file branches to the label DO__IT, bypassing
the prompts. Using REBOOT.BAT in this manner is useful for rebooting the
system quickly. Entering the go parameter means that you've made a conscious decision to reboot the system and that you're aware of the consequences.

Managing Your Configuration

If you are constantly changing and enhancing your configuration, you
are more than likely to modify the CONFIG.SYS and AUTO-

EXEC.BAT files quite frequently. Occasionally, a modified configuration file does not work right, either because you mistyped something or because you're experimenting with certain features to see whether or how they work. But what happens when a new, extensively modified configuration file doesn't work and we've forgotten what the original looked like? If the original file is overwritten by the new one, how can you fall back on the original file so that the system works as it did before? The following trick shows how you can manage your work with configuration files without losing any work.

MANAGING YOUR CONFIGURATION FILES WITH UPDATE.BAT

One of the best ways to manage the updating of your configuration files is to store copies of them in a special directory. If, for example, you're using a hard disk, you probably have a directory, which is called SYSTEM, DOS or something similar, that contains all your MS-DOS system files. Create a directory under your "system" directory called STARTUP and copy into it your CONFIG.SYS and AUTOEXEC.BAT files. Then, so the two files in the new directory aren't confused with those in the root directory, make two copies of each file: First, rename them so that each has the extension .NEW (CONFIG.NEW and AUTOEXEC.NEW), then copy each one so that the new copies each have the extension .001 (CONFIG.001 and AUTOEXEC.001). The copies with the extension .001 represent the first version of the files and they should be left as is so that they can be used later should they be needed. You will always modify the copies that have the extension .NEW.

Next, create the batch file called UPDATE.BAT as shown in the following listing. The UPDATE.BAT file allows you to edit either CONFIG.NEW or AUTOEXEC.NEW by entering UPDATE C for CONFIG.NEW or UPDATE A for AUTOEXEC.NEW. UPDATE.BAT automatically loads the word processor or text editor you normally use along with the appropriate configuration file. Once the file has been edited and saved to disk, UPDATE.BAT automatically queries you as to whether you want to update the root directory copy of the file in question. If no updating is specified, UPDATE.BAT terminates. If updating is specified, UPDATE.BAT copies the file to the root directory, automatically renaming it to the correct name in the process, then queries you as to whether you want to reboot the system. UPDATE.BAT incorporates virtually the same procedure as that used in REBOOT.BAT described previously.

```
REM Insert contents of NOECHO.FIX here
REM Use this procedure to update CONFIG.SYS or AUTOEXEC.BAT
REM from the startup directory to the root directory.
REM
REM Change the assignment to STRTUP_PATH to the directory
REM path you're using to maintain your startup files.
  SET STRTUP_PATH=C:\SYSTEM\STARTUP
  IF (%1)==(a) SET UFILE=AUTOEXEC
  IF (%1)==(A) SET UFILE=AUTOEXEC
  IF (%1)==(c) SET UFILE=CONFIG
  IF (%1)==(C) SET UFILE=CONFIG
  IF (%UFILE%)==(AUTOEXEC) GOTO REVISE
  IF (%UFILE%)==(CONFIG) GOTO REVISE
  BEEP
  ECHO ERROR ON INPUT:
  ECHO Enter UPDATE A to update AUTOEXEC.BAT to drive C, or
  ECHO enter UPDATE C to update CONFIG.SYS to drive C.
  GOTO END
:REVISE
  IF (%UFILE%)==(AUTOEXEC) SET UEXT=BAT
  IF (%UFILE%)==(CONFIG) SET UEXT=SYS
  IF not exist %STRTUP_PATH%%UFILE%.new goto NO_FILE_ERR
  REM WSN is your favorite word processor or text editor
  WSN %UFILE%.new
  ECHO Do you want to update %UFILE%.%UEXT% in the
  QUERY root directory of Drive C:?
  IF not errorlevel 1 GOTO NO_UPDATE
  COPY %STRTUP_PATH%%UFILE%.NEW c:\%UFILE%.%UEXT%/v >NUL:
  ECHO %STRTUP_PATH%%UFILE%.NEW copied to c:\%UFILE%.%UEXT%.
  QUERY Do you want to reboot the system now?
  IF not errorlevel 1 GOTO END
  CLS
  ECHO                              CAUTION
  ECHO ^H
  ECHO About to reboot the system.
  ECHO ^H
  ECHO Make sure that you've saved all of your
  ECHO memory-resident data.
  ECHO ^H
  ECHO Answer N (no) if you haven't yet saved the data,
  ECHO or Y (yes) to go ahead and reboot the system.
  ECHO ^H
  BEEP
  ECHO ^H
  ECHO Are you sure you want to
  QUERY reboot the system right now? (Y/N):
  IF not errorlevel 1 goto END
  ECHO ^H
  QUERY Are you absolutely certain? (Y/N):
  IF not errorlevel 1 goto END
  REBOOT1
:NO_UPDATE
  ECHO %UFILE%.%UEXT% in Drive C: has not been updated.
  GOTO END
:NO_FILE_ERR
```

```
    BEEP
    ECHO %UFILE%.NEW does not exist on Drive Z:.
    ECHO Check the directory and try again.
:END
    REM Clear out unneeded environment variables.
    SET BDOSV=
    SET ANSWER=
    SET UFILE=
    SET UEXT=
```

By naming your configuration files in the manner previously described, combined with using UPDATE.BAT in a special directory (or special floppy disk), you can ensure that you have your old configuration files should you need them. Each time you make significant changes to a configuration file and prove that it works by using it for a while, make a copy of the file with the .NEW extension so that the new copy has the extension .0?? where .0?? is .002 if a file with .001 already exists, or .003 if a file with .002 already exists, and so on. You should back up your configuration files frequently in this manner so that if you need to fall back on one of your backup files, the file with the highest-numbered extension closely resembles the equivalent file with the .NEW extension.

Summary

This completes our presentation of the secrets of configuring MS-DOS. This chapter has uncovered some of the secrets related to commands and functions that can greatly enhance the configuration of your particular MS-DOS implementation, including enhancements of existing commands. Much of the information covered in this chapter either has not been described in the MS-DOS technical manuals or has been inadequately covered in the past.

Secrets of Data Encryption

Chapter 14

Because of the expanding role of computers in our society, some of the information that is stored in computers, or sent between computers, is of a private or sensitive nature. The protection of that information is the topic of this chapter, and the method that is used is data *encryption.*

To encrypt literally means "to make secret." All the programs and devices discussed in this chapter can be used to encrypt data, with varying degrees of security. To enable you to choose the right encryption method for your needs, this chapter explains some of the theory behind encryption, as well as the strengths and weaknesses of the various methods. Finally, this chapter concludes with some tips on using encryption systems wisely and properly.

Ciphers and Codes

For most people the word *encryption* conjures up visions of Sherlock Holmes solving the mystery of the "Dancing Men." In this Doyle short story, little stick figures were used by the villain of the story as a form of secret correspondence.

For students of history, encryption may bring to mind Lt. Comdr. Thomas H. Dyer's brilliant work in cracking the Japanese Imperial Navy code JN-25 in 1940. The ability to read the secret orders of the Japanese Navy had a decisive affect on the course of the war in the Pacific.

In comparing these examples of classic cryptography with modern methods, today's computers make child's play of Holmes' efforts, but interestingly enough, they would not have been much help in 1940. Even today, the solution to JN-25 would remain a challenge. The difference in the security of these two methods is based on the fact that although Sherlock Holmes' dancing men are a *cipher*, JN-25 is primarily a *code*. What makes a code more difficult to break than a cipher? The reason lies in the difference between a code and a cipher.

In technical terms, a cipher operates on a fixed length unit, be it a character, a byte of data in a computer, or even an eight-byte group as is the American Data Encryption Standard (DES), which we'll be studying soon. A code on the other hand, operates on *linguistic* units, such as words, phrases, or even syllables.

In the "Dancing Men" cipher, each letter of a message is replaced by a distinct, unique figure of a dancing man, as shown in Figure 14-1. The cipher consists of twenty-six different figures, each representing one letter of the alphabet. Neither the words in the message nor the order of the letters in the words is altered.

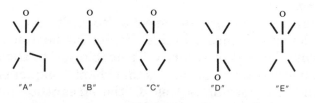

Figure 14-1. The "Dancing Men" Cipher

The Japanese Naval code of 1940 consisted of about 45,000 five-digit numbers representing words and phrases. In addition, special place names were assigned two or three letter codes. (For example, AH was the code for Pearl Harbor, while AF meant Midway Island). To gain even greater security, after a message was encoded (translated using the code), it was then enciphered (translated using a cipher). The process of enciphering a coded message is called *superencipherment*.

Because Holmes' "Dancing Men" cipher is simply a method for substituting characters of the alphabet, its use requires only a knowledge of English and a table showing the proper figure to use for each letter of the alphabet. Given this simplicity, Mr. Holmes was able to solve or "break" the cipher at a single sitting. As a code, JN-25 defined an entire vocabulary and must have filled a large volume. The solution of JN-25 required the efforts of an entire team of cryptoanalysts, who were still adding to their knowledge two years after their initial breakthrough.

We can create a few examples to demonstrate the difference between ciphers and codes. Suppose that we wish to encrypt the words THIS IS A SECRET MESSAGE. One choice of a cipher is to substitute each letter of the message with the letter that follows it in the alphabet. The encrypted text of the secret message then would read UIJT JT B TFDSFU NFTTBHF.

A code, on the other hand, substitutes each word of the message with an entirely different word from a code book. By using a common dictionary as a code book and a code that replaces each word of the message with the word located 100 pages later in the dictionary, the secret message THIS IS A SECRET MESSAGE can be coded to read AFTER PESTICIDE COMPOUND USHER REAPPEAR.

In general, codes are much harder to break than ciphers. One reason for this is that a partial solution is often no help in discovering the remainder of the code. Another reason is that because entire phrases can be represented by a single code word, the coded message appears to be a collection of unrelated words. In spite of their advantages, however, codes are rarely used for computer encryption.

Because codes replace entire words or phrases, they must have many code words and phrases defined. A useful code book could easily approach or surpass the size of a dictionary, making it impractical for personal computers. Another problem is that codes are designed for messages composed of words and phrases, not for computer data. If a code were expanded to contain all the possible combinations of data in a computer, it would be too large to fit in any computer!

The biggest advantage of using ciphers for computer encryption is that they can be expressed as an *algorithm,* or series of steps that converts a normal message into an encrypted message. It takes much less space to store a program to encipher messages than an entire code book to encode messages. Another advantage is that a cipher algorithm encrypts any word or phrase, not just those words that appear in a code book.

Evaluating Cipher Systems

Computer data encryption is based on a combination of traditional cipher methods. The two building blocks of cipher systems are *substitution ciphers* and *transposition ciphers.*

The method used by Sherlock Holmes is a substitution cipher

because it substitutes one character for another. In substitution ciphers, the order of the characters in the message is maintained, although the characters themselves are exchanged for new characters. Substitution ciphers can be quite complex, sometimes using more than one substitution table in various ways. Ciphers that use multiple tables are called *polyalphabetic ciphers* because each table is akin to a different alphabet.

The other basic cipher method, the transposition cipher, actually reorders the characters of the message according to some rule rather than changing the characters themselves.

Character Frequency Distribution

Each of these methods has disadvantages that can only be overcome when they are used in unison. Used individually, each cipher leaves telltale information that can allow a cryptoanalyst to break the cipher and determine the original message.

The frequency with which letters are used in English is quite constant over a large enough sample (see Table 14-1). When simple substitution ciphers are used, such as with Sherlock Holmes' "Dancing Men," the characters may be changed but the frequency of their use remains constant. Usually, you can assume that the most frequently used character is really an E, the next most used character a T, and so forth. Given a large enough sample of encrypted text, a statistical analysis of the message yields the probable cipher.

Transposition ciphers help by concealing the order of characters. However, a cryptoanalyst can analyze and rearrange the characters of an encrypted message while looking for standard English syntax. The cryptoanalyst discards those ciphers that result in incorrect syntax, until the right cipher is discovered. Examples of English syntax are the placement of vowels, rules against multiple consonants, sentence structure, and certain common character combinations such as *ei*, *th*, and *ing*.

Computer ciphers avoid these potential trouble spots by combining methods, for example, using a substitution cipher, followed by a transposition cipher, another substitution cipher, etc. Decoding the message is achieved by reversing the steps used in encrypting the message. This combination of steps is called a *product cipher* because the cipher operations are similar to multiplication. Product ciphers are mostly used by computer encryption systems because performing the steps by hand can be very tedious work, and a single mistake can result in unintelligible gibberish.

Table 14-1.   Frequency Distribution in the English Language

Letter	Percentage of Use
EEEEEEEEEEEEEEEEEEEEEEEEEEEEEEEEEEEEEEEEEEEEEEEEEEEE	13.0
TTTTTTTTTTTTTTTTTTTTTTTTTTTTTTTTTTTTTTTTTT	10.5
AAAAAAAAAAAAAAAAAAAAAAAAAAAAAAAAAA	8.1
OOOOOOOOOOOOOOOOOOOOOOOOOOOOOOOO	7.9
NNNNNNNNNNNNNNNNNNNNNNNNNNNNN	7.1
RRRRRRRRRRRRRRRRRRRRRRRRRRRR	6.8
IIIIIIIIIIIIIIIIIIIIIIIIIII	6.3
SSSSSSSSSSSSSSSSSSSSSSSSSS	6.1
HHHHHHHHHHHHHHHHHHHHH	5.2
DDDDDDDDDDDDDDDD	3.8
LLLLLLLLLLLLLL	3.4
FFFFFFFFFFFFF	2.9
CCCCCCCCCCC	2.7
MMMMMMMMMMM	2.5
UUUUUUUUUU	2.4
GGGGGGGG	2.0
YYYYYYY	1.9
PPPPPPP	1.9
WWWWWW	1.5
BBBBB	1.4
VVVV	0.9
KK	0.4
X	0.15
J	0.13
Q	0.11
Z	0.07

```
0   1   2   3   4   5   6   7   8   9   10  11  12  13
```

Most traditional cryptography systems are designed to encrypt characters from a set of 26 letters. (Even the Japanese Naval Code JN-25 used Japanese words transliterated into English characters.) However, a computer encryption system must be able to encrypt any of the 256 unique codes that can be expressed with one byte. Because of this, a problem can occur when text files are being encrypted. When the majority of the unencrypted data is from the original set of 52 uppercase and lowercase letters (text only), an encryption system that translates the 52 alphabetic characters into only 52 encrypted characters produces a nonrandom distribution. The code breaker need only solve a cipher of 52 characters rather than a cipher of 256 characters. A message composed of only 52 character codes is easier to break than one made up of 256 randomly distributed codes.

- First evaluation point: A good computer encryption system should produce encrypted text without reoccurring patterns that correspond to any natural patterns in the original text. Character and character grouping distribution of the encrypted message should be close to random distribution. (All characters should have an equal frequency of occurrence.)

Repetitious Patterns in the Encrypted Message

The largest aid to a cryptoanalyst in breaking a cipher or code is giving the cryptoanalyst a sample of both the unencrypted data (often called *plaintext*) and the same data after encryption. Through comparison of the two, the cipher can usually be deduced. Although it seems obvious that we want to prevent unauthorized people from obtaining samples of our unencrypted data, this is not always easy to do.

Communications systems often have formal components, much like the traditional STOP in telegrams. Logon and logout messages from operating systems or telecommunications services, operating system prompts (C:>), and so forth, provide obvious repetitive patterns that could be used as a starting point in breaking the cipher. One solution is to eliminate all such messages and prompts. This would reduce the risk but it also makes the computer system more difficult to use. A better solution is to choose an enciphering system that can resist being compromised by short repetitive messages. Such a system must often encrypt multiple characters, as opposed to encrypting a character at a time.

- Second evaluation point: To prevent a cryptoanalyst from deducing the plaintext equivalent of frequently occurring encrypted text, a good computer encryption system should prevent repetitive words and phrases from being encrypted to the same text. This implies that the system should encrypt groups of characters rather than individual characters.

Keys

Even the best encryption system is rendered worthless if an unauthorized party can obtain the *exact* same system and use it to decrypt the secured data. Because commercially available encryption systems can be purchased by nearly anyone, how can security be maintained? Just as a hundred people may buy the same lock, but be safe in the knowledge that they have their own key, so can encryption systems use *keys* to secure their data.

A key is a value that is used in conjunction with the encryption system to customize the cipher so that two users with the same system can be assured of the respective privacy of their data. Keys are logically similar to passwords, except that whereas passwords are only used to gain access to a system or database, encryption keys are used to encrypt the data (lock it) as well as decrypt the data (unlock or gain access to it). Another difference between keys and passwords is that a different encryption key may be used each time data is encrypted. Indeed, it is critical that users of an encryption system be able to select their own keys and change them at will.

The uniqueness of the encryption key is all that prevents an unauthorized party from decrypting and reading secured data. For this reason, the key must be such that it cannot be guessed or found through an exhaustive search of all possible values of the key. The way to prevent an unauthorized party from guessing the key is to choose a key that is random. Names, words, and phrases are bad choices for an encryption key. The way to preclude an exhaustive search of all possible keys is to use long ones.

To understand why the length of the key is so important, consider the following example. A key composed of up to 6 letters has about 387 million combinations. If a computer could check 1,000 combinations per second, it would take just over four days to check all the keys, meaning that the average time to find the key would be about two days. If the length of the key is doubled, to 12 letters, the number of combinations increases to over one hundred thousand trillion combinations (one with seventeen zeros after it)! The same computer would take over 170 million *years* to check all the combinations.

The length of the encryption keys used on computers is usually measured in bits. A 32-bit key (4 bytes) is considered the shortest acceptable key, with over 4 billion combinations. Keys selected by the user are most often entered as numbers or as a string of characters. A number key should be at least 10 decimal digits in length. Character keys (text strings) are usually a little longer, to allow the actual cipher key (used internally by the encryption program) to be based on a combination of bits from the user's text key.

- Third evaluation point: Any computer encryption system must allow the user to choose his or her own encryption key. The size of the key should be long enough to prevent the key from being found in a reasonable time by an exhaustive search.

Reversing Accidental Encryption or Decryption

Accidents sometimes occur when encrypting or decrypting files. Some common occurrences are: decrypting a file using the wrong key, decrypting a file that was not encrypted, and encrypting a file a second time instead of decrypting it. What do you do when one of these mistakes occurs?

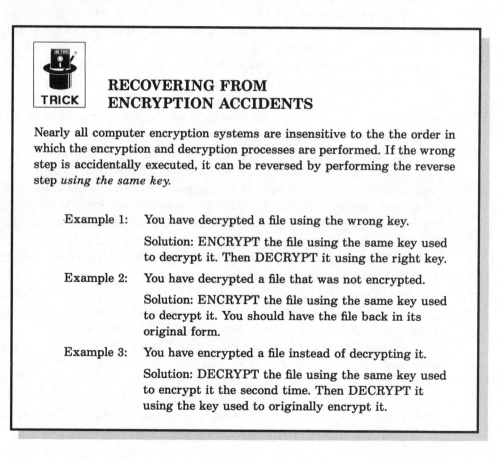

RECOVERING FROM ENCRYPTION ACCIDENTS

Nearly all computer encryption systems are insensitive to the the order in which the encryption and decryption processes are performed. If the wrong step is accidentally executed, it can be reversed by performing the reverse step *using the same key.*

Example 1: You have decrypted a file using the wrong key.

Solution: ENCRYPT the file using the same key used to decrypt it. Then DECRYPT it using the right key.

Example 2: You have decrypted a file that was not encrypted.

Solution: ENCRYPT the file using the same key used to decrypt it. You should have the file back in its original form.

Example 3: You have encrypted a file instead of decrypting it.

Solution: DECRYPT the file using the same key used to encrypt it the second time. Then DECRYPT it using the key used to originally encrypt it.

- Fourth evaluation point: A friendly computer encryption system should also allow the decryption process to be reversed by the encryption process.

The Uses of Cryptography

Data encryption can be used in three basic ways by computer users: storage, transmission, and verification. A primary use in business is to protect data that is stored in a computer system from curious eyes. Examples of this use are for protecting payroll and employment records or new product designs and marketing plans. In another use, encryption is used to protect transfers of sensitive information via public carriers (mail, courier, telephone, or satellite), which are difficult to physically protect. Encryption renders the intercepted data meaningless to the criminal who pirates it. The third use of encryption is for verification and authentication. Electronic Funds Transfers, purchase orders for stocks and securities, and remote access to computing resources are all operations requiring that the receiving party be able to verify the identity of the sending party.

Using encryption to protect the exchange of information or for verification purposes raises an interesting problem. Consider the situation in which you would like to send some private information to a new friend, via modem. You both have compatible computers, modems, and best of all, encryption programs. You can encrypt the data and send it to your friend, but in order for your friend to decrypt the data, he or she must know the right key to use! How do you give the key to your friend without letting everyone else know its value? Someday, the solution will be possible through *public key encryption*, a topic discussed later in this chapter. For the time being, you and your friend must agree beforehand on some method for exchanging keys or use a piece of information outside the scope of the encryption program.

TRICK   **SELECTING KEYS FOR EXCHANGE**

One method of preparing encryption keys for use during transmission is to use a type of code book. This is a list of keys that have been prepared and exchanged beforehand. It can be an actual list of keys, or it can be as simple as a common book that both participants have a copy of.

Before the encrypted data is sent, the participants select from the list the key to be used. The selection can be indicated by its position on the list. For example, 201, 5, 10, 20 can mean "Turn to page 201 of our code book and use the twenty characters starting from paragraph five, word ten, as the key for this transmission."

For better security, a list of random keys should be exchanged because a key based on words chosen from a book is easier to break than a random sequence.

For spur of the moment exchanges, common recollections can suffice to provide a key. For example, "Do you remember the name of the restaurant where we had lunch last Thursday? You do? Good, that name is the key."

The problem of exchanging keys can arise in nearly all encryption situations where more than one person requires access to the data. In a case where company personnel records are encrypted for the sake of security, does the entire company shut down when the only person who knows the key goes on vacation? Of course not. In a case where critical data is stored in an encrypted form, the key must be saved somewhere against possible loss. The key should be written down and placed in a safety deposit box or company safe. If the key is lost, the data is lost!

MASTER TRICK

SHAMIR METHOD FOR SHARING KEYS

Just as banks give only part of the vault combination to any single employee, so also can encryption keys be devised to require more than one person to decrypt the data. Each person is given part of the key, so only when the required number of people are assembled can the full key be determined and the data decrypted. This method, devised by Adi Shamir[1], derives the partial keys from a polynomial of the form:

$$p(x) = a_n x^n + a_{n-1} x^{n-1} + \ldots a_2 x^2 + a_1 x + a_0$$

The size of the polynomial is based on the number of people required to determine the key. If k people are required to be assembled to determine the key, the polynomial is of degree *k-1* (n is equal to $k-1$).

The values of a_n through a_1 are picked at random, and a_0 is the value of

---

[1]Shamir, A. "How to Share a Secret," *Communications of the ACM,* vol. 22, Nov. 1979, pp 612-613.

the encryption key. Each person is given a point on the curve described by the polynomial of the form *(x, p(x))*, where *x* is unique for each person.

When *k* people have been assembled, their points determine the polynomial by solving *k* simultaneous linear equations in *k* unknowns. The solution yields a_0, the encryption key. Note that partial keys may be given to any number of people so that when any *k* people assemble, they can determine the encryption key.

Encryption has other drawbacks besides risking loss of data through loss of the encryption key. By encrypting something, you tell the world that you have something to hide. The appearance of encrypted data in a normally open environment raises eyebrows at the least. If concealment is as important a factor as data security, physical security, such as removing the data from the system, might be a better solution.

TRICK   **HIDING ENCRYPTED DATA**

One method of hiding encrypted data on an MS-DOS system is to make the data blend in. Few people expect executable files (.COM and .EXE files) to be readable, so renaming an encrypted file with the extension of an executable file may throw people off the track. Of course, if the file is executed, unexpected results almost certainly occur.

CAUTION: Do *not* use this method on files encrypted by Borland's Superkey proprietary encryption process! The proprietary encryption method uses the file's name as part of the key, so renaming an encrypted file will change the key, with the result that encryption of the file is no longer possible.

In any type of encryption, remember that encrypting data is similar to putting locks on the front door. It is a delaying action at best. The goals of encryption are to make access to protected data so difficult that compromising the data is not worth the effort, or so that by the time the data is compromised, it is no longer sensitive and therefore is worthless. In most cases when important classified information is being protected, encryption must be considered as an aid to and not a replacement for physical security of storage or transmission.

With all these problems, why consider encryption at all? Because there are cases where it is not feasible to remove your hard disk for the night or to send a courier to Bora Bora with the annual stock report. Once you have decided to encrypt your data, how do you go about doing it?

Implementing Computer Cryptography

The simplest cipher systems implemented on a computer are nothing more than automated traditional cryptography. A basic transposition cipher can be performed using an *Exclusive Or* (XOR instruction) operation on each byte of the message with a corresponding byte from a selected key. A substitution cipher can be created using a "lookup" table, where each byte of the message is replaced by a byte in a table. The Translate (XLAT) instruction of the 8086 family is well suited to this operation. With the addition of multiple tables, a polyalphabetic cipher can be implemented easily. Unfortunately, the simplicity of these methods means that they are not likely to deter a serious code breaker for very long. Better ciphers are required.

Although any method of encryption that can be done by traditional methods can also be done by computer, a computer brings something more to the game. We should not limit ourselves to thinking along the lines of traditional character oriented cryptography. The computer has an advantage over the traditional cryptographer in that the character size can be varied. By this we mean that although the data was most probably entered a byte at a time (from a standard ASCII keyboard), the computer is not limited to processing it in that size. It could be processed a bit at a time or many bytes at a time.

Because one of the ways to enhance security is to avoid leaving any recognizable patterns, computer encryption is often done at the bit level, substituting and transposing bits within the data rather than only at the character level.

Figure 14-2 demonstrates the advantages of encrypting text in groups larger than 8 bits. In this example of a 12-bit cipher, the three character string EOE is shown as encrypting to the three character string XYZ. Unlike an 8-bit group substitution cipher, E does not always encrypt to the same character, which hides the frequency of occurrence of the character E. However, patterns still can appear in the encrypted text because every time the character sequence EOE starts on a group (12-bit) boundary the result is XYZ. If the text were encrypted in groups of 11 bits, only character sequences 11 bytes in length would result in identical sequences of encrypted text.

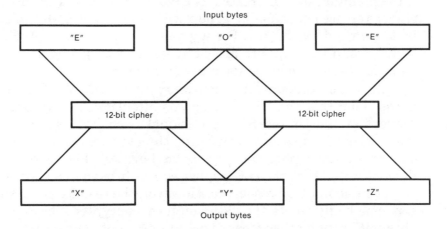

Figure 14-2.   Cipher Group Operation on 12-Bit Boundary

Bit operations operate on data that is an unnatural size for most computers, resulting in time consuming calculations and a much slower encryption system. Only when implemented in hardware do these techniques really pay off in terms of security *and* performance. The *Data Encryption Standard* cipher, or DES, is one that has been implemented in hardware.

DES

Another advantage of the computer over a human cryptographer is that the computer can perform repeated steps with a much smaller chance of errors. The DES cipher takes advantage of this fact and is based on a combination of traditional methods.

The DES cipher is essentially a 19-stage algorithm that encrypts 64 bits (8 bytes) at a time. The large size of the cipher group effectively conceals any information about character frequency. DES also specifies a 56-bit (7-byte) key, which precludes finding the key through an exhaustive search of all possible keys.

Three of the nineteen stages are fixed and are used to perform a transposition at the beginning and end of the algorithm, with a 32-bit swap thrown in for good measure. Each of the remaining 16 stages implements a product cipher based on a different function of the key. Despite the complexity of the operation, DES is a rather simple cipher in terms of cryptography. Experts have noted that the DES algorithm is essentially a substitution cipher using a 64-bit "character." That is, if the plaintext data is treated as a sequence of 64-bit groups, the DES cipher replaces each 64-bit group with a different 64-bit group, which is determined by the key. For a given key k, the encrypted result of a 64-bit group x always produces the same 64-bit group $f(k,x)$ as output: $f(k,x)$ is always the same for a given k and x.

A certain amount of controversy surrounds the DES algorithm. Some claim that the DES cipher was intentionally "weakened" at the request of the United States National Security Agency (NSA) to a point where it is secure enough for the average user, but where NSA can break the cipher for any given key. At this time, it has been demonstrated that the DES cipher *can* be broken in a short time given sufficient computing resources. However, the resources are such that if someone badly wants the data you have encrypted, they can probably obtain it though other means that are best not considered here (primarily illegal activities). All in all, unless your encryption needs are equal to those of the U.S. Government, in which case you should definitely seek professional or government help, the DES method most likely is secure enough.

Readers with programming experience who wish to implement the DES algorithm can find the complete description in a number of books. Two volumes that the authors can vouch for are *Modern Methods for Computer Security and Privacy,* by Lance Hoffman (Prentice-Hall, 1977) and *Computer Networks* by Andrew Tanenbaum (Prentice-Hall, 1981). Be forewarned that the DES algorithm was designed with the intent of being implemented in hardware (which it is, as we shall see). As a result, it is not blindingly fast when implemented in software. One quoted figure given is the execution time of 0.3 to 1.0 *seconds* for the encryption of 8 characters on an Intel 8080 processor (the predecessor to the Intel 8086 family). Superkey, from Borland International, contains a more recent implementation of the DES cipher for the IBM Personal Computer series and compatibles. When used on a standard (4.77 MHz) IBM, Superkey encrypts data at a rate of just under one-half kilobyte per second.

The most important note to novice users of the DES encryption method is that the algorithm is designed to accept a 56-bit key. The temptation to use the low seven bits from eight typed (ASCII text) characters as a key is strong but seriously degrades the security of the system. A key of eight characters in length could be found in a relatively short time by an exhaustive search. Instead, the key should be generated from 56 randomly chosen bits.

Even the DES method can yield giveaway repeating patterns if used carelessly. Long strings of identical characters (such as spaces in text or zeros in data) show up visibly in the resulting encrypted output. The following listing shows the plain and encrypted text for four lines of 64 characters each. (Spaces are shown for clarity only, and each line includes a Carriage-Return Line-Feed pair at the end.) Note that the last seven groups are the same for each line and that the encrypted text of 00000000 is always the same. You should also note that the first group of each line is totally different, even though there was only a one or two bit change from line to line (000 . . . , 010 . . . , 020 . . . , and 030 . . .).

Note that <nl> is *newline,* (Carriage-Return Line-Feed).

Plaintext (ASCII)		Encrypted Text (Hexadecimal)	
DES Group	DES Group	DES Group	DES Group
00000000	00000000	72 86 1C 49 C6 BF 5B BF	72 86 1C 49 C6 BF 5B BF
01234567	89ABCDEF	62 C9 74 51 02 BA C3 EF	00 57 A2 B2 85 25 3E 17
00000000	00000000	72 86 1C 49 C6 BF 5B BF	72 86 1C 49 C6 BF 5B BF
01234567	89ABCD<nl>	62 C9 74 51 02 BA C3 EF	C2 E7 63 D0 36 39 AB 9C
01000000	00000000	BA 2A AC E4 C4 BF 91 E7	72 86 1C 49 C6 BF 5B BF
01234567	89ABCDEF	62 C9 74 51 02 BA C3 EF	00 57 A2 B2 85 25 3E 17
00000000	00000000	72 86 1C 49 C6 BF 5B BF	72 86 1C 49 C6 BF 5B BF
01234567	89ABCD<nl>	62 C9 74 51 02 BA C3 EF	C2 E7 63 D0 36 39 AB 9C
02000000	00000000	D1 FA 0B 98 FD 40 96 55	72 86 1C 49 C6 BF 5B BF
01234567	89ABCDEF	62 C9 74 51 02 BA C3 EF	00 57 A2 B2 85 25 3E 17
00000000	00000000	72 86 1C 49 C6 BF 5B BF	72 86 1C 49 C6 BF 5B BF
01234567	89ABCD<nl>	62 C9 74 51 02 BA C3 EF	C2 E7 63 D0 36 39 AB 9C
03000000	00000000	5C 0C 66 96 B0 A7 BE EB	72 86 1C 49 C6 BF 5B BF
01234567	89ABCDEF	62 C9 74 51 02 BA C3 EF	00 57 A2 B2 85 25 3E 17
00000000	00000000	72 86 1C 49 C6 BF 5B BF	72 86 1C 49 C6 BF 5B BF
01234567	89ABCD<nl>	62 C9 74 51 02 BA C3 EF	C2 E7 63 D0 36 39 AB 9C

In spite of the fact that the DES cipher can create repeating patterns, the complexity of the cipher, and length of the key will prevent all but the most experienced and well equipped cryptoanalyst from breaking the cipher and discovering the key.

Stream Encryption

There is another way to avoid the problem of repeating patterns. The most common actions performed with ciphers are encrypting files and encrypting serial data being transmitted from one computer to another or from a terminal to a computer. In the first case, entire blocks of data are encrypted, which allows greater freedom in combining the data. In the case of serial data, it is most often encrypted byte by byte (unless an entire file is encrypted for transmission and sent in the same manner as an unencrypted file). This susceptibility for creating only 256 different encrypted characters when using byte encryption can be avoided through a technique known as *stream encryption*.

In stream encryption, the encrypted output data can be recombined with the unencrypted input data to further scramble the data. This method, sometimes called *cipher feedback mode*, is often used when terminal (single byte at a time) or bit serial (single bit at a time) data is to be encrypted, such as when sending data over a modem.

One example of stream encoding using the DES cipher is shown in Figure 14-3. Before being encrypted, each bit or byte of input data is first combined with the output bit or byte from the previous cipher operation. Combination is performed with an Exclusive Or operation. The result of the Exclusive Or is used as input for the next cipher operation and also sent to the receiving party.

During decryption, a received bit or byte is decombined using an Exclusive Or with the result of the previous cipher operation. The decombined data is the plaintext message. The received data (before decombination) is also used as the input for the next cipher operation.

Both the transmitting and receiving ends operate their cipher blocks in encryption mode. Both stations must use the same key and begin with their cipher engines in the same state. Because the input data for each cipher block is identical, the output also is identical. The message data is encrypted only by a simple Exclusive Or operation, but the key is of infinite length because it is being generated by the cipher blocks. Infinite key ciphers of this type are very secure because a would-be eavesdropper must know the entire history of the transmission in order to have any hope of breaking the cipher.

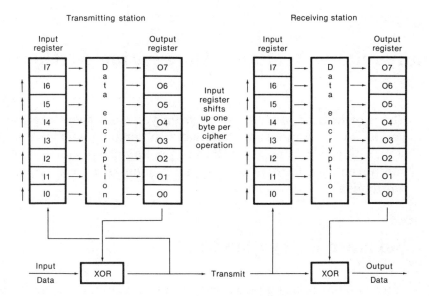

Figure 14-3. Stream Encoding

Because stream encoding is dependent on the entire history of the operation, it is more susceptible to errors. Data communications is seldom an ideal world and transmission errors do occur. A single uncorrected error in transmission causes the receiving cipher engine to deviate from the sending cipher engine, rendering the decoded message into gibberish. The same applies to stream encryption of data stored on disk, etc. If an error were to occur in block encoding, as opposed to stream encoding, only that block would be lost.

Fortunately, error detection and correction methods may be applied to the encrypted data, which helps ensure error-free transmission. It is a bad idea to use stream encryption on an uncorrected data link, such as the average telephone modem connection, but more sophisticated modems or transfer protocols can provide the protection from errors necessary for stream encryption.

Another drawback of stream encoding is that it is time-consuming. To continue using the DES method as an example, the DES algorithm encodes and decodes 64 bits at a time. When used in stream mode, only 8 bits are input or output for every block encrypted or decrypted. The encryption/decryption process takes eight times as long.

As with the DES cipher, stream encryption is best performed in currently available hardware, where the additional delays are less noticeable.

Commercially Available Encryption Methods

Short of having to write a program yourself, there are two ways that you as a user can obtain the means to perform encryption and decryption. You can purchase a software package to perform the task, or you can purchase a hardware component such as an add-on board or external device.

Software Encryption Products

With the burgeoning popularity of encryption, many software utilities are available that include encryption facilities as "accessories." The majority of these facilities are designed for the encryption of files on a disk rather than for the encryption of data during transmission. Of course, nothing is wrong with encrypting a file before transmission. It is just an extra step.

Borland's Superkey

Superkey from Borland International is a memory resident keyboard filter program. Once installed on an IBM Personal Computer series or close compatible system running MS-DOS, Superkey stays in memory filtering the characters and keystrokes entered from the keyboard. It supports key substitution and expansion (key macros), saves previous commands, and performs a number of other useful functions. And somewhat incidentally, it supports file encryption.

Superkey is supplied in two forms. The only difference between them is in the encryption cipher that each supports. One uses a proprietary method developed by Borland for encryption. The other uses the National Bureau of Standards' DES. The proprietary method processes about 4K of data per second on a 4.77 MHz PC or XT. The process is fast and is probably limited by the speed of the disk accesses. The DES method is about ten times slower, processing about a half a kilobyte per second on a 4.77 MHz 8088. Disk accesses are infrequent, leading the authors to conclude that the process is limited by the speed of computation.

The choice of which encryption method to use is made by loading one of the two Superkey program files contained on the distribution disk. The Superkey manual states that their own method is "safe against all but the most sophisticated intruders." Because even the DES method is not totally secure, it is probably not worth the extra time to use the higher security DES method for file storage. However, DES is preferable to the Borland method when transferring files, as we explain later.

Once Superkey is installed, file encryption or decryption is selected by activating the Superkey menu (Alt-/) and typing E for Encrypt. At that point, the user needs to answer only four questions and the process proceeds. The questions are 1) encrypt or decrypt, 2) what file or files, 3) what key, and 4) binary or text mode, which we explain shortly.

First, note that for both the proprietary and DES methods, the order of encryption and decryption is not important because the decryption method is simply encryption in reverse. If you accidentally decrypt a plaintext file, you scramble it as effectively as if you encrypted it. Don't worry, though. You can get the original file back by encrypting it!

Superkey accepts ASCII text keys, (not binary number keys), which might seem to be a limitation when you consider an encryption method such as DES that takes seven full bytes as a key. Superkey corrects for this deficiency by allowing keys up to thirty characters in length! Our advice is that if you feel encryption is necessary, please do it properly and use long keys, preferably with non-English nonsense words or nonalphabetic characters.

Now, about binary and text mode. Superkey allows the user to make a distinction between files that are to be stored on disk and those that are to be sent via modem. If text mode is *not* selected, Superkey encrypts the file in place, overwriting the original with an encrypted version of the same length. In text mode, however, Superkey produces a separate encrypted version of the file, which contains only uppercase letters and the Superkey header and postscript. This file is suitable for transmission via modem even in text transfer mode. The penalty is that the "text mode" encrypted file is about twice the size of the original file. Note also that the Superkey header and postscript advertise the fact that this is an encrypted file.

CAUTION

RENAMING SUPERKEY ENCRYPTED FILES

One last note about the Superkey encryption process. Borland's proprietory method uses the name of the file to be encrypted as part of the key. This means that if a file is encrypted, renamed to something else, and decrypted, using Superkey's proprietary method, the process fails and the result is gibberish. This restriction applies to both binary *and* text mode encryption. Because many files go through numerous name changes when they are transmitted from one system to another (especially on bulletin board systems), this is an undesirable feature. However, the DES encryption method supplied with Superkey doesn't have this problem because the key is based entirely on the user's input. For this reason, the DES method is probably superior when using encryption for file transmission, despite the longer processing time.

The Public Domain Archive Program ARC

Interestingly enough, there are similarities between the techniques used for encryption and those used for data compression. One program that takes advantage of these similarities is ARC. ARC is a "user supported" utility available from System Enhancement Associates, in Wayne, New Jersey. (Refer to Chapter 8 for further information on public domain software.)

Normally ARC is used to compress and archive files on a disk, and it is quite good at that, sometimes reducing file storage space by over 50 percent. ARC has a number of options for adding, removing, extracting, and generally maintaining files in an archive. One of the options enables the user to perform basic encryption on an archived file.

ARC stores all archived files in another (usually large) file called an *archive* that may contain many files. The user can put all the files into one archive or create many archives. A generic operation with ARC has the format:

```
C:> arc [flags] [archive file] [files to be acted on]
```

One of the flags supported is *g*, for garble and takes the form:

```
C:> arc [flags]g[password] [archive] [files to be acted on]
```

The *g* flag and password are required for all operations accessing the encrypted file, except listing the names of the files in the archive. ARC is not particularly sophisticated about the encryption. It simply performs an Exclusive Or on each byte of the file with successive bytes from the password. However, because the operation is performed on a compressed file, which already is altered somewhat, it safeguards the file from the curious and from casual thieves.

ARC does have the added benefit of reducing disk storage, so if your goal is to store files with security from prying eyes, ARC may be the ticket for you. And as we have said, it's free (sort of).

The Public Domain Program PC-CODE1

Another public domain program is PC-CODE1. (Refer to Chapter 8 for more information on obtaining PC-CODE1.) PC-CODE1 also uses a superenciphering method much like the DES. Unlike DES, PC-CODE1 allows the user to control the values of the intermediate keys and allows more steps in the encipherment process.

To use PC-CODE1, the user must select whether keys are to be entered numerically or as ASCII text and select a level of encipherment. The "high" level uses 25 keys, whereas the "low" level uses only 7 keys. The program then generates the actual encipherment keys using the entered numbers as *seeds*. (Seeds are numbers from which other numbers are numerically derived. The derivation process varies depending on the use and implementation.) Once this process is complete, the user selects the input and output filenames, and is given the option of saving the keys on disk for future runs.

PC-CODE1 is claimed to be better than the DES algorithm because it uses longer keys. PC-CODE1 also provides statistics on the effectiveness of the encipherment (called "debug" mode). When using this debug mode, PC-CODE1 checks the output data for giveaway patterns. Functionally, this is a quality program in terms of its encryption feature.

Unfortunately, every rose has its thorns and this is no exception. The current version of PC-CODE1 has two problems. First, it is written in BASIC and it is slow! The documentation states that the addition of a 8087 Numeric Data Processor speeds up the program operation significantly, so that problem may be overcome. The second and more serious problem is that the program is susceptible to crashing when presented with the wrong input. It is not what you would call "user friendly." As a result, although it is probably a good deal for the home hobbyist, caution is advised before using this program in a business environment, especially with users not comfortable with the foibles of computers. The last thing any business needs is unreliable software.

The User-Supported Program The Confidant

A much more polished, if less secure, program is also available as user-supported software. (Refer to Chapter 8 for information on obtaining this program.) Called *The Confidant,* this program's capabilities are very similar to Superkey's. The Confidant has a suggested donation value of $10. At that price, it seems worth a try.

As with Superkey, The Confidant supports both the DES algorithm and a less secure private method. We can understand the need for the private method as The Confidant is slow when processing in DES mode—by the author's calculations, almost 20 times slower than Superkey. Also on the negative side is the Confidant's 16-character key: one half the size used by Borland in Superkey.

However, on the plus side, The Confidant is easy to use and allows the user to specify a variety of sources and destinations: console, printer, or files. Best of all, The Confidant does not have PC-CODE1's tendency to blow up when presented with the wrong input. As an introduction to cryptography, it is almost certainly worth the modest donation.

Note that The Confidant only runs on the IBM Personal Computer series of computers or close compatibles because it makes use of their unique display capabilities.

Hardware Encryption Products

As was predicted when the DES was first adopted, the presence of a standard has enabled hardware chip manufacturers to produce encryption engines in silicon. Two of the products currently available are the WD2001/2 Data Encryption Devices from Western Digital Corporation and the T7000 and T7000A Digital Encryption Processors from AT&T.

Western Digital's WD2200 Encryption Board

The WD2200 board from Western Digital is a hardware encryption engine compatible with the IBM Personal Computer series of computers and those MS-DOS machines that are bus compatible. The heart of the board is the WD2001 Data Encryption Device that fully implements the DES algorithm on a single chip. The board supports stream encoding as well as block encoding, but more importantly, the WD2200 supports DMA (direct memory access) transfers to and from the board, allowing a very high throughput through the DES chip.

This board is ideally suited to users who desire to encrypt or decrypt large amounts of data. In addition, the WD2200 can be used in a network server that provides access to communications channels for other personal computers that may attach to it.

TRANSPARENT DATA ENCRYPTION

The best feature of the WD2200 is that Western Digital supplies a program with the board called SECDRIVE, for secure drive. When installed, the SECDRIVE program *automatically encrypts and decrypts all transfers to and from a disk!* The program uses an eight-character ASCII key, which necessitates choosing a random key with great care and not using only alphanumeric characters.

SECDRIVE may be used with floppy disks, hard disks, and virtual disks. It can support multiple disks with individual keys. Even the directory of the disk is encrypted!

Why is this feature so extraordinary? Because it means that the storage is secure. Temporary files, deleted files, data in partially filled sectors, everything is encrypted. Even the most detailed analysis of the disk fails to yield sensitive data.

Western Digital's WD 4025A X.25 Data Transmission Board

Western Digital has also included the WD2001 Data Encryption Device on their 4025A X.25 Data Transmission Board for the IBM Personal Computer series and close compatibles. Unlike the WD2200, the

DES chip on this board must be accessed under program control, writing and reading eight bytes at a time from the DES chip's input and output registers.

Because of this access method, stream encryption must be implemented in the software driver program for the board. However, because the user is responsible for validating the data that enters and leaves the board through the X.25 interface *before* performing encryption operations on it, it would be inadvisable to make the encryption process part of the transmission process. In other words, because the data packets being transmitted probably contain header information that must be routed prior to decryption and because the software managing the X.25 data link must verify the correctness of the data before it can be decrypted, it is better that the encryption and decryption processes take place separately from the transmission process.

This board does, however, provide great functionality to the user who needs both X.25 data communications ability and the ability to transfer secure data.

T7000 Digital Encryption Processor from AT&T

Although the authors are not aware of any board level products incorporating the T7000 for the IBM PC XT and AT family or compatibles, the capabilities of this chip deserve note. Should a product become available, it is definitely worth the attention of the serious user.

In addition to the standard DES encryption mode of 64 bits in and 64 bits out, the T7000 supports three other encryption modes. One of these is stream encryption (called *cipher feedback mode* by AT&T) with either a single bit or single byte feedback. Yet another mode uses the T7000 to produce a series of pseudo-random numbers that are combined with the input data to secure it from curious eyes. This mode has the advantage that a single bit error in transmission produces only a single bit error in the decrypted plaintext, meaning that the entire transmission is not lost because of a single bit failure. This feature overcomes our hesitation about stream encryption methods.

Even with all these features, the chip is fast: rated at 235,000 ciphering instructions per second with an 8 MHz clock. In the standard DES mode, this equals a throughput of 1.822Mbytes per second. We hope that products incorporating these and other encryption features are commercially available before long for the microcomputer user.

Comments on Computer Encryption

CAUTION

DON'T LOSE THE KEY!

The most obvious comment in the world of encryption applies to encryption keys: *Don't lose your keys!* If you encrypt a file and forget the key, delete the file. If your encryption method is secure, neither you nor anyone else will be able to recover the file. Don't call the manufacturers. They can't help you. If you have a poor memory, write the key down somewhere and keep it with you. If the data must be kept secure, keep the key secure also. Conversations at the water cooler shouldn't include your encryption keys. Leaving the key written on your desk blotter isn't a great idea either. Don't throw pieces of paper into your trash with keys written on them. Companies have lost a great deal of money to thieves who frequent dumpsters.

Choosing the Key

Sloppy operating procedures can negate all of the effort of setting up a secure computing environment. Foremost among these is poor choice of encryption keys. Always assume that a would be thief can obtain a copy of the ciphering procedure. The only protection then lies in the key. We have already stressed the importance of using long, unexpected keys. What are some good choices?

TRICK

TRICKS FOR CHOOSING ENCRYPTION KEYS

For less critical users, good keys can often be found in the world around us. One key used by an acquaintance of ours is the set of Universal Product Codes found on most common items (those funny little bar codes that they're putting on everything these days). These ten-digit numbers can be concatenated to form unexpected keys but are easily recalled by remembering the product names from which the Universal Product Codes are derived. Another method is to use the serial numbers that appear on one dollar bills and other denominations. However, don't tell anyone your method or they may guess your keys by watching what you do.

The best keys are often generated by pseudo-random number generators. However, a bad pseudo-random number generator can get you into a lot of trouble by providing a repeating sequence of numbers that may be easy to break. If you use this method, make sure the numbers provided are large and relatively random. Make sure also that you write the keys down somewhere because the chances of your remembering them correctly are quite small.

Leaving Erased Data on the Disk

Assuming that you have implemented one of the methods described in this chapter for protecting your data, you still may be at risk. How? Because the data that you have just encrypted may reside two other places in your system, still in an unencrypted form. One is in the memory of your computer and the other is in the form of backup files and erased files on your disk.

Taking care of data in memory is the easy part. One way is to use the fill command in DEBUG to clear memory as in this example:

```
C:> debug
-r cs
CS 15FD
-f 15FD:0 L FFFF 00
-f 25FD:0 L FFFF 00
 :  :   :  :  :
-f 95FD:0 L FFFF 00
-q
```

This example assumes that your system has a full 640K memory as it goes through each unused 64K segment clearing all the bytes to zero. Each time the fill is performed, the segment address is increased by 1000 hex. The task can be made easier by using the F3 key to recall the last command, then using the Right Arrow key (number 4 on the numeric keypad) to backspace and edit the segment address.

An easier method is to use the simple CLEARMEM.COM program provided in the following listing. This program can be created by typing the listing exactly as shown, including the blank line, into a file called CLEARMEM.SCR. Then type DEBUG <CLEARMEM.SCR, and DEBUG automatically creates the program CLEARMEM.COM for you. CLEARMEM may be run by typing clearmem at the system prompt. CLEARMEM clears all remaining DOS memory in the system to an interesting pattern of increasing numbers. CLEARMEM does *not* clear extended memory (memory MS-DOS can't use).

```
n clearmem.com
a 100
CLD
MOV   AX,CS
ADD   AX,12
MOV   ES,AX
XOR   DI,DI
MOV   CX,10
REP   STOSB
INX   AX
CMP   AX,WORD PTR [2]
JNE   106
MOV   AX,4C00
INT   21

r cx
1b
w
q
```

This still leaves the problem of dealing with backup files. As you probably know, many word processors and spreadsheets create backup files as they operate, WordStar and SuperCalc being two examples. Instead of deleting the backup file, which only removes the directory entry, the file must be physically destroyed on the disk by writing new data on top of it.

TRICK   **PROTECTING BACKUP FILES**

One method of preventing people from recovering and reading deleted backup files is to encrypt the backup file, then delete it. Should anyone recover the backup file (with Norton Utilities for example), they would be reading gibberish.

The danger is that the backup file may not be the *only* backup created by the program. Some programs, like word processors, create temporary files, which are deleted before the program exits. Even worse, sectors of the temporary files may be reused by other files. The only truly secure methods are to always encrypt the disk with a utility such as Western Digital's SECDRIVE and WD2200 board or to copy all valid files from the disk to another disk, then clear the disk using a program such as Norton Utilities' Wipedisk. Then, the valid files may be copied back to the original disk and encrypted as necessary.

Conceivably, the problem can also be addressed by a program that writes over all unused portions of a disk, including the unused portions of sectors that are used by valid files (which can be determined from a file's byte count). Until such a program is developed and marketed, we either live with a potential hole in our security, resort to the costs of hardware solutions, or take such drastic measures such as clearing our disks every day at the end of work.

Better Security

If the standard methods don't impress you, consider multiple pass encryption algorithms. They add security but also add more time and more keys to remember. The methods described in this chapter defeat the casual thief, and the better methods (such as DES) stop a dedicated amateur. If you feel that your data requires an even higher degree of security, consider both increased physical security and consulting an expert in the field of computer cryptography.

Public Key Encryption

Public Key encryption is most likely the future method of encryption of data for transmission. Unfortunately, current public key schemes are unsuitable for the microcomputer environment, requiring computing resources that are larger by orders of magnitude than those now available. Still, the capabilities of public key encryption make it worth mentioning.

Public key encryption is based around ciphers for which the encoding cipher and decoding cipher use different keys. One key is made public (thus the cipher's name) and the other kept private. Thus, anyone may encipher a message but only the cipher's owner can decipher it. This effectively solves the problems of distributing the cipher key because the public encryption key may be freely sent over unsecured lines.

If we call the encoding cipher *f(x)* and the decoding cipher *-f(x)*, the typical operation is that *f(x)* is distributed and used by a sender on a message *M*, as in *f(M)*. The receiver then calculates *-f(f(M))* and has the original message.

If we add the condition that *-f(f(x))* is equal to *f(- f(x))* (that is, the order of the operations does not matter), this encryption system allows for secure communication between two parties with verification. A message sent from A to B would be enciphered as follows:

```
fB("From A" + -fA(Message)
```

Receiver B then applies *-fB(x)* and finds the message is from A. Applying the public fA(x) operation on *-fA(message)* leaves the plaintext message. Because only A could have created the *-fA(x)* message, B knows that the message is indeed from A.

However, for public key encryption to work, the algorithm must be such that the public key can be calculated easily from the private key and that the knowledge of the public key does not compromise the private key. Current algorithms for this are so computation intensive that they are not feasible for today's microcomputers. Some algorithms operate with decimal prime numbers hundreds of digits in length! As promising as public key encryption is, it will be a while before it is available for personal microcomputers.

SUMMARY OF ENCRYPTION DO'S AND DON'TS

- Avoid long runs of identical character sequences or standard phrases such as "Please Login" or "STOP" that can provide a cryptoanalyst with examples of both plain and encoded data.

- Use an encryption method that encrypts groups of characters rather than single characters. This greatly enhances security.

- If time allows and the transmission and/or storage is free from

> errors, use a "history dependent" encryption method such as stream encoding.
>
> - Remember that deleted backup files can be restored to compromise secure data.

Summary

Note that in most security studies of industrial and educational computer installations, the majority of the passwords were found without resorting to cryptoanalytical methods. Instead, most passwords were found through trial and error, using the names of the users, their families, friends, and pets, and the English words found in any decent size dictionary. One study found a fair number of users with single letter passwords!

The lesson is that the choice of encryption keys is probably the most important aspect of data encryption, even more important than the choice of methods. If remembering the key is a problem, write it down in a secure place, because if you choose a key that is easy to remember, chances are that someone else will find it easy to discover.

Annotated Bibliography

Appendix

Books
Technical Manuals

The following are books and manuals used by the authors as references. You may wish to consult these references for further information on specific topics.

Books

Anderson, D., J. M. Gessin, F. Warren, J. Rodgers. *PC-DOS Tips & Traps.* Berkeley, Ca.: Osborne/McGraw-Hill, 1986.

> This book is somewhat useful. It includes many hints and pitfalls. Starting with two chapters as a tutorial for beginners and ending with a final "advanced topics" chapter (all in 218 pages), it obviously doesn't delve into anything very deeply. It is not suitable for a beginner, not a reference book, and not an advanced book.

Beechhold, H. F. *Plain English Maintenance & Repair Guide for IBM Personal Computers, The.* New York, NY: Simon & Schuster, Inc., 1985.

> A down-to-earth nuts 'n bolts maintenance guide that provides hardly any information on diagnostics and problem isolation but does act as a good guide to anyone wanting to do detailed repair work on a PC beyond the normal board-replacement procedures. It includes good information on how to do soldering and desoldering.

Curtis, C., and D. L. Majhor. *Modem Connections Bible.* Indianapolis, In.: Howard W. Sams & Co., 1985.

> A useful book for learning how to connect various makes of modems to various makes of microcomputers. In addition to numerous diagrams showing how RS-232 cables should be wired for various modem-computer combinations, this book also provides useful background information on how modems work, what the

various data transfer error-checking protocols are and how they work, and how RS-232 cables are typically wired.

Dahmke, M. *Microcomputer Operating Systems.* Peterborough, NH: BYTE /McGraw-Hill, 1982.

A fairly comprehensive guide to operating systems in general, with descriptions of operating systems on small, medium, and large computers. Specific examples are given of popular operating systems such as CP/M (the predecessor to MS-DOS) and multitasking operating systems such as MP/M and UNIX.

DeVoney, C. *IBM's Personal Computer.* 2nd ed. Indianapolis, In.: Que Corporation, 1983.

Dealing primarily with the hardware of the IBM PC and IBM PC XT (2nd edition), this book provides a considerable amount of information not found in other publications, including the IBM *Technical Reference* manuals. Although the book does not include electrical schematics, it does provide extensive mechanical and electrical specifications of the IBM PC units themselves and IBM and IBM-compatible equipment. The last part of the book discusses various types of software that are compatible with the IBM PC series, including different operating systems. It concludes with a good introductory description of IBM PC telecommunications and networking.

DeVoney, C. *Using PC DOS.* Indianapolis, In.: Que Corporation, 1986.

This book is oriented for PC-DOS Version 3.0 and is a sequel to *PC DOS User's Guide,* which was geared for PC-DOS Version 2.0. The book is user-oriented rather than programmer-oriented and does not include coverage of EDLIN, DEBUG, and ANSI ESCape sequences. It probably provides the best coverage of PC-DOS for users. If you could only have one "user-oriented" book, this is probably the best candidate.

Eggebrecht, L. C. *Interfacing to the IBM Personal Computer.* Indianapolis, In.: Howard W. Sams & Co., 1986.

This is a useful book for anyone wanting to learn more about the hardware of the IBM PC and how to interface your own hardware to it. Although only the IBM PC is covered (does not include the XT or AT), this book provides a wealth of information not provided in the IBM Hardware *Technical Reference* manual.

Froehlich, R. A. *The IBM PC (and Compatibles) Free Software Catalog and Directory.* Portland, Or.: dilithium Press, Ltd., (distributed by Crown Publishers, Inc., New York), 1986.

This 924-page, softbound book is one of the most comprehensive guides to learning about locating, selecting, obtaining, and using public domain and user-supported software. It provides useful information on various organizations that maintain libraries of free and low-cost software and includes introductory information for those wishing to use electronic BBSs (bulletin board systems). Also included is an extensive catalog that lists by volume number the library disks available from various organizations. The book includes a directory in index form matching software categories and individual programs to the library numbers described in the catalog. Also included are lists of BBS systems with phone numbers and user groups around the country.

House, K. G., and J. Marble. *Printer Connections Bible*. Indianapolis, In.: Howard W. Sams & Co., 1985.

Like the *Modem Connections Bible*, this is a very useful book for learning to connect various makes of printers to various makes of microcomputers. Numerous diagrams are provided to show how cables should be wired for different printer-computer combinations, showing both parallel and serial (RS-232) cabling when either is supported. Included also are printer switch settings for various modes of operation.

King, R. A. *MS-DOS Handbook, The*. Berkeley, Ca.: Sybex Inc., 1985.

This book assumes a prior knowledge of MS-DOS and computers in general. The first half of the book is oriented toward programmers, the second half toward users.

Kamin, J. *MS-DOS Power User's Guide*. Berkeley, Ca.: Sybex Inc., 1986.

A book that provides a treasure-house of advanced techniques for getting the most out of MS-DOS. It covers such things as advanced batch file features, using BASIC to create menus, password protection, redirection, file management, and more. A useful book and a must for anyone wishing to advance their knowledge and MS-DOS expertise.

Kelley, J. E. *PC Secrets: Tips for Power Performance*. Berkeley, Ca.: Osborne /McGraw-Hill, 1986.

Another book that describes the advanced use of MS-DOS. Although somewhat more basic than *MS-DOS Power User's Guide*, this book also provides many useful tidbits of information that can significantly increase your knowledge of MS-DOS and its various hidden features. Included are many programs that either "fix" certain irregularities in the way MS-DOS runs on IBM Personal Computers and close compatibles or enhance the features of your system.

Norton, P. *MS-DOS and PC-DOS User's Guide*. Bowie, Md.: Robert J. Brady Co., 1984.

A conversational book that describes the different uses and implementations of MS-DOS on various types of microcomputers. Although the information covered is not comprehensive (for example, most of MS-DOS's commands are discussed very briefly), it is the kind of book that a newcomer to MS-DOS can read from cover to cover without dealing with too many technicalities. Appropriate for beginners but not for advanced users.

Norton, P. *PC-DOS: Introduction to High-Performance Computing*. Bowie, Md: Brady Communications Company, Inc., 1985.

An interesting and practical book that is effective at starting at the beginning and graduating to getting the most out of your system. It includes DOS 1.0 through 3.1 and concentrates mostly on 2.0 and up.

O'Day, K., and J. Angermeyer. *Understanding MS-DOS*. Indianapolis, In.: Howard W. Sams & Co., 1987.

A good book for someone getting started with MS-DOS. Although not for advanced users, this book's interesting and nonintimidating approach to learning MS-DOS for the first time makes it highly recommended for someone who *needs* to learn MS-DOS but does not necessarily desire (at the time) to become an advanced user.

PC-SIG Library, The. 2nd Ed. Sunnyvale, Ca.: PC Software Interest Group, (1st ed.) 1984, (2nd ed.) 1985.

The main catalog of the PC-SIG (PC Software Interest Group) that describes its library of public domain and user-supported programs. The first edition covers Volumes (disks) 1 through 100. The second edition has been expanded to include Volumes 1 through 306. Supplements and newsletters are periodically published describing new additions to the PC-SIG library.

Sheldon, T. *Introducing PC-DOS and MS-DOS: A Guide for Beginning and Advanced Users*. New York, NY: BYTE/McGraw-Hill, 1985.

One of the most complete books written on MS-DOS, this book is divided into two parts: a tutorial and an advanced user's guide. Along with the more basic features of MS-DOS, many advanced uses of MS-DOS are presented. Although at first glance, this book appears to be simply a beginner's book, it has many hidden tidbits of information for advanced users. A useful reference for any advanced user's book shelf.

Simrin, S. *MS-DOS Bible*. Indianapolis, In.: Howard W. Sams & Co., 1985.

Designed as a reference book for MS-DOS and its commands, the *MS-DOS Bible* can be used in most instances as a substitute to the MS-DOS user's and technical manuals. The first edition covers MS-DOS Versions 1 through 2. The book is divided into three parts: an information "jump table," a tutorial on MS-DOS and its commands, and a quick reference guide to MS-DOS commands. Several appendixes are included that show an IBM PC extended ASCII table and describe MS-DOS error messages, MS-DOS interrupts and function calls, and useful batch files.

Supplement to the PC-SIG Library: Disks 301 to 454, The. Sunnyvale, Ca.: PC Software Interest Group (PC-SIG), 1986.

A supplement to the second edition of *The PC-SIG Library,* including Volumes 301 through 454.

Waite, M. and C. L. Morgan. *Graphics Primer for the IBM PC*. Berkeley, Ca.: Osborne/McGraw-Hill, 1983.

A good book for learning how to generate graphics on IBM Personal Computers and compatible systems. Its extensive use of color plates and examples makes this book a very pleasant and enjoyable reference work.

Wolverton, V. *Running MS-DOS*. 2nd ed. Bellevue, Wa.: Microsoft Press, 1984, 1985.

> Taking the reader a step beyond the MS-DOS technical documentation, this book describes more concisely how MS-DOS commands are used. Both a tutorial and a quick reference to MS-DOS commands are provided, which, although they do not include undocumented features of MS-DOS, are an improvement over the standard documentation supplied with MS-DOS.

Zarrella, J. *Operating Systems: Concepts and Principles*. Suisun City, Ca.: Microcomputer Applications, 1979.

> A short guide describing characteristics of operating systems in general, with such topics as tasks, processes, system services, communications, memory management, input/output, file systems, and system security. Although no single operating system is covered specifically, this book provides a brief overview of what a typical operating system consists of.

Technical Manuals

COMPAQ Portable 286 Personal Computer Maintenance and Service Guide. Houston, Tx.: COMPAQ Computer Corporation, 1985.

COMPAQ Portable 286 Personal Computer Operations Guide. Houston, Tx.: COMPAQ Computer Corporation, 1985.

COMPAQ 80286-Based Products Technical Reference Guide. Houston, Tx.: COMPAQ Computer Corporation, 1985.

CPYAT2PC User's Manual. San Carlos, Ca.: Microbridge International Inc., (for Version 1.1) 1985.

CUBIT Data Compression Software Owner's Handbook and Guide. Manchester, NH: SoftLogic Solutions, Inc., 1986.

Disk Operating System. Boca Raton, Fl.: International Business Machines Corp., (for DOS 1.10) 1982, (for DOS 2.00) 1983, (for DOS 2.10) 1983, (for DOS 3.00) 1984, (for DOS 3.10) 1984 and 1985, (for DOS 3.20) 1986.

Disk Operating System Technical Reference. Boca Raton, Fl.: International Business Machines Corp., (for DOS 2.10) 1983, (for DOS 3.00) 1984, (for DOS 3.10) 1984 and 1985, (for DOS 3.20) 1986.

Microsoft Word, Using and *Reference to Microsoft Word*. Bellevue, Wa.: Microsoft Corporation, (for Version 3.0) 1986.

MS-DOS Version 3 Reference Guide. 2nd ed. Houston, Tx.: COMPAQ Computer Corporation, 1985.

Norton Utilities, The. Santa Monica, Ca.: Peter Norton, (for Version 3.0) 1984.

Referee User's Manual. Madison, Wi.: Persoft, Inc., (for Version 1.0) 1986.

Sidekick Owner's Handbook. 6th ed. Scotts Valley, Ca.: Borland International Inc., (for Version 1.5) 1985.

Software Carousel Owner's Handbook and Guide, The. Manchester, NH: Soft-Logic Solutions, Inc., 1986.

Superkey Owner's Handbook. 2nd ed. Scotts Valley, Ca.: Borland International Inc., (for Version 1.0) 1985.

Technical Reference (IBM Personal Computer Hardware Reference Library). Boca Raton, Fl.: International Business Machines Corporation, (for IBM PC) 1981 and 1982, (for IBM PC XT) 1984, (for IBM PC AT) 1985.

Turbo Lightning Owner's Handbook. Scotts Valley, Ca.: Borland International Inc., (for Version 1.0) 1985.

WordStar Professional. San Rafael, Ca.: MicroPro International Corporation, (for Version 3.3) 1983.

XTREE. 2nd Ed. Sherman Oaks, Ca.: Executive Systems, Inc., (for Version 2.0) 1985.

Source Information   Appendix B

Sources for Commercial Software
and Hardware

Sources for Public Domain and
User-Supported Software

Th**his appendix contains sources for commercial software and hardware and public domain and user-supported software, including a list of electronic bulletin board systems in the United States and Canada.

Sources for Commercial Software and Hardware

ARISTO Computers
16811 El Camino Real
Suite 213
Houston, TX 77058

Distributer of memory upgrade kits for IBM PC, PC XT, close clones, and early COMPAQ models.

Executive Systems, Inc.
15300 Ventura Blvd., Suite 305
Sherman Oaks, CA 91403
(818) 990-3457

Developer of XTREE (file and directory manager).

Lugaru Software, Ltd.
5740 Darlington Rd.
Pittsburgh, PA 15217
(412) 421-5911

Developer of the Epsilon text editor.

Microbridge Computers International, Inc.
655 Sky Way, Suite 125
San Carlos, CA 94070
(415) 593-8777

Developer of CPYAT2PC, a program that permits the writing of 5¼-inch, 40-track, 360K floppy disk using high-capacity (1.2M) floppy disk drives in IBM AT and compatible systems, without the need for an add-on 360K disk drive.

Personally Developed Software
P.O. Box 3280
Wallingford, CT 06494
1-800-IBM-PCSW or 1-203-237-4504 in Alaska and Hawaii

Produces publication called *The Directory* that lists several programs developed for IBM Personal Computers, sponsored and supported by IBM.

SoftLogic Solutions
P.O. Box 6221
Manchester, NH 03108
(603) 644-5555

Developer of Disk Optimizer, Cubit (file squeezer), Software Carousel (memory partitioning), and Double-DOS (multitasking 2 tasks MS-DOS replacement), all commercial programs.

Software Research Technologies
3757 Wilshire Blvd., Suite 211
Los Angeles, CA 90010
(213) 384-5430

Developer of SmartPath (extended PATH for overlay files) and
SmartKey (keyboard macros) commercial programs.

Sources for Public Domain and User-Supported Software

PC Software Interest Group (PC-SIG)
1030 E. Duane Ave., Suite J
Sunnyvale, CA 94086
Phone: (408) 730-9291

For library of MS-DOS/IBM PC public domain, freeware, and user-
supported software, available on 5¼-inch floppy disks or CD-ROM.
Catalog/directory subscription available.

The FreeSoft Company
P.O. Box 27608
St. Louis, MO 63146

Developer of Ultra-Utilities (also known as The Wizard's
Apprentice).

Electronic Bulletin Board Systems

The following is a condensed list of electronic bulletin board systems
in the United States and Canada. One or two numbers have been

selected from each area code, so we hope that if you're calling a BBS system for the first time, you'll be able to find one within your area code. Most BBS systems contain more complete and up-to-date lists of BBS systems around the United States, detailed lists of local BBS systems, and occasionally have lists of BBS systems around the world. Because these systems change continually, Table B-1 may not be completely accurate.

Most BBS systems support a standard set of communication-line parameters, although occasionally one is found with parameter requirements that are slightly different. If you set your communications program and/or modem to the following parameters, you'll be able to gain access to most BBS systems.

Speed:	1200 bps (bits per second or *baud*)
Data Bits:	8
Parity:	None
Stop Bits:	1

Occasionally, you may find a BBS that supports only a data speed of 300 bps. If you gain access to a BBS that runs only at 300 bps, you must quickly lower the data speed while on line or hang up, change the speed, then call back. Conversely, if you have a 2,400 bps modem, you should be able to switch quickly to the right speed if the BBS you're calling doesn't support 2,400 bps.

List of BBS Systems in the USA and Canada

A list of BBS systems in the USA and Canada is provided in Table B-1.

Table B-1.   BBS Systems in the USA and Canada

Telephone #	St.	City	SYSOP	Name or Description
201-291-4904	NJ	Sandy Hook	Louie Jones	Lighthouse BBS
202-537-7475	DC	Washington	Ken Goosens	FNMA,Soft Xchg,RBBS B
203-334-5778	CT	Bridgeport	Jim Ryan	Mission Control I
205-826-4437	AL	Auburn	Tim Placek	Tiger Board,Auburn U
206-723-2452	WA	Seattle	Tom Philbrick	Seattle BBS,Lotus
209-296-3534	CA	Volcano	Dave Carroll	High Sierra,Turbo,20M
212-340-9666	NY	New York	Rudy Gordon	The Machine,AT,20M
213-376-7089	CA	Redondo Bch	George Peck	
214-239-3073	TX	Rowlett	Dan Kardell	North Dallas

Table B-1 (cont).

Telephone #	St.	City	SYSOP	Name or Description
215-486-6568	PA	W. Chester	Dennis Grady	D.K.G. BBS
216-381-3320	OH	Cleveland	Norm Henke	PC-Ohio,32M
219-277-3341	IN	South Bend	Chuck Harrell	NIPCUG
301-498-7283	MD	Laurel	Phil Grier	PC-DOS RBBS
302-478-3463	DE	Wilmington	Dan North	PC Professionals
303-690-4566	CO	Aurora	Chris Carson	Tips
304-344-8088	WV	Charleston	Bob Ketcham	UserBoard BBS,20M
305-273-0020	FL	Orlando	Asa Fulton	Home of RBBS-X3
308-995-5667	DE	Holeredge	Steve Clark	PC*jr*,Jr-Net
309-438-7370	IL	Normal	George Warren	ISU BBS,Comp. Sci.
312-882-4227	IL	Chicago	Gene Plantz	Superboard
313-393-0527	MI	Detroit	Jon Tara	PCUTIL,Utilities
315-423-1208	NY	Syracuse	Stuart Williams	Syracuse Micro Club,T
316-682-1698	KS	Wichita	George Winters	Kansas BBS,DOS,CP/M
317-842-2208	IN	Indianapolis	Tony Moleta	Indy PC Users Bd
318-635-0253	LA	Shreveport	Brian Kelly	RBBS/Shreveport
319-363-3314	IA	Cedar Rapids	Ben Blackstock	Hawkeye BBS
401-769-0570	RI	Woonsocket	Jim Bardwell	
404-396-5460	GA	Atlanta	Rick Wells	Boogie Board
406-656-8124	MT	Billings	Dave Williams	The 8th Dimension
408-225-1845	CA	San Jose	Gene Lowry	Bigfoot BBS,20M
412-362-1672	PA	Pittsburgh	K. Fitzpatrick	Computer Moron,20M
413-357-8809	MA	Granville	Scott Maentz	New England BBS
414-964-5160	WI	Shorewood	Bob Mahoney	EXEC-PC,248M,10 lines
415-481-0252	CA	San Lorenzo	Terry Taylor	
415-689-2090	CA	Concord	Jon Martin	Home of RBBS-PC West
415-927-1216	CA	San Rafael	PCUG	Marin Sonoma PCUG
416-231-0538	CN	Toronto	Doug Peel	PC-Canada,E-Mail,Ads
416-751-6337	CN	Toronto	Doug Peel	PC-Canada Line 2
419-756-4958	OH	Mansfield	Tom Rothe	Mid Ohio,33M,Goodies
502-426-8381	KY	Louisville	Mike Weixler	On-line Exchange
503-371-4601	OR	Salem	Bryan Burke	Pro-Net BBS
504-895-5259	LA	New Orleans	Pete Smothers	
505-821-7379	NM	Albq.	Dave Staehlin	TBC BBS,30M
509-697-7298	WA	Selah	Pat O'Farrell	PC Biblio,123,Ham
512-659-5470	TX	San Antonio	Bob Trautman	Ultralite Sa.,Pascal
513-831-7557	OH	Cincinnati	John Harrington	Pro-Line BBS
514-989-1567	CN	Montreal	James Ludwick	Le Systeme OnLine
515-683-5193	IA	Ottumwa	Bill Bagley	Indian Hills CC
516-741-6914	NY	Long Island	Andrew Brenner	Railroad BBS
517-337-0261	MI	Lansing	Warren Wolfe	Data Basics
518-455-6208	NY	Albany	Tom Kinney	Rockflr Coll,Govt,Ed
519-837-2469	CN	London	Rob Smith	EMJ OnLine
601-895-7693	MS	Olive Br	John Mahaffey	Electronic BB,DOS,C
602-899-4876	AZ	Chandler	David Cantere	Technoids Anonymous
603-357-2090	NH	Keene	C. VonSchilling	
608-273-5037	WI	Madison	Mike Brown	NICBUL BBS
609-799-4643	NJ	Plainsboro	Frank Petillo	Gandalf BBS
612-623-1156	MN	Minneapolis	Howard Ekman	Terrapin Station
615-870-5155	TN	Chattanooga	Harry Haronian	40M,Chat. Choo Choo
617-353-9312	MA	Boston	Dick Rohrdanz	Boston Computer Soc.

Table B-1 (cont).

Telephone #	St.	City	SYSOP	Name or Description
617-449-4727	MA	Needham	PC Week	PC Week hints,Xchg
617-587-1886	MA	Brockton	Bill Ruby	Shoe City BBS
619-438-5256	CA	La Costa	James Haden	AT,30M,DOS,UNIX
619-561-7817	CA	El Cajon	Jim Brown	45M
701-293-5973	ND	Fargo	Loren Jones	RBBS beta site
703-759-5049	VA	Great Falls	Tom Mack	Home of RBBS-PC
704-332-5439	NC	Charlotte	Bill Taylor	Apple,Mac,IBM
707-447-8393	CA	Benicia	Jeff Brown	West Coast Archive
713-481-0455	TX	Houston	Mike Freeman	The Last Resort BBS
714-861-1549	CA	Diamond Bar	Jim Holloway	Diamond Bar BBS
716-227-1156	NY	Rochester	Don Race	Atari,CP/M,DOS
717-226-6653	PA	Hawley	Randy Gullick	Software Safari
718-238-7855	NY	Brooklyn	Jesse Levine	Atlantic Palisades
801-266-7658	UT	Salt Lake	Fred Clark	Salt Air/Sysops/RBFix
803-548-0900	SC	Ft. Mill	Bill Taylor	
804-296-7591	VA	Charlo'ville	Mike Watkins	ByteLines,C,Pascal,CA
805-526-6147	CA	Simi Valley	Dan Sjolseth	Simi Valley
806-353-7484	TX	Amarillo	Dorn Stickle	Communications
812-824-7990	IN	Bloomington	Robert Cole	PC-Link Central,20M
813-294-6233	FL	Winter Haven	Ingram Leedy	DigiCom BBS
814-238-0955	PA	State Coll	Jim Foster	JMJ,Turbo Conference
816-833-3427	MO	Independence	Bill Bell	Kay-Cee Pee-Cee,20M
817-481-6334	TX	Grapevine	Mark Sehorne	IBM AT
818-240-6006	CA	Glendale	Carl Spencer	Blueprint,Framework
907-344-8041	AK	Anchorage	Jan Zumwalt	PC Club News/Bus SIG
907-428-1025	AK	Anchorage	Jeff Grant	Alaskan Megasystem
912-236-3047	GA	Savannah	Randy Wilson	IBM AT,DOS 3.0 ques.
913-827-3310	KS	Salina	Dirk Speed	23M
914-277-8030	NY	Somers	Steve Haase	Somers BBS
918-584-0703	OK	Tulsa	Brian Tiernan	Macom/Tulsa,38M
919-782-0829	NC	Raleigh	Terry Ray	Buffer,20M

Reference Tables   Appendix C

Hexadecimal to Decimal Conversion

Decimal to Hexadecimal Conversion

I n addition to ASCII (see Table C-1) and IBM ASCII extended cross-reference tables (see Table C-2), this appendix explains how to convert from decimal to hexadecimal and vice versa.

Table C-1. ASCII Cross-Reference

DEC X_{10}	HEX X_{16}	OCT X_8	ASCII	IBM GRA. CHAR.	Terminal Key *
0	00	00	NUL		< Ctrl-@ >
1	01	01	SOH	☺	< Ctrl-A >
2	02	02	STX	☻	< Ctrl-B >
3	03	03	ETX	♥	< Ctrl-C >
4	04	04	EOT	♦	< Ctrl-D >
5	05	05	ENQ	♣	< Ctrl-E >
6	06	06	ACK	♠	< Ctrl-F >
7	07	07	BEL	●	< Ctrl-G >
8	08	10	BS	◘	< Ctrl-H >
9	09	11	HT	○	< Ctrl-I >
10	0A	12	LF	■	< Ctrl-J >
11	0B	13	VT	♂	< Ctrl-K >
12	0C	14	FF	♀	< Ctrl-L >
13	0D	15	CR	♪	< Ctrl-M >
14	0E	16	SO	♫	< Ctrl-N >
15	0F	17	SI	☼	< Ctrl-O >
16	10	20	DLE	►	< Ctrl-P >
17	11	21	DC1	◄	< Ctrl-Q >
18	12	22	DC2	↕	< Ctrl-R >
19	13	23	DC3	‼	< Ctrl-S >
20	14	24	DC4	¶	< Ctrl-T >
21	15	25	NAK	§	< Ctrl-U >
22	16	26	SYN	▬	< Ctrl-V >
23	17	27	ETB	↨	< Ctrl-W >
24	18	30	CAN	↑	< Ctrl-X >
25	19	31	EM	↓	< Ctrl-Y >
26	1A	32	SUB	→	< Ctrl-Z >
27	1B	33	ESC	←	< Esc >

Table C-1 (cont).

DEC X_{10}	HEX X_{16}	OCT X_8	ASCII	IBM GRA. CHAR.	Terminal Key *
28	1C	34	FS	∟	<Ctrl-\ >
29	1D	35	GS	↔	<Ctrl-` >
30	1E	36	RS	▲	<Ctrl-=>
31	1F	37	US	▼	<Ctrl- ->
32	20	40	SP		(Space) <SPACE BAR>
33	21	41	!	!	! (Exclamation mark)
34	22	42	"	"	" (Quotation mark)
35	23	43	#	#	# (Number sign or Octothorpe)
36	24	44	$	$	$ (Dollar sign)
37	25	45	%	%	% (Percent)
38	26	46	&	&	& (Ampersand)
39	27	47	'	'	' (Apostrophe or acute accent)
40	28	50	(	(	((Opening parenthesis)
41	29	51	)	)	) (Closing parenthesis)
42	2A	52	*	*	* (Asterisk)
43	2B	53	+	+	+ (Plus)
44	2C	54	,	,	, (Comma)
45	2D	55	-	-	- (Hyphen, dash, or minus)
46	2E	56	.	.	. (Period)
47	2F	57	/	/	/ (Forward slant)
48	30	60	0	0	0
49	31	61	1	1	1
50	32	62	2	2	2
51	33	63	3	3	3
52	34	64	4	4	4
53	35	65	5	5	5
54	36	66	6	6	6
55	37	67	7	7	7
56	38	70	8	8	8
57	39	71	9	9	9
58	3A	72	:	:	: (Colon)
59	3B	73	;	;	; (Semicolon)
60	3C	74	<	<	< (Less than)
61	3D	75	=	=	= (Equals)
62	3E	76	>	>	> (Greater than)
63	3F	77	?	?	? (Question mark)
64	40	100	@	@	@ (Commercial at)
65	41	101	A	A	A
66	42	102	B	B	B
67	43	103	C	C	C
68	44	104	D	D	D
69	45	105	E	E	E
70	46	106	F	F	F
71	47	107	G	G	G
72	48	110	H	H	H
73	49	111	I	I	I
74	4A	112	J	J	J
75	4B	113	K	K	K
76	4C	114	L	L	L
77	4D	115	M	M	M
78	4E	116	N	N	N

Table C-1 (cont).

DEC X_{10}	HEX X_{16}	OCT X_8	ASCII	IBM GRA. CHAR.	Terminal Key *	
79	4F	117	O	O	O	
80	50	120	P	P	P	
81	51	121	Q	Q	Q	
82	52	122	R	R	R	
83	53	123	S	S	S	
84	54	124	T	T	T	
85	55	125	U	U	U	
86	56	126	V	V	V	
87	57	127	W	W	W	
88	58	130	X	X	X	
89	59	131	Y	Y	Y	
90	5A	132	Z	Z	Z	
91	5B	133	[	[	[	(Opening bracket)
92	5C	134	\	\	\	(Reverse slant)
93	5D	135	]	]	]	(Closing bracket)
94	5E	136	^	^	^	(Caret or circumflex)
95	5F	137	_	_	_	(Underscore or underline)
96	60	140	`	`		(Grave accent)
97	61	141	a	a	a	
98	62	142	b	b	b	
99	63	143	c	c	c	
100	64	144	d	d	d	
101	65	145	e	e	e	
102	66	146	f	f	f	
103	67	147	g	g	g	
104	68	150	h	h	h	
105	69	151	i	i	i	
106	6A	152	j	j	j	
107	6B	153	k	k	k	
108	6C	154	l	l	l	
109	6D	155	m	m	m	
110	6E	156	n	n	n	
111	6F	157	o	o	o	
112	70	160	p	p	p	
113	71	161	q	q	q	
114	72	162	r	r	r	
115	73	163	s	s	s	
116	74	164	t	t	t	
117	75	165	u	u	u	
118	76	166	v	v	v	
119	77	167	w	w	w	
120	78	170	x	x	x	
121	79	171	y	y	y	
122	7A	172	z	z	z	
123	7B	173	{	{	{	(Opening brace)
124	7C	174	¦	¦	¦	(Vertical bar; logical OR)
125	7D	175	}	}	}	(Closing brace)
126	7E	176	~	~	~	(Tilde)
127	7F	177	DEL	DEL	<Del>	

Table C-2.   IBM Extended Cross-Reference

BINARY X_2	OCT X_8	DEC X_{10}	HEX X_{16}	Ext. ASCII
1000 0000	200	128	80	Ç
1000 0001	201	129	81	ü
1000 0010	202	130	82	é
1000 0011	203	131	83	â
1000 0100	204	132	84	ä
1000 0101	205	133	85	à
1000 0110	206	134	86	å
1000 0111	207	135	87	ç
1000 1000	210	136	88	ê
1000 1001	211	137	89	ë
1000 1010	212	138	8A	è
1000 1011	213	139	8B	ï
1000 1100	214	140	8C	î
1000 1101	215	141	8D	ì
1000 1110	216	142	8E	Ä
1000 1111	217	143	8F	Å
1001 0000	220	144	90	É
1001 0001	221	145	91	æ
1001 0010	222	146	92	Æ
1001 0011	223	147	93	ô
1001 0100	224	148	94	ö
1001 0101	225	149	95	ò
1001 0110	226	150	96	û
1001 0111	227	151	97	ù
1001 1000	230	152	98	ÿ
1001 1001	231	153	99	Ö
1001 1010	232	154	9A	Ü
1001 1011	233	155	9B	¢
1001 1100	234	156	9C	£
1001 1101	235	157	9D	¥
1001 1110	236	158	9E	P_t
1001 1111	237	159	9F	f
1010 0000	240	160	A0	á
1010 0001	241	161	A1	í
1010 0010	242	162	A2	ó
1010 0011	243	163	A3	ú
1010 0100	244	164	A4	ñ
1010 0101	245	165	A5	Ñ
1010 0110	246	166	A6	ª
1010 0111	247	167	A7	º
1010 1000	250	168	A8	¿
1010 1001	251	169	A9	⌐
1010 1010	252	170	AA	¬
1010 1011	253	171	AB	½
1010 1100	254	172	AC	¼
1010 1101	255	173	AD	¡
1010 1110	256	174	AE	«
1010 1111	257	175	AF	»
1011 0000	260	176	B0	░
1011 0001	261	177	B1	▒
1011 0010	262	178	B2	▓

Table C-2 (cont).

BINARY X_2	OCT X_8	DEC X_{10}	HEX X_{16}	Ext. ASCII
1011 0011	263	179	B3	│
1011 0100	264	180	B4	┤
1011 0101	265	181	B5	╡
1011 0110	266	182	B6	╢
1011 0111	267	183	B7	╖
1011 1000	270	184	B8	╕
1011 1001	271	185	B9	╣
1011 1010	272	186	BA	║
1011 1011	273	187	BB	╗
1011 1100	274	188	BC	╝
1011 1101	275	189	BD	╜
1011 1110	276	190	BE	╛
1011 1111	277	191	BF	┐
1100 0000	300	192	C0	└
1100 0001	301	193	C1	┴
1100 0010	302	194	C2	┬
1100 0011	303	195	C3	├
1100 0100	304	196	C4	─
1100 0101	305	197	C5	┼
1100 0110	306	198	C6	╞
1100 0111	307	199	C7	╟
1100 1000	310	200	C8	╚
1100 1001	311	201	C9	╔
1100 1010	312	202	CA	╩
1100 1011	313	203	CB	╦
1100 1100	314	204	CC	╠
1100 1101	315	205	CD	═
1100 1110	316	206	CE	╬
1100 1111	317	207	CF	╧
1101 0000	320	208	D0	╨
1101 0001	321	209	D1	╤
1101 0010	322	210	D2	╥
1101 0011	323	211	D3	╙
1101 0100	324	212	D4	╘
1101 0101	325	213	D5	╒
1101 0110	326	214	D6	╓
1101 0111	327	215	D7	╫
1101 1000	330	216	D8	╪
1101 1001	331	217	D9	┘
1101 1010	332	218	DA	┌
1101 1011	333	219	DB	█
1101 1100	334	220	DC	▄
1101 1101	335	221	DD	▌
1101 1110	336	222	DE	▐
1101 1111	337	223	DF	▀
1110 0000	340	224	E0	α
1110 0001	341	225	E1	β
1110 0010	342	226	E2	Γ
1110 0011	343	227	E3	π
1110 0100	344	228	E4	Σ
1110 0101	345	229	E5	σ
1110 0110	346	230	E6	μ

Table C-2 (cont).

BINARY X$_2$	OCT X$_8$	DEC X$_{10}$	HEX X$_{16}$	Ext. ASCII
1110 0111	347	231	E7	⊤
1110 1000	350	232	E8	Φ
1110 1001	351	233	E9	Θ
1110 1010	352	234	EA	Ω
1110 1011	353	235	EB	δ
1110 1100	354	236	EC	∞
1110 1101	355	237	ED	φ
1110 1110	356	238	EE	ε
1110 1111	357	239	EF	∩
1111 0000	360	240	F0	≡
1111 0001	361	241	F1	±
1111 0010	362	242	F2	≥
1111 0011	363	243	F3	≤
1111 0100	364	244	F4	⌠
1111 0101	365	245	F5	⌡
1111 0110	366	246	F6	÷
1111 0111	367	247	F7	≈
1111 1000	370	248	F8	°
1111 1001	371	249	F9	•
1111 1010	372	250	FA	·
1111 1011	373	251	FB	√
1111 1100	374	252	FC	η
1111 1101	375	253	FD	2
1111 1110	376	254	FE	■
1111 1111	377	255	FF	

* Those key sequences consisting of "<Ctrl->" are typed in by pressing the CTRL key, and while it is being held down, pressing the key indicated. These sequences are based on those defined for the IBM Personal Computer series keyboards. The key sequences may be defined differently on other keyboards.

IBM Extended ASCII characters can be displayed by pressing the <Alt> key and then typing the decimal code of the character on the keypad.

ABBREVIATIONS:
DEC = Decimal (Base 10)
HEX = Hexadecimal (Base 16)
OCT = Octal (Base 8)
ASCII = American Standard Code for Information Interchange

Hexadecimal to Decimal Conversion

Figure C-1 shows how the hexadecimal number 7D2F is converted to its decimal equivalent:

```
7  D  2  F   hexadecimal

                              Fh = 15d ─────────▶  15d   x       1d  =      15d
                              2h =  2d ─────────▶   2d   x      16d  =      32d
                              Dh = 13d ─────────▶  13d   x     256d  =    3,328d
                              7h =  7d ─────────▶   7d   x   4,096d  =   28,672d
                                                                       ──────────
                                                                       32,047  decimal total
```

Figure C-1.   Converting a Hexadecimal Number to Decimal

Each hexadecimal digit is always 16 times greater than the digit immediately to the right.

Decimal to Hexadecimal Conversion

The process is reversed when you convert decimal numbers to hexadecimal. Start by selecting the leftmost digit and determine its significance in the number (thousands, hundreds, etc.). Then the decimal is divided by the hexadecimal value of the first digit's relative position. (That is, if the first digit is in the thousands position, divide by 4,096 [hexadecimal equivalent of 1,000 decimal].) The result is the first hexadecimal digit. Then the remainder is divided by the hexadecimal value of the next digit's relative position (for example, divide the hundreds digit by 256 because 256 is the hexadecimal equivalent of 100 decimal). Figure C-2 shows how the decimal number derived in the previous example is converted back to hexadecimal.

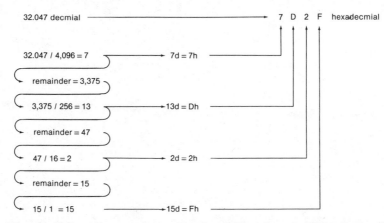

Figure C-2.   Converting a Decimal Number to Hexadecimal

Secrets of
Diagnostics

Appendix

T his appendix provides a list of error codes (see Table D-1) that may be generated by the ROM BIOS in IBM Personal Computer series or compatible systems or when running IBM Diagnostics, IBM Advanced Diagnostics, or compatible software. The error codes normally consist of three to four digits, although in some cases they are accompanied by other codes. In three-digit error codes, the first digit represents the device number. The remaining two digits, other than 00, represent the actual error condition. In four-digit error codes, the first two digits represent the device number. The remaining two digits, other than 00, represent the error condition. The device number plus 00 represents successful completion of the test when running diagnostic software.

Table D-1.   Diagnostics Error Codes

Code		Description
0XX		MISCELLANEOUS ITEMS
	010	Undetermined problem
	020	Power problem
1XX		SYSTEM BOARD
	101	Main system board failed
	109	Direct memory access (DMA) test error
	121	Unexpected hardware interrupts occurred
	131	Cassette wrap test failed
	199	User-defined configuration incorrect
2XX		MEMORY
	201	Memory test failed
		Displayed in the form XXXXX YY 201 where XXXXX represents the memory bank and YY represents the bit (actual chip)

Table D-1 (cont).

Code		Description
3XX		KEYBOARD
	301	Keyboard did not respond to software reset correctly or stuck key failure detected; if stuck key detected, the scan code for the key displayed
	302	User-defined error from the keyboard test
4XX		MONOCHROME ADAPTER/DISPLAY (MDA)
	401	Monochrome memory test, horizontal sync frequency test, or video test failed
	408	User-defined display attributes failure
	416	User-defined character set failure
	424	User-defined 80 x 25 mode failure
	432	Parallel port test failed (monochrome adapter)
5XX		COLOR GRAPHICS ADAPTER/DISPLAY (CGA)
	501	Color memory test, horizontal sync frequency test, or video test failed
	508	User-defined display attributes failure
	516	User-defined character set failure
	524	User-defined 80 x 25 mode failure
	532	User-defined 40 x 25 mode failure
	540	User-defined 320 x 200 graphics mode failure
	548	User-defined 640 x 200 graphics mode failure
6XX		5¼-INCH FLOPPY DISK ADAPTER/DRIVES
	601	Disk power-on diagnostics test failed
	602	Disk test failed
	606	Disk verify function failed
	607	Write protected disk
	608	Bad command disk status returned
	610	Disk initialization failed
	611	Timeout—disk status returned
	612	Bad NEC—disk status returned
	613	Bad DMA—disk status returned
	621	Bad seek—disk status returned
	622	Bad CRC—disk status returned
	623	Record not found—disk status returned
	624	Bad address mark—disk status returned
	625	Bad NEC seek—disk status returned
	626	Disk data compare error
7XX		8087 (PC XT) OR 80287 (AT) FAILURE
8XX		(Undefined)
9XX		PARALLEL PORT (LPT1)
	901	Parallel printer port LPT1 test failed
10XX		ALTERNATE PARALLEL PORT (LPT2)
	1001	Alternate parallel printer port LPT2 test failed

Table D-1 (cont).

Code	Description
11XX	ASYNCHRONOUS SERIAL PORT (COM1)
1101	Asynchronous serial port COM1 test failed
12XX	ALTERNATE ASYNCHRONOUS SERIAL PORT (COM2)
1201	Alternate asynchronous serial port COM2 test failed
13XX	GAME CONTROL ADAPTER
1301	Game control adapter test failed
1302	Joystick test failed
14XX	GRAPHICS PRINTER
1401	Graphics printer test failed
15XX	SDLC COMMUNICATIONS ADAPTER
1510	8255 Port B failure
1511	8255 Port A failure
1512	8255 Port C failure
1513	8253 Timer 1 did not reach terminal count
1514	8253 Timer 1 stuck on
1515	8253 Timer 0 did not reach terminal count
1516	8253 Timer 0 stuck on
1517	8253 Timer 2 did not reach terminal count
1518	8253 Timer 2 stuck on
1519	8273 Port B error
1520	8273 Port A error
1521	8273 Command-read timeout
1522	Interrupt level 4 failure
1523	Ring indicate stuck on
1524	Receive clock stuck on
1525	Transmit clock stuck on
1526	Test indicate stuck on
1527	Ring indicate not on
1528	Receive clock not on
1529	Transmit clock not on
1530	Test indicate not on
1531	Data set ready not on
1532	Carrier detect not on
1533	Clear to send not on
1534	Data set ready stuck on
1536	Clear to send stuck on
1537	Level 3 interrupt failure
1538	Receive interrupt results error
1539	Wrap data miscompare
1540	DMA channel 1 error
1541	DMA channel 1 error
1542	Error in 8273 error checking or status reporting
1547	Stray interrupt level 4
1548	Stray interrupt level 3
1549	Interrupt presentation sequence timeout
16XX	(Undefined)

Table D-1 (cont).

Code	Description
17XX	**FIXED DISK**
1701	Fixed disk post error
1702	Fixed disk adapter error
1703	Fixed disk drive error
1704	Fixed disk adapter or drive error
18XX	**I/O EXPANSION UNIT**
1801	I/O Expansion unit post error
1810	Enable/disable failure
1811	Extender card wrap test failed (disabled)
1812	High order address lines failure (disabled)
1813	Wait state failure (disabled)
1814	Enable/disable could not be set on
1815	Wait state failure (enabled)
1816	Extender card wrap test failed (enabled)
1817	High order address lines failure (enabled)
1818	Disable not functioning
1819	Wait request switch not set correctly
1820	Receiver card wrap test failure
1821	Receiver high order address lines failure
19XX	(Undefined)
20XX	**BISYNC COMMUNICATIONS ADAPTER**
2010	8255 Port a failure
2011	8255 Port b failure
2012	8255 Port c failure
2013	8253 Timer 1 did not reach terminal count
2014	8253 Timer 1 stuck on
2016	8253 Timer 2 did not reach terminal count or timer 2 stuck on
2017	8251 Data set ready failed to come on
2018	8251 Clear to send not sensed
2019	8251 Data set ready stuck on
2020	8251 Clear to send stuck on
2021	8251 Hardware reset failed
2022	8251 Software reset failed
2023	8251 Software "error reset" failed
2024	8251 Transmit ready did not come on
2025	8251 Receive ready did not come on
2026	8251 Could not force "overrun" error status
2027	Interrupt failure—no timer interrupt
2028	Interrupt failure—transmit, replace card or planar
2029	Interrupt failure—transmit, replace card
2030	Interrupt failure—receive, replace card or planar
2031	Interrupt failure—receive, replace card
2033	Ring indicate stuck on
2034	Receive clock stuck on
2035	Transmit clock stuck on
2036	Test indicate stuck on
2037	Ring indicate stuck on

Table D-1 (cont).

Code	Description
2038	Receive clock not on
2039	Transmit clock not on
2040	Test indicate not on
2041	Data set ready not on
2042	Carrier detect not on
2043	Clear to send not on
2044	Data set ready stuck on
2045	Carrier detect stuck on
2046	Clear to send stuck on
2047	Unexpected transmit interrupt
2048	Unexpected receive interrupt
2049	Transmit data did not equal receive data
2050	8251 detected overrun error
2051	Lost data set ready during data wrap
2052	Receive timeout during data wrap
21XX	ALTERNATE BISYNC COMMUNICATIONS ADAPTER
2110	8255 Port a failure
2111	8255 Port b failure
2112	8255 Port c failure
2113	8253 Timer 1 did not reach terminal count
2114	8253 Timer 1 stuck on
2115	8253 Timer 2 did not reach terminal count or
2116	8251 Date set ready failed to come on
2117	8251 Clear to send not sensed
2118	8251 Data set ready stuck on
2119	8251 Clear to send stuck on
2120	8251 Hardware reset failed
2121	8251 Software reset failed
2122	8251 Software "error reset" failed
2123	8251 Transmit ready did not come on
2124	8251 Receive ready did not come on
2125	8251 Could not force "overrun" error status
2126	Interrupt failure—no timer interrupt
2128	Interrupt failure—transmit, replace card or planar
2129	Interrupt failure—transmit, replace card
2130	Interrupt failure—receive, replace card or planar
2131	Interrupt failure—receive, replace card
2133	Ring indicate stuck on
2134	Receive clock stuck on
2135	Transmit clock stuck on
2136	Test indicate stuck on
2137	Ring indicate stuck on
2138	Receive clock not on
2139	Transmit clock not on
2140	Test indicate not on
2141	Data set ready not on
2142	Carrier detect not on
2143	Clear to send not on
2144	Data set ready stuck on
2145	Carrier detect stuck on

Table D-1 (cont).

Code	Description
2146	Clear to send stuck on
2147	Unexpected transmit interrupt
2148	Unexpected receive interrupt
2149	Transmit data did not equal receive data
2150	8251 detected overrun error
2151	Lost data set ready during data wrap
2152	Receive timeout during data wrap
22XX	CLUSTER ADAPTER
23XX through 28XX (Undefined)	
29XX	COLOR PRINTER
30XX through 32XX (Undefined)	
33XX	COMPACT PRINTER

Index

E